insidetracks

insidetracks

a first-hand history of popular music
from the world's greatest record producers and engineers

Richard Buskin

FOREWORD BY BRIAN WILSON

SPIKE
AN AVON BOOK

AVON BOOKS, INC.
1350 Avenue of the Americas
New York, New York 10019

Copyright © 1999 by Richard Buskin
Foreword © 1999 by Brian Wilson
Inside back cover author photo by Mike Grogan
Interior design by Kellan Peck
Published by arrangement with the author
ISBN: 0-380-80745-9
Library of Congress Catalog Card Number: 99-94879
www.spikebooks.com

First Spike Printing: September 1999

SPIKE TRADEMARK REG. U.S. PAT. OFF. AND IN OTHER COUNTRIES, MARCA REGISTRADA,
HECHO EN U.S.A.

Printed in the U.S.A.

OPM   10 9 8 7 6 5 4 3 2 1

FOR MY OWN GREATEST HIT, MELANIE,
AND CO-PRODUCER, DOROTHY-JEAN.

ACKNOWLEDGMENTS

∎

Over the years many people—including publicists, editors, managers, and personal assistants—have helped set up the interviews that are featured in this book, and to each of them I owe a debt of gratitude. While they are too numerous to list here, and a fair number of them no longer work for the same people or with the same companies, I would like to say a special thank-you to David Stark, Kristofer Englehardt, Randy Poe, Jerry Schilling, Jean Sievers, David Leaf, Joe Hosken, Zenon Schoepe, Dennis Muirhead, Debra Pagan, Pat Nelson, and Bobbie Marcus for their greatly appreciated efforts in this regard.

The aforementioned interviews have been reproduced in the form of monologues, yet, while some of these express conflicting opinions, I have still done my best to check all of the names, dates, and other details that are mentioned, and to this end I would also like to thank Jeff Mintz, Allen J. Wiener, Ernst Jorgensen, Mark Lewisohn, and Josiah Gluck for their help in ascertaining the facts or, where doubts still exist, at least trying to determine the most likely scenario.

As an artist, composer, and producer, Brian Wilson has created timeless musical masterpieces whose influence is immeasurable and whose legacy is a testament to the human spirit. He is a personal hero of mine, and so I feel honored and privileged to have had Brian contribute the foreword to this book.

A special note of thanks goes to my agent, Linda Konner, whose ongoing advice, assistance, and efforts on my behalf single her out as one of the best in her field.

And last, but obviously not least, I of course wish to express my heartfelt appreciation to all of the interviewees who appear in this book. In several cases an interview was granted to tie in with the promotion of a record or the marking of an anniversary, but in most it came about simply as the result of a gracious response to my own request, and for that I am extremely grateful.

CONTENTS

■

FOREWORD:
a word from brian wilson
xi
INTRODUCTION
xv

INDEX

FOREWORD: A WORD FROM BRIAN WILSON

When Richard Buskin asked me to write the foreword for his book on record production, I was honored. So many of my all-time favorite records were produced by people he interviewed, such as Leiber & Stoller, Sir George Martin, Quincy Jones, Bones Howe, Gus Dudgeon, Jerry Wexler, Tom Dowd and Phil Ramone, and I know you'll be fascinated to hear how they did it.

For me, making music has always been a very spiritual thing. I think anybody who produces records has to feel that, at least a little bit. Producing a record—the idea of taking a song, envisioning the overall sound in my head and then bringing the arrangement to life in the studio—well, that gives me satisfaction like nothing else. And I still get quite a charge seeing my name on a record: "Produced by Brian Wilson."

The first record I produced that you might have heard was the Beach Boys' *Surfer Girl* album. Before I made that record, from the fall of 1961 through early 1963, I spent a lot of time in the studio, observing people like Nik Venet and, especially, Phil Spector. From Spector more than anybody else, I learned how to think as a producer. I saw how he took terrific songs ("Be My Baby," "Then He Kissed Me") and by using the best musicians in the world (Hal Blaine, Carol Kaye, Jay Migliori, et al), a great arranger (Jack Nitszche), wonderful engineers (Stan Ross & Larry Levine) and the hottest singers (like Darlene Love, Ronnie Spector, and LaLa Brooks), he was able to make records that really hit me in the gut.

What did I learn from watching him? Well, I saw how when

you combined instruments, like a piano and guitar, you got a new sound. Phil also used echo, and since then I've always loved echo, to make the sounds "swim." Most of all, I understood the difference between writing a song and producing a record. To make a great record, it definitely helps to start with a great song, but as I saw and heard at those Gold Star sessions, a record has to be a total sound experience for the listener. So the idea became, for me at least, to try to make the listener feel the way I did when I first wrote the song. To do that, I realized I would have to produce our records.

For example, "Surfer Girl" was the first song I ever wrote, and we cut a demo of it back in 1961. When I produced the record of "Surfer Girl" in 1963, I finally knew how to take what I heard in my head and recreate that feeling in the studio. There's a lot of love in that record.

As a producer, I've always been fascinated by sound. I love learning what instruments are capable of doing so I know how to use 'em—a harp on "Catch a Wave," a fuzz guitar on "Little Honda," an accordion on "Wouldn't It Be Nice," a Theremin on "Good Vibrations," a DX-7 on "Love & Mercy." But I've never tried something new just to be different. I only use a sound or a production technique if it's appropriate, if it blends in properly— if it helps me to express feelings. If an instrument stands out . . . like "Look at me, I'm a Theremin" . . . I wouldn't use it.

How we recorded the vocals was also a big part of our sound, and if I had to choose one thing that really made the difference, it was when we started double-tracking. It gave the leads real punch and made our backgrounds sound like a choir.

The other thing that I did back in those days that's pretty rare today is that I tracked live. By that, I mean that I would gather all the musicians in the studio, teach them the song and my arrangement. They would play it live, all the way through, until I had a take that I was happy with. For me, the key was feel. It didn't just have to be perfect; more important, it had to *feel* right.

In the 1960s, we cut on three-track, so the instrumental track would be on just one track. That meant we were mixing it live as we recorded. On my records, a big thing for me was clarity of the instruments. I had my own way of miking, and in the live mix, some parts I had written would be drowned out; you couldn't always hear every instrument. But you could always feel them.

Something you have to learn is to trust your instincts; to never settle until you have the record exactly as you want it. It also helps a lot if you have an engineer who you can really rely on, like I did with Chuck Britz. But in the end, only you—the producer—can really know when it's right.

For example, another thing I did was to mix in mono, but not because I'm deaf in my right ear. I mixed in mono to control the way the listener heard my records. I didn't want speaker placement or balance control knobs on the amplifier to change what you heard.

Of course, when you're also writing the songs and singing on your productions, there are major advantages. I could write to our strengths as a group, arrange the tracks to best showcase our voices, choose the lead vocalist that was right for each cut. When I'm in a writing cycle, when I've finished a song, I have a pretty good idea in my head how I want the record to sound. The hard work is making it happen.

But I don't mean to say that producing is a job. It's a life. When I was producing the Beach Boys' records full-time, I ate, slept, and breathed music. I couldn't wait to get into the studio and cut. Back then it was so much simpler. I could write a song on Monday, track it on Tuesday, put down the vocals on Wednesday and by the weekend, be playing a dub (acetate) on the radio. In the sixties, getting music to your audience was much more straightforward. From what I'm hearing now, I think in the future, distribution of music on the Internet will help me communicate more regularly as an artist.

Of all our sixties productions, the three that stand out for me are *Pet Sounds,* which I call our love album; "California Girls," which I think represents our best overall achievement and is an example of how I used what we called "dynamics" to get that kind of symphonic sound; and last, "Good Vibrations," which was really different for me. Back in 1966, I had started composing and recording little pieces of music, knowing I would find a way to fit them together to make a whole song. I remember at the time, people around me didn't really understand what I was trying to do. They were impatient. But I was determined not to rush it. That's an important lesson: If you believe in what you're doing, don't let other people stop you.

Now, if you're going to become a producer and I could give you just one last piece of advice, it would be to remain open to creativity. To be a great producer, music has to be a big part of your soul. And when it comes to making music, if I could invent a way to get it from my heart into yours, without doing all that hard work, I would be very happy. But until that day, we have to go into the studio and just do it.

The good thing about that is that the studio is still a wide-open adventure; there's still so much for all of us to learn about making great records. Believe me, there's no one big secret. But as you read this book, you'll see that over and over, the best producers all share one thing—they love music. And they live to make it. Just listen to what these producers have to say, and then listen to their records. And always, try and listen with your heart.

And in the end it comes down to creativity and passion. The people interviewed for this book have it, so there is a lot you can learn from their experiences. I know I can't wait to dig in, so let's get to the main course—the "Inside Tracks" on modern record production. Enjoy!

INTRODUCTION

■

Aside from a few notable exceptions, producers and engineers are the recording industry's unsung heroes. Ask most members of the general public what a record producer does and you'll prompt either a blank expression or a vague response along the lines of "He decides if a record is good enough to sell." As for the recording engineer, from the job title alone most people will deduce that this individual operates the studio equipment, but that hardly tells the whole story.

In actual fact, the engineer is the person who attains not only the desired sound but also the right effects to help enhance it. It is a job that has expanded tremendously over the years along with the huge advances in recording technology, and the engineer's increased role has been reflected in the acknowledgments that have generally appeared on records only since the late 1960s. Meanwhile, although the producer rarely has the final say in the marketability of a finished record, it is his job within the daylight-starved walls of the studio to help arrange the music and coax the best performances out of the artists. Given the temperamental nature of many of these artists, this latter task can also call upon said producer's skills as a nursemaid and part-time psychotherapist. There are undoubtedly easier ways to earn a living.

Still, one thing that producers and engineers tend to have in common is their undeniable love of music, and it is the highs they experience in the recording studio—those exhilarating moments when the blending of artistic effort, musical material, and technical input produce great results—that enable them to endure much of the nonsense that is dealt out by either the performers or the record company honchos. When they give interviews to promote a new release, producers and engineers obviously try to focus on the more upbeat aspects of the related project, and these can be interesting to a journalist such as myself and informative to the readers. However, when I also get them to talk about *past* efforts they often feel far less obligated to, well, let's just say "accentuate the positive." The distance of time enables them to divulge once-guarded secrets and truly speak their minds, and the resulting anecdotes can make terrific reading. This is what I hope you'll find within these pages.

For several years people have been suggesting that I compile my interviews into a book, but I wanted to hold off until I had the kind of material that would provide an all-encompassing view inside the recording studios. Now I do, and so I've assembled many of what I consider to be the most interesting, insightful, and amusing interviews that I have done during the past two decades, based upon not only the tales they tell but also the variety of personalities whom they discuss and the different time periods they cover. Indeed, the producers and engineers featured herein transport us from the early 1940s, when the routine was to record four songs in one three-hour session, to the late 1990s, when sonic perfection is often of the essence and the welter of technological toys can both help and hinder the lengthy creative process. As they talk, we share their experiences in the fields of jazz, folk, pop, rock, rhythm 'n' blues, country, classical, soul, disco, techno, heavy metal, rap, hip hop, and grunge. The result, I think you'll agree, is a sort of musical potpourri—dip in, pick a star, and learn something.

While I've enjoyed talking to a wide range of music artists down the years, I have invariably gleaned far more interesting information from my conversations with the people who are positioned on the other side of the recording console, industry professionals who are not nearly so image or publicity conscious and whose memories are often far more accurate and objective than those of the musicians. However, I do say "often" because, as you are about to see, different interviewees' recollections about the same artists and identical events can sometimes contrast sharply, and so it is ultimately up to you to decide whose memory—if any—is most worthy of your trust.

The words have all been recorded. Here are the stories.

Richard Buskin,
Los Angeles, California, 1999

insidetracks

sam phillips

■

If you wish to identify one of the main people who was responsible for breaking down the barriers between white and black music, melding country with blues and creating the art form that we know as rock 'n' roll, then Sam is the man. During less than a decade, and in tandem with fledgling artists such as Elvis Presley, Howlin' Wolf, Carl Perkins, Jerry Lee Lewis, Johnny Cash, and B. B. King, Sam forged the basis for so much that was to follow, and he achieved much of this while running his own small Sun Records label and a tiny studio located at 706 Union Avenue, close to downtown Memphis, Tennessee. In 1998 Sam took the time to talk with me about the events that had such a radical impact on the first century of recorded sound.

"I cannot truly judge what the first rock 'n' roll record was because that would be unfair, but if I go along with the view of a number of people who are more qualified to look upon this objectively, then I think that [Jackie Brenston's] 'Rocket 88' was the first. This takes nothing away at all from Bill Haley or Elvis or anybody, but in the sense of the term 'rock 'n' roll'—which to me wrapped up black and white youth and vitality—it really was the first rock 'n' roll record.

"I sure can recall that session. That's when I had to tell Ike [Turner] that I wanted to know if he had somebody in his band who could sing. Ike was singing and of course he was a hell of a talent—he was playing the piano at that time—but I knew his voice was not quite what I was looking for. I don't want to say that ultimately I couldn't have done something with Ike, but anyway he told me that Jackie Brenston had a song called 'Rocket 88.' Jackie played the tenor sax, and I put a mike in front of him and, man, as a singer he was a natural. Then there was the busted woofer in the speaker [guitarist Willie Kizart's amp having fallen off a car roof rack], which I stuffed paper into just to try to make us a usable amplifier, and that, together with the saxophones and the guitar,

1

made a very unusual sound. 'Rocket 88' is, till this day, an exciting record, and that piano intro which Ike played on it is still a classic.

"Being raised as a country sharecropper's son at the bend of the river in Florence, Alabama, in the Muscle Shoals area, I was very, very aware of the musical capabilities of untried black people. You've heard a lot of times about being in the cotton fields and all that, but this was literally true. We lived on a farm at the bend in the river where the soil was good for raising cotton, and my daddy hired and worked with a lot of helpers on the farm, because he was a tenant farmer himself. So, I was aware of how black music affected me as a child, and I also knew how white people talked about black people in those days when they would make music. Of course, a lot of times they would say it in a laughing manner— you know, 'Man, he can get it, can't he?'—but even when I was seven, eight, nine, I followed that type of thing.

"A blind negro named Uncle Silas Payne came to live with us when the white family he'd been with couldn't feed him anymore during the Depression—we didn't have much more ourselves—and he taught me rhythms on his knee, and he sang me songs that he made up in his head about molasses and pancakes, and he would just fascinate me. Then there was a shoeshine man by the name of Sam in North Florence; his back was broken and he was probably less than five feet tall, but he had a natural spirit and a rhythmic instinct. I'm not just talking about popping the rag on your shoes, but he'd tap his knee, tap his toe, tap his shoe. These things influenced me so that I knew there was a cross-pollination going on between blacks and whites, because I and other people—adults and young people—would not have been as fascinated by black music if there hadn't been something very natural and very interesting about it. I knew that young people were more likely to be very, very objective about it, and as it proved, I was totally right about that, because that's why we got so much flak later on concerning 'white children falling in love with niggers.' I don't know how many times I heard *that!*

"At the same time, I think that there was a real, real close association between country music and rock 'n' roll. I remember the first record I ever heard in my life, on an old Victrola with a steel needle, was a Jimmie Rodgers song; I don't recall if it was 'Blue Yodel No.1' or 'All Around the Water Tank' [this is from the first line of "Waiting for a Train"]. With his Southern accent and the way he sang the blues, I can tell you, there was really more cross-pollination between Southern white music, Southern white gospel, and black gospel. I don't believe there's any relationship in any other category of music that comes closer than the country blues, especially the type that Jimmie Rodgers started in the twenties and thirties. He was a person who contributed so much, and he kind of parted the waters so that we could see the dual influence.

"Back in the early fifties I was looking to create something different. I was by nature an explorer, and I loved music, period, otherwise I would not have attempted to do what I did with raw talent. As a child on the farm in Alabama I had been exposed to music that was in one way or another not 'developed,' so the last thing that I thought about when I went in the studio at any time was cutting a hit record. Now, I had sense enough to know that if these things didn't sell and I had no money then I couldn't stay in business very long, but I had no ulterior motive of getting rich or of doing my artists wrong in any way from a business standpoint. I wanted to develop these artists, work with these artists, get their natural instincts out and capture that, and then I knew it was up to me to go out and work my ass off and sell it.

"From the beginning I was very much interested in exploring some paths that had not been trodden and looking for the hidden possibilities. I knew that these people had not been 'overly exposed' because most of them had never had an opportunity to even be in a studio, and so what I tried to do with each artist was to find his natural honesty in terms of what he liked to do, regardless of what category of music it might fall into. I did not want him doing something to please somebody behind the control room glass. It was about trying to develop confidence, knowing that any audition was extremely difficult even for professionals—then as now—let alone for people who had never been tried or proven.

"You also knew that you almost had to be a psychologist, doing the things that we did at the time, because there was a great lack of confidence as to whether or not these artists would be accepted, exactly what they were supposed to do, and whether I was really telling the truth when I told them, 'No, it didn't cost you anything to have an audition,' and 'Man, I want what you naturally feel. Do it to the best of your ability and we'll go from there.' The artists who I worked with all had a certain basic honesty in their music, and after assuring and working with them, and gaining their confidence and their trust in me, I think they then really knew that they had somebody who was working with them in the common interest of seeing what they had.

"To me simplicity and naturalness are the key ingredients for a good recording, and I still feel that way even with forty-eight tracks today. Well, after I gained the confidence of these people I think that they then felt that they could do 'their thing,' whatever it was. That didn't mean we were going to accept it as it was, but I had the ability—or else I certainly would not have gotten into this type of work the way that I did—to spot these things, and deep down in their hearts they really truly knew that although I had white skin I had a lot of instincts that they had, and I was going to give them an opportunity to display their talents and I would be proud of them.

"The common thread that we had among the black as well as the white artists was that we were able to establish a feel whereby we were looking for what might potentially be unique about them. Howlin' Wolf was one of the most interesting people who I ever worked with. I was really impressed with the fact that his voice was so different, so unusually 'bad,' but so honest that it fascinated me, and the Wolf and I worked together better than I did with any other artist. I just enjoyed working with the Wolf. When he went to Chess [Records] I don't think they really ever gave that psychological bent that the Wolf needed. In my view very few people honestly had that ability, and Wolf was one of those people who had to believe that you believed in him. I'm not saying that the Chess brothers didn't—I'm not speaking disparagingly about them—but they never did capture his potential, and had I continued to have the Wolf [on Sun Records] I think he would have been a mammoth seller in the white community as well as the black.

"I had a lot of different things that I wanted to do with the Wolf. This Wolf had really a lot of potential that you just didn't hear on the few records that were out both on Sun and on Chess. I had other routes and other approaches—like I did with Elvis Presley—that I wanted to attempt with the Wolf, but after he left and went to Chess Records I didn't get to do my laboratory work with him.

"I have been accused of having had my attention diverted from making blues records by working with Elvis, and to an extent it's true, but it was not for the reason that people might think. I had a very small operation, and by that time I knew that there was an awful lot of excellent rhythm and blues records—or, as they were mainly called then, 'race records'—being produced by so many different labels. I had felt all along that, as long as the artists were black, you were going to get a limited amount of play on the air. In fact, I had found that out and I knew that, because I had been in radio myself since the forties, and I had thought that if there was a way for some white person to perform with the feel of a black artist . . . I did not want anybody who did not have a natural feel, but I said to myself—and this is true—'Man, if I can find a white person who can give the feel and the true essence of a blues-type song, black blues especially, then I've got a chance to broaden the base and get plays that otherwise we couldn't.' And man, did that prove to be a phenomenal philosophy!

"With Elvis as the catalyst, and later on, Carl Perkins' 'Blue Suede Shoes,' there's no question about it; it opened up so many doors. Now look; you've got as much play on black artists as you've got on white artists—or more—and while I don't say that it never would have happened, people of vision and unselfishness like me were responsible for that.

"For the record—and it's unfortunate that this has been misrepresented, because [assistant] Marion Keisker meant so much to me and helped me so much when I didn't have the money to hire help at the studio—Marion did not make Elvis's personal recording of 'My Happiness' and 'That's When Your Heartaches Begin' on tape. I made it directly to the acetate. However, in no way does that detract from what Marion did in terms of helping me in the office. There again, another story that is incorrect is the one about Elvis coming back and doing another demo ["I'll Never Stand in Your Way"/"It Wouldn't Be the Same Without You"]. I've been shown the record with the Memphis Recording Service sticker on it, and I cannot account for that, but the only record that Elvis ever made as a demo was that so-called one for his mother's birthday. We of course later found out that her birthday had long since passed! I mean, it wouldn't make any difference if that second 'demo' was recorded at Sun, but it just is not true. At this point I don't know where it comes from, but I just know that he never made another direct-to-acetate 'personal' record.★

"Anyway, when Elvis came in and he performed those first two songs I was blown away by this guy's talent. By that I don't mean that I heard the finished thing, but I just heard some instinctive things about this person's intonations and stuff—of course, man, we didn't talk about 'intonations' and all of that jazz, but that's what I was hearing and feeling! You know, that's how you communicate, and so it didn't take a genius to recognize that this person Elvis had real potential. Now, the one thing that it took me a while to make up my mind on was that he sang those ballads, and I just knew that we could not do ballads and this sort of thing with Elvis, because there were people who were so well known—Dean Martin, Bing Crosby, Eddie Fisher—selling tons of records on major labels.

"I knew that just could not be the route to go with him, and when I got through making that first little record I told Elvis that I was going to the maximum security prison in Nashville to record the Prisonaires and that I had heard that they had some other songs over there that had been written by other prisoners. One of them was supposed to be extremely good, and I hadn't heard it but a friend of mine—whose uncle worked out there as a guard—had, so I said, 'Let me see what they've got and then I'll give you a call when I get back.' I therefore had Marion write his address down, how we could reach him, this sort of thing, and I went on to Nashville and I came back with one song that was a beautiful

---

★This whole issue remains a gray area. Published interviews with Elvis Presley, Scotty Moore, and Marion Keisker conform to the opinion that Elvis made the recording of "My Happiness"/"That's When Your Heartaches Begin" soon after he quit school, around June or July of 1953. Furthermore, even though Elvis arguably performs more confidently on this demo disc than on the one featuring "I'll Never Stand in Your Way"/"It Wouldn't Be the Same Without You," the fact that "I'll Never Stand in Your Way," written by Hy Heath and Fred Rose, was not even copyrighted until late 1953 appears to confirm that Elvis did record it after the "My Happiness" disc, probably in January of 1954. Could Marion have made the recording when Sam wasn't around? Sam categorically refutes this. Nevertheless, whether or not this was the case, there was apparently a gap of a year rather than a matter of months between Elvis cutting the "My Happiness" demo and his first documented Sun label recordings.

number called 'Without You.' It was a ballad, but it was several months before I called Elvis in to hear this.

"When he did listen he was just knocked out with it—of course, he would have been knocked out by just about anything given the opportunity to make a record!—and that's when I asked him if he had a band of any kind or any boys he could play with. He said, 'No,' because Elvis had been kind of a real loner, an independent person, very shy, and he didn't play any gigs, so that's when I decided to call [guitarist] Scotty Moore, who I had worked with on different things and who I knew was a very patient person, and he suggested bringing in Bill Black, who played a good slap upright bass. I wanted as few people as possible and still get a rhythm going. Elvis was pretty good on the rhythm, but I had to get Scotty away from the [more intricate] Chet Atkins influence—not that it wasn't great, but I didn't want it for what we were going to do—and I told Elvis, Scotty, and Bill, 'We want to look for things that we can do in a medium to real up-tempo.' I said, 'We've got to approach this thing to try to get the attention of younger people,' and I knew that tempo had a lot to do with that back then, rather than just a great lyric and beautiful melody.

"We were in there doing our best, and in the meantime they would get together and work on stuff. I told them, 'Never get too uptight. Just kick things around, come in, and if I say, "No, I don't hear it this time," that doesn't necessarily mean that y'all are not right and I am, but I'm the one who's going to make the decision! However, I don't want you to become discouraged if you have to make a number of trips here.' I named a whole bunch who had come in many different times before we found out what they really sold. So, they would go and work out together, and then one of them would call me—usually it would be Scotty and sometimes Elvis—and say, 'Man, we'd like to come back in and see what you think.'

"That went on a number of times, and so, again contrary to what may have been written, it wasn't anything at all like Elvis hanging around the studio so much to convince me of a damned thing. I was already convinced, and then it was up to me to see if I could find, one way or the other, the route to make absolutely certain that I didn't go the wrong route with Elvis. My honest opinion was that he might be that white guy who could get the overtones and the sexual feel in there without anything being vulgar, just that actual thing that gets hold of somebody and says, 'Hey, listen to me!'

"I think a great part—if not the major part—of my success was working with my artists, and I have always considered that God gave me one thing if he didn't give me anything else and that was a good ear. I would do anything in the studio to alleviate as much tension as I could, yet I wanted them to really have that feel, that spark, like they're ready to come out of the gate at the Kentucky Derby, while at the same time not injuring themselves in the process. All of these things are so important, and I owe all of my success to that psychological bent. I knew that I had to do my very dead level best to go in the right direction, and that's why it took so many months before we finally came up with the very thing that we should have, which was 'That's All Right (Mama)' and 'Blue Moon of Kentucky.'

"The door to the control room was open, the mikes were on, Scotty was in the process of packing up his guitar, I think Bill had already thrown his old bass down—he didn't even have a cover for it—and the session was, to all intents and purposes, over. Then Elvis struck up on just his rhythm guitar, 'That's all right, mama . . .' and I mean he got my attention immediately. It could have been that it wouldn't have sold ten copies, but that was what I was looking for! There was no question in my mind. I didn't give a damn what the song was. That was the *sound,* the *feel,* even the tempo. I think we moved the tempo around, but we didn't do much to that song, man. We did a couple, three, maybe four takes on it, and we had something that we had been looking for for months.

"When I heard 'That's All Right (Mama)' it opened a whole new door. Elvis being as young as he was, I thought, 'My god, this guy knows "That's All Right"!' 'Big Boy' Crudup had had that thing out seven years before, and so on 'Blue Moon of Kentucky,' man, we certainly weren't going to do a bluegrass version and try to outdo Bill Monroe. No, we knew that we had to work with up-tempo stuff to get the attention. Then we could kind of play around maybe with slower things or things that might border on being good ballads. When it all started to come together [a "Blue Moon of Kentucky" session tape captures Sam exclaiming, "Hell, that's fine! That's different! That's a pop song now, nearly 'bout!"] it was just kinda like you've been looking so long, say, for something and then there it is! I guess that's how a scientist would feel in the laboratory, looking for something that had been so elusive and, boy, there it is under the 'scope!

"Elvis had sex written all over him from the day he walked in the door. I don't mean anything about him being good-looking, because he really wasn't as good-looking as he would develop a little later on, but he had sex written all over him, and the right kind. When this man opened his mouth it had sex, when you saw him on stage you couldn't take your eyes off him, and that was even as a male. I don't want to use the word *charisma*, but this guy—and I'm talking about him in a total, total personal way, in addition to fantastic talent as far as his singing was concerned—had a certain ability for contact, and to a measured degree he could give you that sexual feel, or whatever feel was needed, if a song indicated that it had that potential.

"Judging my own stuff is the toughest thing in the world to do, but I think 'Mystery Train' is a masterpiece. It is one of those things that is so instinctively, innately there. You can play that thing all day in an office full of people and it wouldn't get in the way no matter what they're doing, or you could play it at the sexiest party and somehow or another it's got that freedom about it. You can't beat the right vamp, and this thing has got a vamp in it that is just outstanding. Even right at the very end, where Elvis thought that this wasn't going to be the take, you know; he just went off and shouted 'Woo-hooo!' as I was fading that thing out, because he really didn't think it was going to be a cut, and hey, I didn't know for sure, but I knew that we didn't need any more takes! So, that just shows you that when you really open up and instinctively feel that you've got nothing to lose, boy, you might be surprised by what you can do.

"I've never liked the term *rockabilly*. I've always thought *rock 'n' roll* was the best term, because it became all-inclusive of white, black, and the whole thing, whereas *rockabilly* tended to just want to lend itself so specifically to white. It also promoted the feeling that maybe we were stealing something from the blacks and wanted to put it in a white form, so I never did like *rockabilly*. However, I really think that what we came up with, between Elvis, 'Rocket

88,' and Carl Perkins' 'Blue Suede Shoes,' was the basis for rock 'n' roll.

"As for the 'Sun sound,' I liked to use very sparse instrumentation—not just for economic considerations, although I certainly had every reason to—and I was the first one to employ slapback [echo], feeding the tape back through the board. You see, the human ear doesn't like hearing something that is aurally so different to the point of being strange. It likes something different so far as the total confluence of the sound and the song and how it's done. I knew that people had heard records on jukeboxes in live little restaurants and dives, and what I tried to do with that type of echo and the sparse instrumentation was to make the sound not too foreign to the average ear. The acoustics of the room [on 706 Union Avenue] were good, but miking has an awful lot to do with the finished product. Of course, everything at that time was monaural, and I'm big on miking and I'm big on using the right mike, although I couldn't buy real expensive microphones.

"I was not going to sell Elvis's contract and did not want to sell it, but I made a demand that I didn't think [RCA Victor] would go for and they did. I only did it because I knew I had [Carl Perkins'] 'Blue Suede Shoes' in the can—nobody else knew this even though I really had a lot of confidence in it—and I needed the money to do something with it. Steve Sholes, who I did the deal with, was a very honest, very wonderful person. He didn't propose to be a great A&R [Artists & Repertoire] man, didn't propose to know sound, but he knew how to keep people together and get them to work, and he said, 'Sam, I would give anything if you would come with us.' He just thought I had something that was so different that he didn't believe anybody in his organization had that exploratory feel when working with new talent. However, I told him, 'Steve, I love you and I would love working with you. You'd stay out of the way, but I do know that in a big company—and I have been contacted by others—I might not have the freedom that I would need to do the crazy things that I would like to try. There might be certain limitations that wouldn't permit me to either fail big or succeed big.' I said, 'That would just spoil my whole life, as I'm only doing this because it is something that I believe so completely in. You don't get in this game and work like

I do for the money. You have to have the money to operate, but this is as much a part of my life as breathing.'

"I also told Elvis, 'This isn't being defiant to anyone at RCA, because Steve Sholes is a wonderful person and he will let you work, and so will Chet, but you be sure to run your sessions.' Still, one of the engineers who worked over there at RCA and did a number of the sessions on Elvis told me later on, 'Man, we worked to try to get your sound until we were bleeding out of the eyes! Forget the ears—Hell, our ears just went crazy!' He said, 'We never did get what we felt was you, but we did our best.' I said, 'Well, Elvis was the person who had the latitude, and although he wouldn't have had any idea about going in there and turning the knobs, he would know when he heard a good sound, because he had a good ear himself.' Anyway, they did some pretty good things on Elvis—I mean, 'Don't Be Cruel' was the first thing that they did that really had that instinctive Elvis thing about it. 'Heartbreak Hotel' was okay, but when I was driving into Cullman, Alabama, from Florida and heard 'Don't Be Cruel' on the radio I said, 'Hey! Man, he's arrived with RCA!' I just knew that they had unlocked the door, and I could hear that this was Elvis directing the session all the way.

"I worked with Carl Perkins similarly to the way I worked with Elvis, and I always thought that Carl could have been a great, sustained country artist. I cut 'Turn Around' with him before I cut 'Blue Suede Shoes,' and it was one of the finest country records you ever heard. Carl had a great ability, especially in terms of his guitar playing; it had rock written all over it, and when I heard 'Blue Suede Shoes' I thought he really ought to go into the rock vein. He had written this song and he had the line 'Go, man, go.' Well, that was a common term used in the vernacular of country people, and I said, 'Carl, why don't you just say, "Go, *cat,* go"?' Aside from getting the sound that I wanted that's all I did, but it was one of the things that kept it from being mainly a country record.

"On the other hand, Johnny Cash could have gone by the wayside if I had tried to make a 'rocker' out of him. Johnny Cash had folk all over him. When he came in for his audition Johnny basically apologized for not having more musicians. He said, 'Mr. Phillips, the next time we come in I'll have a steel player and probably a fiddle player,' but after we got through with the audition and I'd heard the 'band' that he did have I said, 'Johnny, let's just play around here a few more sessions before we think about adding anything to the "instrumentation" of your "band"!' I mean, Luther [Perkins] could literally play one string at a time, and I loved that! It blew me away. Johnny would get disgusted with Luther—he'd get in and have a great feel on a cut with a good vamp going, and Luther would take a break and hit the wrong note, and Johnny would get so upset because Johnny had done a good job in his mind. Luther's hair looked like it would stand on its end when he'd make a mistake, because he was scared to death, but I loved Luther and I loved all three of those guys, [bass player] Marshall Grant and Johnny.

"Man, you're talking about a classic sound! There's not another one like it. I mean, there's vamps and there's vamps, but there isn't that sound. Really, Johnny was disappointed when I told him there was just really no way I could sell these darned good Southern gospel songs that he had written, but I knew that I had enough on my plate to try to sell him. He wasn't country, he wasn't rock, and so I thank God that I didn't try to make something out of him but what he was.

"Roy Orbison was another case in point. Anybody who heard him would have known that he had an unbelievably beautiful voice. In fact, his voice was even more 'polished' than Elvis'—and I don't like polish; I'm not one of these people who tries to dress things up too much—and I knew that his home would mainly be with ballads, but, like with Elvis, I also knew at that particular time that there was no point in him coming out and trying to compete with all of these established singers like Eddie Fisher and Dean Martin. So, 'Oobie Doobie' could be classified as a novelty record, but it was also a tempo'd thing, and we had to get the young people's attention. The only reason I let Roy go was not because we had a fight, but I couldn't get around to recording everybody and doing everything, and I never sold stock in my company because I knew that I had to control it and run it like I wanted to. If it succeeded, fine, and if it failed then that was my problem.

"Again, it sure did not take a genius to know that Roy Orbison could sing, and eventually, if I had kept Roy, there is no doubt that at the right time we would have done our share of ballads. However, Roy Orbison also played a very different type guitar, and so I would have actually done more rhythm things than were done later on by him while certainly emphasizing his ability as a ballad singer, but it would have had to come at the right time.

"In late 1956 I took possibly the first vacation that I'd ever had in my life when I, my wife, and our two young sons took off and went to Daytona, Florida, for a week. Jerry Lee Lewis had been trying to see me, and while I was away he and his father had apparently sold eggs to buy gasoline to come up here [to Memphis from Ferriday, Louisiana]. You might think, 'Man, was anybody that poor in the fifties?' Well, *they* were. Anyway, he had missed me, so one day he came in to Sun, and Jack Clement—who I had hired by that time to take a little bit of the load off me on auditions and so on—recorded a demo of him doing 'Crazy Arms.' When I got back Jack told me about this guy who had been looking for me. He told me that he'd put him down on tape and that he was a piano player, and I said, 'That's what I'm looking for!'

"I really was looking for an artist who could be a lead piano player and hopefully a vocalist, too, and damn if Jerry Lee Lewis wasn't like that. I really do think that the guitar is the greatest instrument on the planet, but there were so many guitarists by that time that I wanted a piano. So, when I heard this demo of Jerry Lee Lewis I said, 'Where is that cat? Get a hold of him and get him in here! I want to talk to him,' and we were doing a session with Jerry Lee Lewis within a matter of two to three days. I was just blown away. The guy was different. You know, Jerry still sings a little bit nasal, but the expression, the way he played that piano and how you could just feel that evangelical thing about him . . . Man, was I looking for that, and there it was!

"I always let people do their thing, but I had a way of somehow or the other suggesting things that if they worked they worked, and if they didn't we didn't do any damage. That was very important. You have to keep in mind that I was working with novices, and I didn't want to undermine the potential or the confidence that they had or that I could develop in them. So, when I made suggestions I had to be very careful about that. I don't mean I had to go in and soft-soap; I was pretty plainspoken, but they could tell by the way I worked that I was more interested in getting the potential out of them. I never played the big-shot producer who'd had this hit or whatever. They equated with me that I knew where they were coming from because I had been there myself.

"I absolutely think that the technical limitations of the time contributed towards making more successful, heartfelt records. It made us mike things more carefully, and it made sure I didn't convey to the artists, 'Well, Lord, you do it, and if you miss then that's the only chance you're gonna have!' No, I think that having the sparseness and the lack of ability to overdub absolutely contributed to how well things turned out. Of course, we didn't know it at the time; it just made things a little more difficult to set up and that sort of thing, but I was always a mike nut anyway—I would experiment with positioning and I knew which microphone worked best with each instrument—and I really think it was a blessing in disguise. It had the duality of getting more of a natural sound as well as the fact that nobody laid back and said, 'Gosh, I can come in tomorrow and overdub.' There just was no such animal. I mean, hell, you just cut another damned track, y'all!

"It changed the world, what we did at that little studio. I'm taking nothing away from all of the other great independent labels, but what we did managed to cut through the segregation to such an extent that it was way beyond what I had even hoped we could do. That not only affected this nation, it affected people around the world, and it absolutely had a lot to do with encouraging communication between people of different races."

chetatkins

Not everyone has a street named after him, but if you stroll around Nashville's Music Row you'll find Chet Atkins Place. Such is the reputation of the legendary country guitarist and producer. The artists Chet has either produced or played with over the course of five decades include Elvis Presley, the Everly Brothers, Hank Williams, Les Paul, George Benson, Paul McCartney, and Mark Knopfler. The man's influence has been enormous, and he has 40 million album sales and thirteen Grammy Awards to show for it.

"Sometimes I look at myself in the mirror and think, 'How in the hell did I do that?' I'm from up in the Smoky Mountains, a terrible place, and we almost didn't make it through the Depression, but I made a success and I don't know how the hell I did it. I hear my influence in other musicians' work, and I can't believe that either. They're all over the world, and I guess it's because I was first.

"In the beginning I was paid $35 a week by RCA to do the things that my boss, Mr. Sholes, wanted me to do around the studio. He had this dream of building a studio in Nashville and having me run it, and that finally happened in about 1954. That was at 1525 McGavock Street, and we had a couple of homemade RCA recording machines, an echo chamber that consisted of a sewer pipe that went up two stories, and a Hammond-sprang reverb. Lawrence Hammond owned the patent on the B3 [Hammond organ] until he died, so nobody could use it, but this engineer took a reverb out of a B3 and we'd run band voices through that. It was illegal, of course, but we got a good echo sound.

"We recorded Elvis' first national hit, 'Heartbreak Hotel,' at RCA in Nashville, and you know, Elvis made a hell of a record. He was a cut above anybody I've ever seen. Everything he did was different. Instead of tapping his foot he'd shake his leg and turn on the girls, and even in the studio he'd get down pretty much and give a full performance. He was not shy! He was shy in a social sort of way, but when he performed it was like 'Screw the world!'

He didn't listen to any of the critics. At one point during that first session I called my wife and told her to come straight to the studio. I knew she'd never see anything like this again. It was so damn exciting.

"As it happens, the reverb in that studio was no good. The ceiling was concave, and so when you'd hit a bass note it would go up there and roll around for days before finally coming back down. It was just a bad design. You don't need a ceiling like that. Shortly afterwards, in about 1957, we built Studio B, and I can still remember RCA's chief engineer, Mr. Miltonberg, drawing the design for that on a paper napkin. Now it's referred to as 'the legendary Studio B,' but in truth it was like all studios in those days. It wasn't worth a damn. It shouldn't be legendary. It's only legendary because Elvis and a lot of great artists recorded there. Mr. Miltonberg designed it really badly. I remember it had the toilets around the front of the building, things like that. Miltonberg was the guy who, in New York, would take my records and dub them off on other records and they'd have distortion. He was a bad dude. I think he must be dead by now and I'm glad.

"Eventually, on the strength of Elvis' success, Steve Sholes was promoted within the RCA organization and I took over the country roster. My first signing was Don Gibson, and at his first session he recorded 'Oh Lonesome Me' and 'I Can't Stop Loving You.' He'd actually written both songs in a single afternoon. Anyway, the demo of 'Oh Lonesome Me' had been recorded in a little room and it had this distinctive thumping bass drum sound. I said, 'Wow, who's playing that bass?' and Don said, 'Troy Hatcher'. Well, I knew Troy, so I said, 'Bring him down here. We'll use him on the record.' He turned up with this great big drum, it was almost like a marching drum, and so we put a mike on that—which had never been done before, as far as I know—EQ'd [equalized] it so that it was real hot on the record, and hell, it was a hit all over the world. So, after that I got confidence and I figured I could make a record as well as anybody else. I thought, 'If I hear a song and like it then the people will easily like it,' and they did.

"In terms of recording methods I'm a lot more technical now than I was then, but in those days I still knew the difference between distortion and cleanness. If I heard something wrong I'd ask a lot of questions until I could dig up the problem, and that actually caused me to have a lot of enemies within the record company. I'd made some hits and they kind of resented that—'You can't get close to the microphone! You might pop a "P"!' If you popped a 'P' in those days there was a possibility it wouldn't play on the jukebox and a lot of records would be returned. I had an engineer who believed in that theory all the time, so he left. He got kind of sick of me picking on him I guess, and then the next session was one with Jim Reeves, and he got right into the microphone and whispered the lyrics. I remember, Mr. Sholes called me and said, 'How did you get that sound?' and I said, 'Hell, he just wanted to get up close and inside the microphone and I let him! He did it, I didn't do it.' You see, Jim had been a disc jockey and radio announcer, and he knew about mike technique probably more than I did. He knew how to get intimate when the mike was in front of him.

"Eventually, after I'd notched up hit records as a producer and for my guitar playing, I was able to get more of my way with RCA. I had it written into my contract that the Nashville studio would get the same standard of equipment as those in New York and Hollywood had, and that was good in case I needed something. I'd say, 'It's in my contract. Get me one of those.' By that time, you see, I'd started hiring people to help me, because one day I went to work and at one point I looked down and my shoes didn't match. I thought, 'Buddy, you've been on the job too long,' and so after that I started to delegate responsibility. . . . Because your shoes should match!

"Today they build studios with almost complete isolation on each musician. They sit in little cages and listen on headphones. In my opinion that's not so good for the creative process. Before we used to gather around the piano. We'd all gang around Floyd Cramer and run over the tunes a few times, and the musicians would get ideas for fills or for rhythm licks, and that was more fun. I know that still goes on, but it's not the same.

"The heart and the feel are everything when making a record. The sound doesn't matter too much to me as long as you're doing something that touches your heart. I've seen guys producing and they'll work half a day trying to get a sound on one instrument, but I think that's kind of futile. So's talk about a 'Nashville sound.' There's no damned 'Nashville sound'! It's the musicians who sing and play the backing, but it's always been there. People love musicians who come from the South and play or sing with a Southern accent; harmony groups like the Jordanaires. If there was a 'Nashville sound,' that's what it was. That kind of thing happened gradually. You know, with Jim Reeves we'd try different instrumentations, and if we had a hit we'd continue in that direction. Me and Owen Bradley, who was another producer out here, we were just trying to keep our jobs. I'd been fired from every damned job I ever had, so I was trying to keep from being fired by making a hit. . . ."

bobthiele

■

One of the major producers in the world of American jazz, Bob Thiele worked with such giants of the industry as Duke Ellington, John Coltrane, Louis Armstrong, Count Basie, Charlie Mingus, and Coleman Hawkins. As head of A&R at Coral Records during the 1950s he also signed and produced pop artists like Buddy Holly, Jackie Wilson, the McGuire Sisters, and Teresa Brewer, whom he would later marry. It was in a retrospective mood that he sat down and talked with me in 1988, eight years before his death at the age of seventy-three.

"George David Weiss and I had written this song, 'What a Wonderful World,' for Louis Armstrong. That was a rough period; it was the late sixties and there was Vietnam, protests, and everything else, and George and I decided to have Louis sing about how good things really could be. I did the lyrics, George did the music; we helped each other and finished the song over the course of about two or three days.

"I went down to Washington to see Louis while he was working there and he liked the song, so we went ahead and booked studio time for him together with a sixteen-string rhythm section. I was with ABC [Records] at the time, and the president of the company, Larry Newton, showed up at the session. I was in the control room, and he came in and said, 'What the hell are you doing? You're crazy!' You see, Louis Armstrong had just had a big hit with 'Hello, Dolly!' which was a Dixieland-type arrangement, and now here we were, recording a ballad with strings. He said, 'This record isn't going to mean anything,' and finally he became so upset that he threatened to cancel the date and throw everyone out. I said, 'Well, you're going to go down in history, Larry, as the only man who ever threw Louis Armstrong out of a recording studio!' He got really mad, and a couple of friends of mine who were at the session had to restrain him out in the hallway, because he was just going berserk. He shouted, 'You're fired!' and by that time I was a nervous wreck.

19

"Still, we finished the date and things cooled down as the days went by. One of the vice presidents called me and said, 'Come on back to work. This is ridiculous,' so I did. Then, at one of the subsequent sales meetings, they played all of the new product that was going to be released, and when they put on Louis' 'What a Wonderful World' Larry said, 'This is a piece of shit. It isn't going to sell at all.' That led to another argument, but he was right in a way, because when the record did come out it sold maybe 1,500 copies. However, when it was released in England by EMI it sold about 650,000 copies. It was number one over the Beatles and the Rolling Stones, and it stayed at the top for several weeks.

"Louis had made this record because we were good friends, and I'd paid him union scale, which was like $250. He didn't care. Anyway, we got a telex from EMI asking us to rush out a Louis Armstrong album with the title *What a Wonderful World*. All we had were four sides, so Newton called me and said, 'Bob, get your friend Louis to do eight more sides and let's work the same deal.' I said, 'Well, I'll see what I can do.' Now, during this whole sequence of events Louis' manager, Joe Glazier, had heard about what was going on, and so when I called him and told him we'd like to get Pops [Armstrong] in the studio again to do eight more sides he said, 'You tell that bastard at your company that he can have eight sides for $25,000.' I passed this on to Newton, and Newton said, 'Well, tell him to get lost.' I said, 'What about EMI?' and he said, 'To hell with EMI. It doesn't matter. Forget it.' After that we received a telex from South Africa, a telex from France, a telex from . . . everybody wanted a *What a Wonderful World* album. Not too surprisingly, after a couple of weeks Newton finally agreed to the $25,000 payment.

"Now, you know how Louis Armstrong was always considered such a friendly, jovial, happy-go-lucky sort of guy, with that big smile of his? Well, we wanted to rush out this project, and because of his work schedule, the only place where he could record at the time was in Las Vegas. So, I sent Louis the songs that we wanted to do, and then about a week later I flew out. I went up to his hotel room, and he was in there with his wife, together with a band boy named Bobby. I said, 'How are you doing, Pops?' He said, 'Fine. Everything's going well.' I said, 'You got the songs, didn't you? Because we've got studio time booked in a day or two.' He said, 'I don't have any songs.' I said, 'Well, I mailed them to you.' So he said, 'Bobby, if the songs came in, where did you put them?' Bobby said, 'I think they're in that suitcase over there on the table.' Louis' wife stood up to go over to the suitcase, but Louis shouted, 'Sit down! I didn't tell you to go get them! I want Bobby to get them!' He was coming on as a real mean guy, and I started to get a little shaky.

"Anyway, things got straightened out. He took a look at the songs, he could read music and he knew what to do, so we got to the session, and I believe we planned to record all of the songs in one day. Well, when we got to the last song Louis undoubtedly didn't like it and he hadn't even attempted to learn it. I was in the control room, he was out in the studio, and all of a sudden I could hear him say, 'Bobby! Let's get the fuck out of here!' For a second I thought he was talking to me, but actually he was speaking to his band boy. Every other word was 'fuck,' and he was saying, 'Get my fucking horn! We're getting outta here!' As he walked through the studio he said, 'Fuck everybody!' and as he walked past the string section he said, 'Fuck all you guys!' I finally opened the door as he was walking past the control room, and I asked him, 'Pops, what is it?' and he screamed, 'Fuck you, you white motherfucker!' It was real horrible, you know. I'd known Louis for fifteen years, and he'd always come across as Mr. Showbusiness, a nice guy, but I certainly discovered that he could really go off the deep end.

"I had first met Louis as a fan. You see, in all the years that I've been working in the recording business I will still go out and listen to music. I love jazz, and so even as a kid I would go and see Louis and Duke Ellington play, and I was probably a little pushy at getting to meet them, introducing myself and saying how great I thought they were. I initially got to meet Duke backstage at Carnegie Hall in 1938, and eventually we became friends and the relationship just blossomed. He was a beautiful man, and over the course of the years we worked several times together. At Impulse! [during the 1960s], he made a record with Coleman Hawkins—they had never recorded together before—and then he agreed to do an album with John Coltrane.

"It was really a major feat to get these two artists together, and the funny thing is that Duke was the kind of guy who usually tried to get everything in one take. Even if there was some slight problem with the balance or one of the musicians hitting a sour note he would say, 'Look, if the overall feel is there, that's great, let's keep that one.' Coltrane, on the other hand, was such a stickler for perfection that he would record the same song over and over again. I mean, he could make ten to fifteen takes on the same tune. Yet, when these two guys came together, I'll never forget how beautiful it was after they'd worked on the first tune, 'In a Sentimental Mood.' At the end of the first take I looked out of the control room window and I knew that Duke was satisfied, and I just felt that Coltrane was gonna say, 'Well, we'd better do it again.' So, I quickly ran out into the studio and said, 'What do you think, Duke?' and he said, 'That's it.' I said, 'Come on, let's go tell Coltrane,' and so before John could open his mouth Ellington said, 'John, that's it. There's no reason to do it again.' That settled that issue!

"For me the two most important figures in the world of jazz music—the innovators—were Louis as a soloist and Duke as an orchestral giant, arranger, conductor, and a great piano player, and so I really sort of dedicated most of my listening activities to them. Then, as I grew older, I realized that I somehow wanted to record great jazz music. I was hearing a lot of musicians at little clubs and jam sessions, and many of them were great players who were unheralded and not recording. I felt that they should be heard, and so in 1939 I formed the Signature Records label for that very reason and worked with people like Coleman Hawkins, Lester Young, and Erroll Garner. At the same time, deep down I could always see myself in the studio recording Louis Armstrong and Duke Ellington some day, but then in the 1950s I moved on to Coral Records, which was a subsidiary of Decca, and did a lot of straight pop records.

"From the standpoint of pop music—as opposed to rock 'n' roll—probably my most successful years were when I was head of A&R at Coral. We made the first records with Steve Lawrence and Eydie Gorme, we signed the McGuire Sisters, we had Lawrence Welk, and I remember a manager named Al Green taking me up to the Apollo Theater to hear a black vocal group [the Dominoes] that Jackie Wilson was in. He wanted me to sign the group, and I said, 'Nah, but I'd love to just sign that one guy. He knocks me out!' Al didn't care, so we agreed to sign Jackie Wilson and then later, when I went to the Taft Hotel to pick up the contract, I was told that Al had died during the night. However, a kid named Nat Tarnapole—who would become Jackie's manager—brought me the signed contract, so the deal went through!

"We went into the studio with Jackie, and the first record we made was 'Lonely Teardrops.' It was unique in a way, because it was R&B but we did it with a big band, not a tight little rhythm and blues band but a big orchestra, and of course that became a big hit, and so I continued to work with Jackie. In the beginning he was a great guy, but then he went downhill through drugs.

"At around the same time as we were doing 'Lonely Teardrops' the Buddy Holly situation came about. Norman Petty had produced this record with Buddy in Clovis, New Mexico, called 'That'll Be the Day,' and it had been turned down by every company in the business. I was last on the list, and when I heard it I said, 'Hey, this is great! I want to put it out.' We bought it for like $2,500, but beforehand I remember going to the president of the company, Milton Rackmil, and saying, 'Look, I want to buy this and we ought to put it out.' Well, Rack played it at a meeting to a few people, including a PR guy and a sales guy, and they all said, 'You can't put that out on Coral. It'll destroy the image of this classy pop label!' Fortunately, I remembered that Coral's parent company, Decca, also owned the Brunswick label, which was really not being used, so I said, 'Okay, let's put it on the Brunswick label.' They finally agreed to that, we put the record out, and, my god, it just took off. It was a tremendous hit. So, we signed the Crickets— which Buddy was a member of—and we continued to make more records with Norman Petty, who would send us the tapes from Clovis, New Mexico. Then I got the idea of putting Buddy Holly on Coral while leaving the Crickets' sound on Brunswick. That way we could develop Buddy as a solo artist, and as things turned out he became very big.

"Buddy happened to be a very nice, appreciative kid. He was always thanking me, and he said that he'd love to record in New York City, so I said, 'Well, look, when you come up we'll do it.' Eventually he did make the trip, and Norman wasn't around, and I therefore took charge of the session at Bell Sound when we recorded 'Rave On' and 'That's My Desire.' In fact, Buddy knew that I'd already written some songs, and he asked me to compose one for him, so I and a girl named Ruth Roberts wrote 'Mailman, Bring Me No More Blues'—I used the pseudonym of Stanley Clayton, as in those days it would never do for the A&R guy to have his name on a song—and we sent it to him down in Clovis. Buddy then told Norman that he wanted to record it, and that was his way of paying me back for releasing 'That'll Be the Day.'

"On one occasion Buddy, Norman, and the boys invited us to Clovis, and so their music publisher, Murray Deutsch, and I flew off and landed somewhere in Texas. Clovis was like this hick town, and I don't think it even had an airport. Still, when we arrived we were given a big welcome—they had a band playing, we were given cowboy hats, and it was pretty wild—and we stayed for about three days at Norman Petty's house. Now, another good thing that came out of that trip was the song 'Sugartime.' We were on [Petty's] porch and the guy who wrote the number was sitting on the front steps, playing the guitar and singing it. I told him it sounded good, and he said, 'Boy, I'd love to record it.' I said, 'I'll tell you what; don't play it for anybody else, because when I get back to New York I want to do it with the McGuire Sisters.' He agreed, and so that's what we did, and of course 'Sugartime' became a giant hit. That's how things would happen back then, one just bouncing off the other. I found all of the artists during that period a pleasure to work with. They really were a bunch of nice people, and they also had faith in my judgment.

"It was because of my success doing pop records that I was also able to make jazz recordings. The heads of the major companies were not jazz enthusiasts, but they would say, 'Hey, let's keep Bob happy by allowing him to go do his jazz records. They're not too expensive, and let's just hope that he keeps producing these great pop hits by the McGuire Sisters, Lawrence Welk, Teresa Brewer, and whoever.' After that my discovery of people like Jackie Wilson and Buddy Holly only helped to solidify my position with Decca, and as a result I was able to produce a lot of jazz records.

"I was with Decca from about 1953 to 1960, and I learned more about the business during that time than any other. You see, the great thing about being head of A&R in those days—even though we did things quickly, recording four sides in three hours—is that you were the guy who really made all of the decisions with respect to songs, with respect to the sound and the arrangements, with respect to what records came out and when they came out. You controlled everything. Today everything is done by committee. I mean, nine guys have to get together before they can even put out a record. . . ."

jerry**wexler**

■

A native New Yorker who started out writing for *Billboard* magazine, Jerry was the man who coined the term *rhythm and blues*
to replace the title of "race records" on the black music charts.
After joining the independent Atlantic Records label during the
early fifties, he helped to build it into one of the giants of the
industry, while bringing black music to the masses courtesy of
his work with artists such as T-Bone Walker, Professor Longhair,
Big Joe Turner, Champion Jack Dupree, Ray Charles, Ruth
Brown, LaVern Baker, and the Drifters. The 1960s saw Jerry
largely define the role of the hands-on producer with soul singers such as Aretha Franklin, Wilson Pickett, and Solomon Burke,
and during the second half of that decade and into the seventies
he was also instrumental in developing Muscle Shoals into a
major recording center, working with the likes of Willie Nelson,
Dire Straits, and Bob Dylan. In 1998 Jerry and I discussed his
views on record production, as well as aspects of a career that
has gained him innumerable plaudits and awards, including induction into the Rock & Roll Hall of Fame.

"For me there are three different types of producer. First there's
the documentarian, and that would be Leonard Chess. Let's say he
would hear Muddy Waters in a bar on a Thursday night with his
band; well, he would bring him into the studio on the weekend
and reproduce what he heard in that bar. Then there's the Phil
Spector type, where the whole thing is conceived in his brain.
Every atom, every little platelet is previsioned by him, including
the role of the artist; that would be your songwriter/musician/
engineer. And then the third type I have no name for, but I can
define it as 'serving the artist.' Most of the producers in this last
category are original jazz fans and record collectors: John Hammond, Chris Strachwitz, Ahmet and Nesuhi Ertegun, Bob Thiele,
Alfred Lion. It's not just that they love the music, but they bring
a heavy load of information with them.

"You know, if I am thoroughly immersed in everything from

26

King Oliver through to the New Orleans Rhythm Kings and Bessie Smith and Jelly Roll Morton, and then on to swing with Count Basie and any number of small bands that I've heard—man, I've got a bag full of licks and riffs that you just don't have unless you're coming from this place! That's because I'm a record collector. I might be in a session and need a rhythm pattern, and I'll take a lick that I heard on a Clarence Williams record which I picked up in 1939 called 'Black Mountain Blues' in which I heard a tuba and the bass clef of the piano, single note in unison. Unbelievable! That stuff gave me the chills! I was a kid then, and I had no idea that this would ever have any meaning for me except as entertainment. However, years later I would be in the studio, looking for a lick or a hit or an idea or a sonority, and I'd actually use that.

"We brought something to the game, we brought something to the table, which was information, and it comes more from jazz than from the blues. That was our diction, but here's what is strange: these people had backgrounds in jazz and became producers of all kinds of music, whether it was rhythm and blues, pop, Tex-Mex, whatever. It wasn't so much that they became jazz producers, because by definition jazz producers don't do that much hands-on work in the studio. Neither do folk producers, whereas with pop and R&B producers there's a lot of hands-on.

"When Bob Dylan came to me and asked me to do that first gospel album, *Slow Train Coming,* I had no idea what I was in for. All I knew was that the genius had done me the honor of saying that he wanted me to produce an album with him. However, it soon transpired that he wanted the structure and the sonority that he had heard in Ray Charles, Aretha Franklin, and Wilson Pickett records, as opposed to Woody Guthrie rambling and scrambling down the road with his guitar on his back and making eleven-and-a-half-bar mistakes. He wanted that structure.

"That was in 1977. Many years before, around 1972, Bob came by a session that I was doing, and we took a break and went back to my office, we lit up a cheroot, and he said to me, 'Man, I've done the word thing, now I want to do the music thing.' I wasn't sure what he meant, it was just idle chatter to me, but sure enough, when he came to me many years later I understood what he meant. When you listen to *Slow Train* it surely sounds different to anything else that he ever did. I'm not saying that it's better, but if Dylan hadn't gone through that Woody Guthrie/Rambling Jack Elliott phase, making mistakes on chords and going into odd meters and so on, he wouldn't have been Bob Dylan. He had to do that, but now he was saying, 'I want a taste of Otis Redding.' So, that's what we did, but ordinarily do you think notable producers of folk records like Manny Solomon and John Hammond did very much in the studio? I don't think so.

"People often ask me, 'What do you think of So-and-so as a producer?' and I say, 'I can only go by his records, because I have never been in a studio with him.' Producers aren't in the studio with other producers! Still, among the producers of pop music I think the most prolific were Bob Thiele and Milt Gabler. Bob Thiele accounted for more records than anybody else, and I don't think people realize that about Bob. For his part, Milt went from Commodore to Decca and worked with whoever was there, but especially, to his credit, with Louis Armstrong and Billie Holiday.

"We had such an incredible string of successful records at Atlantic Records. There were literally hundreds of small labels in the early days, starting in the forties, dealing in rhythm and blues and in country; King, Federal, Exclusive, Aladdin, Imperial, Chess, and on and on and on. They're all gone. There isn't one of them left even though we all were the same size, and the reason for us surviving was not because we knew how to manage money, but (1) we kept turning out and selling records, and (2) we recognized the need to expand from this narrow alley of R&B into the big rock field. There was a recognition of repertoire, because you couldn't exist for five decades on R&B alone. It's just not possible. If we hadn't gone into the English thing, into the Buffalo Springfields and the Sonny and Chers, there wouldn't be any Atlantic Records.

"Back in the fifties and early sixties we were greatly complimented. People used to talk about the 'Atlantic sound.' However, there's no more 'Atlantic sound,' because whatever went into the 'Atlantic sound' soon became available to everybody. Today, the way that we are going with synthesizers and all of these gimmicks, a lot of people feel that the use of machinery—of click tracks, drum machines, and so on—is dehumanizing music, but I feel the next step may be the utilization of electronic devices to build in the little human element; the extra breaths, the little pause, the slightly out of time note. I think that's the next step and it'll probably happen. I mean, when we were doing mono, man, we had to be good, because we had to mix it on the spot and it had to be right, right then and there. We couldn't remix it and make it the way we wanted it, and a lot of that credit goes to Tom Dowd.

"Good music is good music. The basic elements have to be there, comprising rhythm and intonation. Those are the two things; it's got to be in time and it's got to be in tune, whether it's 'How Much Is That Doggie in the Window?' or 'Got My Mojo Workin.'" Whatever it is it's got to have those qualities, and then there's the general quality that people never talk about; it's called sonority, and that is the way the sound leaps off the record and goes into your ear. As [jazz guitarist] Eddie Condon once said, 'Do you want music pouring into your ear like honey or do you want it to come in like broken glass?' So again, intelligible lyrics, a good hook, a good rhythm pattern, a good melody—that works. It worked for Bing Crosby and Perry Como just as well as it might have for Neil Young.

"I remember once, a disc jockey named Jimmy Bishop of Philadelphia came to my house in Long Island and stayed the weekend, and we were playing Otis Redding's 'Satisfaction.' We were talking about who was the best soul singer—Sam Cooke, Wilson Pickett, Jackie Wilson—and he said, 'Solomon Burke with a borrowed band!' Personally, I think the greatest singer who ever lived was Sam Cooke. I mean, he moved his voice like an instrument and he had charisma. When he sang in front of an audience he would move in a certain way and he would hit a lick, he would do one of his bends and at the same time he would slap his side, and women would fall over like tenpins. They'd just faint. Jackie Wilson had some of that, but Sam Cooke was the man.

"Different people I've worked with were great. I mean, I can't say that Solomon Burke was better than Wilson Pickett or that Wilson Pickett was better than Ben E. King. They were all fantastic. You can't line them up and put them in order. You know, all of this business now where they have the '100 greatest novels,' '100 greatest plays,' 100 greatest whatever; I can't play that game. I loved Solomon Burke and I loved Wilson Pickett.

"Otis Redding called me a week before he went down in that plane. He said, 'I want you to do my next album,' and I said, 'Otis,

that could be very political. I don't want to have any problems
with [East] McLemore Avenue [Stax Recording], with [owner] Jim
Stewart and everybody.' He said, 'You won't.' I said, 'Well, how
come?' You see, the Stax sound was a fantastic thing, and Otis and
Steve Cropper had really milked it. Now he wanted another sound;
he wanted the sound that we had behind Wilson Pickett and Ray
Charles and Aretha Franklin. There was a different kind of beat
and a different way in which the horns were stacked. So we talked
about that, but then he went under. . . . He was one of the greats.

"I can't think of anything I ever did where the music didn't
resonate with my own personal tastes. There are bands that I signed
yet did not have the slightest desire—and made no attempt—to go
into the studio with. I only ever worked with one white rock
group and that was the Sanford-Townsend Band; Barry Beckett
was the co-producer and we had a hit called 'Smoke from a Distant
Fire,' but that represented a slight deviation from my normal work.

"T-Bone Walker was probably my favorite blues player. I love
the architectonic structure of his solos—every phrase has shape,
every phrase is a coherent statement of its own as opposed to, for
example, the overwhelming majority of rock guitarists. T-Bone
represented a deeper thrust into the blues than what you might call
mundane rhythm and blues. He played Texas blues, which was a
form in which other instruments were involved, and there were
also jazz influences in his playing.

"He was of a vintage where bluesmen played in juke joints or
after-hours joints where workers came from turpentine camps or
from cutting sugarcanes. They came in for a good time on a Saturday night, and that music was for dancing, so it might involve a
drum and a piano as well as T-Bone's guitar, as opposed to the
straight Delta bluesmen such as Robert Johnson, who didn't play
in combination with other instruments as a rule. Nor could they
be danced to because of the constant shifts in scale signatures, time
signatures, and so on. I mean, a Delta blues player—an early Muddy
Waters or early Elmore James—being free to go wherever he
pleased, might play twenty different licks in one go, any one of
which could be a rhythm pattern for a whole record.

"Champion Jack Dupree, on the other hand, was really more
of an R&B man than a bluesman. There were very few piano
players who played solo without another instrument; with a few

exceptions most of them were part of a band. Well, the session I did with Jack Dupree, 'Blues from the Gutter'—and you've got to believe me, it took a lot of courage to use that title in those days [1958]—featured a combination of blues and jazz men. The alto player, Pete Brown, would alternate between Fifty-second Street, playing with jazz people like Frankie Newton and [Hot] Lips Page, and the fleshpots of Newark for the low-down New Jersey blues. At the same time you also have to remember that in Champion Jack there were a lot of New Orleans influences, and there were very few solo pianists in New Orleans except for people like 'Stack-A-Lee' Archibald [real name Leon Gross]. So with Jack there was a whole mixture.

"Working in the studio with these old-time blues players was difficult but doable, because they were very amenable. They wanted to do everything they could, although not specifically to please me, because I always viewed myself as a man who was serving the project, and I always hoped that this came across. I was there to serve them, and I think that they felt it. Trust was very rarely an issue. It was more of a concern when I went south to Memphis and Muscle Shoals and started to work with the players there, because this was like repeat activity; I'd be back time and again working with the same cadre of wonderful Southern musicians, and it was necessary for them to really build up some trust in me.

"There's a thing now in Memphis on Beal Street called the Blues Walk of Fame where they put gold notes down [on the sidewalk] with people's names engraved on them. Recently they invited me there to be so honored, along with Sam Phillips, Steve Cropper, and Little Milton as the other inductees, and it was one of the most emotional and happiest occasions I've experienced. You know, I've gotten a lot of hardware—Grammys, the Rock & Roll Hall of Fame, and so on—but nothing's touched me as much as this. So many people came by for the occasion; they came from Nashville, they came from Muscle Shoals, Eddie Hinton's mother drove 250 miles from Birmingham because she loved the way that I treated her son, and there was so much love in that room it was unbelievable. Well, all of this came about in a strange way, because there was more of a gulf between me and let's say Jim Stewart and Roger Hawkins and David Hood and Barry Beckett than there would be between me and Aretha Franklin. They didn't know who

I was or what I was, and so it took a lot of years to build up that trust, but I believe I really won them over.

"Working at Muscle Shoals was by far the best period for me, from the middle sixties through the seventies. I feel that going to Memphis and Muscle Shoals and watching the way that they made records organically, inductively, from the bottom up, taught me what the components of a piece of music are. I didn't even come close when we had all of that success in the fifties and early sixties. I think my understanding was broadened and deepened so much by watching records being made from scratch rather than deductively from written arrangements. Oh, man, it changed my life! There was such an interaction between me and the musicians, and there was never anything like it in New York or L.A.

"It was more of a culture shock for them than it was for me. Like 'Who is this Jew carpetbagger coming down from New York to tell us how to play our music?' But you know what? There's an abiding love now. That's very important to me, and this induction into the Blues Walk of Fame was sort of a capper for it."

malcolm**addey**

∎

An in-house engineer at the EMI Studios on Abbey Road in North London from 1958 until 1968, Malcolm clearly remembers the days when a suit, shirt, and tie were de rigueur clothing for the recording artists as well as for the technical staff (although women usually wore dresses). After working with various middle-of-the-road pop acts, he eventually became jaded with the British music scene and relocated to New York to immerse himself in projects relating to film, commercials, and his first love, jazz. More than forty years in the business, his numerous recording and mastering assignments for radio and jazz labels are like a throwback to the days when it was standard for songs to outnumber the hours that it took to record them.

"There were about ten engineers working at Abbey Road during the late fifties, and two of them were specifically doing pop: Peter Bown and Stuart Eltham. They were my mentors. It was getting too busy in the pop department and they needed a third person, so they looked around and pointed to me. When Cliff Richard came in to do his first session Peter Bown was scheduled to be the engineer, but Peter was a huge fan of classical music and he wanted to go to the opera that night, so he was there for about the first five minutes and then he said, 'Okay, Malcolm, you're doing fine,' and off he went!

"The first song that we did was 'Schoolboy Crush,' which was originally intended to be the A side of Cliff's debut single. Then we got around to recording 'Move It' and things started to get very interesting as far as I was concerned. Ian Samwell wrote the song, and he literally wrote the lyrics right there on the floor of Studio 2. It was probably the first in-session pop songwriting that ever took place in England. Now that song's regarded as the first true all-British rock 'n' roll record, while back then, having been associated with such a hit, I wasn't an assistant or a junior anymore. All of a sudden I was a full engineer and everybody wanted to use me! That kind of rise was absolutely unprecedented, and I feel sort of good about it.

"We copied a lot of things from Capitol, and EMI's affiliation with them in the States perhaps gave us a little bit of an edge over some of the other companies. I know that some of the sounds coming out of Decca's London studio, for instance, were absolutely appalling on the pop side. They didn't have a clue how to make a pop record. So, we did have that edge and we also did a lot of experimental work.

"During my early years at Abbey Road the studio manager was Chick Fowler. Actually, his name was Edward Fowler—no one ever called him Chick to his face. He was a very imposing-looking white-haired gentleman, and very nice, too, especially as he was reponsible for me being hired in the first place! Anyway, one day I wanted to try something different from the established guidelines. It was for Helen Shapiro's first session, 'Don't Treat Me Like a Child.' This had been scheduled in a hurry so it was in the big, echoey Studio 1, but I grouped all of the musicians tight together and put screens around them, and then I decided to experiment; I wanted to limit [the high-frequency signals of] the voice. You see, Eltham, Bown, and I were very, very good listeners. We used to get piles of American records sent to us from EMI's head office in Manchester Square—mainly on independent 45 [rpm] labels, as opposed to Capitol's records, which sounded great but weren't that innovative—and we'd spend whole mornings analyzing them, how certain sounds had been achieved and so on.

"Now, I didn't agree with Eltham and Bown about every-thing—I was the young kid, so I kept quiet—but I could tell that on a lot of those records the vocals were definitely limited on the sessions. Well, there was a golden rule at EMI, and that was to never limit on the session. This came from Capitol, strangely enough. Peter Bown had visited the Capitol Tower in 1956 or 1957 to study their work methods, and when he'd returned he'd said, 'Capitol definitely does not limit on sessions. They do it only on the mastering.' Okay. So much for Capitol. It was silly.

"The only limiter we had in those days was an old EMI one, which was a dog. It was called the RS 114, and the maintenance people just hated it, but I wanted it. Back then at EMI the mainte-nance engineers did the setup in the studio—a hangover from the days when that newfangled device, electricity, came in—and on this particular day Jimmy Johnson was the maintenance guy. Well, when he heard that I wanted to use the RS 114 he came running up to me—it was about six-thirty in the evening, half an hour before the session was due to start—and said, 'Malcolm, I cannot possibly put a limiter on this session!' I said, 'Why not?' 'Because there's a memo, dated such-and-such, which states that under no circumstances shall limiters be used on recording sessions!'

"Barry Waite was the assistant manager, so I rushed up to his office with Jimmy alongside and I said, 'Mr. Waite, I want to use a limiter on Helen Shapiro's vocals, but Mr. Johnson has told me that this isn't allowed.' Puffs of smoke were coming out of Waite's ears, and he turned to Jimmy and said, 'Well, there may well be this memo, but when a balance engineer wants to use any piece of equipment on a recording session there's absolutely nothing we can do. He must be allowed to do so.' At that point Jimmy harrumphed his way out of the studio, I got to use the limiter, and even though I could never have foreseen it, that record went on to be an absolute smash hit for Helen. Of course, after that it was a case of 'don't knock the rock'—I'd obviously displayed a streak of genius!

"The way that I looked at it was that there's a brick wall. Obviously the loudest thing on the record is going to be the vocal, so you make the vocal hit the wall and you build the rest around it. Don't forget, in those days a great deal of store was put into what one could do 'upstairs'; in other words, the mastering room. I did not adhere to that as much as some people did. Some producers thought it was the panacea—'Leave it to the mastering'— whereas the mastering could ruin it, of course. In fact, the mastering wasn't all that good in our place; we were struggling greatly. Malcolm Davies had a big job of copying all of those American records without the proper equipment. After all, those guys were using 1-kilowatt amplifiers and stuff like that to get the level with no distortion. And do you know what amplifiers we had with our lathes? Twelve-watt Leak amplifiers! Our design engineers would say they were 'adequate.' Well, we weren't looking for adequate. We were looking for knock-your-socks-off at the jukeboxes!

"In those days overdubbing was strictly illegal when union musicians were involved—you couldn't overdub musicians or vocalists or run a track of any kind, unless, for instance, you made special arrangements with the MU because the singer had lost his or her voice. As a result, you'd get the occasional musician who was a real lefty and who would come nosing around to see what machines were rolling. Well, we could have had a machine rolling in the back room for all they knew, but believe me, our little console was not rigged for doing split mixes! You were lucky to get one mix out of that thing! I mean, we didn't even have a vocal booth in any of our studios, so there would always be a little leakage if we were recording a loud voice. We'd just put screens up and say, 'Sing a little quieter.'

"There's that old story about Sir Winston Churchill once visiting Abbey Road and thinking that he was walking into a hospital. Well, I have to say that when I first went there for my interview I thought exactly the same. I looked down this long corridor and it was really intimidating. It did look like a hospital, with that drab fifties decor, everything painted a pale green, cream, and brown, and all of these people walking around in white coats. I thought, 'This is very weird!' Now, we recording engineers never wore white coats. We did wear suits—and as a concession on Saturdays we were allowed to wear sports jackets and trousers!—and the same rules applied to the maintenance guys. However, in their case they also wore white coats to protect their clothing, and I think that was perfectly reasonable.

"Don't forget, all of this dated back to the days when recording engineers were not musical in the sense that we are today. They were literally lathe operators who had come out of the factories. Many of those old guys were still at Abbey Road when I first arrived there; people like Bob Beckett and Dougie Larter. They were nearing retirement, but it was wonderful to be around them, to hear their stories about 'recording with a pack on the back, walking through the jungles of Africa'! Originally, they'd all had musical backgrounds, but now, operating lathes with all that oil, they were like engine drivers, so of course they wore white coats!"

leiberandstoller

■

These days the word *legendary* is an overused epithet, but it can certainly be applied to the pioneering professional achievements of Jerry and Mike, both in their capacity as producers and as the composers of some of the rock era's most memorable and evocative songs. Not that they have confined themselves to just the one genre. Rhythm and blues, jazz, country, and cabaret have all been part of their oeuvre, and their landmark work with Elvis Presley, the Coasters, the Drifters, Willie Mae Thornton and Peggy Lee—among many, many others—has justifiably earned their induction into the Songwriters' Hall of Fame, the Record Producers' Hall of Fame and the Rock & Roll Hall of Fame. Still collaborating on a wide variety of projects following the success of their Broadway musical *Smokey Joe's Café*, L&S spoke with me on several occasions at the tail end of 1998 and start of 1999.

JERRY LEIBER

"I moved from Baltimore to Los Angeles when I was eleven years old and I was set on becoming an actor. When I turned fifteen I joined the Circle Theater, a little theater group that had been started by Constance Collier and Charlie Chaplin, but I didn't get to do too much except sell Cokes and sweep the floor, so after a couple of seasons I got fed up and quit. When I was sixteen I also got a job at night as a busboy, and the short-order chef there was a Philippino cat who had a tiny radio that was always tuned into the blues stations, so I started listening to music that I hadn't heard since I was a kid. You see, my mother happened to have a grocery store in a black neighborhood of Baltimore, and when I heard the blues again I realized how much I loved that music and how much it meant to me. Meanwhile, my sister's husband was an aspiring songwriter and his father was a very established composer by the name of Lou Porter, and when Lou started taking me around the studios where he worked I got the writing bug. So, a combination

37

of listening to those old blues records and hanging out with my brother-in-law's father set the tone for my future aspirations.

"I started writing songs with a drummer in my junior year at high school, but he always had trouble making enough time for us to get down to business. After four or five months we had only written a few songs, and when I put it to him he said that he just didn't have the time, but he had saved a phone number for me from a gig that he had played the week before in East L.A. He said, 'The piano player was real good and I thought he might just be the guy for you.' So he gave me Mike Stoller's number and I called him the next day.

"Mike was a guy of very few words—he's changed quite a bit since then—and he was like a very hip, laid-back jazz musician. So, when I called him up and said, 'Are you Mike Stoller?' he said, 'Uh-huh.' I said, 'You play the piano, right?' He said, 'Uh-huh.' I said, 'Can you read music?' He said, 'Uh-huh.' I said, 'Can you write music?' He said, 'Uh-huh.' I said, 'Well, word has it that you might be interested in writing songs. Would you be interested in writing songs?' He said, 'Nope.' That was my introduction to Mike Stoller, but I didn't take no for an answer. I really needed somebody to work with, and so I just stayed on the phone with him for twenty or twenty-five minutes and I finally convinced him to let me come over to his house for a few minutes and talk to him.

"At that time he was a very retiring kid, very quiet, and when I went over to see him he was only talking about jazz, Dizzy Gillespie, Bird [Charlie Parker] and all of those cats. I knew very little about bebop, but I knew a bit about boogie-woogie piano players and blues singers. I had my spiral notebook with me and Mike said, 'You write your songs in that book?' I said, 'Yes.' He said, 'Do you mind if I take a look at it?' So, I handed him the book. He was sitting on the couch, the piano was in the far corner, and as he started ambling towards the piano and leafing his way through the book he stopped at the third or fourth page and said, 'Hey, man, these aren't songs. I mean they're not "blue-moon-in-June" songs. These are the blues,' and he looked at me and smiled, and he said, 'I love the blues.' He sat there at the piano and started to noodle, play a line, play a lick, and before we knew it we were writing songs.

"In the beginning our writing was both spontaneous and simultaneous. Mike would be sitting at the piano, jamming something rhythmic, and I'd just start yelling and he would catch the spark. All of the early pieces were more or less eight or twelve-bar blues— with the exception of a song like 'Kansas City,' which I had originally envisaged in the same vein before Mike gave it a real melody—and sometimes I would insist on what I thought was a better note and sometimes he would insist on what he thought was a better word. In any event, the debate would always result in something that we both thought was better. Later on the songs were planned far more meticulously and they were more carefully constructed, the lyrics being laid out in a very precise form according to cadence and rhyme, while the music would be composed to accommodate that.

"In the early days, with singers like Jimmy Witherspoon, Charles Brown, Floyd Dixon and Amos Milburn, we would be working alongside such notable record session cats as Maxwell Davis, Johnny Otis and Jessie Stone. These great men were responsible for everything that happened in the studio. They often wrote the songs, they always wrote the arrangements and they invariably played their instruments in an incomparable way. They brought their talent, their experience and their maturity to our sessions, and for two young guys who were just starting out that was invaluable.

"Anyway, the late, great Lester Sill, who was our mentor, arranged for us to go to a Johnny Otis rehearsal where different vocalists would be auditioning for us, and among the singers were Mel Williams, Little Esther, 'Big Mama' Thornton and Little Willie Littlefield. Johnny, who had a terrific twelve-piece band, was always looking for new material because he was producing these people for three or four different labels. So, we went to his place, which was sort of a large converted garage, we listened to the various singers perform, and when Big Mama got up and sang she knocked us out.

"I said to Mike, 'That's it, let's get out of here, let's write her a song,' and when we got into the car I started singing these kind of dummy phrases and pounding on the hood of his car with my right hand, which was out of the window. I was pounding this kind of buck-dance beat and I was singing, 'you ain't nothing but a hound dog.' Actually what I started singing was more suggestive than that, as I was trying to get something like the Furry Lewis phrase 'Dirty Mother Furya.' I was looking for something closer to that but I couldn't find it, because everything I went for was too coarse and would not have been playable on the air. Mike said, 'You know, "hound dog" sounds pretty good to me.' I said, 'That's kinda polite!' but he said, 'Well, I think it's just right, man. I think if you go the other way you're gonna sell that record to ten collectors, whereas if you stay with "hound dog" it could have a much broader appeal.' So, I wrote three quarters of the lyrics on the way to his house, and when we got there Mike went to the piano and set the buck-dance rhythm, and ten or fifteen minutes later I wrote down the finished song, which was essentially a raw shout. We then got in his car and went back to Johnny's place.

"We walked in with the song, and as Big Mama was breezing by she snatched it out of my hand. She said, 'Oh yeah, well what's this?' She was being playful and she started to croon 'Hound Dog.' I thought that she was putting me on, because the way that she was singing the song—which should have been very funky and insinuating—was completely inappropriate, so I said, 'Mama, it don't go like that.' Well, she looked at me, and if looks could burn I would have been a cinder. She said, 'Oh? How do it go?' I said, 'Well, if you let me . . .' She said, 'I let you. You do whatever you want,' and then she said, 'Hey, white boy, don't tell me how it go. I show you how it go.' She put one finger inside the left side of her mouth and one finger inside the right and she pulled it like kids do when they're making faces, and then she stuck her tongue out and she waggled it so fast that it looked like it was going to take off. She did this to the band, and the band fell off the stand, howling with laughter, and she said, 'That's the way it go! It go like that!'

"Johnny Otis came over and he said, 'What's going on here?' and I shrugged and said, 'I don't know. Something must be eating her.' He said, 'Mama!' and she looked over and you could tell right away that there was immediate respect. He said, 'Do you want a hit?' Reluctantly, she replied, 'Mmm-hmm,' and he said, 'Well, these two boys write hits. Now stop the nonsense and let him'— and this is funny, because he wasn't in on what had been said— 'show you the way it go.'

"Mike went over to the piano and sitting there was Devonia

Williams—known as Lady Dee—who was wearing an elegant outfit and high heels, but who was so haughty looking that he did not want to approach her. We soon found out, however, that she was a sweetheart of a person, and she made room for Mike and he sat down while I got up on the stand with the band. I sang 'Hound Dog,' and after we finished the musicians all applauded. Then, as I was coming down off the bandstand, Big Mama fixed me with another look, but this time it was as if to say, 'I guess you're okay.'

"The next day we went into Radio Recorders [in Hollywood] and when I looked out from the control room I saw that on drums we had the road drummer [Leard 'KC' Bell], and right away I knew we were in some kind of trouble. Johnny Otis had played the drums when we'd rehearsed the song the previous day, and it was the beat that he'd laid down that had helped Big Mama to learn how to sing it. Now, however, Johnny had decided to work the session from the booth, and so I told him, 'This is not going to work, man,' and I explained that when we'd rehearsed it in his studio he had been playing the drums to a buck-dance beat that created a certain rhythmic pulse. This had supported the vocal as well as the guitar solo that Pete Lewis played. Johnny said, 'You think it matters that much?' I said, 'Yeah, I think it matters to the point where it's the difference between a hit and an okay record. This is an okay record, but if you go out there and play drums maybe we'll make a hit.' He said, 'Who's going to supervise the recording?' I said, 'Mike and I will.' He said, 'Okay man.' He was completely affable about it, he got on the drums, in one take it was all over and it was one of the biggest rhythm and blues hits in the history of the music business.

"Elvis' version of 'Hound Dog' was based on an adaptation by Freddie Bell and the Bellboys, whom he'd seen performing the song in Vegas to a skiffle country rhythm which was a kind of nervous shuffle. That wasn't true to the way we'd written it, and neither were some of the lyrics that had been added. You see, Big Mama's version was basically the story of a woman kicking a loafer and a goldbricker out of her house, whereas Elvis' rendition took on a coy, tongue-in-cheek, country folk attitude. Revised lines such as 'You ain't never caught a rabbit and you ain't no friend of mine' made the song literal, whereas beforehand 'hound dog' was metaphoric.*

"Only Big Mama's recording realized the intention of the writers and arrangers. It's the real McCoy. Presley's version, on the other hand, is a send-up, plain and simple. Nevertheless, after you've heard something ten million times you kind of believe that's the way it ought to be, and that's what happened to the world at large. They heard Elvis' version and they were converted. It totally outsold Big Mama's version, which had been number one on the rhythm and blues charts for countless weeks, and it's hard to argue with that.

"Elvis was a natural. Only a few ballad singers in the history of popular music were as good as Elvis and one was Bing Crosby, another was Frank Sinatra and still another was Dean Martin. When Elvis sang 'Love Me' and 'Don't' you could hear the strong influence of Dean Martin, although Presley seemed more convincing. You know, Dean Martin was pretty good too, but it all stemmed back to Crosby who had that really lyrical, low, round baritone. There again, when it came to rhythm stuff Presley was uncanny. The first time I saw him dancing on television I knew he was going to be a great artist, because he had great rhythm and great timing.

"We had been commissioned by Jean Aberbach of [music publishers] Hill & Range to write the score for a new Elvis Presley film, and we had traveled from California to New York supposedly to deliver it. We checked into a two-bedroom suite at the Gorham Hotel, and Mike was so excited about the jazz acts that were in town that he said, 'Hey, let's take off a couple of days first and go around the clubs.' So we did that, and on about the fourth or fifth day, after having received a number of phone calls asking for the score, the doorbell rang, we opened it and there was Jean Aberbach.

"In his unmistakable Viennese accent he said, 'Where is the score to my movie?' We said, 'You're gonna get it.' He said, 'I

---

*As originally written by Leiber & Stoller and performed by Big Mama Thornton, "Hound Dog" basically had a woman telling her lover, "You ain't nothing but a hound dog, quit snoopin' round my door. You can wag your tail but I ain't gonna feed you no more." On the other hand, the line "You ain't never caught a rabbit and you ain't no friend of mine" was one of several concocted for the version performed by Freddie Bell and, later on, Elvis Presley.

know I'm going to get it. I'm not leaving here until I do get it!' He pulled up a large couch, pushed it in front of the door, and stretched out on it with his coat draped over him like a blanket. Then he closed his eyes, so Mike and I had no choice. We went to the rented piano in the hotel room and in about four or five hours we wrote four songs: 'Jailhouse Rock'—which became the title of the film—'Treat Me Nice,' '(You're So Square) Baby, I Don't Care' and 'I Want To Be Free.' Up until that point the script hadn't called for a musical number set in the jail, but we said, 'Let's do one! This is a musical, not *Scarface!*'

"It soon became apparent to us that we weren't going to be able to get Elvis to perform in another bag, as Sinatra was able to do when he went from the swing and straight pop songs of the forties to the musical comedy numbers that he sang in films like *Guys and Dolls*. I used to go to the Actors' Studio and watch scenes, and I always thought that with the right kind of coaching Elvis Presley would have been as good an actor as James Dean. I felt he had the raw material. I was in touch with certain people in New York, and one time the great agent Charlie Feldman suggested making a movie of Nelson Algren's *A Walk on the Wild Side*, with Feldman himself as the executive producer, Elia Kazan directing, Budd Schulberg writing the screenplay, James Wong Howe as the cinematographer, Mike and myself writing the score, and Elvis Presley playing Dove. He had lined up a crew that was second to none, and I was so excited I could hardly sleep. I thought, 'This is it. This is what we have been waiting for,' and so I set up a meeting with Jean Aberbach and his brother Julian, and when I told them the idea there was this deadly silence.

"After a few moments Jean politely asked Mike and me to step out of his office while he contacted the Colonel. Then we were summoned back and Jean reported on the Colonel's response to our request. In short he'd said, 'If you ever interfere in any way with the business of Elvis Presley, not only will you not be able to find a job in New York or Los Angeles or Chicago, you will not be able to find a job in the music business anywhere in the world.' Well, they didn't know it at the time, but, even though it meant giving up millions of dollars, we decided to quit there and then. There was an end to opportunity and new ideas, and we had lost our incentive.

"Still, the coup de grâce came after I had been struck by walking pneumonia [in late 1958]. I was in the hospital for about a week on the critical list, and when I finally got home I found twenty-five to thirty telegrams from both Colonel Parker and the people at Hill & Range stuffed into my letterbox and all saying the same thing: 'You and Mike must come to California. Elvis is ready to record.' My doctor said I had to stay home for at least two weeks, and so I called Parker's office at MGM and I told this to his secretary. Two, maybe three days later I then received a special delivery letter from Parker with a note saying, 'Dear Jerry, We expect you here by the weekend. Enclosed you'll find your contract for the new movie score and the recording sessions that are to follow.' However, behind the cover letter was this blank page with just the space outlined for Parker and I to sign and date. There was no contract. So, I spoke with him on the phone and when I pointed out to him that there had been a mistake he said, 'What mistake?' I said, 'Well, there's a page for the signatures but I don't see any contract,' to which he said, 'That's the contract.' I said, 'Tom, there's nothing written on the page,' and he said, 'Well, boy, you just sign it. We'll fill it in later!' I said, 'Man, who do you think you're talking to? Some Oakie from Memphis?' I said— and here I wasn't being totally honest—'I'm a New Yorker, man. I don't go for this shit.' There was a long silence and then he said, 'Boy, I don't think you're going to be very happy that you said these things to me.' I called Mike up and told him and he said 'Screw him!'

"Eventually we took on some very heavy professional obligations at Atlantic and we couldn't possibly supply all the needs there for material. You know, as just kids freelancing we could find artists, write a couple of songs, and go in and record them, but at Atlantic they gave us a roster of three, four, five artists, and they all needed to be recorded, so at best we could maybe write one or two songs per artist per date. Therefore, when we were doing the Drifters, I would call up, say, Doc Pomus and Mort Shuman and tell them, 'We're cutting the Drifters in three weeks. We need a hit song, man. They already have four ballads, so why don't you work on something with a medium rhythm tempo?' and they would come back with 'Save the Last Dance for Me.' They knew what I meant.

"If my memory serves me correctly the initial idea to use strings on 'There Goes My Baby' was mine. I would make contributions to musical and arranging ideas just as Mike would make contributions to lyrical ideas. Well, with 'There Goes My Baby' I suggested that there should be something very large, moving, and melodic in terms of the string section, and Mike responded to that right away and we just put the elements together. It's not like strings had never been used on pop records before, but they had never been used with these rhythms and this kind of material.

"The only act we wrote all of the songs for was the Coasters, and that was because no one else could write them. In fact, the writing and production of their records was a natural extension of what I had been doing during the early part of my life. I had been an actor and a comedian, and I'd grown up on radio, sketching out routines that I thought were funny and then setting them to music. Still, for me there was no difference between producing our own material and producing material that had been written by other people, aside from the fact that sometimes I might have a few more ideas and a little bit more objectivity with someone else's music.

"Take our composition 'Is That All There Is?', which was first introduced by Georgia Brown on a BBC TV special in 1966. We tried to record that song with a number of different artists before hitting paydirt, and even then there was some last-minute drama. To start with, we presented it to Marlene Dietrich. Burt Bacharach was her accompanist and arranger back then, and we really wanted Marlene Dietrich to record 'Is That All There Is?' so I asked Burt to set up an audition with her and he did. We met over lunch at her apartment and Burt played her the song. I sang it and when we got to the end she said, 'Have you ever seen my act?' I said, 'No,' and she said, 'I am glad you are telling the truth, because I would know if you were lying. After all, if you had seen my show you'd know that this song is about who I am, not what I do.'

"In 1968 we presented 'Is That All There Is?' to Peggy Lee and she immediately fell in love with it. She said, 'If you give this song to any other singer I will have you terminated,' and although she giggled and we didn't take her literally, it was clear how serious she was about wanting to record it. She said, 'I know you wrote this song for me. It's the story of my life.' Peggy played Mike and me Randy Newman's first album, for which he had written all of the songs and orchestrated them with Van Dyke Parks. She was very excited about the possibility of having him arrange 'Is That All There Is?' and, when we heard his record, so were we. So, Mike called Randy up and asked if he'd be interested in doing the chart, and he said that he would be thrilled. Mike then sat with him and gave him his ideas, and that's how Randy came to write the arrangement. In fact, going to someone else gave us a fresh approach on the song and the objectivity that it needed.

"We did the session with Peggy Lee, but during the course of it something happened that had never happened before and I came close to throttling somebody. You know, Peggy does two, three, maybe four takes and that's it—she's not in there like Elvis Presley with thirty or forty takes—and she's a consummate pro and she doesn't brook any bullshit. She wants to do the job, get it over with and go home. Well, on this particular date there was something wrong on every take, and having worked with Peggy a number of times I knew that she was being very patient. We recorded and we recorded and we recorded, and finally we hit paydirt. Take 36 was the best take of anything I had ever made in my life outside of take 1 of Big Mama's 'Hound Dog,' and Mike and I both knew it at that very instant, and everybody in the band was also smiling. It was perfect.

"The technician was a young kid, and at first I had been nervous about using him because he'd earned a reputation for being one of Ken Kesey's Merry Pranksters [a hippie troupe that had taken a well-publicized, LSD-drenched bus trip through California in 1965]. However, when we'd spoken to each other he had sounded very bright and very able, and so I'd let the fears blow away. Now he's playing take 36 back to us, and we're listening and we're listening and there's nothing. We don't hear a thing. Suddenly he looks at me and his face is ashen. 'Oh my god,' he says, 'I've put it on in "erase" mode.' He had erased the best take of our lives. What could we say to Peggy? She was out there with her hands on her hips waiting to hear the playback, and she knew that it was the greatest take she'd ever made. Finally she put her coat on and she left, and I took the tape over to another studio and spent three and a half weeks making forty-eight edits between eleven different takes to get the performance. That's what was put out on the record, and although it is good it does not compare to that one take which was wiped. That's the only time in forty-nine years that this has happened to us, and it had to be then."

MIKE STOLLER

"I gave up on the idea of being a jazz musician when I was sixteen or seventeen because I realized that I just didn't have the chops and that my musical taste outstripped my technique. I can improvise better when I am writing rather than performing.

"Starting in 1940, when I was seven, I went to an interracial summer camp in New Jersey. Like many camps, it sounded like its name was American Indian—WO-CHI-CA. However, that stood for Workers' Children's Camp. It was there that I first heard a black teenager playing boogie-woogie on the piano and fell in love with that wonderful music, and by the time I was eight or nine years old I was playing pretty good boogie-woogie myself. When Christmas came around I would beg my parents to get me boogie-woogie records by Pinetop Smith, Albert Ammons, and Meade Lux Lewis, and when I was ten or eleven a neighbor introduced me to [pianist and composer] James P. Johnson, who gave me a few lessons.

"Running into another white guy of my age who had similar musical tastes to me was totally unexpected. He called me and he said, 'My name is Jerome Leiber,' and we went through a little kind of waltz on the phone where I said I really didn't want to write songs because I was sure it was something that I really wouldn't like. He said, 'Whaddya like?' and I said, 'Bird, Prez [Lester Young], Thelonious Monk, Stravinsky and Bartok.' You know, I was more or less telling him to get lost, but he was persistent, thank goodness. He said, 'Well, nevertheless, I think we ought to meet to discuss it,' and I really thought he was talking about something I would hate. However, when he came in and showed me his notebook and I saw a line of lyrics, then a line of ditto marks and then a rhyming line, I said, 'Wait, these are 12-bar blues!' I went to the piano and we started writing, and it was a total shock to me because I thought he would be writing the worst kind of commercial junk!

"I knew something about the literature of blues, because a lot of the records that I had bought for the instrumental boogie-woogie had a vocal song on the other side. That was probably the side that the record companies were pushing, and so while I was buying them for the instrumental side I was still familiar with the content and with the language and poetry of blues, and it was a real surprise to find out that this young white fellow named Jerome Leiber wanted to be a songwriter almost exclusively in that idiom . . . so we started writing.

"Usually what happened in the beginning was a kind of spontaneous combustion. We'd be in a little smoke-filled room in my house, and Jerry—who is a very funny guy—would stalk around screaming some phrases based upon whatever inspired him, and that was usually me jamming at the piano. If something sounded good we'd stop and we'd examine it and we'd work on it, and while he was the words and I was the music he'd fire a line, I'd fire a word or a line back sometimes, and he would say, 'Yeah, that's great, but don't go down on that note, go up on it,' and we'd get into big fights about whether the note went up or down or whether the word was *and* or *but*, and out of all of that came some songs, and some of them I guess were pretty good. I think there were more pretty intense fights at the very beginning, but as Jerry frequently says, 'Leiber and Stoller is the longest running argument in the history of the music business.' Nevertheless, we are indeed not only collaborators and partners but also the best of friends, and we have been for forty-nine years.

"Lester Sill, who was a wonderful man, initially introduced us to the Bahari brothers at Modern Records, and that is where we met Jimmy Witherspoon, who did the first performance of one of our songs in December of 1950 at the Shrine Auditorium [in Los Angeles]. Then, in 1951, Lester took us to New York and he introduced us to Ralph Bass of King and Federal Records and Bobby Shad of the Sittin' In label.

"After we formed our own Spark label [in 1954] we were selling a lot of records in Los Angeles but we were very underfinanced. We started a record company, a publishing company and a sales company on about $3,500, and we had a tiny little office which had a desk, a sofa, a piano bench, a piano and, behind a lattice separator, a filing cabinet and a john. You could reach out with both hands and touch either wall, and we would put the sofa on top of the desk and then we'd rehearse with The Robins [who would later become the Coasters] when Lester was out, so nobody could answer the phone. That's the way we were making records, and we were able to sell things like 'Riot in Cell Block #9' and 'Loop-De-Loop Mambo' by the Robins; over 100,000 records in L.A. and a few in San Francisco and that was it.

"When we started having some success with Spark Records, major labels—particularly on the West Coast—like Capitol and Decca would ask us for songs, and we would present them with songs but they would make records that didn't sound like blues records. You know, they sounded like some kind of swing music and they missed the point, so we were forced to say, 'Look, we have to make our own records because we know the way they're supposed to sound.' That's how we became 'producers,' although no one had thought of that title yet, and in that respect at Spark we were like many guys who owned record companies. A lot of them, like the Chess brothers, were in the studio making records, but we did more because we also wrote the songs and did the arrangements. It was quite some time after Atlantic hired us to make records for them that we started to get credit for making the records.

"At first the response [from Jerry Wexler] was, 'Well, how many times do you want your name on the label? You wrote the song and we tell everybody that you made it. We tell Waxie Maxie our distributor in Washington that you made it . . .' and we said, 'But it's not on the label.' Atlantic finally saw the point when we made some records of songs we hadn't written, and, as far as I know, it was they who came up with the credit 'producer.' That, of course, means something entirely different in the record field than it does in film-making, because if one used the same terminology we would be directors—'Directed by Leiber and Stoller'—but they came up with this label 'producer' and it stuck, and eventually the whole industry went the way of independent productions.

"Ahmet Ertegun's brother Nesuhi, who was a true jazz aficionado and a real scholar, heard our stuff and liked it, and he was sending samples to Ahmet and to Jerry Wexler. They persuaded us to give up our record company and make records for Atlantic, and they paid us a royalty just for making them. As producers, I mostly worked on preparing the music, doing the arranging, and playing the piano, while Jerry [Leiber] worked with the singers on interpretation, and we'd rehearse them for at least two weeks and then go in and cut four sides. While I was playing piano out on the floor

Jerry would be directing from the booth, and that's the way we worked.

"In 1956 I received my first big royalty check: $5,000 for the song 'Black Denim Trousers and Motorcycle Boots.' I thought I'd never see that much money at one time ever again, so my first wife and I decided to take a three-month trip to Europe. Towards the end of it we boarded the *Andrea Doria* in Naples to sail back to New York, but en route it collided with the *Stockholm* and within an hour it was listing at a forty-five-degree angle. It looked as though we'd had it, but eventually a freighter rescued us and, when we made it back to New York, Jerry was waiting at the dock. We embraced and he said, 'Man, I've got great news. We have a smash hit!' I said, 'You're kidding,' and he said, 'I'm not. It's "Hound Dog."' I said, ' "Hound Dog"? Big Mama's record?' and he said, 'No, it's by some kid named Elvis Presley.' I said, 'Elvis who?' I didn't know who he was, but then a day or two later I heard the record.

"The following year we were doing the recording sessions for *Jailhouse Rock* at Radio Recorders. Actually we were functioning as producers without title or compensation, but Elvis knew the records that we had made and he wanted us to be present in the studio, so I played piano on 'Treat Me Nice,' we worked with the band, and Jerry worked on tempi, making suggestions to Elvis. Well, a fellow from MGM had popped in to watch what was going on, and he asked Jerry if he would play the role of the pianist in the movie. Jerry said, 'I'm not a piano player. Mike is,' but the guy said, 'That's all right. You look like one,' so Jerry agreed. Then, on the morning that shooting was due to begin, I went into our office and Jerry said, 'Man, I've got this horrible toothache. I've got to go to a dentist. Why don't you go over to the film studio in my place?' I said 'But they asked for you,' and he said, 'They won't know the difference.' I said, 'Are you kidding? Of course they'll know the difference!' He said, 'Look, I can't make it,' so I went, and all they said to me was, 'Take off the beard. It's a scene stealer.' That's what I did, and what followed was several weeks of film work at minimal scale, appearing alongside Scotty Moore, D. J. Fontana and the late Bill Black.

"We moved to New York in '57, and for three years we would write at home, in Atlantic's waiting room, in the studio or in a corner up at Hill & Range. We didn't have an office until we set one up on 57th Street in 1960, and then a year later we moved into the Brill Building. Throughout that time we wrote to amuse each other rather than follow the market. With 'Yakety Yak,' for instance, I was just playing some funny kind of rhythm pattern on the piano and Jerry shouted, 'Take out the papers and the trash.' I yelled back, 'Or you don't get no spending cash,' and the song was finished in about half an hour. It was spontaneous. It just happened.

"While several of the songs that we wrote for the Coasters were not as steeped in the blues as some of the other songs that we'd written, at that time we were still writing numbers that were close in form to the blues. I mean, 'Love Potion No.9' is not exactly twelve-bar blues in the traditional sense, but it is also not of the same genre as, say, 'Yakety Yak' or 'Charlie Brown.' In fact, 'Love Potion No.9' was something that we were going to do with the Coasters, but the manager of the Clovers—who was a friend of ours and had gotten a job as the head of United Artists Records—called us and said, 'Man, I need a hit for the Clovers.' So we gave him 'Love Potion No.9' and we went in and produced it.

"We were working on 'There Goes My Baby' and I started to play a line, and Jerry said, 'That sounds like violins.' I said, 'Hey, why not? Let's try it,' and so we recorded it with an R&B rhythm section, five fiddles and a cello simultaneously. When Jerry [Wexler] and Ahmet [Ertegun] heard it they thought it was horrible, but we said, 'There's something about it that's interesting,' and when it came out it was a number one hit on both the pop and R&B charts. That gave us the idea of utilizing a lot of rich orchestral colors as well as Latin and Brazilian percussion instruments together with the [South American] baião rhythm, and that became a kind of signature of the new records we were making.

"As time went by the record company became concerned with the cost of the recording sessions, because we went from using a five-piece band to having twenty or so musicians in the studio— or even close to thirty on some occasions—and the idea of us going a half hour overtime panicked them. I remember them calling us on the carpet, so to speak, after the session that we did with Ben E. King when we went half an hour or an hour overtime to get four songs done. Ultimately, of course, it turned out all right, because two of the songs became smash hits; 'Spanish Harlem' and 'Stand By Me' were done at the same session.

"One day Lester Sill called us and said he had this talented fellow who would like to hang out with us as a sort of apprentice. We had never heard of Phil Spector, but as a favor to Lester we flew Phil from Los Angeles to New York and signed him to a writing and production deal. Also, to provide him with some extra income, we hired him as an additional guitar player on many of our recording sessions. At that time we were already using as many as four guitars on our big sessions for artists like the Drifters, so Phil became the fifth guitarist, and after the sessions were over he would listen to all of the playbacks and also attend the mixing sessions to watch and listen to Jerry and I as we made final mixes.

"Later, Phil started his own record company with Lester— called Philles, after Phil and Les—and he had an enormous string of hits, many of which he cowrote with Jeff Barry and Ellie Greenwich. Then, in 1963, when Jerry and I were on our way to Bell Sound Studios to record the Drifters, we bumped into Phil on Broadway. He was just in from Los Angeles, and we told him that we were recording the Drifters and asked him to come by later and hang out. In fact, we said jokingly, 'Bring your guitar and maybe we'll put you on the contract and pay you scale!' So, he did come by, and he played a fine guitar solo on 'On Broadway.'

"After a couple of years of running our own Red Bird label, producing or supervising production and teaching our protégés, we decided to withdraw from the mainstream of pop writing and record production. Our next major effort was Peggy Lee's 'Is That All There Is?' and then in the early seventies we went to London, where we produced Stealer's Wheel, Procol Harum and Elkie Brooks. By then the attitude among recording artists had become very relaxed, studios were taken for full days, and there was no restriction about having to get four sides in three hours, which is what we grew up on. That's why in the early days we did a great deal of preparation, working with the Robins and later the Coasters. We'd work for weeks in order to get the harmonies and the backgrounds right. We didn't want to waste any money in the studio because it was expensive—even though by today's standards it was next to nothing—and I think that our records for the most part show that kind of preparation.

"Thirty-five, forty years ago there weren't such rigid playlists, and if disc jockeys liked something they could play it and it might catch on. Of course, it's claimed that the evil involved there was the potential for payola, which was true, but in addition to that there were times when a disc jockey just liked a record. He played it and suddenly it became a hit in one city, and then other cities picked up on it. Today that's not likely to happen, and everything is now also geared towards album sales, whereas years ago we used to go in and make four sides, pick the two best, and put them out on a record, and you could have a hit without an album. Your profit as a record company was not nearly as big, but it was better for songs.

"These days a lot of recordings start with a click track and a bass, and guys who are on a great record may never even meet each other. That's a very different experience from something that is done simultaneously and it produces a very different result. When Jerry and I started it was 'go for broke.' You know, if the vocalist sang a wrong word you either left the wrong word in when the track sounded great or you stopped it and started again from scratch. You had no ability to redo the vocal without redoing the band, and although you gained a lot from the ability to do that with the advent of multitrack, you lost something very special from the situation where everybody was going for broke. . . . But hey, it's a brave new world, and it's changing all the time!"

mickie**most**

■

Artist, producer, publisher, record label exec, and studio owner, Mickie has pretty much done it all during more than forty years in the music business, and it was the blues and R&B that first drew him in before rock 'n' roll encouraged him to pick up a guitar. On the *London Sunday Times* list as one of the Top 200 most successful people in Britain, he resides in palatial splendor in his native North London and makes the art of the hit maker sound ever so simple.

"I have always preferred making singles instead of albums, and I think that's because I can still remember those days in the mid-fifties when albums were too expensive for me to buy. They were for people who had money to burn! In fact, one of the only albums that I bought back then was the first by Elvis Presley, and I still play that today, so I've certainly had my five bob's [fifty cents'] worth out of it! Most of the albums would just have one or two songs that you liked and the rest was throwaway, so we were really hot for singles and we lived in this world of jukeboxes. That was our entertainment. Any café that had a jukebox and a pinball machine was Las Vegas for us in the fifties, and I don't think I ever grew out of that.

"My girlfriend was from South Africa, and when she returned there her family said I would have to follow her if I wanted something more permanent. They thought I wouldn't bother but I did, and they then made it clear that I would have to spend four years there as they didn't know me, which seemed sensible. Well, during those four years I had a lot of hit records as a singer, and I also produced the records as there weren't any producers in that very small market. That's how I learned to produce.

"I did my four years and then I came back to England in '62, and in '63 I discovered the Animals. I was on tour with the Everly Brothers, Little Richard, and Bo Diddley, and after we'd played a show in Newcastle we went to this club called the Club-A-Gogo and onstage were the Animals. I thought, 'Ah, this is what I've been looking for ever since I've been back!' At that point the music scene was really bland, with people like Eden Kane and John Leyton, but the Beatles and their like were also just starting to hit, and so I was fortunate to be in the right place at the right time.

"The record companies didn't like the idea of you doing things that were outside the norm, but I just signed the groups to myself and I financed them, offering them a royalty and a deal, and then it was up to me to make this deal work. Fortunately, I had already been recording with EMI, and they were interested in what I was doing. They had a label manager there working for Motown named Derek Everett, and he liked my work—the first record that came out was a hit, the second record was number one all over the world, and after that I never had a problem.

"The Animals got a tour with Chuck Berry on the strength of a Top 20 hit that we'd just had with a record called 'Baby Let Me Take You Home,' and they would perform 'House of the Rising Sun' onstage. I thought it should be their next single, so after they'd played a show in Liverpool they got on the sleeper overnight to London and I picked them up early in the morning along with their drum kit, amplifiers, and all their gear. We were booked into Kingsway Recording Studio for a three-hour session from eight until eleven, and by eight-fifteen, take 2, I said, 'That's the one!' Then, in the remaining two hours and forty-five minutes, we made the album.

"That consisted of songs that they wanted to record, really. Songs that they had rehearsed and played many times as part of their repertoire, so I said, 'Okay, go for it!' We did everything live, straight to mono, and that's how it all started. After that, for me, it was a case of hit after hit. The next one was 'Tobacco Road' with the Nashville Teens, followed by 'I'm Into Something Good' with Herman's Hermits.

"I had this Goffin and King tune, 'I'm Into Something Good,' which was really catchy, and I really thought it needed somebody youthful-looking. Herman's Hermits' management had called me many times and asked me to take a look at them, so I said, 'Send me a photograph,' and as soon as I saw the photo I envisaged Peter Noone as a young [President] Kennedy. I quickly went up to Bolton, where the band was playing, and they were doing all of the pop R&B stuff such as 'Mother-In-Law,' 'Poison Ivy,' and so on.

I'd brought 'I'm Into Something Good' with me, and they just fitted it really well, so I told them to learn the song by Sunday and we would record it then. That's basically what happened, and it was as simple as that.

"I used to spend every other week in New York or Los Angeles, scouring around places such as the Brill Building for material. I had all of these appointments set up for me, so when I arrived there on a Sunday night I'd have my schedule and then from Monday morning to Friday evening I'd visit publishers and listen to tunes. On Friday night I'd return to London, record the material the following week, and then go back to the States the next Sunday. That's all I did for five years.

"The progression normally comes from America with regard to what is dictated in terms of beats per minute. American black music is the only black music. British black music is really white. For something to be a hit there has to be that bit of magic. The song, the recording; the whole thing has to add up in my mind to a hundred, and when I hear it I just go, 'That's it!' At other times I might hear a great song but the arrangement isn't doing it for me, so I'll rework it, and often that'll turn out to be what is needed. I just seem to have the ability to do that, I don't know why. There again, there are also times in your life when you're wrong—perhaps it was the wrong timing for the record, it came out too early or too late, we didn't pick up the airplay, whatever—but if it doesn't succeed it doesn't succeed, and making excuses is a negative. You just have to say, 'Okay, I goofed. I've got to try harder next time.'

"Of course, after 'House of the Rising Sun' all of the sessions that I was ever involved with took longer than fifteen minutes! I mean, that was just one of those freak things, but still, as far as I'm concerned, once a performance is on tape it's just pointless to keep going on. With ['House of the Rising Sun'] I realized I'd got it, and I must have got it because the record's sold millions and millions for more than thirty years. I'm sure if I'd spent another two weeks doing it I would never have made it any better. It would probably have got worse.

"Still, as we moved towards the late sixties things were changing technically. We went from mono to stereo, four-track to eight-track to sixteen-track, and things obviously began to take longer, but I personally like to be in and out of the studio. I just can't keep things up for that amount of time, really; it's just too long. Also, as you get older you don't want to waste so much time doing something that you used to do in three hours. We used to do a whole single and maybe a spare B side in a three-hour session—certainly we'd get the master done—and even all of those Donovan records, some of which were quite complicated, were done in three hours.

"Having said that, I think there are records that suit the lengthier kind of sessions. A lot of the dance and rap records suit it, because you've got programmed material, and once you've got the vibe right on the program it remains right. So, you can do overdubs and so on and maintain the energy, but I do believe that when you're performing group music the recordings sound and feel better when everything is played together. If they're good players and they're well rehearsed they should play in time, and that will produce a better feeling. After all, most people buy records because they feel and sound right—musically, they don't understand, and why should they? They're not musicians. But instinctively they know.

"By the late sixties Clive Davis was the main man at CBS, and I'd been recording for them for about five years, bringing them Donovan, Lulu, the Yardbirds, and so on. We had a very good relationship with Epic Records, but for some unknown reason Clive apparently felt that singles were past it. He thought that people would stop buying singles and just buy albums, but I didn't share that belief at all. I always thought that the single was kind of the flag waver for the album, so when I formed the RAK Records label in late '69 I decided that, as all of the major companies were now leaning towards dumping singles and signing artists with the album concept in mind, I would take care of the singles market myself. As it turned out, the first twenty-seven records that we issued on RAK all made the Top 50.

"I was recording an album—that never got finished—with Jeff Beck at Motown in Detroit when I first saw Suzi Quatro. The manager of a group called Cradle invited us to see them in our spare time, and they were pretty good, but it was the bass player who caught my attention. She was not singing at the time, she was just standing at the back, but she played very well, and I thought that she had something. So I told the manager that I was not interested, although if the group didn't make it and it should break up, then give her my number in London and I'd like to talk to her. Well, sometime later she phoned and said that the group had broken up, so I sent her some money, a contract, and a plane ticket, and that's how it happened.

"As for Hot Chocolate, Errol Brown and Tony Wilson came into my offices in the early seventies with some songs, and I recorded 'Bet Your Life I Do' with Herman's Hermits and 'Think About the Children' with Mary Hopkin. Then they brought me another song called 'Love Is Life,' and I said, 'Well, why don't you do this yourself?' They didn't really have a group, so we brought in a lot of the musicians that I was normally using, and it took a long time to get this record right because we had to create a sound, a Hot Chocolate sound.

"It was a case of trial and error. I kept trying things, and it was almost like being a chef really, introducing different ingredients, throwing them away and starting again. Eventually I got this kind of organ-guitar thing going, this riff, and that's what they got known for. Anyway, that record was a very big hit. The second and third weren't so big—they were a bit too Caribbean, too calypso-ish, and I told them that although the songs were all very pleasant I didn't think they were going in the right direction. I said, 'You've got to write something really black, otherwise there's not much more I can do,' and the next song that they wrote was 'Brother Louie,' which was a black record. That got them back on the path, and then we had all of the big stuff that followed, like 'Sexy Thing' and 'Everyone's a Winner.'

"Before sampling and synthesized sounds, when we were in the studio we relied heavily on the rhythm section, and then if we wanted to sweeten the tune up a bit there were only three or four things we could do; we could either use strings, brass, reeds, or voices. There was nothing else, other than the percussion, and so if we wanted to make a sound that didn't exist in those days we'd have to do so through echoes and mixing sounds together. We did that a lot with Donovan and with the Yardbirds; you know, putting amplifiers in cupboards and microphones in the toilet, and tape running all around the studio for those very long delays. That kind of thing was interesting, but now there's no limit. There are so many preset sounds to play around with that you can't make a decision. It's very confusing.

"Still, the first thing you have to understand about the music business is that there are no rules. You never can tell what's coming next. It could be anything. Back in 1964 I had a deal with MGM. They had Herman's Hermits and the Animals. Then I had a further deal with Epic for the next five artists that I produced. You see, EMI distributed MGM's records in England, and the president of the company came over and said, 'Hey, man, why haven't we got the Beatles?' So, Len Wood, who was running EMI at the time, looked down the charts and said, 'Well, have these ones, the Animals.' It's funny how these things start.

" 'I'm Into Something Good,' 'Tobacco Road,' and 'House of the Rising Sun' were all number one hits in America, yet, six months before, I'd played these records to a lot of companies in New York, Philadelphia, and Los Angeles, and not one of them would take any of the three, saying they didn't think they were right for their market! It wasn't difficult to hear that these records were in for a shot, so I was laughing really. It didn't depress me at all, but the only thing was that I expected these people in America to know. I couldn't believe how much they didn't know, and nothing has changed. They're clueless, and the proof of this is that if they knew what was going down they would all be multimillion-aires, wouldn't they? I mean, the guys in A&R departments would be riding around in Lear jets if they got it right all the time, but they're not!"

sirgeorgemartin

∎

When I interviewed George in 1987 it was just prior to the twentieth anniversary of the release of the Beatles' landmark *Sgt. Pepper* album, and he had recently been involved in the transfer of the band's catalog to CD. Reacquainting himself with the original master tapes had helped to stir the celebrated producer's memory, and he proceeded to recall how his own role had evolved along with the Beatles' musical artistry.

"As far as the music was concerned, John Lennon was always looking for the impossible, the unattainable. He was never satisfied. He once said to me, in one of our evenings together when we were reminiscing, 'You know, George, I've never really liked anything we've ever done.' I said, 'Really, John? But you made some fantastic records!' He said, 'Well, if I could do them all over again I would.'

"Looking back, some of the plopping sounds that we got on the mikes were pretty awful, but I was out to get *performance*—the excitement of the actual live action—and technical things like that didn't worry me too much. Sometimes the engineers would express disdain that I wasn't worried, but it was important to get the feeling rather than anything else. The small vocal and instrumental mistakes that you might hear on the Beatles' records were never intended, but they did it that way. It was live and things such as that sometimes slipped my attention. Once something went through and I saw it was there I didn't think it was worthwhile calling them in again to replace a line; life's too short!

"We didn't set out to specifically give an album a different sound from the last one, but there was this eternal curiosity that the boys had to try something new. They were growing up, and they were like plants in a hothouse. When I first met them George and Paul were nineteen and twenty years old, kids. In just over a year they became world stars, and so their normal kind of growing-up period was taken away from them by the pressures of fame. They therefore grew up in the studio with me, and up to the point of *Pepper* they were expanding their ideas. Consequently, they were thirsty for knowledge, curious to find out what else they could have, and with their fame came the opportunity to experiment. So George heard of a Rickenbacker twelve-string, wanted to have one, and he got one. Then everybody wanted one.

"Once you started something, for a while it almost became the fashion. For example, once I'd turned John's voice around on 'Rain,' played his voice backwards to him and put it on the track, it was 'Great! Let's try everything backwards!' So George started doing backwards guitar solos, there was backwards cymbal on 'Strawberry Fields,' until that was exhausted and it was on to the next gimmick. It was a healthy curiosity to find new sounds and new ways of expressing themselves.

"In order to record the backwards guitar on a track like 'I'm Only Sleeping,' you work out what your chord sequence is and write down the reverse order of the chords—as they are going to come up—so you can recognize them. You then learn to boogie around on that chord sequence, but you don't really know what it's going to sound like until it comes out again. It's hit or miss, no doubt about it, but you do it a few times, and when you like what you hear you keep it.

"Aside from Paul's bass playing none of the Beatles were the world's greatest musicians, but the *sound* that they produced was absolute magic. Ringo, for instance, gets a sound out of his drums which is all Ringo. His time-keeping isn't rigid, clinical, and of quartz-controlled accuracy, but he's got tremendous feel. He always helped us to hit the right tempo for a song, and gave it that support—that rock-solid backbeat—that made the recording of all the Beatles' songs that much easier. His tempos used to go up and down, but up and down in the right way to help the song. His use of toms was also very inventive. The 'A Day in the Life' timpani sound on the toms was very characteristic.

"Obviously, in those days we never had the studio effects that there are now, but we used to try different things. That was always fun, and it made life a little bit more interesting. The most notable case was 'Yellow Submarine,' of course, where you can hear the noise of bubbles being blown into tanks, chains rattling, and that kind of thing. We actually did that in the studio. John got one of those little hand mikes, which he put into his Vox amp and was able to talk through. So all of that 'Full steam ahead . . .' you hear was done live while the main vocal was going on, and we all had a giggle.

"We weren't averse to putting recorded effects in, too. There were all sorts of sound effects that you could get on record, so in the case of 'Good Morning, Good Morning,' for instance, there was a whole farmyard of animals dubbed in from a disc.

"For his part, John Lennon never liked his own voice, and I could never understand this because I thought his voice was terrific. He always wanted it to be mixed down, and on 'Tomorrow Never Knows'—which borrowed lyrics and inspiration from the *Tibetan Book of the Dead*—he wanted me to make him sound like a 'Dalai Lama singing from the highest mountaintop,' while still being able to hear what he was singing. Of course, it was an impossible task, except that he obviously wanted a kooky effect, and artificial double tracking was the only thing we could think of. Needless to say, in those days we didn't have machines like harmonizers or anything like that, so what I did was to put his voice through the Leslie rotating speaker of the Hammond organ. That gave it the effect you can hear, and to my knowledge that was the first time anyone ever did that.

"Before the Beatles came along I ran [EMI's] Parlophone Records label, and I was responsible for all of the finances and all of the contracts. Then, once the Beatles came along, 1962 went into 1963, Brian [Epstein] and I became firm friends and talked in terms of me producing his stable of artists, and I got on a golden treadmill—which actually turned out to be a copper treadmill for me, being that EMI was making all the money—where I was in the studio all of the time. In 1963 I just recorded and recorded and recorded, every day, every weekend, and the administrative side of my job was falling away because I had so much work to do. That was the year that I had thirty-seven weeks out of fifty-two at number one, and I never wanted to work that hard again. Consequently, that was the beginning of me not being involved in the Beatles' financial affairs.

"Their original contract that I signed them to was a miserly one. It secured them to EMI for five years, and after the first year I went to the managing director of EMI and said, 'Look, you should double their royalty.' He said, 'Why?' and I said, 'Well, because we've got them for another four years, they're giving us so much and they're not getting enough in return.' He said, 'Okay, I'll double their royalty if you get another five-year option out of them.' I refused and said, 'No, if you want to do that you do it yourself. I'll give the Beatles the money but I won't ask for any more from them.' They only had an old penny per single between the five of them—including Brian—so when the contract was renegotiated at the end of the five years Brian went directly to Sir Joe Lockwood, the head of EMI, and did a better deal.

"I was always very much my own boss at Parlophone and always a bit of a maverick, and although I never had much money I did have my own way . . . and I will say that EMI let me have my own way. So when it came to planning anything for the label I had the final word. If I wanted to spend five months on doing an album, that was up to me. My neck was on the chopping block if I didn't make it, but I did make it, so there was no problem. I'm sure there was panic in the offices of EMI when we took four months to record *Pepper,* but nobody could say anything to me or threaten me because it was in my charge. They couldn't do anything about it.

"I must say that I never seriously lost my nerve at any point during the *Sgt. Pepper* project, but I did harbor very slight reservations about the orchestral sequences on 'A Day in the Life.' One part of me said, 'We're being a bit self-indulgent; we're going a little bit over the top,' and the other part of me said, 'It's bloody marvelous! I think it's fantastic!' I was then thoroughly reassured before I put the thing together when I actually let an American visitor hear a bit of 'A Day in the Life.' When that happened he did a handstand, and I then knew my worries were over.

"After the project was finished, I felt we could extend that. I thought we could make another album that would be a little bit more controlled, in fact, while still allowing for the Beatles' originality and ingenuity. I tried to get the boys to accept that there had to be a definite form in the records, and Paul would listen to me but John wouldn't.

"Things began to get difficult during the making of *The White Album.* The boys came back from India, and they had thirty-two songs that they wanted to record. I listened to every one of them, and a lot of them I didn't think were great, and I told them so. I said, 'Look, recording thirty-two songs is silly. Let's get down to fourteen or sixteen songs, eliminate the dubious ones, and concentrate on making really great tracks.' They wouldn't have that, however. They said, 'Well, let's do them all and then you can turn them down if you want to.' They then proceeded to record all at the same time—George would be in one studio, John would be in another, and Paul in another—and so Chris Thomas and I had to run between them to try to get the right recordings. It wasn't until long afterwards that I discovered that the reason for them wanting to have thirty-two tracks recorded wasn't entirely artistic. Their contract, which had been renegotiated by Brian, stipulated that it would expire within a certain period of time or within a certain number of titles recorded. Therefore, the more titles that they recorded, the quicker they got out of the contract. Meanwhile, I was naive enough to think that their decision was just artistic.

"Personally, my favorites among all of their albums are—working backwards—*Abbey Road, Pepper, Revolver,* and *Rubber Soul,* and I also have a sneaking affection for the first two [*Please Please Me* and *With the Beatles*]. I think we all knew that *Abbey Road* would be their swan song, but I look back on it as a happy time. We had been very unhappy during *Let It Be*—that was a miserable experience—and I never thought we would get back together again. So I was quite surprised when Paul rang me up and asked me to produce another record for them. He said, 'Will you really produce it?' and I said, 'If I'm really allowed to produce it I'll really produce it. If I have to go back and accept a lot of instructions which I don't like, then I won't do it.' But Paul said they wanted me to produce it as I used to, and once we got back in the studio it really was nice.

"The boys tended to record their own items, and sometimes we would work in different studios simultaneously. There again, for the tracks where more forces were needed the other boys would come in. 'Because,' for example, was very much a John song, but it needed the combined singing of the three men [excluding Ringo], so obviously it became a joint effort. Between us we also created a backing with John playing a riff on guitar, me duplicating every note on an electronic harpsichord, and Paul playing bass. Each note between the guitar and harpsichord had to be exactly together, and as I'm not the world's greatest player in terms of timing I would make more mistakes than John did, so we had Ringo playing a regular beat on hi-hat to us through our head-phones. We had no drum machines in those days, so Ringo was our drum machine. After that the three boys sang the whole song together in harmony, and then we overlaid another three voices and then another three voices, so we had a nine-part harmony all the way through.

"*Abbey Road* was kind of 'Sgt. Pepper Mk. II,' and I thought this time around we could make an album that was a little more controlled and boast a definite form, a continuously moving piece of music. However, while Paul went along with the idea, John didn't. So it became a compromise, with one side of the album very much the way John wanted things—'Let it all hang out; let's rock a little'—and the other being what Paul had accepted from me: to try to think in symphonic terms, and think in terms of having a first and second subject, put them in different keys, bring back themes, and even have some contrapuntal work. Paul dug that, and that's why the second side sounds as it does. It still wasn't quite what I was looking for, but it was going towards it.

"They each learned a great deal in the decade we were to-gether, and all of them became excellent producers. Still, when you get as rich and famous as the Beatles everyone thinks you're fantas-tic—and you are, of course—and everybody tells you so. A lot of people don't mean to be sycophants, but they are, and they wouldn't dream of saying anything untoward. There aren't very many people who are able to say to the emperor, 'You aren't wearing any clothes, Jim,' but that's one thing I've always been able to do."

norman**smith**

■

Originally a composer and musician, Norman engineered the Beatles' first five albums, yet, as per the convention up until the late sixties, the records never credited him for his work. Later on he discovered a fledgling band named the Pink Floyd and produced their seminal recordings, before then securing his own chart-topping success as that gravel-voiced pop star Hurricane Smith.

"As a jazz musician I'd been in and out of recording studios, but it was very, very difficult to earn a living. Being that we were expecting our first child, my wife and I decided that it was time I got down to a proper job and earned a more consistent wage, and so, when I saw an advertisement in *The Times* for a recording assistant required at the EMI Studios on Abbey Road, I applied along with about 200 others. The age ceiling at that time was twenty-eight and I was thirty-four, but I lied, and fortunately I was one of three to be taken on.

"I had to start right at the bottom as a gofer, but I kept my eyes and ears open, I learned very quickly, and it wasn't long before I got onto the mixing desk. In those days every prospective artist that came in had to have a recording test, and that's what we started doing as engineers, because we couldn't really cock anything up. Normally, each of the producers at EMI had their own assistants and they would be the ones to keep an eye on the potential talent, and that's what I was doing when one day, of course, this group with funny haircuts came in. . . .

"At their recording test the Beatles didn't make a very good impression, apart from visually. I mean, we heard nothing of John and Paul's songwriting ability. They had tiny little Vox amplifiers and speakers which didn't create much of a sound at source. Of course, every sound engineer wants some kind of sound at source, which he can then embellish and improve, but I got nothing out of the Beatles' equipment except for a load of noise, hum, and goodness-knows-what. Paul's was about the worst—in those days we had echo chambers to add onto the reverberation, and I had to raid the Studio 2 echo chamber in order to fix him up with a sound so that we could get something down on tape.

"Afterwards we brought them all up into the Studio 2 control room, and for about half an hour we laid into them about their equipment and the fact that we needed to get some decent sounds. They didn't respond at all, and so George Martin then asked them if they had anything to say to us. Perhaps there was something they didn't like. Well, George Harrison looked George Martin up and down and said, 'Yeah, I don't like your tie.' With that I just creased up. I'd always admired the Liverpudlian accent; it sounded very humorous, and that just about confirmed it for me. Afterwards the rest of them joined in with the wisecracks, and that was far more impressive than the musical side of things. When they left George Martin said to me, 'Well, what do you think of that lot?' and I said that I'd never seen anything like them. They were so different.

"At that time there was an enormous number of groups coming in for tests, and none of them really showed any potential or anything visually different, but of course these guys did. I said, 'For that alone we should sign them. Just because of their humor and the way they present themselves.' So George said, 'Well, I'll think about it,' and of course shortly afterwards he did sign them.

"When they returned to record 'Love Me Do' we did, in fact, have a very hard time. George [Martin] didn't even come in for the first part of the session. It was his assistant, Ron Richards, and myself who attempted to get the damned thing done, but it took a few weeks to finish it. Now, two sessions may not sound like a long time, but it does when you consider that we did the Beatles' very first album [*Please Please Me*] in one day.

"George Martin specialized more in producing comedy material, and so he often left the pop records to Ron Richards, but in the case of the Beatles I think he got involved largely because of [their manager] Brian Epstein's influence. They had a pretty good rapport—as did I with Eppy; he was a very nice man—and Brian really wanted George to come in and give his okay to 'Love Me Do.' Then, once the single got into the charts and sold well, here was confirmation that we did have a hit act on our hands, and therefore the boss of Parlophone had to take over from hereon in.

"At the recording test we had heard Pete Best's drumming,

and frankly I thought it was okay. I therefore think—and this is just speculation on my part—that there must have been something else involved in the group's decision to get rid of him. For some reason they really wanted Pete out and Ringo in; whether that was political or due to friendships, I don't know. Ringo himself was never a great drummer, even at the height of their fame, and he himself knew that, but he was adequate for the Beatles, and of course the main thing about Ringo was his personality. On the other hand, I personally didn't see any reason why [session man] Andy White was brought in for 'Love Me Do,' because a little boy could have played the drum part on that song!

"The truth of the matter is that, to the best of my memory, Paul had a great hand in practically all of the songs that we did, and Ringo would generally ask him what he should do. After all, Paul was no mean drummer himself, and he did play drums on a couple of things. Ringo, for his part, came up with the odd thing, and he did have an off-the-cuff ability.

"To be honest, it was only because 'Love Me Do' did better than we expected that the Beatles got the chance to do an LP, and thank God they did, because that enabled their writing ability to come out, and after that they had many, many number one hits. Still, although saying that they recorded their first album in one day sounds impressive—and I suppose it was—you also have to remember that they had a whole day booked in the studio and at that time that was pretty rare for a pop group. Normally an artist would only have a few hours booked, and so perhaps an album might be recorded in about ten hours or so, but over the course of a few days.

"Having said that, I really don't know how the Beatles' voices held out for that entire session—in fact, John's very nearly didn't for the last number, 'Twist and Shout.' Paul found it pretty easy to sing, but John was always under a bit of strain, given the timbre of his voice. I remember they did have a large jar of cough lozenges—Zubes—as well as a carton of cigarettes, and he just went for it. Due to the state of his voice we knew we had to get 'Twist and Shout' in one take, and fortunately we did. There again, if you listen to it, perhaps the sore throat and the hoarseness improved the performance. It's a terrific performance.

"EMI always gave us—the engineers—the chance to experiment on our own in the control room if we had a certain kind of sound that we were after. We could go in and try different ideas, and out of that did come certain things, such as tape delays, ADT [artificial double tracking], and other things of a semitechnical nature. Actually, back then the sound engineers were judged—quite unfairly, in my view—by the number of hits that they'd worked on. Consequently, once the Beatles broke through I was also walking on water at Abbey Road and I could do no wrong, so I could more or less do exactly as I wanted. Before then Ron Richards and myself had been struggling to get hits with people like Shane Fenton, who later became Alvin Stardust, and Paul Raven, who would become Gary Glitter—and so the Beatles made it for me, and from then on I was the number one engineer.

"Up until the time when I became a sound engineer the other engineers would always use screens. Everything was screened off so that the separation was good on each mike, but I didn't like that idea for the Beatles once it had been decided that I was going to record them. I wanted to set them up the way that they looked, in line with their attitude and how they approached things, and it seemed to me that they would be far happier if they were set up in the studio as though they were playing a live gig. I therefore threw all of the screens away, and the Abbey Road management warned me that I was taking a little bit of a chance, but the Beatles performed as they did onstage and although the separation on each mike wasn't terribly good, it did contribute to the overall sound. We also got a bit of splashback from the walls and the ambience of the actual studio, and in my view that helped create what the press dubbed the 'Mersey Sound.' I'd receive phone calls and letters from America asking how I managed to get all of that sound on tape.

"You see, as far as my side of it was concerned—and all of the other engineers, for that matter—we were sort of restricted. The material had to be transferred from tape onto acetate, and therefore certain frequencies were very difficult for the cutter to get onto disc. I mean, if we did, for instance, slam on a lot of bass, it would only be a problem when it got up to the cutting room, but at the same time we were all a little bit frustrated that we couldn't get certain kinds of sounds that we would have liked. Instruments like the sitar were terribly, terribly difficult to record due to the range of sound frequencies—the meter would be bashing over into the red, and so you didn't get any value for money.

"During those years we were limited as to how much bass we could put on a record without causing too much difficulty for the disc cutter. Well, Paul McCartney would often ask me for more bass frequencies, and I'd say, 'All I can give you is 2 dBs.' After that they would call me '2 dBs Smith,' as well as 'Normal.' Of course, there was more equipment becoming available as time went on, and then there was the contribution of all six of us—or five of us, not counting Ringo—so all of that contributed to the progression of sounds, as did the kinds of songs that were coming across. Don't forget that their writing was changing, too, and this demanded a different sort of approach.

"Still, believe it or not, I once very nearly had one of my own compositions recorded by the Beatles—I had always been interested in songwriting, ever since I was ten years old. Anyway, it was a Friday evening; I shall never forget it as long as I live. They'd recorded thirteen songs for the *Help!* album, but we always aimed for fourteen, and so they said, 'Well, what are we going to do now for this last one?' They were running through different ideas and discarding them, and I was sitting up in the control room with George Martin and [music publisher] Dick James, so I turned to George and said, 'I happen to have written a song for John, and it's in my inside pocket.' He said, 'Well, tell them over the talkback.' I said, 'No! I can't do that! You tell them. But don't get them all to come up. Only Paul.'

"So, George Martin asked Paul to come up, and he told him that I'd written a song. He said, 'Really, Norm?' I said, 'Yeah, I have actually.' 'Well, let's hear it then! Come down . . .' I said, 'No, no, no. I'm so nervous about it. Let me go across to Number 3 with you and I'll play it to you.' So that's what I did, and he really did think it was good. He said, 'That's terrific, Norm! It sounds good for John.' I said, 'Well, no offense, Paul, but I've written it for John.' 'Oh, right. Let's get John in.' So John came into Number 3, I performed it again, and he said the same. 'Yeah, smashing. We'll do that.' I couldn't believe it!

"When we returned to the control room both Paul and John asked me to record a little demo over the weekend in time for the session on Monday, and that's what I did, but in the meantime

Dick James immediately offered me £15,000 to buy the song out-right. Well, of course, back in the mid-sixties that was a terrific amount of money, and to me it was staggering, being that I had about fourpence in the bank! I was about to say, 'I'll take it,' but George Martin was sitting behind Dick James, and he was shaking his head as if to say I should ask for more, so I went, 'Well, I'll tell you what, Dick; I'll think about it and I'll let you know on Monday.'

"When Monday came I was sitting with my demo at the mixer a couple of hours early, but when the guys came in they said 'Hello' and walked straight down into the studio. I thought, 'That doesn't look too good,' and then Paul spoke over an open mike and asked me to come down. I went down, and Paul said, 'Look, Norm, don't be upset about this, but do you realize that on this album we haven't done a song for Ringo?' Ringo always had a song, so they now had one for him to record, and Paul said, 'We promise you that we'll do your one first on the next album.' Well, the next album was *Rubber Soul,* by then their attitudes had changed, and so that was the closest that I ever got to having one of my songs recorded by the Beatles. As for what it was called, that produces another ache in my heart, because not only could I never ever find that damned manuscript or the little demo that I gave them, but I can't even remember the blasted title either! It was a good song with a solid beat, almost like the solid beat of 'Twist and Shout,' but with a bit of romance, too. . . . I try not to think about it too much.

"By the time of *Rubber Soul* we were dealing with completely different types of songs, and, to be honest with you, the attitude towards not only the recording but also each other was beginning to show not too nicely. Up to that time we'd had a kind of family setup between the four guys, George, and myself. It was superb, and you can probably imagine what a great time it was to be part of all that. Also—and I don't want to take anything away from anyone—production of the Beatles was very simple, because it was ready-made. Paul was a very great influence in terms of the produc-tion, especially in terms of George Harrison's guitar solos and Ringo's drumming. It was almost like we had one producer up in the control room and another producer down in the studio, and of course John Lennon also knew what sounds he wanted.

"When *Rubber Soul* came around it was taking a lot longer to record each title. I could see the friction building up, and I didn't like it at all. I thought, 'To hell with this,' and I told George Martin, 'I don't like what I see and I want to get off this train.' He said, 'They're going to be very upset about this,' but I said, 'Well, that's the way it is.' Anyway, a few days later what should appear by special delivery but a solid gold travel clock from Aspreys inscribed with thanks from the Beatles. That was a sweetener to stay on, and initially I agreed, but it was nevertheless very difficult and I still didn't like what I could see coming up, particularly between Paul and John, who were the main force really. I could see them drifting apart, and I did not like that one little bit.

"Fortunately, EMI had offered me a job as an in-house producer, and so I was able to go anyway. Meanwhile, Geoffrey Emerick had started as a button pusher, and the boss at Abbey Road asked me to coach him and get him ready to take over as engineer for the Beatles, which I did. I told him that if he ever got into trouble he could call me, and a few times he did ask for my advice. However, I left engineering completely behind and I moved full-time into production. Obviously, I could still put in my four penneth with regard to the technical side, but as a producer I was soon working with Pink Floyd and by then I had too many other things to worry about . . . such as Syd Barrett.

"To be honest, in the beginning I'd never even heard of the Pink Floyd. An agent called Brian Morrisson told me about them and said that they were causing quite a stir, particularly with their stage lighting. He asked me if I'd like to go and see them, and I said, 'Yeah, I would,' because at that point I still didn't have too many artists under my belt that were worth anything. So I went and saw them, and I can't in all honesty say that the music meant anything at all to me. In fact, I could barely call it music, given my background as a jazz musician and the musical experience that I'd had with the Beatles. After all, with the Beatles we're talking about something really melodic, whereas with Pink Floyd, bless them, I can't really say the same thing for the majority of their material. 'A mood creation through sound' is the best way that I could describe Floyd.

"There was something about Syd Barrett's songs which was indescribable—nondescript—but obviously had that Barrett magic for an awful lot of people. Some of his songs were interesting as far as I was concerned, but more for the question, 'Well, why the hell did he write that?' You know, 'What inspired him?' Nevertheless, we got along as well as anybody could with Syd Barrett. He really was in control. He was the only one doing any writing, he was the only one who I as a producer had to convince if I had any ideas, but the trouble with Syd was that he would agree with almost everything I said and then go back in and do exactly the same bloody thing again! I was really getting nowhere.

"I never actually saw Syd taking drugs in the studio, but he had the kind of character that, even if he hadn't taken any, you'd think he was on drugs. He was a peculiar person. You couldn't really hold a sensible conversation with him for longer than thirty seconds. Roger Waters had the best rapport with Syd, but even he found it difficult. I remember them being on [BBC TV's] *Top of the Pops* with 'See Emily Play,' and beforehand I took them into Number One Studio purely to rehearse what they would do on television for the first time. I was almost choreographing them—silly little old me, thinking they would actually stick with my choreography! Of course, that all went out of the window thanks to Syd. He wasn't happy about doing *Top of the Pops;* he didn't like singles—he only liked doing albums—and it was while waiting around for an appearance on [BBC Radio's] *Saturday Club* that he walked out of the door and went missing. That really was the first sign of his complete mental breakdown, and he never did come back into the studio anymore after that, meaning that I had a hell of a hard time with the recordings.

"As musicians, the Floyd were capable enough, but again Nick Mason would be the first to agree that he was no kind of technical drummer. In fact, I remember recording a number—I can't now recall which one—and there had to be a drum roll, and of course he didn't have a clue what to do. I had been a drummer, and so I had to do that. Nick was no threat to Buddy Rich! Roger Waters, on the other hand, was an adequate bass player for what they did, but to be honest he used to make more interesting noises with his mouth. He had a ridiculous repertoire of mouth noises, and we used that on one or two things.

"So, they were capable, but I had a great struggle with them after Syd Barrett went funny and left. They tried very hard to write material—I remember them writing a song about apples and oranges, which I dressed up and released as a single, and that sold about six copies. It was around the time of the *Saucerful of Secrets* album, and I really did think that it was all over. We still had to keep the singles coming for the audience that they had established, but the songs that were being composed by the other three guys were, to say the least, lacking in commerciality. Their recording career was going down the drain fast, and then along came Dave Gilmour and things started to pick up again. They were able to get back to what Pink Floyd was all about and reestablish themselves, and the rest is history.

"After producing *Atom Heart Mother* I was the executive producer on *Meddle*. You see, these guys now knew what they wanted, and so it was silly for me to contribute anymore. I thought I'd done my bit with them and encouraged them to produce themselves—they were producing tape loops at home and bringing them in to me—as well as to be resourceful in the studio. Having done that, it was time for me to retire gracefully and offer to help them if they needed my advice at any time. However, they didn't, because Roger—a bit like Paul McCartney—had the makings of being a good producer, and Dave Gilmour showed this ability as well, and I personally think that the two of them together were a greater force than Syd Barrett ever was.

"Anyway, I was getting near to Hurricane now, and so everything else went out of the window in terms of my producing. After one particularly boring afternoon session with Floyd I asked them to count me out of the usual trip to the restaurant for dinner, and I went down into Studio 2 and started tinkling away on the piano. I've always written my songs by getting a chord sequence first of all, and I came up with a sequence that I really liked, along with just this one line: 'Don't let it die.' I hadn't realized that Floyd's engineer, Tony Clark, was still around, but he said it sounded good, so I asked him to record me. I then took that away and eventually managed to write the lyrics, and when I did the demo I tried to imitate John Lennon's voice as best I could, because I thought the song would suit him.

"Well, I was in my office one day and who should walk past but Mickie Most. I played my little demo to him and afterwards he said, 'Who's that, then?' I said, 'I won't tell you yet. Just tell me what you think.' So he listened to it again and then he said, 'If anybody brought that in to me to release I'd take it straightaway because that's a top 3 hit.' I said, 'You're joking!' He said, 'Who's that singing?' I said 'Well, it doesn't matter who's singing. It's for John Lennon.' He said, 'Forget John Lennon. Who's that singing?' I said, 'It's me. Now you're going to change your mind, aren't you?' and he said, 'No, I'm not, actually. I didn't know you could make that kind of noise.' I said, 'It's the only kind of noise I can make!'

"Mickie said I should release the recording as is, and I told him that I wanted to add some strings, so he told me to do that and then release it. He wanted his own company, RAK, to publish it, but being that I was employed by EMI I had to give them first option. I played the recording at a sales meeting, and the remarks weren't very nice, with some people saying it sounded like a strangulated John Lennon. It got the thumbs-down, and so I told EMI's head of marketing that I wanted to buy the tape back—it had only cost about £80 [$200] to make, because I'd played everything on it except the strings—and that Mickie Most wanted to release it. Well, Mickie was held in very high esteem, and so after they heard this the EMI top brass now wanted to release it themselves. I didn't want them to, but in the end I agreed that it wouldn't look very good if an EMI producer released a single on RAK, so I let them release the song on the understanding that Mickie would publish it, and that's what happened.

"My wife and I were on holiday in Corfu at the time of the song's release, and while we were there I received a telegram to say that it had entered the charts at number eighteen. Soon after that it jumped to number two, but as I was still away I couldn't do *Top of the Pops*. At that time [1972] I had long hair, and so Mickie had the brilliant idea of finding someone who had hair like me and having the back of his head photographed. That's all that people saw when they did the chart rundown on *Top of the Pops!*

"As for the name, Norman didn't have much of a ring to it, but I wanted to retain Smith, and after trying different ideas I saw the old movie *Hurricane Smith* being advertised in the *TV Times* [listings guide]. As it happens, a group already had that name, and halfway through the labels being printed for 'Don't Let It Die' their lawyer contacted EMI and said we couldn't use it. In the end they thrashed out a deal whereby whoever got a hit first would retain the name. . . . I got the hit.

"The follow-up single didn't do anything, but then I came up with the tune to 'Oh, Babe, What Would You Say?' and I gave it to Roger Cook and Roger Greenaway to write the lyrics. They were writers of the year, but it took them weeks to get back to me, and then, when they did, I couldn't believe the lyric which these two guys had concocted. I think it was called 'I'll Take Tea If That's Okay,' and it was about this guy who had a hang-up with alcohol, leading to the line 'so I'll take tea if that's okay. . . .' Well, you know where that ended up: the bin! After another few weeks I myself wrote the lyrics to 'Oh, Babe,' and while it went to number four in Britain it made number one in America. I was fifty, and there I was on the *Tonight Show* with Johnny Carson and doing a concert tour in my frills and flares!''

geoffemerick

■

At the age of twenty Geoff made his debut as the Beatles' recording engineer by conjuring up the hallucinatory sounds on
"Tomorrow Never Knows," and his contribution to the band's
landmark *Sgt. Pepper* album the following year earned him a
Grammy Award. Full of fresh ideas, devoid of preconceptions,
and ably assisted by his colleagues at Abbey Road, Geoff was
a true innovator in his field, and he has adhered to the tried-
and-trusted methods ever since.

"George Martin and I worked so closely together over the years
that we knew exactly what the other was thinking and wanted. It
was a great working combination, just incredible. In fact, everybody
used to think it was a little bit odd sometimes, because we'd virtually go through a session and not say two words to each other. We
didn't need to. We just got on with our own jobs and it worked
out fine.

"From the time that I started working with the Beatles on the
Revolver album there were hardly any vocals or instruments that
weren't doctored in some way, and I have to say that a lot of this
was pretty innovative. You see, up until that time the technical
approach had roughly been that if something didn't look right on
paper then you couldn't do it. Without any disrespect, that was
like the BBC approach, because if something was being broadcast
and the vocal happened to be sibilant the offending engineer would
be hauled onto the carpet and told off. These were the guidelines
according to technical people who weren't really doing the job in
practice—'You can't do that, because you're going to overload that
stage in that amplifier,' and so on.

"The things that we were doing in the mid-sixties were considered horrendous and would never have been allowed by EMI eighteen months earlier. We were basically driving the equipment to
its limit. On the *Sgt. Pepper* album, for instance, 'A Day in the Life'
was a milestone recording. We put a lot of tape echo on the vocal,
and that sound always suited John's voice. He could hear it in his

headphones, and he used that echo for rhythmic feel on a lot of the songs that he performed. He had a cutting voice that used to trigger the echo so well.

"There was a great feel about 'A Day in the Life.' It was very exciting, especially when the day came to dub on the orchestra. Everything had been building up to that. At the end of the track, by careful fader manipulation, I gradually built the orchestra up to reach its climactic peak, and my technique for something like that back then was a little bit psychological. I brought the sound up to a point and then, about halfway through the crescendo, slightly faded it back in level without the listener being able to discern this. That gave me more room for maneuver, so that I could push the level up to its maximum over a longer period of time instead of shoving it straight up there to start with. It was all a case of having a feel for the music rather than just concentrating on the technical side. People couldn't understand how, after a certain point, the sound got louder and louder but the meters hardly moved. For that famous final piano chord I had to fade the level up and up and up as the chord decayed in order to get every last drop of sound. That's why the hiss and amplifier noise increase right at the end.

"George Harrison's Indian track, 'Within You, Without You,' presented problems in the recording technique because hearing very quiet instruments being amplified almost like electric guitars caused concern to the musicians, who had never heard them that way. The tablas, especially, sounded so different being close-miked and compressed. That a great track. There again, another thing that I recall about the *Pepper* album is the sound of the rhythm parts on the 'Sgt. Pepper' theme at the beginning and during the 'Reprise'; the way that the bass drum and snare sort of thundered out. No one had heard the bass drum sounding that way before, and that was largely achieved by padding it with chunky woolen sweaters to give a really hard and solid effect. Later on we would take the front skin off the bass drum, but this was before that idea came about. Stuffing the drum with cushions and rags to deaden the sound has now become a normal practice, but in those days it was novel.

"*Pepper* was a very personal project, and everyone had become very close to it, but we never realized the impact that it was going to have. We knew that it was different, but that could have gone one way or the other. You know, it could have been stamped as awful. Thankfully, it wasn't. For me that album is still the thing that I'm most proud of and get the most excitement from. A lot of people think that *Abbey Road* is a better album, but *Pepper* is better to me. Still, it's amazing that *Abbey Road* was put on a pedestal of its own, considering what it had to live up to. Most people said that the Beatles would never be able to follow *Sgt. Pepper,* but they did with *Abbey Road.* On the other hand, the *White Album* meant nothing to me, nothing at all. I hated it. Because of all the personal tensions I walked out halfway through, but that record just never meant a thing—and it shouldn't have been a double album either.

"By the time of the *White Album* all four Beatles rarely recorded in the same room at the same time, and so it didn't seem all that odd when Paul, George, and Ringo got together at the start of '94 to do the overdubs for 'Free as a Bird' [John's vocal-and-piano cassette home demo of one of his songs]. They did a couple of run-throughs in order to work out who was going to play what, and then, when it came to the actual recording, everything was done one at a time. It was much the same when they did 'Real Love' the following year, and, in all, each of the songs took about two and a half weeks to complete. We didn't work long hours— usually it was from midday to, like, seven at night, five days a week—and I have to say that a lot of the session time was actually taken up with good conversations about the past. In fact, I think that [producer] Jeff Lynne was quoted as saying that the conversation was more interesting than the actual sessions! They were just reminiscing about the old days, and it was great.

"I tried to clean up the actual sound as best as I could, but in terms of employing effects I really didn't dare attempt to try anything. Basically, the sound that you hear on there is the sound that was on John's cassette—which was really Lennonish—albeit a hundred percent cleaner after I faded stuff up and down. There were no clever tricks added to that. Jeff [Lynne] just tried to space out the gaps between the words in order to make the whole thing fit together more rhythmically, but that was it. We originally tried to overdub straight to the vocal tape, but there were too many variants, so we just spun in a few words and lines. This applied more to 'Free as a Bird,' as we had to open it up in order to put Paul and George's new verses in.

"We didn't want to add any sort of modern devices to the mixes, and the same applied to the entire *Beatles Anthology* project [comprising three double-CDs' worth of outtakes]. Originally I had been Norman Smith's second engineer, and he had really taught me my job, so, knowing how he had worked, I sort of bore that in mind when I was mixing the first two *Anthology* sets. It's hard to put a finger on how his sound varied from mine—maybe it was just a bit softer, more mellow—but on *Anthology 1* and *2* I tried to mix as I thought Norman would have done.

"Personally I'm anti-computers. They've got this de-noising system at Abbey Road to remove all of the hiss and crackles, but first of all there was no noise on the original tapes, and secondly it screws the sound up in my opinion. That's why I made sure they didn't use the de-noiser on the second and third *Anthology* sets. It was more useful on *Anthology 1* because that made use of a load of old tapes, but even then it was like listening to the first Edison recording on a cylinder where some surface noise tells you it's dated, and then removing this and leaving a terrible phasey swish across it. I think they went a bit too far in that respect. They should have left a bit of surface noise on it. If that was the way it was recorded, then that's the way it is and that's the way it should be."

al schmitt

■

The winner of six Grammy Awards as Best Engineer, Al has recorded and mixed over 140 gold and platinum albums during a career that stretches back to the early fifties. Elvis Presley, Frank Sinatra, Michael Jackson, Madonna, Quincy Jones, George Benson, Tony Bennett, Sam Cooke, and the Jefferson Airplane are just a few of the acts who have benefited from his skills.

"Having been taught to do everything mono and directly to disc before the advent of tape machines, I learned all about miking techniques and how to balance quickly. It all had to sound right at the same time because you couldn't fix it in the mix, and I still prefer to work that way. My idea of a good time is to be in the studio with sixty-five musicians or more.

"One of the nice things about being successful in this business is that you get to work with successful people. They have the finances to hire the best musicians and work in the best studios with the best equipment, and so after that you've got to be stupid not to get the best sound. At the same time, these kids are starting out working with a guy who doesn't know how to tune his drums, they're using this little schlocko board and a bunch of cheap microphones, and then they wonder why their stuff doesn't sound as good as Al Schmitt's. Well, there's an obvious reason: I've got all of the benefits.

"When I was six and seven years old my father used to take me to my uncle's studio, Harry Smith Recording, at 2 West 46th Street in New York, which was the first independent facility on the East Coast, and I'd watch these big bands being recorded with just one microphone. It was the musicians who would be moved around. Soloists got up, came down and played their solos in front of the mike, and then went back and sat down, and I can also remember looking out there and seeing all of the guys with no shoes on so that they wouldn't make a noise when they were stomping. . . .

"Back in the early forties the studio was recording onto acetate with a glass base. They couldn't use aluminum because all of the aluminum was going towards the war effort. Anyway, by the time I was eight I was spending entire days there, watching Art Tatum rehearse on the piano—I'd sit next to him and he would show me little boogie-woogie licks—and meeting anyone from Duke Ellington to Orson Welles. Then, much later on, after I'd returned from the forces in the early fifties, I worked full-time at Apex Studios, recording Atlantic acts with my mentor, Tommy Dowd.

"When I was first there we would record direct to sixteen-inch transcription disc. We had two turntables to play things back, and I can remember Tommy and I trying to do edits. We'd have a couple of takes and we'd cue them up on each of the turntables. Then, at a certain point, we would do these cross-fades, going from the two sixteen-inch discs to another disc. It would take maybe five, six, seven attempts, and so, as you can imagine, it was great when tape came in.

"On one occasion Tommy was putting all of this stuff together on the mono master tape and I said, 'What would you do if I did this?' I was kidding around, but by accident my hand actually hit the Record button, and he looked at me and I looked at him and we both jumped to stop the machine, but I had already erased what was on there. I can't remember who the artist was, but we spent hours piecing four or five little outtakes together. No one ever knew what had happened, but that taught me a lesson to never screw around in the recording studio.

"One Saturday, about three months after I had joined Apex, I was alone in there, working on the little voice and piano demos that we offered to the general public. The last booking was at two in the afternoon, and it had been made under the name of Mercer, but when the time arrived these musicians suddenly started coming in with their instruments and I said, 'Wait a minute, there's some mistake here. This is supposed to be just a little demo with voice and piano.' As it happens, it was Mercer Records which had booked the session, and it was for Duke Ellington's band! I tried to call my boss, but I couldn't reach him; I couldn't reach anybody. So, I had this notebook in which I'd written down every setup and every microphone that had been used during the sessions that

I'd watched, and I found a session that we'd done with a big band and went into the studio and started to set things up.

"Duke sat next to me, and I kept saying, 'Look, I'm not qualified to do this. Someone made a mistake here and I can't get hold of anybody. I'm totally unqualified,' but he kept patting me on the back and saying, 'Don't worry, son, we're gonna get through this. Just relax!' Now, if somebody had told me the night before, 'Yeah, tomorrow at two o'clock you're going to record Duke Ellington,' I think I would have freaked, but as it was thrown at me at the last minute I didn't have a chance to collapse! I had to do what I had to do or run away and never show my face in this business again. So I did it, and it came out fine.

"Today if you just do the tracks on two songs in three hours it's unbelievable, whereas back in the fifties and sixties we would complete four songs in three hours. We even completed an entire Ray Charles album with twelve songs in just seven hours! One of the advantages of those days was that we guys went from one date to the next, dealing with all different kinds of music. I mean, I can remember a specific day when I did Ike and Tina Turner from nine to twelve in the morning, Henry Mancini in the afternoon, and then Sam Cooke at night. I would do three dates every day practically, and the work was always varied.

"You couldn't keep going over a song until everybody got it right. As long as the feel was there, that was it. Let's face it, if you listen to some of the great old Frank Sinatra records he's not in tune on all of them, whereas today he would be absolutely in tune on every note, because we could tune him. We couldn't then, but it was all down to performance and feel. Singers had to do their vocals live, so they had to learn microphone techniques. As a result I was often able to set the fader and not even worry about the vocalist. People like Rosemary Clooney, I did a bunch of albums with her and it was great. I'd set her microphone and she'd lean in on the low notes, back off on the high notes and just do her own thing, so I could concentrate on the orchestra, talk with the conductor, and balance the sound right there in the studio.

"For me that was the best era. Recording was a lot of fun. I can recall making records at Coastal Studios with Bobby Shad. We'd finish, make these masters, send them off to the plant, make acetates, and then we'd drive up to a radio station in Harlem. We'd give them the record, get in the car, be driving back down, and we could hear the record on the air. This was two and a half, three hours after we'd finished! Today you finish a record and you wait six months for it to come out. You get those after-record blues. But I also have to say that the people who deserve the credit get the credit, and that wasn't always the case.

"In the second half of the fifties I did a lot of jazz sessions with guys like Chet Baker, Gerry Mulligan, and Thelonious Monk, and then I started to do some pop records when I moved to California in 1958 and worked at Radio Recorders. Well, I was engineering a Connie Francis session, and the producer was Morty Craft, and after we'd done a couple of songs he left. Even during those first two songs he'd been on the phone most of the time! Anyway, after he left I was there with the arranger, David Rose, and at some point we decided that we'd double Connie's voice on a song called 'My Happiness.' For that we had to bring in another tape machine, and so we played back what we had done, recorded her voice onto the other machine, and when the single came out it was a smash. There again it was also produced by Morty Craft, who had been in a bungalow at the Beverly Hills Hotel when it was being done!

"Another time a very famous musician and a wonderful, wonderful man named Neil Hefti was producing a session that I was engineering, and he totally forgot about it. This was at RCA, Marti Page was the arranger, Sammy Davis Jr. was the artist, and the song was 'What Kind of Fool Am I.' Again, when the record came out it was still produced by Neil Hefti. That's how it was in those days.

"I'd often find myself engineering and trying to get the performance while all of these producers were on the phone throughout the sessions. Then there were the times when we'd hit the talkback and say, 'Okay, guys, we're on the honor system.' This meant, 'When you make a mistake raise your hand and we'll try to fix it,' because the producer himself couldn't hear it! Back then many producers were just guys who decided they wanted to be in the record business. It was amazing. Half of them weren't musicians, but they were getting all of the money, all of the recognition, and having all of the fun while we engineers were working our butts off. So, that's when I decided that I also wanted to be a producer.

"I engineered people like Ray Charles and Elvis Presley when I was on staff at RCA. I did all of Sam Cooke's recordings, and I also ended up producing his last records. As an RCA producer I signed the artists, found the songs, and ran the sessions. The only thing I couldn't do was engineer, and that was because the union wouldn't allow it. I would tell a guy what to do, but by the time that I told him and he did it, it was too late. So, I would sometimes reach over and grab the fader myself, but that was a no–no and I would be turned in and read the riot act. Boy, did the business ever change over the years!

"By the mid–sixties things were really getting crazy. This was towards the end of my time at RCA, and the whole scene was turning upside down. I'd be doing orchestral overdubs with Eddie Fisher from two until five, then I'd go up to my office and meditate a little before working with the Jefferson Airplane until four in the morning. After that I'd grab a little sleep, come back in and do my paperwork, relax a bit, and then it was back to Eddie Fisher. Can you imagine? It was very weird. I loved Eddie, he was fabulous to me, but he wasn't particularly my cup of tea, so I quit RCA and went independent.

"I produced four albums for the Jefferson Airplane: *After Bathing at Baxters, Crown of Creation, Bless Its Pointed Little Head,* and *Volunteers,* and it was a great experience for me. Janis Joplin; the Mamas and the Papas; Crosby, Stills, and Nash—all these people would come and hang out. There was a lot of partying, heavy drug use, and plenty of debauchery. It cost me a marriage, but I had a good time.

"We all got along really well. I loved Grace Slick; she was absolutely incredible. She worked hard, she was always there, she had an awful lot of talent, and she was incredibly good–looking. One day she would come in looking like a little Brownie Scout, and then on another she would be wearing contacts in her eyes with mirrors on them, so when you looked at her you saw yourself! It was bizarre.

"*After Bathing at Baxters* took five and a half months, and I had never, ever worked for more than two weeks on a project. We'd play stickball in the studio, they had tanks of nitrous oxide in there, somebody would be continually rolling joints, they'd bring their motorbikes into the room, and it was just lunacy. At the same time we did some strange stuff, reversing tapes, multi–ing things together, bouncing down; all things that we'd never done before. We didn't have the automated mixing consoles then, and we left the tracks on most of the time, so if you're wearing headphones you can hear somebody taking a hit off a joint, people talking, and so on. We left that kind of stuff in for those who really wanted to get into it.

"There was one night when I was working on a live album by the Airplane offshoot, Hot Tuna, at a little venue in Berkeley [California] called the New Orleans Club. I was at the bar, and I had a glass of apple juice while the equipment was being set up, and then I finished my drink, went back into the remote truck, and sat down beside the engineer, Alan Zetz. The next thing I knew the truck started to expand and I started to see all of this sparkling shit happening, and finally I turned to Alan and said, 'You're on your own. I'm outta here!' My apple juice had been spiked with LSD and I was totally out of it. I mean, when Tom Donahue got married up at the Jefferson Airplane's house, they spiked the wedding cake! Old ladies were walking into the Golden Gate Park, totally tripping out. That's how they did things back then.

"I continued to produce for several years and then I started to do more and more engineering and realized that this was my first love. I mean, that's why I got into this business. I didn't get into this business to produce records, I got into it to engineer records and to try different things with sound. So, that's what I did from the end of '70 until around 1983, when I had a serious accident. I fell off a ladder onto the back of my head and lost my hearing in my left ear. I worked as the music supervisor on a couple of films, but for three years I hardly did a thing, and that was probably the most frightening time of my life. I thought my career was over and I didn't know what I was going to do. I eventually started to drink pretty heavy, isolate, and feel sorry for myself, but then one morning I went out to get the newspaper and I heard this bird singing. Something about it sounded different, and I suddenly realized I could hear again in both ears. Apparently the nerve had healed itself, and it was like putting two wires together. I had been a cocky son of a bitch prior to the accident, and I think this was God's way of humbling me a little bit.

"Still, I have to tell you, as much as sound is important to me as an engineer, it is the performance and the feel that sell the record. I know a lot of bad-sounding records that were huge hits because they moved people emotionally, and some records that sounded perfect but didn't sell shit. I still feel that people have trouble relating to things that are perfect.

"There's a story where Steely Dan walked into the control room and saw me mixing with the monitors off, just using the meters. Then, when I turned the sound up, it was perfect and they were going, 'Jeez, the fucking guy mixes without even listening!' However, that's folklore. What really happened was that I'd already done the mix and had turned the monitors off, and I was just checking the meters to see what was going on. That's how legends are born. . . ."

ron lenhoff

■

The chief engineer at King Studios in Cincinnati, Ron engineered all of James Brown's legendary recordings there from 1966 to 1972. He had started in the music business in 1955, the same year that Brown signed to King Records, and their working alliance ended when the facility closed and the Godfather of Soul switched to the Polydor label. Originally an electronics specialist, Ron quit the music business despite Brown's pleas to follow him to New York, yet he was still happy to reminisce when I talked with him fifteen years later.

"Most of the time, working with James Brown, it would be down to the first complete cut. He'd say to me, 'Ron, are you ready?' and if I said, 'Yes,' he would cut it. After that, if he got all the way through it without stopping, I'd better have it on tape! I never ran into the situation where I didn't have it on tape, but I sure as hell always worried about it!

"My first involvement with James was when I was asked to remix a mono recording that he'd made in New York of 'Papa's Got a Brand New Bag.' It was terrible. It was so muddy you could hardly hear all the instruments. It took me two days of copying, recopying, editing, EQ-ing, and editing again just to brighten it up. Still, the music was really good, and after that we got to work together a lot.

"You know, by the late sixties James was looking for hit songs to help get him back on the charts, and so whenever he was doing a concert in or near Cincinnati he would come by King late at night and record maybe three or four tracks in just as many hours. Don't forget, at King we had the facility to record, mix, master, press, and label the discs, so the finished product could be ready for shipping within twenty-four hours.

"James was well known for turning up at recording sessions without having written any songs. He'd just have the ideas in his head and when he came in he'd improvise right then and there. He could also play the drums and the keyboard instruments, so he understood exactly what he wanted. He'd build a pattern with the musicians aound the bass and drums, and then bring the guitar in. All the musicians had worked with James for a long time, so they knew what he wanted, and once he got the rhythm section going he would start working on the horns. All the time he was doing this I was setting up sound levels, EQ-ing, that sort of thing. It usually took him anywhere between a half hour and two hours to get everything together, depending on whether the musicians saw right away what he was after or whether he had to pull a few teeth . . . which he had to do on occasion.

"Working with all the people I did, even at other studios, I never ever saw anybody work in a session like James. He knew what he was going for and he wouldn't accept anything but that. When he left the studio he was happy. I never ever had him come back after a session and say that he didn't like it. You see, James wasn't a hard taskmaster during the session as long as you gave him what he wanted, which is the same as almost everyone else I know. The only guy I ever met who wasn't like that was Louis Armstrong—if anyone made a mistake he would just say, 'Oh, well, don't worry about it. We can do it again!' But I can't say there was ever any time I didn't enjoy working with James. He and I seemed to know what each other wanted, and I guess that's why we worked so well together.

"The only time that he ever did anything other than hand-hold the microphone when he was singing was when he did overdubs. Otherwise he'd often write the lyrics just before he was about to do the vocals, and then he'd go straight into it. When he hand-holds the microphone it's like he's onstage. It isn't a studio performance; it's a stage performance. He had a great mike technique right from the very first time I met him, so we didn't really get the problem of his voice phasing in and out. Once in a while we might have trouble with the mike banging around in his hands, but not very often. Fortunately, this would usually happen on what would have been an outtake anyway. We didn't always get everything the first take, but the first complete take that he was satisfied with. If he was happy with it we'd have it on tape. I knew I had to work that way.

"We did add echo, but that was usually done on the session, and at that time it was one hundred percent live echo. We'd use anything to give him an edge, and later on we did use echo plates. Both James and I preferred to always aim for as clean a sound as possible, with plenty of separation on the instruments. I'd play with a lot of stuff, and if I thought it was going to be too far out for him I would let him listen to it before putting it on tape. More often than not his stuff was cut pretty straight, and very seldom would I go back to do anything to it later. The only thing I edited for him, and it became a pretty good-sized record, was a track called 'Baby Don't You Weep.' That was a live recording and it ran for twelve to fourteen minutes. King Records' A&R guy Gene Red was a very fine musician, and we sat down and between the two of us edited it down to a little less than three minutes.

"We would only overdub occasionally and usually this would be an entire number into a performance on a live album—I won't say which. Sometimes we'd drop in another live number and sometimes a studio recording with the crowd overdubbed, either from a concert or even from a game at the ballpark. The problem of putting something in from another live performance is that the acoustics more often than not are different. It becomes difficult that way, but it can be done, it has been done, and I've done it.

"The first thing I would try and do was copy the acoustics, not by dubbing anything but simply by EQ-ing. When I got to the point where I could punch up the live tape and punch up the studio tape, and run them at the same time sounding close, I would then put it all on another tape and work on it from there. Sometimes it meant going three, four, or five generations before I got what I wanted, but, there again, in those days you'd really want to dirty up a studio recording for a live album. It wasn't like today, when the equipment on the road enables a live recording to sound almost as clean as a studio recording.

"I remember one studio that James discovered outside of St. Louis just before he went over to Polydor, and he wanted to do a session there. There were all of these disused salt mines, and in one of them some guy had built a studio. It had a little fifteen-foot-by-twenty-foot control room with all of this equipment crammed into it. Nothing had been done to the walls of the place—it was just like they had carved it out of the salt, no acoustic treatment at all—and it really was beautiful. James wanted to do a rehash of 'Honky Tonk.' The console was eight-track but it didn't have equalizers or limiters, and so we had to start patching this and patching that. I finally got everything set up, and we did four songs—three of them instrumentals, including 'Honky Tonk'—and they were all hits on Polydor. It was a weird, weird studio, but it had a great sound!

"Another time, after he'd done a show in Nashville, James asked me to engineer a session for him there. Well, there were no flights available, so I jumped in the car and drove all the way. It took me five hours to get there, and as soon as I arrived at the studio James and the musicians were ready to record, so we cut four tracks and then, before I left, James told his manager, Bud Hopsgood, 'Give Ron ten percent of that last song.' The song was 'Sex Machine,' so we wrote up the songwriter's contract and I've been collecting on it ever since!"

roy**halee**

■

Roy started his career with an audio stint at CBS Television in New York in the 1950s, prior to securing a job in the editing department at Columbia Records. From there it was a short walk to the studio, and, once ensconced in that environment, he made an auspicious start and never looked back, aside from occasions such as this 1997 interview.

"My first recording session in the studio at Columbia Records was on the album *Another Side of Bob Dylan,* and that was very fortunate because at the time Columbia didn't have any rock 'n' roll artists per se. They either dealt with classical or what they called 'legit pop acts' such as Tony Bennett and Johnny Mathis. Dylan, on the other hand, was their first folk rock act, and on the strength of that job I got a bit of a reputation in the city. Shortly afterwards we did 'Like a Rolling Stone.' A six-minute single was unheard of at that time, and basically I don't think they really liked it at Columbia Records. It was foreign to them, but then, when the damned thing took off, it turned a lot of heads and he exploded.

"After that I began to work with outside clients such as the Lovin' Spoonful on hits like 'Summer in the City'; the Cyrkle, who had a number one record with 'Red Rubber Ball'; and the Dave Clark Five, as well as the Yardbirds when they had Jeff Beck and Jimmy Page both playing lead guitar. The Yardbirds session I was involved with was when they cut 'I'm a Man.' I remember being very impressed with the guitarists because they used little amplifiers at low-volume settings, which was the exact opposite of what everybody else was doing, yet the sound in the control room was, of course, enormous. Evidently they were hip to the idea that if you play a little softer you get a bigger sound when it's recorded.

"I always made musical suggestions while I was taking care of the technical side, but in those days that was expected of us, and Columbia didn't even give engineering credits. Sometimes I would be doing the producer's job as well, and I also wouldn't get credit for that. In fact, I later produced the records of an act named

Peaches and Herb—there was no other producer around—and I never got an engineering or a production credit! Still, I'm not bitter about that, you know, because that was part of the gig, that was part of the training, and I was grateful to be able to do it. I was having a good time, and it's only when you grow a little older that you realize you were being taken advantage of. I mean, I didn't get any royalties, I didn't get any credit, I didn't get anything, but what I did get was a lot of experience doing a lot of different acts. Jazz, rock, classical . . . man, you name it and I was able to get my hands on it. I even worked on show material with forty-, fifty-, sixty-piece bands, a chorus, and soloists all live. It was invaluable. These days I think it's almost impossible for an engineer to have that many opportunities, but I broke in doing that stuff.

"The first time I met Paul and Artie [Simon and Garfunkel] was in 1964, when they came in to do an audition for a producer called Tom Wilson. The company then signed them and released that audition as their first album, *Wednesday Morning 3AM*. That contained the original acoustic version of 'The Sound of Silence,' and later I went back into the studio with Tom Wilson and overdubbed that track with electric guitars, bass, and drums. Paul was away in England, and Artie was probably teaching somewhere, so they didn't know anything about this, but then it was released and it hit big. The record began to catch on in Boston—it was a monster there, and it spread across the country—and then the SOS went out for Simon and Garfunkel to come back and make an album. So, that's how that all started.

"Paul and Artie really helped me a lot, because they started the idea of the producer-engineer. At that time engineers were not producers and producers were not engineers. You could work with bad producers, but there were also some very, very good producers who did their schtick—which was the music—and basically left the engineering to the engineer. Simon and Garfunkel, on the other hand, obviously felt that I was really producing their records with them and that I should be credited for this and paid a royalty. Aside from Tom Wilson, both Bob Johnston and John Simon had also produced them. In fact, Bob Johnston produced Dylan, too, and at around that time I was on practically all of Bob's sessions. I thought he was a good producer; very exciting, he got a lot of emotion going in the studio, which impressed me at that time as other producers were not getting the musicians fired up. There's a certain talent in that. Still, for whatever reason, Paul and Artie wanted to make their records with me.

"As I said, in reality I was producing the records with them. I could get involved musically, and I started to get very close to Paul, who would bounce songs off of me—'What do you think of this? What do you think of that?' and so on—and things therefore evolved to the point where I was a member of that group. On 'The Boxer,' for instance, it was my idea to put the brass and voices on the end and to mix the pedal steel with a little trumpet part similar to the one that I'd heard on the Beatles' 'Penny Lane.' That was actually kinda neat, because the pedal steel was recorded down in Nashville and the little Bach trumpet was done in a church at Columbia University, where all of the voices were overdubbed. We therefore used two remotes to achieve one sound, and for me that was really interesting.

"Musically, engineering-wise we were a team, and as a result of that we were able to do a lot of innovative stuff. Quite honestly, if a regular producer had been involved he wouldn't have known what the hell was going on! You know, linking up two eight-track machines to make sixteen, and going out and making work tapes. The second eight-track would be used as a work tape to go and overdub voices in the church; do it as a remote, bring it back to the studio, and overdub on it. That wasn't being done at the time, so it was great. It was innovative and very, very creative from an engineering standpoint.

"At that particular time I was still on staff at Columbia, and all of the technical restrictions and guidelines that were imposed on engineers made things very, very tough. There was a union there, and I was always stepping on their toes, although not on purpose. You know, going way back to the beginning when I was editing, a lot of times a producer would come in and leave a classical musical score with me. It would say, 'Edit here, edit here, edit here, edit here . . .' and I actually got into trouble with the union for reading the score! That wasn't my job. But hey, those were the rules, and, as a result of that, Clive Davis, who had taken over as the boss of Columbia Records, asked me to go build a studio in San Francisco and work out there.

"We had a lot of acts there—Janis Joplin and several others—

and I wouldn't have the union problems that existed in Nashville, L.A., and New York. In fact, they eventually had to close all of those studios—particularly the Hollywood one, which was a disaster—as they just couldn't compete with the independents. The rules were so strict. They'd walk out and take a union lunch hour in the middle of a recording session. It was maddening. Because of that, when Columbia would try to sign acts the artists would say, 'Well, fine, we'll sign, but we don't want to work at your studios. We want to have the freedom to work elsewhere.'

"As a result I did go out to San Francisco and I opened the Columbia recording facility, which was a legitimate studio with a union, but a much more liberal union atmosphere. I stayed there for five years and cut Blood, Sweat and Tears as well as Paul's first album and Artie's first album after they broke up, but finally I had to leave because of the lack of musicians. I found myself traveling down to L.A. all of the time. I mean, trying to do overdubs with the San Francisco Symphony Orchestra, I'd put headphones on them and they would freak out! They couldn't relate to it at all. In L.A., the players were possibly not as good, but at least they would sit down and wear headphones and it was like they were in their living room.

"So, I left Columbia and went to ABC Records in Los Angeles, where I was head of A&R, and that was a mistake. It was a record label that was floundering and going out of business, but I stayed there for eight months and signed Steven Bishop and worked with Rufus and Chaka Khan, and then when ABC folded I hung around in L.A. and did some independent records. Boy, what a cruel town that was. When I was head of A&R people there would call me every five minutes, but then when I was on the street again I was a bum! I was forced into going independent, and I should have done that in the first place. The doors opened up, and all of a sudden I realized, 'My god, there's a wealth of talent out there that would love to work with Roy Halee!' The next thing I knew, I was getting calls and turning down a lot of work.

"I did some good things in L.A., but I had to get out of there. I felt too bitter about the place, so I came back to New York, I came home. Still, I worked on *The Notorious Byrd Brothers* with the Byrds while I was on the West Coast, and Simon and Garfunkel's *Bridge over Troubled Water,* so it wasn't all bad. I've always loved working with those guys, and happily I've been involved with Paul again on his Broadway show. That's a whole other world. He wrote a lot of songs for it and two of them are just out of this world, man. Paul Simon at his best, I think. Just fabulous.

"You know, Paul's a great guitar player, he's studied the guitar, he's studied classical guitar, and he's a very gifted guy. Very, very smart and very competitive, and that has always come through in his music. He was the main creative force behind Simon and Garfunkel and he's still creating. There again, Artie contributed a lot to the production in terms of the arrangement of the voices, and his input was very valuable.

"The *Graceland* album was really a total change for Paul. Before that project he would always come into the studio with a song, or at least the sketch of a song, bounce it off of Artie or me, and lay it down as a demo. For instance, I have a demo here of 'Bridge over Troubled Water' before the song was really finished, with Paul, as usual, playing it on guitar. Then we would go into the studio with a rhythm section and it would become a finished song. However, with the *Graceland* project it was more of a case of collecting grooves of South African music on record and then making the decision to go over there and do some cutting.

"It was a very tough project to do but a very pleasant experience. We worked with several different bands in Johannesburg, and when I set the musicians up they'd like to work very close together. At the same time they also had to be isolated so that we could do a lot of editing—let's pull out the guitar here, let's remove that— in order to make songs, because they were just grooves. We had to have the flexibility to erase. So, there we were, in a studio that we didn't really know, and I couldn't put the players in little rooms all over the place with headphones. They had to be close together with eye contact to get the feel and the groove going, yet also isolated in terms of the sound, and that was my job. It took a lot of experience. At this point in my life I've run into just about everything, and there are ways of setting up a rhythm section and achieving good isolation without having to put them in closets all over the place. The right choice of microphones and levels certainly helps, and so that's what we did.

"When I had to work on some of the Simon and Garfunkel compilation CDs, the tapes that Columbia supplied me with were second-, third-, and fourth-generation copies, and just deteriorated to the point of being ridiculous. The company would lose tapes or they wouldn't want to make the effort to find them, and the story I always got was, 'We can't supply the originals so you'll have to work with these.' Well, some producer there went on a crusade and literally worked for two years to find all of the masters, and they found them in Nashville, they found them in L.A., and they found them in New York. The result was that they remixed a lot of the stuff from the original masters, and the sound of what they sent me to listen to was just unbelievably good.

"It was a revelation, and it brought back a lot of memories: of how the bass harmonica was miked on 'The Boxer'; of Hal Blaine playing the congas with that AMS sound on the backbeat, courtesy of an echo chamber being opened and closed by hand; of the bass drum pattern on 'Bridge over Troubled Water,' which could only be achieved with 3M tape machines because the head spacing enabled it to come out in that rhythm; of Paul and Artie actually in the echo chamber at Columbia on 'Only Living Boy in New York' . . . yeah, a lot of memories!"

bruce**botnick**

■

From the Chipmunks to the Doors, Joe Perry to the Beach Boys, and the Frankie Avalon/Annette Funicello beach party movies to *Rambo, Basic Instinct,* and *Total Recall,* Bruce has virtually done it all. During a career that has spanned four decades this Los Angeles–based producer-engineer has scaled the rock 'n' roll heights, made a successful transition into film sound track work, and retained a detailed memory of the landmark sessions with which he has been involved.

"I've got to figure that I've been very fortunate to work with a lot of great people over the years, that a lot of great music has gone under the bridge, and that I've been able to make something that people want to listen to. I don't know that I see the same color red or color blue as everybody else, but it seems that I have been fortunate enough to be given a gift whereby what I hear is what a lot of people like to listen to.

"The first thing I did with the Beach Boys was *Pet Sounds,* and that was done at Sunset Sound. It was recorded in stereo but released in mono, and that's because Brian [Wilson] was deaf in one ear and he never mixed in stereo. In fact, a lot of other times when I worked with Brian we did the tracks in mono. The standard setup was grand piano, harpsichord, stand-up bass or electric bass, electric guitar, a couple of acoustic guitars, drums, and maybe two percussion instruments. That was also [engineer] Jack Nitzsche's basic nucleus for the Phil Spector sessions, and the same group of musicians even played on *Pet Sounds*—Hal Blaine on drums, Carol Kaye on bass, and so on—although Dennis [Wilson] also played the drums.

"Brian was great as a producer. He knew exactly what he wanted. He'd go out into the room, play the piano, and show everybody the exact feel that he was after. I remember when we did 'Good Vibrations,' I worked on that two or three times. I mean, Brian would go to Gold Star and he'd do a version. Then he'd come over to Sunset Sound and do the verses, and we'd cut those in and throw away the Gold Star verses, literally cut them and throw them in the can. Then he'd listen for a while and maybe go to Western to recut the choruses and put them in, before returning to me and recutting the choruses again so that I would put those in. After that the same thing would happen with the bridge, and so that's how the finished song really came about. It was just piece by piece, because Brian would be very satisfied with the verses but not satisfied with the chorus, and then he'd be satisfied with the chorus but wouldn't like the bridge, and then he'd like those two together and maybe not like the verses! He wanted certain sounds to happen and so he'd keep recutting it, and, as it turned out, the majority of what ended up on the record is what I did.

"In 1966 I recorded the first Doors album. At that time I was doing all of the West Coast recordings for Elektra Records. They had a lot of confidence in me as I'd already done Love for them and Tim Buckley, and so it was natural for them to just bring the Doors in. You've got to understand, that first album [*The Doors*] was done in seven days. It was just another session with a new band that had been signed, and Paul Rothchild was the producer as he had been on staff with Elektra for years.

"The band's material was wonderful. I had an immediate affinity for it without anyone telling me, 'Wow, this is heavy!' Everybody knew what to do and the whole thing was very, very simple. There were very, very few mikes—for the most part it was all recorded live in the studio, with Jim [Morrison] in the vocal booth at Sunset Sound in order to keep the separation.

"It was very much a collaborative effort, and Paul would get in my territory and I would get in his. It wasn't a case of the producer controlling the band and controlling the mixer. He was just the one who kept his eyes on the road—somebody had to do it—but otherwise his approach was much the same as mine.

"In the mid-sixties we still hadn't got to the point where the studio was the place in which to write. Everything was written, they had been playing it live, so when you rolled tape you got a performance. Maybe you'd overdub some things to expand it and enhance what was there, but there wasn't too much of that. We recorded to three tracks of a four-track machine, and the only overdubs that we did were some Fender bass with Larry Knechtel and sometimes another vocal from Jim. Apart from that the bass and drums were on one track and the organ and guitar were on another track. Then, when we mixed it down, we had latitude. In fact, I've gone back to the tracks since then and found that I still have great latitude with just two tracks of information!

"When I was involved with the *Best of the Doors* album, listening to those old recordings after thirty years was like hearing them for the first time, especially since we'd originally left off some of the words that were considered too colorful back then. When you hear the whole song it takes on a different light, and also, being that the two-track tapes have lost high-end over the years, getting back to the first generation of multitrack was really quite something. We also went back to them when we did the movie *The Doors,* and they were pretty impressive. I mean, tape hiss? What was that? You didn't hear it. It didn't exist. If you cut hot you cut cleanly!

"Anyway, that first album was a very big success, and then we came into the studio to do the second one, *Strange Days.* The Turtles—whom I also worked with—had given me a mono acetate of *Sgt. Pepper* about three months before it came out, and I listened to it, I played it for Paul, I played it for the Doors, and we couldn't believe it. I mean, the creativity, the experimentation and the fact that they didn't stick to the norm was so groundbreaking, and that really influenced us to let go and to really try new things. As a result, I think *Strange Days* is pretty innovative.

"We did some backwards things, we did forwards things, and we did sideways things. There was backwards piano, backwards drums, you name it. At Sunset Sound Recorders there was just myself and one other person, and so we were our own maintenance men, even though technically we didn't know what we were doing. We cut our own discs, we set up our own studios, and we were our own bosses, so we didn't have anybody telling us, 'You can't do this.' It's like on 'When the Music's Over,' for instance, I took Robbie [Krieger]'s guitar solo off the microphone, took it out of one mike preamp into a pot that was feeding another mike preamp, and then ran the knobs against one another until I got it to break up just right. I would literally overload the tubes and get them to glow, and while some studios at that time would have shut me down that was never the case at Sunset Sound.

"During that album we also had one of the first Moog synthesizers brought in, put Jim's voice in, and he played it against his vocal. The keyboard would cause the envelope to open and close, and it was doing some really cool things. Then there was the 'farkle,' which I came up with for the Doors—although Van Dyke Parks came up with the name—and which consisted of masking tape that was folded and folded and folded so that it resembled a fan. It was maybe an eighth of an inch long, and it would go around the capstan. This fan would cause a bouncing sensation, and so, as the tape went through, it would make a kind of gurgling sound. Using that on reverbs or vocals, you could create some pretty wild sounds—after all, we didn't have the electronics back then so we had to use our hands!

"A lot of people were doing similar things without anything being published or anybody talking to one another. It was just a very, very creative time, and most of us were having a lot of fun. Making records and hearing them on the radio was exciting, making enough money so that you could do it again was exciting, and getting paid for having fun was exciting. However, I have to say that, even when we went to eight-track on *Strange Days,* the performance was still everything. Nothing was different as far as the approach was concerned, but having more tracks just allowed us to keep things separate while also allowing us a little more hindsight as far as the mix was concerned, even though I now sometimes wonder how valid that was.

"After a while we had a little problem that was dogging us and which took up more of our time than the recording did—you know, Jim's run-in with the law—and we didn't get rid of that until we made the last album, *L.A. Woman.* It's very hard to be creative when you've got a court case staring you in the face, but, all things considered, I think they did incredibly well. Most artists are limited by the fact that their fans like to hear the same guitar solos and so on as on the records when they see them in concert. However, the Doors had a lot of freedom because, although there was a framework, everybody knew that there was free expression within the band. So, they could extend a solo if they wanted, eliminate a solo, or do whatever they wanted, and people would accept it. They were very fortunate in that respect. Very few bands could do anything like that.

"Obviously, in the studio we were trying to make a better and better sound, and we did get to a point where it became too cerebral, so by the time that we went to make the *L.A. Woman* album both the Doors and I felt that we really wanted to just throw off all the shackles and get back to what we did originally: just be very primitive in our approach, very relaxed, get the performances down, and if something didn't sound exactly right then that was okay. That's what we did, and it worked out just fine.

"Paul Rothchild was no longer on the scene. He just couldn't get it on for one more album, and neither could they. The six of us actually went into Sunset Sound Recorders to see if we could 're-light the fire,' but it was obvious after a couple of days that it wasn't working. They weren't inspired at all, and they didn't give a hoot. Paul couldn't turn things around and he basically said, 'Folks, I've done all I can do. I don't feel I can do it one more time.' So, we all talked about it and they said, 'Well, what can we do?' I said, 'Hey, let's make the record ourselves. We'll go over to your place and I'll produce it with you,' and that was it.

"I thought of using their rehearsal room for the recording because that was where they felt very comfortable and so the sessions wouldn't have that studio type of feel to them. As a result we did that album in ten days. The goal was to go in there and, if it was working, great, and if it wasn't, we'd go home. We didn't sit there and try to beat it. We didn't do a hundred takes; two takes, sometimes just one, or maybe as much as four takes, all depending on what was happening. We'd do some editing and fix things that were really obviously bad, but otherwise we'd leave it and just try to keep a raw edge, relaxed, no pretension. I prefer to get a performance and only fix it if there's something wrong, rather than do lots of takes to make it perfect, because how we communicate with music is through emotion, not through perfection.

"Jim stood in a bathroom doorway with a microphone in his hand and he sang. He was a very easy person to record. He had a lot of presence, a big voice, and when you have somebody with a big voice it sounds full even when he gets soft. The more that he performed on the road the more that he really didn't want an expensive microphone. He'd literally hang on the mike, his hand pulling it down in front of him while his foot was on the base. After a while, when an expensive mike is being treated like that it becomes a problem. I don't like the way that foam rubber pop filters sound, so we had to be careful, especially when Jim was inebriated, because if you get moisture on the capsule then the sound goes. I'd always ask him to perform a certain distance from the microphone, and then I started making pop-filters out of ladies' stockings glued over wire frames. However, when they were fresh he was getting stoned off of the glue on the mike filters!

"When I started doing movie work in the early eighties I suddenly found myself not having to take work home and not having to serve as a full-time psychiatrist. I've always been a fan of recording live in the studio, but unfortunately nowadays you can't do that with rock music unless you're doing a concert or unless you rehearse a band for weeks before going into the studio. On the other hand, one of the main things that I love about movie work is that it is still live for the most part. That allows me to go back in my mind to the past and to review what I was doing. It's a great exercise, and I plan to keep on doing it."

vandykeparks

■

Despite asserting that he "came from a long line of piano instruction that goes back to Beethoven and beyond—I'm the last of the line, the last leaf on the vine," Van Dyke started out as a child actor before becoming a session player during the mid-sixties. An accomplished musician, composer, lyricist, producer, and arranger, he has produced various major artists and written several notable film scores, yet it was as Brian Wilson's compositional partner on the Beach Boys' aborted mid-sixties opus *Smile* that he gained his greatest fame and notoriety. Some people would later praise the offbeat material for its daring innovation, while others—including the disgruntled band members—accused Van Dyke of luring the head Beach Boy down a commercially suicidal path. Either way, the shelving of the project left both men dejected and disillusioned, and it would be thirty years before they would collaborate again, Van Dyke writing and producing an album titled *Orange Crate Art* as a vehicle for his longtime mentor.

"I made it through the sixties by the skin of my teeth. Basically, however, I would do it all over again as I did it then, albeit in maybe half the time. I would like to compact the sixties into, say, a five-year period!

"In the beginning there was a great deal of excitement and portentousness about *Smile,* and that had been forced on Brian. The word *genius* was being lightly bandied about, but I don't think there's anything genius about Brian Wilson or anyone who ends up in the music business. If you're a genius you'll be doing things in a much more challenging field of endeavor, and in a much more contributive way than the self-serving manner which the music business entails. However, I think that genius can be a collaborative act, and if that amounts to an ability to draw enough collaborative forces together to produce something truly phenomenal, then I would say that Brian Wilson has hallmarks of genius.

"Back in the mid-to-late-sixties there was just too much for him to bear, compounded with all of the other difficulties that he had prior to me arriving on the scene, and I believe even today that I could have been part of the solution. I don't believe that I was part of the problem. Almost without premeditation, it seemed to me, Brian asked me to write lyrics for him. There was certainly nothing premeditated on my part, but in passing, [producer] Terry Melcher—for whom I had been doing sessions—mentioned to Brian that I was a competent lyricist. In truth I wasn't a competent anything at that point, and I was somewhat amazed, but I was ambitious, and in accepting the offer to work with Brian Wilson many would argue that my ambition outreached my ability, and I have no disagreement with that.

"I knew that Brian wanted to do music that was American in terms of its topic, and I'm sure it was easy for him to divine when meeting me that I was absolutely alarmed by the magnitude of the 'British Invasion,' as well as by the sense of apology that Americans felt culturally simply because we were involved in an ugly act of aggression in Vietnam. I think that Brian rushed into a relationship with me as I was the exception to the rule, but in terms of having an idea as to what the Beach Boys should do to escape the triviality of fast-car-and-faster-women song lyrics, I was the gullible partner in that experiment.

"This has been a matter of conscience for thirty years now, and I've looked back on this situation and tried to figure out what else I could have done, and, quite frankly, I still don't have an answer. Basically, I think it was an improbable project from the moment I stepped in. It could have gained focus, but when I sensed that it had no focus and was a threat to the Beach Boys' esprit de corps, I resigned. I'm not sure if that's because I thought that I would be fired if I didn't resign—I think I could have stuck it out, but I wasn't interested in victory at any cost.

"At that time the press was attributing a far greater social and cultural importance to pop music than it had ever had. All of a sudden everybody was looking for the meaning, and, as Brian began losing his privacy to all of the attendant publicity, we were no longer working alone. In my opinion music was an inferior thing after Bob Dylan's success encouraged people of inferior ability that they, too, could share in the revenues of this new medium with a message. The whole thing was a sorrowful event.

"I had a great enthusiasm in the first month of working with Brian, and that produced 'Heroes and Villains,' it produced 'Surf's Up,' it produced 'Wonderful,' but things stopped being so wonderful fairly quickly, and I was in that deteriorating social olio for the next three to four months. A lot of people—especially the members of the band—did nothing but develop alliances, and they were like bettors at a gaming table. In fact, the people who were calling the shots couldn't play the game, and it became a less-musicalized experience for me. All I had wanted to do was find some refuge and work on some music in any way, and I was happy to do it as a lyricist even though it was a new job for me.

"If we'd had the benefit of obscurity then I feel the results could have realized Brian's expectations for success, and in a way I think it did. I mean, even with its pathos and its somewhat schizophrenic nature, there was enough song material on tape to draw the Beatles out of their roost and down to the studio that we were using. In fact, it's fair to say that they were heavily influenced by the courageous innovations that Brian introduced, and he did these at enormous social expense, losing the loyalty of his own group in the process. Sad stuff, huh?

"We started in the spring of '66 and it ended in the fall. When I later heard 'Heroes and Villains' as a 45 [rpm] single, the tune was in a sequence that I had never heard it in before, and, to be honest, I didn't think it would go to number one. I thought maybe it might reach number eight. It didn't have the torque that I thought it would have, and, although I was elated to hear it on the radio, I was shocked by it and somewhat disappointed. Brian is still recovering from that whole experience, and it took me a long time to recover from it, too.

"Still, I went on to produce and arrange for other people, to work as a minor bureaucrat in a record company, and to get assignments as a film scorer. However, there is nothing that I love as much as making a record, and every five years or so I get to the point where I want to explore my own feelings and subject them to the rapacious, vulgar public gaze. I use the record as a point of personal clarification and admission, and so that's what *Orange Crate Art* is all about.

"I originally came up with the title song, and I was about ready to step into a studio to demonstrate the tune for Lenny Waronker [then president of Warner Brothers Records] when I read that Brian had just done some background voices for Linda Ronstadt. So, of course, I thought that if he was willing to sing for her then he would probably sing for me, and I felt a compassion for what I saw as the inertia of an able veteran. It alarmed me, it maddened me, and it became my celebrated interest. I wanted to get Brian into a studio again, and that's what motivated me to finish this record.

"I therefore gave him a call, went to his home, and with great trepidation I took the song, hoping that I had placed it in the right key and that the words were not offensive and that the chords were interesting enough for him to sing. Brian liked the results immediately, and being that I only had to go through about five people to get to him that meant I had fairly easy access. Thereafter I put his voice on all but a lead vocal—we did five doubled vocal tracks in two and a half hours—and that first effort is what we presented on the record.

"The melody is carried by a falsetto voice, and so the chest voice that would have carried the tune is absent. The reason for this is that I told Brian that I was going to be adding my own voice on at some later date, and so I deceived him with that tune and I then followed suit with about three or four of the other songs. By that time he turned to me and said, 'Whose record is this anyway?' I said, 'Well, it's our record, Brian. It's either your record or it's my record, I don't care.' He said, 'You know, it could be our record. We're doing this, aren't we?' I said, 'Yes, we are, and quite frankly, I don't have anything in mind and I don't know where it might take us, but I just think that we should trust this process.' So, the record actually represents a great deal of price-less trust, and it was a conscious decision on my part to have his name listed before mine because he is my senior, to be sure, in all ways in the record business.

"His mid-range is tired, world-weary, but there's an innocence about the falsetti. I was interested in his range of operations, and I wanted to make sure that whatever we got on this record was a reflection of the potential of his youth. So, with Mike Frondelli's fully informed mixes, as well as the other [mix] work that Ed Cherney had done, we put great emphasis on the background voices. . . . I was conscious that if I wrote melodies that had some degree of complexity or range or ambition, and if I could carry that off, it might awaken Brian's own curiosity in melodic force and remind him of what he is capable of doing. That was a secret desire of mine because I love Brian's melodies, and so it was a good workout for him.

"The guy worked like a son of a bitch. Some things come easy to him—range comes easily—but many times he would leave after a small amount of work had been done, and the record took a long time to complete because he was in the middle of a lot of personal difficulties. You see, Brian didn't learn these songs before he came to the studio. I didn't go over to his house and slouch at a piano and lay it on him. None of that happened. Brian and I don't play golf together. We don't go bowling together. It would be nice to think that we could someday, but as it is we found ourselves on a personal collision course at a studio with some unknown material plunging into space together! So, what with Brian's frequent inability to concentrate and perform the music, we had to take the approach whereby each sentence was recorded and doubled one at a time before the next sentence was then recorded and doubled.

"I subsequently heard Brian sing whole verses of these songs, and I think that was his way of signaling to me that he liked the material and that he had taken possession of it. He probably also realized that what I warranted may be true, that I couldn't have done the record without him and he couldn't have done the record without me. Before this project began Brian had been wounded by the fact that his previous psychiatrist [Dr. Eugene Landy] had helped design his last record for a million dollars and Warner Brothers had deemed it unreleasable, and he had shrunk from any ambition as a recording artist, so by letting me do the vocal arrangements, by letting me write the songs, by suffering my pestering, I think Brian found a way to stay operative in the studio and associate with new music, albeit not perhaps on the level of what has been shown as his own songwriting accomplishments. I think that had a tremendously positive effect on him, and of course, from my own primitive perspective, I had the greatest voice available in popular music to ornament my songs and give them the recognition that his reputation brings.

"We were both unhappy with how things had been left before, and so the record represents a sense of closure at this point. We have finished a project together and now we could do something if we wanted to with a greater sense of abandon. Naturally, I would like to reconstruct the possibilities that would have been suggested some thirty years ago. Maybe that's unrealistic and wishful thinking, but I would love to write words for Brian's music. In personal terms this record has been an absolute triumph of our primitive will to survive, and just in that alone it has been a wonderful experience."

bones**howe**

∎

Dayton Burr Howe picked up the name of Bones as a skinny kid in high school and went on to become a producer and engineer of distinction. A man whose career stretches all the way from the mid-fifties to the present day, he was involved with early experiments in stereophonic sound and helped redefine the industry by being among the first independent recording engineers. Bones has numerous motion picture sound tracks to his credit, and has worked with artists ranging from Tom Waits, Jack Kerouac, and Lenny Bruce to Elvis Presley, Ella Fitzgerald, Frank Sinatra, Jerry Lee Lewis, the Mamas and the Papas, the Turtles, and the Fifth Dimension. As he himself emphasized in 1996, this is quite a variety for someone whose musical roots always lay in jazz.

"When Eddie Brackett and I were staff engineers at United-Western Recording Studios in the early sixties, I discovered that we were carrying two thirds of the workload. I was working almost around the clock, and we decided that we had as much to do with the quality of recordings that were coming out as any individual musician. Therefore, if we were being hired as engineers we should be paid the same as the musicians, which meant about $15 an hour as opposed to $5 an hour.

"It was Thanksgiving of 1962. I was twenty-nine years old, and I decided to quit my job and go independent. I went to see Bill Putnam and Tony Perry, who were the owners of United, and I gave them two weeks' notice, and they said, 'What? Where are you going?' I said, 'I'm not going anywhere.' They said, 'Who's hiring you?' I said, 'No one's hiring me. I'm going to become an independent engineer.' So they said, 'But you can't do that,' and I said, 'Well, watch me! I'm gonna do it.' Two weeks later I left, and three days went by before I got a phone call at home from United, asking me how much I would charge to go back in and do some production work. I told them my rate was $15 an hour, and inside of a week they were hiring me back as an outsider, at three times what I'd previously been earning.

"I worked hard to establish myself in the business, and sometimes the breaks came my way. Bill Putnam had been doing all of Frank Sinatra's recordings at United, and one night before Sinatra arrived for a session Bill hit his head on a mike boom while trying to move a microphone and he went down. We carried him up to his office and put him on a couch, and he told me that I would have to do the session. So, I went back into the studio and was working things out with [arranger] Billy May and the band when Frank arrived, and after going upstairs to see Bill Putnam he came into the booth and said, 'Let me know when you're ready,' and he was really, really nice about things. Then he went out and sang 'Granada' and 'Moonlight on the Ganges' and all of those tunes. I ended up doing three dates with him, and Bill Putnam subsequently did the mix.

"Sinatra was notorious for always turning up about an hour to an hour and a half after a session began, because he'd want the band to already be warmed up. We'd record four songs in three hours, and he was a man of very few takes. His favorite expression was 'If that ain't it, I don't know what is!' That meant 'It's over!' Still, he was great. He was really, really helpful, he wanted to be sure that the band was comfortable and that everybody was happy, and he just wanted the recordings to be good. And they were. As a vocalist he was the best. I was a huge Frank Sinatra fan, and he didn't disappoint me. He bent notes until they sounded right and he was just a great musician.

"Most of the band singers were great musicians, because they weren't separated from musicians. They traveled with them, they were on the bus with them, they talked with them, and they learned the life with them. Male or female, they all were part of that gang of people. It's like being part of a baseball team. They spent a lot of time together, and Frank absorbed all of that musicianship. He had a great musical attitude, he had great ears, he listened to other people, and he learned how to breathe from watching Tommy Dorsey play.

"For my part, I was a record buyer before I was a record maker, and so I knew how he was supposed to sound. That applied to most of the bands and singers whom I worked with. I owned their records and I knew their sound. As a self-taught musician I learned the discipline that you have to practice, you have to listen, and you have to play, and so when I was going from job to job as an engineer I did a lot of analytic listening in between and spent a lot of time in the studios watching other guys mix, to see how they handled the various sound problems.

"I remember sitting in Studio A at United Recorders and watching Phil Spector produce Ike and Tina Turner's 'A Love Like Yours' and 'Save the Last Dance for Me.' Phil's usual engineer, Larry Levine, didn't know the room, and so they decided to get me in. Larry was at the session, however, and he sat there with me and gave me the magic formula for all of those things that Phil did to get the 'Wall of Sound.' I remember we took the echo send, delayed it through a tape machine, and then sent it to an acoustic chamber. So, it was tape delay, but not the kind of tape delay that you had on the teeny-bop records where you had the straightforward echo effect of the voice repeating and so on. In this case you had live sound going to the chamber and you had delayed sound going to the chamber at the same time, and the result was that it repeated in the chamber so that when it came back it was just a big blur. I always said that it sounded like Philip recorded those tracks in the bottom of an empty swimming pool!

"Tina sang live, and the whole rhythm section was in the room at the same time. Phil was notorious for never giving the band five because he didn't want anybody to move. He knew exactly where he wanted the instruments positioned, and it would take him such a long time to get the balance exactly the way he wanted. There'd be, say, a mandolin mixed in with the guitar section. I mean, can you imagine him with a synthesizer? He would have driven the synthesizer player nuts trying to find sounds. As it was he had the band play the chart over and over and over again, like a tape loop. You know, the minute they reached the end they'd play it again, and he would go out and change people's parts. It was a great lesson in that kind of hands-on production.

"It would sometimes only be zillionths of an inch of change to make the difference that Phil wanted, but he'd know when it all fell into place. The amazing thing about it was, when that happened, it did have an incredible sound, and I'm not sure that some of that wasn't just down to the musicians getting beat by playing it over and over and over again, so that the sound began to all melt together. Studio A was full of people, and it was a lot of fun. As I knew the room I was left to set up the miking, but then when the recording was completed Larry Levine took the three-tracks and mixed them back at Gold Star, so I didn't really have that much to do with the outcome. You see, even in those days there was the beginning of the remix engineer!

"The amazing thing is that when I left United most of the people that I had worked with and thought would hire me never called, whereas the people who I thought would never call me actually did. For example, Lou Adler and I had done a record with the Everly Brothers, and I subsequently did a bunch of the Jan and Dean records which Lou initially produced before Jan [Berry] became the producer. Then Lou formed a company called Dunhill Records, and he called me to do all of his sessions, so I did [Barry] McGuire and the Mamas and the Papas with him as well as Johnny Rivers, and this took me through to the mid-sixties, when I began producing on my own.

"Lou once joked that we should have cut a hundred songs during the first Mamas and Papas sessions and then never gone back into the studio! The first album was very businesslike; they had all of the songs written, we went in, we recorded them, and everything was done very quickly. The second one was a little more difficult; the songs were written but then John [Phillips] didn't like the way they sounded and began to change them, Cass [Elliot] wanted to sing something a different way, and stardom took a hold and everyone wanted to have their say. So, the second album inevitably took a lot longer and there were a lot of all-night sessions. At the same time they were also receiving these immense royalty checks from the first album and they were spending money hand over fist. In fact, at one point there was even a competition among the four of them as to who would spend the most money during any given week.

"That having been said, there was a lot of drinking going on in the studio. Cocaine hadn't really come around to the pop world yet; it was still a jazz drug. Denny [Doherty] would put away a bottle of Crown Royal every night, and the bottle was in a blue velvet bag, so we started storing the microphones in the blue velvet bags. Behind the control room window there was this line of bottles along the shelf and a bunch of bags for the mikes!

"My earliest success as a producer was with the Turtles' 'It Ain't Me Babe,' but I continued to work around the clock as an engineer, and then on the Friday before Christmas of 1966 I told Lou that I was going to be out of the studio by midnight and I would be with my family until the first of the year. Lou, however, was a single guy and every day was the same for him. Making records was his life, and I knew that. We were working on this record by Johnny Rivers but I felt that I'd given him enough notice. Well, on the night that I was supposed to stop working I walked into the studio and there was this Triumph motorcycle in there. Rivers said, 'It's for you,' and I said, 'Wait a minute, guys. You're not going to buy me out of the holidays by giving me a motorcycle. I don't want the motorcycle, I don't want it around my house, I don't want my kids growing up on a motorcycle, it's not going to work, and at midnight I'm out of here!' Sure enough, midnight came and Lou was asking everyone to stay on for another session, so I told him he'd better find another engineer, I picked up my briefcase, and I walked out of the studio.

"Lou was furious, and far as he was concerned that was the end of it. He didn't talk to me or call me at all. It was a divorce. He finished the Rivers record and that gave me time to think. I was burning the candle at three ends: I was trying to produce the Turtles and find other artists to produce; I was doing all of this engineering for Lou and whoever else called me up; and I was also playing drums on certain people's demo sessions. I was meeting myself going in and out of the door, and so I really had to decide on what I was going to do. That was what led to me being a full-time record producer and working with the Turtles, the Fifth Dimension, the Association, and so on. Meanwhile, in May of 1967 I also got an 'all is forgiven' phone call from Lou and that resulted in me engineering some of the sound at the Monterey Pop Festival.

"So many things were happening at the same time. I went into partnership with Steve Binder, who was a TV producer and director, in order to create variety specials for television, and we called the company Binder/Howe Productions. The first thing that we did was a Petula Clark special with Harry Belafonte as the guest star, and that caused quite a bit of controversy because after the last song that they did Belafonte reached out and took her hand. Well, no one had ever seen a black man take a white woman's hand on American television, and there was a huge hue and cry from the advertising agency. For a while that turned Steve into the enfant terrible of the industry, but then we got a call from Bob Finkel, an executive producer at NBC, and he asked us to do an hour-long Christmas special with Elvis Presley.

"For me this would be a great opportunity to see Elvis again. Back in the mid-fifties I'd worked on a number of his sessions when he first came out to Radio Recorders in Hollywood, and I had the tapes in my garage for a while and then sold them back to RCA after they'd thrown them out. They were actually two-track safety tapes, with Elvis' voice on one track and everything else on the other, and when RCA threw them in the Dumpster I retrieved them. The company's procedure in those days was that the minute that the mono masters were equalized and released, they then had what they called an 'EQ master copy' and they threw all of the safety copies and two-tracks away! So, I retrieved those and kept them in a box for about thirty years before I sold them back. In fact, RCA didn't even know that they existed until I told them. . . . Every big record company which amasses huge libraries of tape has that problem.

"Elvis was great. I'd been the mixer on a couple of sessions with him when his usual guy, Thorne Nogar, wasn't available, and I'd also done a session when he came out of the army. I'd been there because his people had wanted a familiar face for him when he arrived in the studio, and it was astounding because he came in his uniform. I mean, he was out of the army and there he was, in his uniform with all of his guys!

"To me, Elvis was the first self-produced artist. In the early days he would always choose the songs, bring his own musicians, work on the arrangements with them, and Steve Sholes—the RCA guy who supposedly produced the sessions—basically ran the clock. Well, by the time of the '68 special [Elvis' manager] Colonel Parker was running things, and his idea was for Elvis to sing twenty-four Christmas songs, say 'Merry Christmas, everybody!' and that would be it! During our first production meeting Steve turned to me and said, 'It's a crime,' so—remembering how I used to play the song demos from the booth out to Elvis in the studio and he would choose the ones that he wanted to record—I said, 'We should speak to Elvis about this and tell him that, what with all of the films that he's been making, it's been a long time since people have seen him perform live.'

"We went and had a meeting with Elvis when the Colonel wasn't there, and Steve told him what I'd said and suggested that, while he could still do a couple of Christmas songs, it would be great if he'd sing things that were more contemporary. Elvis loved this, and in the end he convinced the Colonel. I was the music director on the show, and, during the prerecord sessions in Studio 1 at Western Recorders, Elvis sang all of the songs live with a hand mike and did knee-drops in front of the string section. None of them could believe it. He always came dressed to the nines, and he was a great, great vocalist. He could imitate anybody—Fats Domino, Frank Sinatra, you name it—and I still think he was the most exciting performer to ever go onstage. He was absolutely captivating to watch.

"On the other hand, prior to taping the live segment of the show where he sings in front of an audience, Elvis had said that he was nervous about going onstage. He hadn't done so for quite a few years, and he said, 'In between there have been the Beatles and the Rolling Stones, so I don't know if people are going to laugh at me.' He was very serious about it. He had a good sense of who he was—and a great sense of humor about it—and if you look at the beginning of the live segment, as he reaches for the mike you can see that his hand is shaking. However, about sixteen bars into that first tune Elvis knew that he had the audience where he wanted them, and from that point on he was on a roll. He was absolutely amazing.

"Elvis had really wanted to be a part of the production, meet with the writers, and help with the creative process, and so every day he would come to our offices in the 'glass elevator' building on Sunset. He'd arrive in his Cadillac with the guys; there was underground parking, and he would come up in the elevator or by the back stairs. We had been warned from the start that the one thing we couldn't do was expose him to the public, otherwise he'd be mobbed. We'd have to send out for food, and Elvis's big thing in those days was that he drank a lot of Pepsi-Cola and smoked these Dutch cigars, so we made sure we had those in, too.

"The guy was literally cooped up, and meanwhile every Friday and Saturday night during the late sixties the Sunset Strip was like a parking lot, with people banging tambourines in their cars while their radios blared as they drove up and down. Those were the folk rock days, and one Friday night during the writing of the show Elvis said that he'd love to go out and see what was going on. So, we got in the elevator and went down, and we walked out and leaned against a brick planter on the corner of Sunset and Larabee. Elvis stood there in his tight pants and his blue hair, and although one person jokingly said 'Hey, Elvis,' as he went by—as if he'd seen an Elvis look-alike—not one person recognized him. In a way it was kind of sad, but I think he also liked the idea of not having to worry about dealing with crowds of people.

"Elvis once paid me a wonderful compliment. He said that I had a better feel for music than any producer he had ever worked with. I always cared more about the artist's performance than I did about the engineering. I was the first engineer who didn't separate people. I kept them close together, and I believed the way that you got good separation was by way of a good choice of microphones and good microphone placements. The rhythm section was one sound anyway, and so it needed to be recorded that way. I always felt that I was there to serve the music, and I built a whole philosophy around that, and I think that's a good part of why artists have wanted to work with me.

"I myself loved the total free association of working with Tom Waits. I made the *Heart of Saturday Night* album with him, and then his manager had the idea of recording a live set. We decided to have him read his poetry backed by a rhythm section, and instead of finding a venue we could turn a studio into a nightclub, complete with tables, chairs, and a stage. So, that's what we did inside the big room at the Record Plant on Third Street [New York], and then we invited guests for two nights of two shows each. A lot of Waits' friends and fans turned up, along with record company people, journalists, and a stripper named Dwana whom Tom had hired for the opening act. There was standing room only. We had beer and pretzels, and everyone had a good time, and out of it we recorded the double album *Nighthawks at the Diner*.

"The last time that I collaborated with Waits was on *One from the Heart* back in 1982, and I've got to say that Tom is the only artist who I've ever worked with that I miss. We had so much fun together. There again, it ended on a very rational note, and it's a sort of an open-ended thing. Tom called me up, we went out for a drink, and he said, 'I'm trying to write my next album and I want to do something really different, but I've gotten to know you so well that I'm aware of what you like and it's hard for me to write songs when I find myself thinking, "Bones won't like this." So I think I'll have to produce the next record by myself.' I said, 'Tom, that's the most rational reason I can think of for a producer and artist not to work together. I would not want to be the person standing between you and your art. I know what you want to do; we've made these kinds of records before.' It's what I call 'junkyard music,' where he bangs on different things to get a sound, and I said, 'Quite frankly, I don't want to make that kind of record with you.' Still, he knew—and still knows—that I'll always be around if and when he wants to make the kind of records that I am into."

lamont**dozier**

∎

In collaboration with Eddie and Brian Holland, Lamont wrote and produced some of the most memorable pop songs of all time. Between 1963 and 1968, Berry Gordy's Motown label struck paydirt as the Supremes, the Four Tops, Marvin Gaye, Martha and the Vandellas, Junior Walker and the All Stars, the Miracles, the Marvelettes, and the Isley Brothers scored an astounding number of chart successes thanks to the red-hot team of Holland-Dozier-Holland, yet the trio themselves were only modestly rewarded for all of their efforts. They subsequently fared better with their own Invictus and Hot Wax labels, before Lamont moved from Detroit to Los Angeles in 1972 and enjoyed solo success both as a singer and as a composer for numerous major artists. I spoke with him in 1998, soon after he and the Holland brothers had started writing together again for the first time in over twenty-five years, penning a stage musical titled *Holland-Dozier-Holland: The True Motor City Music Story,* which would serve to set the record straight about life at Hitsville during those halcyon years of the 1960s.

"So many people have tried to define the 'Motown sound,' and if it's anything, it's gospel and classical music merging together. Also, if you listen very closely, you'll hear a sprinkling of country and western in there. I was raised on classical and gospel music, that's all we ever heard in our house. My grandmother wouldn't allow anything else—unless it was Tony Bennett or Nat 'King' Cole or Frank Sinatra—and so I had this stuff ingrained in me. At the same time, being indoctrinated into the gospel way of thinking, I wound up being a lead singer at church. A good friend of mine, Aretha Franklin, was there, and a lot of influences were around. So the Motown sound definitely has those elements in it. If you listen to the chords of 'Reach Out (I'll Be There)' or 'I Hear a Symphony' or 'Stop! In the Name of Love,' there are very intricate patterns, and to my knowledge those structures that we were using had never been explored before.

"In terms of the bulk of the music and what people remember of the Motown sound, many of them give a lot of the credit to H-D-H, but then you've got the Temptations and what Smokey was doing, 'The Way You Do the Things You Do' and 'My Girl,' Norman Whitfield with Marvin Gaye's 'I Heard It Through the Grapevine,' and then Marvin when he started doing his own productions, so Motown has got all of these facets to it. You really can't pinpoint where it started or how it started. It just evolved over the years, from 'Please Mister Postman' and 'Shop Around' to 'Forever Came the Day.' I could name a bunch of songs that were semiclassical, semicountry, jazz.

"A jazz musician I know used to buy the stuff, and he would say, 'Man, how did you do that? That jazz reference is very clever!' and I'd say, 'Jazz?' But that's what he heard in the music. The gospel stuff is very apparent, with the tambourines and the organs and the way the piano was pushed, and then you have your classical influence there. The chord progressions were also very poignant, and so it's a combination of very many things that make up the Motown sound. All of the elements of music are there, there's a little bit of something for everybody, and that's why everybody bought it.

"When I first got to Motown in 1962 I met Brian Holland. He was working with Robert Bateman producing acts such as the Marvelettes, for whom they had written 'Please Mister Postman,' but Robert Bateman had become somewhat leery of his future at the company and he didn't want to be there anymore. He had taken on some other projects in New York, and so he suggested that Brian and I should team up.

"We wrote stuff for various [Motown] artists, and some of it started to get attention. I was a singer there, too, but Berry told me, 'Look, if you really want to be successful and make some money at this thing the writing and producing aspect of it is the way to go.' So I took his advice, and shortly thereafter Eddie Holland—who had several records out on the label—decided that he didn't want to sing anymore. That was not his thing really. He's basically an accountant type, and he didn't like to be up onstage, jumping around! That was just silly to him. He liked to be in the background and he could write lyrics, so we brought him in, and that's when things started to click for us.

"We took on more of a workload and the chemistry just gelled. The three of us working together could get a lot more accomplished. I'm a lyricist and a melody man, so I would split my energies. I would work with Brian first, getting things together in terms of the melody and the idea—I was basically the idea man in the group, and I came up with a good seventy to seventy-five percent of all the ideas for the songs. Brian was a recording engineer as well as a melody man, and so I would team up with him to produce the track, and then I would start a lyrical idea and give it to Eddie to finish. He in turn would teach the song to the artist, and so you might say that we had our own little factory within a factory. We were able to turn out a lot of songs that way.

"All of the guys working for Berry had a budget, and they had to come up with something out of that budget. You got your shot and you had to come up with something that sold. We called it 'Motown College.' He just let us do what we wanted to do. He trusted us. We were all talented people and he believed in us, otherwise he never would have brought us in to do what we wanted to do, to do what we felt, so it was very interesting that way. Being a songwriter, he knew that standing over somebody while they're working is just nerve-racking and you're not going to get much done. He or she has to have some leeway, and he understood that. He's very good at knowing what a creative person needs in that respect.

"We became so good at what we were doing and we were selling so many records and breaking so many artists that, in addition to having our assigned artists, we also started to release what we wanted to release. You know, we became that prolific that Berry trusted us to the point where he would say, 'What are you guys putting out on Diane now?' We'd say, 'Well, we like the song 'Stop! In the Name of Love,'" and he'd say, 'Yeah, I heard that. I liked that, too. Great, you're gonna go with that?' We'd say, 'Yeah,' and that was the conversation.

"We were on such a roll it was amazing. *We* were astounded! I remember having a conversation with Brian; I said, 'Man, I don't know what this is, but I don't think this stuff is ever going to end!' I said, 'I get the feeling that we've stumbled into something here that's worldwide and lasting,' and he said, 'Yeah, man, I think so, too. It's awesome. I get a weird feeling, man, like somebody has zapped us!' It was like, 'Okay, you got the power,' so to speak! I mean, how else can you explain it? And as the years went on and the success continued I knew that there was a bigger picture here and a bigger thing happening, and I truly give God the credit. We just happened to be in the right place with the right chemistry, and, for whatever reason, it was time for Motown to happen. After all, we weren't the only ones for whom it started to happen: Smokey [Robinson] was the first; and then there was Brian with Robert Bateman; and subsequently Brian, myself, and his brother; and then it just went through the roof with the Supremes and the Four Tops and so on.

"Nobody knows what a hit is. I mean, you just do what you feel. We had such a closeness together and we all would just stop and look at each other in the office when we hit this certain chord, and we'd go, 'Yeah, that's it. . . .' Bam! We'd all have that feeling, and where that comes from God only knows, because what you're doing is selling a feeling to get to people of all races from all over the world, and they pick up on what you're feeling and they know where you're coming from. Well, to get them to feel that way there's got to be somebody else in the picture, quiet and invisible, sitting on our shoulder and leading us down this path. Motown became such a legendary company, what with everything that it stood for at the time and what it put into the mainstream of life for all people around the world, that you have to say that God or that power which touches people was there in the room when we were creating this thing and it chose us to be the recipients.

"It just fell into place. Brian would play half the song sometimes; he'd play [the intro to 'Reach Out (I'll Be There)'], and then I'd jump in, push him out of the way, and sing, 'Now, if you feel that you can't go on. . . . ' We would feel it like that on the spot. Then he would jump back in with 'Here's the bridge. . . .' We would literally be sliding on and off the [piano] stool: I'd slide him off and go 'Darlin' reach out . . .''; he'd slide back in for 'I'll be there . . .'; and that's the way we would do a lot of the stuff. It was a beautiful experience and one I'll never forget.

"Sometimes we would repeat ourselves. I remember in one instance we got a call telling us that Columbia were releasing an old Four Tops album and trying to take advantage of the momentum they had gained [since leaving Columbia]. 'I Can't Help Myself' had fizzled out, and Columbia was just sitting back and waiting to jump into that space, because they figured that we didn't have anything else, and we didn't. So we had to rush the band into the studio, and I came up with 'It's the Same Old Song,' which was similar to 'I Can't Help Myself.' I found a way of turning the bass figure around, but basically the chords were all very similar, and so I added a few chords on top of the high part just to give it some new nuances. We did that and had it out on the street in five days, and we squashed the Columbia record.

"Then there were the songs that weren't recorded by the people they were intended for, but a hit for somebody else. 'Where Did Our Love Go' was written for the Marvelettes and they refused to do it. The [backing] track was cut in [lead singer] Gladys Horton's key, which was kind of low, but they didn't like it and so, without bothering to recut the track, we just went in and got Diana Ross to do the vocal, even though she had this high, shrill voice at the time. You might say that the Supremes were low down on the totem pole of artists needing assistance, but we decided to just give the song to them. Then they found out that it had been rejected by the Marvelettes and they were really pissed. They were sitting around in the studio cursing, and they didn't want to do it, but they went along with it.

"Diana was already feeling unhappy about doing this song because of the key, and a lot of things were said, but she came off sounding very sultry as a result of that key. I was trying to teach them intricate harmonies for the background and I just was getting nothing, so I suggested singing 'baby-baby' [in a fairly quick tempo], and the only way Diana could do it was to sing 'baybeh, baybeh' in that low and sultry way. All of a sudden that was her sound, whereas previously she had been up in the air. Usually we would have put it in the higher key that she was used to singing in and it wouldn't have come off the same way. Those kinds of moments in the studio you can't explain. Nobody plans them, they just happen, and all of a sudden that became their blessing and started them on a string of hits.

"With us they had a bunch of number ones in a row, and we were looking at each other and saying, 'What the hell is this?' It was very eerie because no one had ever done anything like this, and being the first made you feel kinda funny. The Supremes, on the other hand, never acknowledged that 'Where Did Our Love Go' maybe wasn't such a bad song, and when Brian and I picked them up at the airport after they had gone on an extensive tour they came off that plane, man, and I didn't know these girls. They had a way of walking and talking that was almost funny to us: 'Oh, hi, darling!' I mean, 'star time,' you know? I thought, 'Give me a break!' Brian looked at me and we kind of smiled at each other, but they were into it.

"They were riding this crest, and then right after 'Where Did Our Love Go'—bam!—'Baby Love'—bam! We didn't have an album of songs, so we had to get right in the studio, and when Berry heard 'Baby Love' he said, 'Hmm, this is kinda different. I think it could be a Top 20.' Nobody knew it was going to sell however many millions. It was incredible, and it launched their career and then the hits came one after the other.

"All of the lead singers—Diana Ross, Marvin Gaye, Levi Stubbs, and so on—were great artists, and they had such a handle on what they were doing. With Levi Stubbs it would be one take. I mean, they'd be given the song, they'd be told what to do, they'd learn it in a day or two, come in, and—bam!—they'd be out of there! If they weren't like that they'd never be signed in the first place, so all of the artists were very good in that regard. The talent was there and that made the work much easier. It meant we were able to crank out a lot of stuff, because otherwise, boy, if the talent was kinda lousy or just mediocre we wouldn't have been able to do that.

"It really was like working at a factory. In the early days we all had to clock in and clock out, but eventually we had learned our craft to the extent that we didn't need to punch clocks anymore. We also had quality control. We didn't have an A&R meeting, we called it a 'quality control meeting,' and we actually used to get people off the street to come in and listen to the new material. Eventually, through word of mouth, people got to know that on the first of the month or every couple of months we would have one of these listening parties, and so they would hang out in front of the Hitsville building and then we would bring them into the studio, give them Coca-Cola, potato chips, and hot dogs, and play a bunch of stuff for them to rate. That was in the earlier stages. Later on we did away with that and had a nucleus of staff in the

A&R department that was unmatched by any company in the world, but early on we did everything to try to be on the ball and keep up with what people wanted to hear. We were trying to give people things that would touch them emotionally, and we didn't think that because we were black we would only do this for the black population. We had all mixes, all races of people in there, because Motown embodied the notion that music is a language of its own and it crosses all barriers.

"The pressure of having to compete with the Beatles, who were also turning out one hit after the other, absolutely spurred us on, and I heard that we did the same for them. In fact, from my understanding, before Brian Epstein died he and Berry had a talk about John and Paul coming to do some stuff with the Hollands and myself. They had all of these weird titles for an album—*Hands Across the Ocean, The Beatles Meet the Detroit Hitmakers,* and all kinds of crap—but it never materialized. I think Epstein and Gordy couldn't quite get it together on who would do what, what we could call it, and whose ground it was going to be done on, so it just fell apart. However, we still remained friendly rivals from afar, and we always kept our ears out for what they were doing. You need something to keep you on your toes.

"When we were riding this crest of success we had to keep coming up with the goods. I mean, we weren't in the best of shape health-wise, because eventually everything takes its toll. The problems of not getting enough rest mean that you get tired, a little anxiety sets in, and then you find yourself talking to a therapist because you're mentally exhausted. For Brian and myself it got to be pretty rough there. Also, given the emphasis that was placed on Motown as this all-powerful force, we didn't really get the credit that I thought we should have, and eventually we left because of some of that, but mostly because of the money part.

"We were given tiny statutory rates. The mechanicals were so low it was ridiculous, and we didn't receive any of the publishing; that was all taken from us, so we didn't get the chance to share in all of the money, the billions of dollars that this company was making, and we became disenchanted. We tried to talk about it and come to some agreement, but any time we brought up the subject it fell upon deaf ears. I mean, we were making this machine richer and richer and richer, and we were the ones who were getting less and less of the pie. So we eventually just left and started our own company. Nevertheless, we're still trying to get past royalties that are owing to us, because you need to get compensated for work that can destroy your mind and body and drag you down into the depths of depression.

"It just isn't fair to not get what you worked for, what you made yourself sick for in a lot of cases. I mean, you put your life, your being, and whatever you're about on the line, and then somebody says, 'Okay, two for you, five for me, three for you, fifteen for me.' We need to put that kind of thing to rest, I think, and start paying creative people for what they do."

jimmy**miller**

New York–born and bred, Jimmy enjoyed some of his greatest success on the other side of the Atlantic during the sixties and seventies, producing classic recordings by the Spencer Davis Group, Traffic, Blind Faith, and the Rolling Stones, en route to amassing no less than eighty-eight gold records. A casualty of the then-heady rock 'n' roll lifestyle, he eventually became jaded with the business and withdrew during the early eighties. He made a comeback at the start of the following decade, and in 1990 I spoke with Jimmy, four years before his death at age fifty-two.

"Around '63, '64, I went on the road as a singer and got a recording contract with Columbia, and when I went into the studio I realized that that was what interested me most. So, I soon started writing songs with a young arranger friend of mine and cutting demos of other artists performing our material, and in 1966 I met [Island Records founder] Chris Blackwell. He heard the masters that I was trying to place, and he took one called 'Incense' over to England, put it out, and it was quite successful. He then asked me to go there and work for four to six weeks with the Spencer Davis Group—featuring eighteen-year-old Stevie Winwood—who at that point were unknown in America even though they'd had two hit records in England. So, I went over in September of '66, and the first session I did was 'Gimme Some Lovin'. It was my first worldwide hit as a producer, it broke the Spencer Davis Group in America, and six weeks became eighteen years.

"When Steve left to form Traffic I produced them as well. In those days we would employ effects in the recording, but they were more or less manually done. We'd use the mellotron, which was a keyboard with tapes inside it that would imitate the sounds of other instruments, and we'd also use tape echo and tape phasing. We pushed the studio equipment to its limits in order to create something different, but just when we thought that we were being very brilliant *Sgt. Pepper* came out and we all went, 'Oh, wow, what have *we* been doing? We're just kidding around!' It made everyone in the industry, producers and engineers, sit up and have a rethink, and to this day I still listen to that album in amazement, knowing the equipment that was available back then. Still, once all of the effects had been played out I remember Steve Winwood saying that on the next recording he did he wanted the band to get back to basics and sound like it did onstage.

"One night, while I was with Traffic in Studio B at Olympic, I ran into Mick Jagger. The Stones were in Studio A, and so we invited one another to drop by each other's session. Well, he came by our session at a beautiful moment when we had just cut a basic track which we were all excited about. We were giving it a loud playback and the vibes were wonderful, but when I later dropped by the Stones' session it was rather bogged down and Mick was complaining to me that he couldn't be on both sides of the control room glass at once. So, I just gave him some words of encouragement and told him to hang in there, and about two days later I received a phone call inviting me to his house. He told me that he liked what I'd been doing with Spencer Davis and Traffic, and asked if I would like to produce the Stones' next album. That was to become *Beggars Banquet*.

"Musically they were just coming out of their psychedelic period, which hadn't been too successful for them, and I think that was lucky for me, because I didn't insist that they change direction but they were ready to do so, as was evident from the new songs that they played me. What they had written was rock 'n' roll, yet I subsequently received a lot of credit for getting them back on course, so I benefited a lot from being in the right place at the right time. There again, I think it's fair to say that being American also helped, because—as was the case with many successful British bands during that era—they had been raised on American records, and so with regard to me it was almost a case of the grass being greener. In fact, through their personal record collections Mick and Keith turned me on to American blues artists that I had never heard of, so they gave me quite an education.

"For whatever reasons, it was a successful relationship, and it worked very well for a few years. I was a big fan of theirs ever since I'd heard 'Satisfaction,' so initially I was in awe of the band and could hardly believe that I was going to be in a position to work with them. As things turned out it was not always easy—they could take a long time over certain things—but it was always a pleasure, especially when they'd eventually hit those magic moments as they inevitably seemed to do. The first of those just happened to be on the very first track that I produced for them, 'Jumpin' Jack Flash.'

"In interviews I've seen Mick talking about them recording the backing track for that song on cassette, but to my memory he's mistaken. That took place on 'Street Fighting Man.' They played the demo to me on an old Phillips mono cassette, which was sort of state-of-the-art in those days, and I remember Keith commenting on how distorted his acoustic guitar sounded and saying that he wished we could get that sound in the studio. So I said, 'Well, why not record your acoustic on a cassette?' and the result was that we recorded the basic track that way, including Charlie's drums and me playing some percussion. You know, there we were, spending good money for time in a top studio, and recording onto a £20 cassette machine! We then transferred that onto one track of the four-track tape and went on to overdub other instruments. You can't really tell that a cassette is being played in there when you listen to the finished record, but if you ever took that track out the whole sound would change and become very sterile.

"My own favorite among the five albums that I produced for the Stones is *Let It Bleed,* but I know that Keith's is *Beggars Banquet.* You see, Keith was a workhorse on *Beggars Banquet* because as the only guitarist he played every slide, every rhythm, every lead, and so it should be his favorite album. By then Brian [Jones] was having a lot of chemical problems and a lot of emotional problems, and I was always sympathetic towards him. He was not really contributing to the band, but whenever he felt like playing he would show up at the studio, and this would be maybe every four or five sessions.

"I remember one instance when he had bought a sitar earlier in the day, so he felt like playing it. We were doing a Robert Johnson–type blues song, and there was no place for the sitar, but he was insistent that that's what he wanted to play, so I put him in a separate booth and recorded him on a separate mono reel. In those days we were using four-track, and we couldn't afford to devote one of those tracks to him, and neither could we combine him with anything else, so I was just placating him, but the others would come up and say, 'Why don't you tell him to get the fuck outta here?' I'd say, 'Well, at least he's shown up and he's trying. He may not have the right instrument, but don't you think it's worth trying to encourage him to get it back together?' They would say, 'Look, you're new to Brian. We've been putting up with this shit for three years now.' So, I had a lot more patience, but in the end there was very little that he did contribute.

" 'Jumpin' Jack Flash' was originally intended for *Beggars Banquet*—it was one of the first tracks that we cut—and Mick, being as pragmatic as he is, came over to my flat shortly after we started the album and said, 'Well, I think I've got the single.' He played a cassette of the song, which initially had the line 'I *feel like* Jumpin' Jack Flash . . .' and he was jumping all around, and I said, 'Mick, *you're* Jumpin' Jack Flash! Besides, it's less wordy that way, so it'll be better. Just sing 'I'm Jumpin' Jack Flash . . . ' and he said, 'Yeah, yeah, good idea.' The demo was acoustic, but once the song went electric I was a little afraid of it sounding too much like 'Satisfaction,' because it basically had the same riff but with a turnaround on it.

"I have to give Eddie Kramer a lot of credit for the sound that we got on *Beggars Banquet,* but shortly thereafter he went to the United States to help run Electric Lady Studios, and so Glyn Johns—who had worked with the Stones before—came back to engineer on *Let It Bleed* and *Sticky Fingers,* and then his brother Andy Johns recorded *Exile on Main Street* in the south of France while Joe Zagarino did the mix. Joe passed on very young, and I remember him saying, 'You know, Jimmy, if I were to drop dead tomorrow I feel my life would be fulfilled because I got to work on this project.' He was a lovely man.

"I listened to *Exile* about a month ago, and considering the conditions in which we recorded it—down in the very dank basement of Keith's chateau—it really is better than I recalled, and that's largely thanks to Joe's mixing. I was never happy with the sound of that album, especially after *Let It Bleed* and *Sticky Fingers.* The Stones at that time were tax exiles and could not record in England, which meant that we had to give up our normal home at Olympic. They had recently built their mobile truck, and we had used it a little bit on *Sticky Fingers,* particularly on 'Bitch' and 'Sway,' which had been recorded at Mick's house in the country. What with its giant hall and wood flooring, that happened to be a very good acoustic environment.

"For *Exile,* however, we suddenly found ourselves in this concrete basement with very little ventilation during a hot summer in the south of France. The sound was really harsh, and no matter how hard we tried, no matter how many different microphones we tried and no matter how many different positions we tried, we could never get it right. To make a long story short, we ended up taking the tapes to L.A. and doing the mix there, and ever since I have thought, 'Oh, boy, I bet if we'd had the technology that we have today we could have made it sound so much better.' Anyway, about a month ago I was at somebody's house, and he made me relisten to it, claiming that it was his favorite Stones album, and afterwards I had to agree with him for the reason that it was so basic. I said, 'Well, best to have been left alone!' I mean, there was no intent to record it badly, but somehow the end results worked, and they certainly pleased many of the fans as well as the critics. In fact, I was recently in a state-of-the-art studio with a solo artist and he asked me to reproduce that *Exile on Main Street* sound! We had to work hard to try to achieve that, and in the end I don't think we succeeded.

"At the same time that I recently heard *Exile* I also listened to a couple of tracks off of *Goats Head Soup.* That was the last album that I did with the Stones, and I think that the mixes and the sound on that are absolutely diabolical. By then Mick and Keith were falling out of favor with each other, and it was no longer a case of Mick and Keith's songs but Mick's songs without Keith's help and Keith's songs without Mick's help, and I think that was largely responsible for the downward curve that the Stones were embarked on at that point. Beforehand—on *Let It Bleed,* for example—the two of them would have bits and pieces of songs and they would get together in a corner of the studio and finish them off while we all sat around and waited.

"As a producer I pretty much let the engineer get the sound together, and I might add my own suggestions if there's a particular sound that I'm after or if there's something that I would like to change. Then, after we've got the sound and the band has done a run-through, I invite the band in to have a listen and give me their input. Well, when it came to the Stones, Mick was always very quick-witted. For example, if we were having a problem with the bass but we'd got the sound as good as we could for the moment, I would bring the guys in to have a listen and they'd all say, 'Yeah, yeah, that sounds good,' but on his way out Mick would inevitably turn around and say, 'You will work a little more on the bass part, won't you?' In other words, there was nothing that you could ever put over on him, and I liked that.

"Mick and I always fought a bit over his vocals. I thought they should be up-front, but whenever we were mixing he would come in and say, 'Too much voice, too much voice.' I'd say, 'You're kidding! You can hardly hear it!' and one day I was sitting with him away from the studio and I said, 'Mick, why are you always asking for less level on the vocals? I mean, aren't you confident about how your vocals sound?' He said, 'No, it's not that,' and he described how, when he was growing up and listening to negro blues songs, there would always be a bit of a contest to recite the words because the artists often sounded like they had a mouthful of mush. You couldn't work out the words to a song by hearing it now and then on the radio, so you would have to go out and buy the record and play it over and over. Pragmatic as ever, Mick now believed that if people wanted to get the words to his own songs—including rock 'n' roll bands who wanted to perform cover versions onstage—mixing down his vocals would make them more prone to buy the records! I had thought that, like a lot of other singers, he just wasn't crazy about the sound of his own voice, but actually he was way more calculating."

eddie**kramer**

■

Long-term associations with Jimi Hendrix, Led Zeppelin, and Kiss, as well as assignments for the Beatles, the Rolling Stones, Traffic, David Bowie, the Small Faces, Peter Frampton, Carly Simon, Joe Cocker, Johnny Winter, and Bad Company, have characterized Eddie's varied career as an engineer and producer. A native of South Africa, he studied classical piano, cello, and violin as a child, before developing a taste for jazz and moving with his family to England at age nineteen in 1960. Within a few years he was assisting on sessions involving anyone from the Kinks and the Undertakers to Petula Clark and Sammy Davis Jr., and gaining a musical education that would help nurture the versatility that he would later become famous for. I spoke with Eddie in 1997, shortly after he had remastered and remixed several Hendrix albums, some containing previously unreleased material.

"My whole vibe on recording really comes from the musical end rather than the technical side of things. I was never really a 'technician.' The whole musical idea behind what I do is very, very critical because I use the classical recording technique, and the classical infusion of ideas is very important to the way in which I record rock music.

"Back in the early sixties I had a great time at Pye Studios. It was the center of recording in England, and one of the things that really made it interesting for me was going out on the road and recording classical performances. The studio's owner, Bob Auger, was probably the preeminent live classical recording engineer back then, and it was with him that I learned how to record an orchestra. Later on it was that technique that I applied to recording rock 'n' roll. I would watch how Bob did it, and he was amazing—you know, he would record the London Symphony Orchestra at Walthamstow Town Hall on three-track with a mobile one day, and then come into the studio the following day and record Petula Clark or the Kinks. So, there was this tremendous variety in terms of artists and music, and just by watching Bob I learned a tremendous amount with regard to the basics. That's the kind of stuff that kids today don't know, don't learn, and probably don't want to.

"That whole year at Pye was so important for me, but I still wasn't happy because I wanted my own place, and that's eventually what happened. I had my own studio in '65 which I ran for about a year, and it was quite successful. . . . Well, economically it was a disaster, but sonically it was great! I sold the business to Regent Sound and then in '66 I was asked to join Olympic. This was before it had even been built, and I have to say that the early years at Olympic represented probably the most productive period of the sixties. We worked on a phenomenal amount of stuff with phenomenal artists, not to mention all of the movies, the jingles, and the symphony orchestras. At Olympic I had another mentor in the form of [studio manager] Keith Grant, who had previously worked under Bob Auger, and I did some really nice sessions with him. A couple of these were with the Beatles. I assisted Keith on the recording and mix of 'Baby, You're a Rich Man' and then I myself engineered the backing track and some of the vocals for 'All You Need Is Love.'

"With 'Baby, You're a Rich Man' we had a point to prove. You know, they'd booked us because they couldn't get into their [Abbey Road] studio, and Keith and I just had to prove to the world that we were as good as EMI or better. We recorded and overdubbed and mixed that entire song in one night, starting at nine o'clock and finishing at three in the morning. Not bad!

"John Lennon was a fantastic vocalist, and he was to the fore on both of the songs that we worked on. The guy was at the top of his game, it was his song, he'd know how he was going to sing it, he had complete command of the material and the direction, and he'd open his voice and it would be there. I didn't have to do anything! It's like recording any great artist—like Hendrix's guitar or John Bonham's drums: stick a bloody mike up and away you go! It's not rocket science. After a time, however, you get pretty used to that—'Oh, okay, Traffic.' Stick a mike up and away you go; Small Faces, the same; Hendrix; it didn't really matter. Obviously, they were all different and they all had different requirements, but the approach was the same. I mean, people say, 'Oh, give me that Led Zeppelin sound,' but you can't, because it was a special time and Bonham was a special drummer. He was a big bugger, he hit the drums bloody hard, he tuned them in a peculiar or great way according to how you want to describe it, and he was just amazing. It didn't matter where you recorded or how you recorded, it would always come out sounding like Bonham.

"Anyway, during the 'All You Need Is Love' session John Lennon sat next to me, we rigged up this talkback mike on the console, and he sang into that, so he sang into the bloody headphones. The four of them came into the control room and said [in a thick Liverpudlian accent], 'Oh, yeah, well, we need to do this song, y'know, for a TV show,' and it was incredible, because they filtered out into the studio and Paul picked up Keith Grant's string bass, George Martin played harpsichord, George played lead guitar, and Ringo sat at the drums, and then once they got going they didn't stop! They'd go to the end of the song and then John would count, 'One-two-three,' and they'd be off again. No stopping for half an hour. Then they came into the control room, picked the take they liked, said, 'Okay, that's the one. Do us a rough mix,' and 'See you later!' Pretty amazing. I have to tell you, it was the only time in my life that I was ever really nervous on a session, and I didn't dare ask if I could take photographs. Because, you know, I used to keep my camera with me all the time, but I just didn't have the balls to ask them to take a picture.

"You have to imagine the scene outside the front door of Olympic Studios in those days. The Beatles would hang out on a Stones session, and that was heavy enough, but outside there'd be John Lennon's painted Rolls and Jagger's Bentley, and as buses passed by you'd see them slow down and the drivers would comment to each other about what was going on. Meanwhile, aside from assisting Keith Grant, I was also fortunate enough to work with some great producers, such as Jimmy Miller with the Stones.

"Those were very memorable sessions for me because they were the first time that Jimmy had worked with the Stones. They had previously worked with [manager-producer] Andrew Oldham and with Glyn Johns, and they didn't want that and neither, thank God, did Jimmy. He and I had already worked together with Traffic and I'd had a blast, and now here we were with the Stones and the first track we worked on was 'Jumpin' Jack Flash.' We recorded the band in a circle on the floor of the studio using Jimmy's cassette machine. Then, after the track was recorded, we played it back through a little Phillips speaker, and I put a mike in front of that and recorded it onto one track of the four-track. That was very revolutionary. It gave the song a raw sound, and if you listen to the intro you can hear the wow of that guitar. The machine was bloody horrible.

"It was a lot of fun to be breaking new ground. Jimmy Miller was a sweet man, and he made everything so enjoyable. He was a funny guy and the reason for me producing records. Watching him work, it was amazing to see how he got the band completely nuts. He got them really wound up. He was always cracking jokes, and having an American there was neat. 'Wow, he's an American dude! Cool, man!' He had just such a different vibe and a totally different approach. He was really exciting to work with and very creative. He played drums and he played percussion and he got into the lyrics and he just totally vibed the band up. Jimmy was a one-off guy. He was basically a showoff. Having come from show business, he was an actor and a comedian, so there was this instant rapport with the artists. I thought, 'This is for me, I know I can do this,' and he was very encouraging in that respect.

"Prior to Jimmy being involved with the Stones I recall a session where Andrew Loog Oldham was producing. They were recording 'Let's Spend the Night Together,' and I was assisting Glyn Johns. Mick was in the middle of a vocal, and all of a sudden I looked out across the studio and saw that the double doors were open and there were these two bloody great big cops standing there. They were motorcycle guys with the leather boots and so on, and they were just standing there with their hands behind their backs. I said, 'Glyn, the fuzz are here,' and the panic in the control room was like a Chinese fire drill! Doors were flying open, gear was being thrown down the toilet, and people were waving tape boxes around trying to get rid of the smoke, and of course Oldham had a leather briefcase which was like a walking pharmaceutical. Without missing a beat Glyn spoke to Mick through the head-phones and said, 'Look, the law's behind you. Just be cool.' So Jagger says, 'Oi, you two, come over 'ere!' The cops said, 'Who, us?' and they sheepishly walked over to where he was standing. He said, 'Look, I'm having a bit of a problem with my headphones. Can you help me to hold them on?'

"So there were these two bloody great cops with one finger on each headphone trying to help him with his vocal, and then in the middle of all this Mick says, 'Wait a minute, stop the tape, I've got an idea. Can I borrow your truncheons?' I swear to God these two cops gave him their truncheons, and if you now listen to the rhythm part in the middle of 'Let's Spend the Night Together' and can hear what sound like claves, those are the policemen's truncheons being bashed together by Mick! As it turned out, all that the cops had wanted were autographs. The front door had been left open downstairs, and they'd seen all of the cars outside, so they decided to check things out.

"The tools that we had at our disposal in those days were very simplistic. We had EQ, reverb, tape delay, compression, our imagination, and that was basically it. We had to plan every step of the way. We were working four-track, and so the preplanning of our moves was absolutely critical. Still, it's amazing to me when I now think about how long it took to mix a bloody record. I mean, there's the classic story about Jimi Hendrix losing one side of *Axis: Bold as Love* and us just mixing that in a weekend! We didn't even think twice about it. In a general sense I think the recording industry's become too hung up on minor details.

"I remember Jimi coming into the studio and not only did he have three or four hours to put something down on tape but his producer, Chas Chandler, would be saying, 'Jimi, keep it it short. None of these nine-minute segments.' Well, that forced people to condense their creativity into a little package, a little three-and-a-half-minute gem, and that was good for Jimi and also good for us as the facilitators of the sound. We had to be quick on our feet, we always had to think two or three steps ahead—which I still encourage kids to do—and we had to be precise and have our act together, and yet at the same time also be free and experiment.

"Everytime we rolled tape we were doing something new, and the twists and turns of the sessions would dictate the way we'd be going. However, there was a very important structure, and that came down to the restriction of time and the restriction of equipment. That forced us to be creative; to just let our imagination go while also being aware of the boundaries. There's that thing about 'letting your imagination run wild' and that there shouldn't be any boundaries, but there are. I think every great creative artist works within a boundary; he just pushes those boundaries further each time.

"When Olympic first opened I was the new kid on the block. Jimi had just made some initial recordings at De Lane Lea and also at CBS Studios, and basically Chas was unhappy with both of those places. So, he checked out Olympic and booked some time, and the studio manager said to me, 'Oh, Eddie, you do all of that weird shit, don't you?' You see, my reputation there was for working with experimental jazz groups and anything strange or classically oriented, and it was because of that that I got the gig with Jimi! 'You've got Jimi Hendrix coming in. You know who he is?' 'Oh, yeah, the American guy with fuzzy hair who's freaking everybody out.' I had heard of him, but I hadn't heard him play.

"He was a very shy, self-effacing man, and we just hit it off immediately. He was always great in the studio, from the time we first met until the last time we worked together. Very focused, very prepared. As time went on he became more meticulous, wanted to do more takes, and the number of tracks grew; somehow or other we skipped eight-track and went straight from four to twelve-track and then to sixteen. Well, the more tracks the merrier for Jimi. I mean, he'd go on recording for days, and each solo would be pretty damned good. At the same time, he hated the sound of his voice. He was really insecure about it and would constantly say, 'Oh, man, I can't sing!' I had to build him this three-sided booth facing away from the control room so that nobody could see him sing.

"In the beginning Chas was a very, very strong influence, and he kept him on a short leash in terms of the way that the songs were going. Still, Jimi was there for every decision and probably influenced those decisions a lot more than one might think. The two of them would stay up all night working on the arrangements, and while Chas may have been in charge of the first two albums, it's Jimi's creativity which you're hearing. Nevertheless, Chas was very, very important in the overall scheme of things, but about a month and a half into *Electric Ladyland* he left in disgust because there were too many hangers-on in the studio. It then fell to me to kick everybody out, and I have to say that, in spite of *Electric Ladyland* being a rambling kind of album, it still stands up.

"Jimi was in charge of production after Chas left, and he was able to stretch out and do longer songs. He was also able to come in with his buddies at midnight and experiment with jam sessions. However, in spite of the fact that things looked very loose on the surface, everything was very, very structured underneath. Jimi knew exactly what he was looking for, and he knew the right combination of musicians that would work in a certain situation. So, there was a plan. It wasn't all casual. It may have seemed that way on the surface, but having looked at it very carefully—having looked at his notes, having looked at his lyrics, and having looked at the photographs and the footage—and gotten a really good impression of what Jimi was doing during that time period, I think that he really had his shit together with regard to the studio end of things. So, my technical help would be to keep the session running fluidly and to make sure that his sound didn't get lost.

"For instance, on 'Voodoo Chile' there was a carefully thought-out campaign on Jimi's part to entice the right combination of musicians into the studio, along with the right attitude at the right moment. He knew that if he strolled into the studio I would have my act together sufficiently to be rolling tape within a matter of minutes, and that was a key element to the capturing of the moment. So, on the surface there was a very casual kind of vibe, but underneath it all I was sweating; I knew I had to get that piece of music on tape. That was my mission, as it is for any engineer.

"Basically, while he was opening his mouth to sing or putting his finger on the fret it was my job to make what he was doing sound bigger, better, fatter, wider, longer, you name it, and to that end I would employ phasing, tape delay, compression, EQ, and panning. In fact, panning was the thing that I really became known for. I panned the shit out of everything! You know, if it moved it got panned! I'd kind of add to the dimensions that I heard when I first listened to something. When I hear the music I get a picture in my head and I just run with that.

"No one I work with is probably going to be at Hendrix's level, and I accept that, but if it's well played then I enjoy the music and I enjoy the moment. It doesn't matter who's playing; if they are well rehearsed, they know their instruments, they know their music, and they're trying to communicate something and make it enjoyable, I love it. I love music, period. That's what I'm there for. If I can facilitate putting a good piece of music down on tape I'm happy. After all, I was really lucky. I thank God that I was able to be there in the right place at the right time and record these fantastic musicians. I hope I get the chance to do some more, but there are not too many Hendrixes around."

glyn**johns**

■

From the Beatles to the Rolling Stones, Led Zeppelin to the Who, the Kinks to Eric Clapton, and Linda Ronstadt to Nanci Griffith, Glyn's career has been a case of the best working with the best. As a top-flight freelance engineer in the 1960s, he received no credit for often doing the work of the producer, yet his contributions were unmistakable and he has since gained due recognition for his subsequent production outings.

"I'm fairly strong-willed as a person and in the way that I work, but I never seek to overrule artists out of hand unless I think they are making an enormous boo-boo, in which case I have to stand up and put my foot down. In the main my job is to represent the artists to the best of my ability and to show them in their best light. The fact that we are working together means that we have a mutual respect, and so if they feel really strongly about something I'm not going to argue about it. If they don't want to do a particular song, for example, then I'm not going to push it, because to me it's not that important. You can't make artists do something that they don't want to do, and there's little point in it anyway.

"I have a reputation for making albums rather than just singles, and I think that's a far more interesting way of working and far more real. I don't really like the teenybop market. Still, having said that, I absolutely avoid projects that would see me being stuck inside the studio for a year. I've never done that. I would go potty, and there would be something seriously wrong if it took that long anyway. I was dragged towards that situation all the time with the Stones and that's why I chose to stop working with them. I was bored to tears. I could make six albums in the time they were making one, and I still don't think they've got a clue how to make records.

"The way that they work seems to suit them, but I sat there for years watching what I considered to be the finest rock 'n' roll rhythm section that I'd ever heard in my life disappear up its own arse every night. There are a lot of artists like that, and I think it's

141

a drag, and it's an even bigger drag for those who have to be around while they're doing it. They'd end up with something that was a third as good as it had started out being, because it was overplayed, and everyone—apart from perhaps the composer—was bored as hell.

"A band like the Stones makes its own rules and I accept that, but it was very frustrating to work with a bunch of musicians who in my view were capable of far more than they mostly ever got on record. Unfortunately, very few people are able to speak their mind about it. After all, if you're not there someone else will be, and it was no great loss to them when I went. They just got someone else who was prepared to sit there and either wait eight hours for them to turn up or work three consecutive twenty-four-hour days, but to me that isn't productive and it isn't anything other than a waste of precious time.

"When I started working with the Stones I was a very keen fan of R&B, so I was interested in their early recordings and somewhere in my subconscious I understood the sound. Therefore, when it came to the first session that I ever did with them it was very simple for me to get it, and after that we ran the gamut of everything. We'd go into the studio saying, 'We're absolutely not going to get a sound like we've had before. We want to come up with something completely unusual.' This was the pressure that the Beatles were exerting. They were making records that sounded different, and so the Stones felt that they had to do the same, and as a result they went through their acid period and so on, and while that particular example wasn't much fun, at least it did make me have to work. I basically think that I was good at recording rock 'n' roll. I was very enthusiastic and I was very lucky to record some of the rock 'n' roll that the Stones came up with, and certainly they influenced me as much as I influenced them with regard to the sound.

"For six or seven years I was the only freelance engineer in the business, and so all of the acts that I worked with for much of the sixties regarded me as an engineer, even though I had been coproducing their records ever since the first time that they'd walked into a studio. No one had ever noticed, because I had been thought of as the engineer, and the producer had been thought of as the producer, yet Andrew Oldham couldn't produce an apple and a bleedin' orange most of the time—although he did make some good records—and that was across the board for most of the producers who I worked with. In the case of the Kinks and the Who, for instance, Shel Talmy was certainly in the right place at the right time. He found the bands and I actually engineered the records, and I in fact think that as a result I contributed bloody more than he did. However, he was sitting in the seat at the time, and I don't regret that in the least.

"For their part, the Stones used me as a freelance recording engineer through all of the different producers whom they worked with, and so when it came to thinking of me as being anything else it was very difficult for them to do that. What's more, having said that, they didn't know how to make records; their experience of recording was, in fact, really limited. It was mostly limited to working with me as well as Dave Hassinger in America, and to Andrew Oldham producing them until Jimmy Miller entered the scene. Well, Jimmy Miller was a lovely guy who didn't contribute very much in my view. He just frustrated me a lot of the time, and to my mind he wasn't a great record producer at all. Neither was Andrew Oldham. Consequently, during all of the time that I worked with the Stones their knowledge of producers per se was practically zero. I don't think they really understood what a record producer did, and therefore when the time arrived for me to stand up and say to Mick and Keith, 'Look, I've already been producing for years, so if you want to continue working with me I think I ought to coproduce with you,' I was virtually laughed out of the room. 'You're not a producer, you're an engineer! Shut up and get back behind the desk!' That's when I started to think, 'I'm out of here. . . .'

"Several years earlier, Chris Farlowe's hit, 'Out of Time,' had been coproduced by Mick and me, and Mick had got the credit. That was just one of those fiddles. I'd been retained to produce it with Mick and I hadn't been given the credit; a case of Andrew Oldham maximizing the use of Mick as a producer. There again, with Led Zeppelin I was retained as the coproducer of their [*Led Zeppelin*] record with Jimmy Page, and I was given a verbal deal and they went back on it. They turned around after the fact and said, 'Oh, no, you didn't produce it,' and refused to pay me. So, that's why I only did one Led Zeppelin album, even though they actually had the liberty to then come back and ask me to do the next one! I mean, they certainly coproduced the *Led Zeppelin* album, but there's no question at all that I coproduced the record with them. Listen to it; it's got me all over it, and if anybody's got half an earhole they can even tell what I did. Just compare the album that I made with them to the next one and my contribution is obvious.

"On the other hand, with the Beatles' *Get Back* project [eventually retitled *Let It Be*] it wasn't specified as to what capacity I was being retained in. I was just asked to work with them, and it became fairly clear as I walked in the door that they wanted me to produce, but that was never really stated. George Martin wasn't there and I was. Anyway, one night I took the tapes with me to Olympic and I ran off some mixes of what they had been doing in the rehearsals. I then had an acetate cut the next day and I said, 'Look, this is just an idea, but I think the album could be like this because I think it's wonderful.' I gave each one of them a copy, and when they came back in the next day they all pooh-pooh'd it and said, 'No, that's totally ridiculous.' So I said, 'Okay, forget it.' End of project.

"We started *Abbey Road* almost immediately afterwards, and a few days later I went off to America to do something else. Then, when I came back home to England, I got a call, and Paul and John met me at EMI and said, 'Okay, we think we should go with the idea that you had all those weeks ago,' and they gave me the tapes and let me loose on my own to go and make an album. So, I went and put an album together, had acetates cut and gave them one each, and they all came back and said that they loved it. This was while we were working on *Abbey Road*. Then [business manager] Allen Klein said, 'We can't release the album, we've got to make the film first. The album should be the sound track to the film.' Well, the film was a year in the editing—which was a complete disaster area—and by the time that it was delivered the Beatles had broken up and John Lennon hated my version of *Let It Be*. Without the consent of anyone else in the band, he gave the master tapes to Phil Spector, who he'd recently befriended, and he told him to go and make an album, so Spector took the tapes and overdubbed these schlocky strings and choirs.

"My idea had been that, as the Beatles had proven themselves to be the masters of the 'produced' record, it would be wonderful to release all of this completely live stuff without an overdub on it. It was very, very raw and yet it was still great. It showed their humor and it was like a bootleg album, but it was good, and I thought it would be a pretty neat idea to release something that was completely the opposite of what everybody had come to expect from the band. That is why they thought I was off my tree when I first gave them my rough version, because it was too much for them to deal with, but I thought that Spector's record was embarrassing. Still, I didn't lose too much sleep over it. I was working my arse off twenty-four hours a day, seven days a week, so I didn't pay a lot of attention to what was going on.

"There had been a lot of bad publicity about in-fighting between the members of the band, and my version of the record basically took that and chucked it out of the window. It really showed them getting on well. I mean, at the start of the project they'd had some problems among themselves, but they didn't stretch beyond that. Even when it was unpleasant between two of them it certainly never extended to anybody else. They were always excellent with everyone, from the tea lady to whoever, and they were fantastic to work with. I had a great time."

john**kurlander**

■

An Abbey Road in-house engineer for just under thirty years, John started out recording rock, pop, and "easy listening" orchestral sessions before carving out a niche with show recordings and then becoming the studio's chief classical engineer. As such he worked with many of the world's top conductors and opera performers, and since going freelance and relocating to Los Angeles he has also immersed himself in a wide array of major movie sound track projects.

"When just one of the Beatles was on a session it would be absolutely great, with two of them it would be okay, with three of them the atmosphere would get a bit tense, and when the four of them were together it would occasionally be unbearable.

"Towards the end, because of all the tension and the kind of hours that the Beatles liked to work, the assistants weren't exactly lining up to be on their sessions. Just before I started at Abbey Road, Richard Lush had been the second engineer on *Sgt. Pepper,* and then for the *White Album* John Smith and Mike Sheady did the job, followed by Alan Parsons on *Let It Be.* Well, when it came to *Abbey Road,* I was given the assignment, and I remember asking Richard Lush incredulously, 'Why isn't anyone else doing this one?' to which he said, 'We've done our stints, now it's your turn. . . .'

"There were times when the *Abbey Road* album degenerated into solo projects, with, say, Paul recording in Studio 2 and John in 3, and so Geoff Emerick and Phil McDonald would be called upon to do the engineering and Alan Parsons and myself would assist them. It was interesting; if there were only two Beatles in the studio at one time along with George Martin, Geoff Emerick, and myself, then it would be a case of the five of us just working together. However, when John, Paul, George, and Ringo were all together something would happen and they would become 'the Beatles.' They would close ranks as the Beatles, and so George Martin, Geoff Emerick, and myself would then close ranks as 'the production team.' That didn't mean we were taking sides and arguing; it was more like

146

there being these two cliques, and as a youngster it kind of surprised me that George Martin was in our camp rather than theirs. The Beatles were incredible as a self-contained musical unit, but the chemistry worked in a negative way insofar as the atmosphere was concerned.

"Still, if working with them was like being thrown in at the deep end, that was nothing compared to the greeting that I got when I sat in on my very first studio session. I lived around the corner from Abbey Road, and I started there as an assistant in September of 1967. After joining you would often have to work in the tape library for about a year, but I was out of there by Christmas, and during that period I learned who everybody was and how the tape system worked, and occasionally I would also be invited to sit quietly at the back of the control room and watch a session involving whatever act was in that day. Well, on that first occasion Tony Palmer was producing and Peter Vince was engineering, and although I didn't know it when I walked in, Tony Palmer had an extremely vulgar mouth. So I was sitting there, timidly watching everything that was going on, and Tony Palmer looked around, gave me a cursory look, and turned back to Peter Vince and said, 'Who's the new c—t?' There I was, just seventeen years old, trying to make a good impression, and I was dumbstruck! I soon realized that Palmer was like this with a lot of people. He would turn to the assistant engineer and say, 'Hey, c—t, play the tape,' and while that obviously wasn't on I actually think it was more common in those days to hear really foul language in the studio.

"The studio manager, Allan Stagge, was really unpopular with the staff, and there was almost a reign of terror. There were rules back then as to when all of the sessions had to end by, and every night between about eleven-thirty and midnight he would come back and check to see if people were still working, and if they were he'd often tell them to bring the session to a halt—the Beatles, of course, were an exception to every rule, and so they were allowed to exceed Stagge's curfew! There was an uneasy atmosphere and a lot of us were worried about our jobs being on the line, so one of the engineers concocted this story that Allan Stagge was introducing a test for all of the young engineers, and that if you didn't pass it you were out. It was a load of nonsense, but this guy came up with a bogus test that was asking questions combining recording terms with trigonometry! It was actually quite funny.

"Well, a few years later I was engineering a pop session with a first-time producer named Neil Harrison, and just as we were setting everything up he turned to me and said—I'll never forget it—'Please set the EMT echo plate to πr^2 over c!' I said, 'I beg your pardon?' and so he repeated it: 'Please set the EMT plate to πr^2 over c.' At first I thought he was joking, but then I realized he was absolutely serious, and he continued to trot out these instructions: 'Give me some EQ at a frequency of 52 kilohertz set to a cosine of 0.72'; 'Limit the vocals at a tangent of 45 degrees from the base of the hypotenuse'; 'Compress the snare with a sine of 1.29 to the square root of 57. . . .' I thought, 'What the hell is he going on about?' but then I spotted him taking a peek at this crib sheet that he was holding just beneath the console, and I said, 'Can I take a look at that?' When I saw it I realized it was a throwback to that bogus test that we'd been given!

"Apparently, Neil had been assisting a producer named Roger Ferris, who had been a tape operator himself at the time that the test was doing the rounds. Things hadn't worked out, Roger had been fired, and Neil was going to be his replacement, and this really pissed Roger off. Neil had never been in a studio—he had been trained more as an A&R guy—and so when he told the departing Roger that he was going to produce a session at Abbey Road and would like some technical tips on what to do, Roger had decided to set him up. He'd told him that he would have to gain the confidence of the engineer who he was working with or else he'd look stupid, and therefore to 'help' him he had written two pages of this trigonometry nonsense! We almost peed ourselves, but Neil Harrison didn't last long as a producer.

"When the Beatles were in the studio there would be this incredible parade of really famous people from the world of entertainment coming in almost every day to hang out for a few hours. In fact, there weren't many times when they were alone. It was as if life carried on, and we would do bits of recording in between them going about their daily routine and bits of business. I remember after John and Yoko had a car crash in Scotland, a bed was set up for Yoko in a corner of the studio and again she would be there with a group of visitors. So, they would be recording with open mikes, and Yoko and her visitors would have to be asked to stop talking while the red light was on.

"When we were compiling the *Abbey Road* album, that short track which ends it—'Her Majesty'—was originally cross-faded between 'Sun King' and 'Polythene Pam.' So, the last note of 'Sun King' was the first note of 'Her Majesty' and the last note of 'Her Majesty' was the first note of 'Polythene Pam.' We put it together in the middle of the night, and when he heard it Paul said, 'No, it doesn't work there, I don't like it, chuck it out.' Well, being that the track was already cross-faded and this was only a demo assembly of the album, I wasn't going to undo the cross-fade and restore the original. So I just cut 'Her Majesty' out, leaving the last note of that song over the first note of 'Polythene Pam,' and instead of throwing 'Her Majesty' away I put twenty seconds of red leader tape at the beginning of it and wrote 'Unwanted version of "Her Majesty" after red leader.' Then, the next morning, while we were all asleep, [engineer] Malcolm Davies cut a reference of the record, and again he had the same attitude as I had—don't throw anything away—so he just stuck on 'Her Majesty' as a separate track twenty seconds after the end of all of the other songs. The band therefore listened to the album, and just when they thought it was all over this track suddenly came in at the end, still missing the final note. This appealed to them, especially as it would leave the album sounding totally unfinished, and so they used that same rough mix with the last note missing. A lot of things would happen by accident that way and they would say, 'Yeah, I like it,' and then later on everyone would write about how brilliant it was.

"After the Beatles broke up I worked with John, Paul, and George on some of their solo albums. I worked on *McCartney,* and when Paul would try to describe how he wanted something to sound, if Geoff or Phil asked him to be more specific he would usually say, 'Just make it sound good!' That was his most common reply. I also did the odd session on George's *All Things Must Pass,* and one day, while he and [producer] Phil Spector were doing something in Studio 3, they needed a rough mix of 'My Sweet Lord.' I therefore went into Room 4—which was a little remix suite—with Spector, and although I'd done virtually nothing up to that point engineering-wise, over the course of twenty minutes he dictated to me how to achieve his famous 'Wall of Sound.' It was like, 'Put on the tape. Lift that fader. Run that tape echo. Spin the echo around . . . a bit more, bit more, bit more . . . that's it. Right, now add a bit of reverb to it . . . a bit more . . . that's it. Now let's bring in this track. . . . ' I did everything, but I was like a puppet as he dictated the whole process step by step. In terms of the kind of delays and the kind of reverbs that he was using, I think there was a formula, but in all other respects he did it by ear. It was amazing. Within twenty minutes he had dictated how to turn a very dry eight-track recording into his trademark sound.

"When I started engineering I worked with Mickie Most for a few years, and then I did a lot of middle-of-the road and show recordings with Norman Newell and, later on, John Yap, who had his own label for show recordings. During the seventies, Norman and I did a load of albums with [music hall pianist] Mrs. Mills, and they were all variations on the same 'good time' theme, with names like *Mrs. Mills' Piano Party, Mrs. Mills' Banjo and Piano Party, Mrs. Mills' Christmas Party, Mrs. Mills' Wartime Songs Singalong Party,* and on and on. We'd roll them out one after the other, and she used to sell a lot of records, and whenever she was in the studio there would always be a very amenable, familylike atmosphere. Her name was Gladys, and at the beginning of each session the second engineer, Richard Langham, would go up to her, give her a big kiss, and then get out the tape box and start writing out the details, and on one occasion he turned to her and said, 'So, what are we doing today, Glad? Another fucking party?' She just burst out laughing. She loved it.

"I ended up doing countless West End [London] musicals, but I always dreamed of doing a Broadway musical, and the first one that I got to do was *On Your Toes.* It was the early eighties, the conductor was John Mauceri, and, quite unusually, he was also one of the show's coproducers. We were in the RCA Studios in New York and the title track is this eight- or nine-minute song-and-dance number which we recorded live: orchestra, lead vocals, chorus, and dancing. About six minutes into the piece there were four tap dance solos, and each time we got to the fourth of these the featured girl always just missed a step and lost the rhythm of it. We did another take and another take, and every time she got to that point she blew it.

"Everyone came into the control room for a playback, and we

told Mauceri that while most of the number was fine we still hadn't got the tap dancing sequence. He said, 'Play it to me,' so we did, and then in front of the whole orchestra and chorus—about thirty-five people—he just turned around, pointed to the girl, and said, 'Look, you're out, we'll go in and record it again, and you [pointing to someone else] dance her part.' Everybody was shocked, the girl started to well up with tears, and she said, 'That's not a very nice thing to do,' to which Mauceri replied—and this is the quote of my career—'You've done it four times. If you were going to get it right you would have got it right by now.' Ever since then, when I'm on a session doing an overdub with someone who's clearly nowhere near getting what we want, somewhere in the back of my mind I'm thinking, 'That's once . . . that's twice . . . ' Obviously, there are things that will become progressively better as you do multiple takes—the Beatles were often a case in point—but there are also occasions when, having done something four times, you know that even if you do it two hundred times it will never get there! So, I learned a hell of a lot from John Mauceri's comment, and quite often now we can do something four times which is nowhere near the mark and then say, 'We're not going to get this today. Let's come back and do it tomorrow,' and the next day we'll get it in one.

"While I was doing the show work I also became involved with classical sessions. I started off recording provincial English orchestras and then progressed to the international scene. When Chris Parker retired in 1985 I took over as chief classical engineer at Abbey Road, and that brought me into contact with all of the biggest names: Domingo, Perlman, Pavarotti, Kiri Te Kanawa, and so on.

"I was at La Scala in Milan in the late eighties to record the rehearsals and performance of an opera featuring Pavarotti. Ricardo Muti was conducting. Now, over the course of my career my weight has gone up and down, and at that time I was a forty-two waist. Meanwhile, it had been on the news that, as Pavarotti had a new girlfriend, he'd been on a diet, and while it was making him quite tetchy he was very proud that, for him, he'd lost a lot of weight. Anyway, we were recording this rehearsal and I needed to adjust a mike that was close to him, so I left the control room, which was in the basement of the [opera] house, and walked up towards the stage. Where I came out was on the audience level, so I then had to get up on a chair and climb onto the stage. Muti was standing around with his arms crossed, as if to say, 'How long's this going to take?' and I was getting nervous, and because of that I lost my footing and almost fell off. Pavarotti immediately lunged forward and, in attempting to grab me, got hold of the back of my underpants. I said, 'Oh, thank you very much,' got up, and started to adjust the mike, and he said, 'We have the same underpants!' I said, 'Yeah, fine, okay,' and he said, 'No, we have the same *size* underpants!' and while Muti was hanging around waiting, and in front of the La Scala orchestra, two hundred chorus and the other soloists, he then proceeded to pull out the waistband of the back of his underpants to prove that, on that particular day, he was, in fact, wearing a pair of Jockey Y-fronts size forty-two! For me it was a disgrace that I was still wearing a forty-two and for him it was a major achievement! I just returned to the control room completely embarrassed, and then, as if that wasn't bad enough, when he came in later for a playback, he made sure that all of the people who hadn't witnessed this thing were made aware—'Look! John and I are wearing the same underpants!'

"At around that time I did a series of albums with a Spanish conductor named Luis Cobos which were very, very popular in Spain and South America, and we worked practically all over the world together, recording different orchestras. On one occasion he urgently needed something to be mixed in New York, but through a series of misunderstandings I flew to London at the exact same time as he flew to New York, and—no matter whose fault it was—the result was that he had gone there for nothing and I owed him one. Well, the way that he got his pound of flesh back was to ask me to fly to Moscow for the next album. This was pre-glasnost, when the old Soviet Communist regime was still running things, and I really didn't want to go, but because of the screw-up over the New York trip I reluctantly agreed.

"I was so paranoid about the visit that I thought I was just going to disappear without a trace and never be heard of again, and I have to say that going through Immigration really was a harrowing experience. Anyway, we had an interpreter with us, and when we arrived at the state-controlled studio for a date with the Moscow Radio Orchestra we ran straight into this very bureaucratic studio manager. With the assistance of the record company executive and our interpreter, I launched into my normal routine of, 'Okay, so the session starts at ten. At seven o'clock I want to do this, that, and the other; I want the machines lined up by eight-thirty; I want this level, that level, this one at so many dB's over, with this amount of headroom; I want these microphones . . .' and I gave him this whole list of how I wanted it to be done. This was duly translated by our interpreter, and the bureaucratic studio manager looked me straight in the eye and said, 'No' or *'Nyet!'*

"Whenever you work in different countries you get a slightly different attitude. In England it will be 'Yeah, okay, mate, we can do that'; in America it will be 'Yes, we can do that, but it will cost you'; and with Luis in Spain it was 'Sí, señor, mañana.' But I'd never come across a flat 'No!' I was very, very indignant at first, but then I tried to compromise on the setting-up arrangements and technical requirements, and after about three days I found myself completely compliant with everything that I was told to do. So, if I'd say, 'I need to do this, that, and the other,' and they said, 'No, we will do it this way,' I would say, 'Oh, okay.' It wasn't about giving up or dropping standards, but there was clearly no point in arguing . . . comrade!"

ron**and**howard**albert**

■

Frank Zappa, Eric Clapton, Crosby, Stills & Nash, The Rolling Stones, Jimi Hendrix, Joe Walsh, James Brown, Johnny Winter, Jimmy Page, Joe Cocker, Buddy Miles, the Allman Brothers . . . as producers, engineers, record company execs, and studio owners in Miami, Florida, the Albert brothers have worked with all of these artists and many more, yet they themselves have retained a fairly low profile. That is why I interviewed them in 1997, convinced that there had to be some interesting stories among the miles and miles of tape that these guys had played with down the years. I was right. There were.

RON: "Making records has always been a wonderful experience for us. Everything's a hit in the studio. There's no such thing as a flop while you're in there, and unless there's some personal crisis, we're all in a good mood, having fun, and doing what we want to do. Having said that, the acts that sustain themselves are the ones with the true talent, and there's a real fine line between enormous talent and dislikable personalities. It seems that the crazier they are, the more talented they are, and once you've figured that out and are able to deal with it on a rational basis, then you don't notice their lunatic shortcomings as much as their ability.

"Frank Zappa was an enormously talented musician, and he surrounded himself with enormously talented musicians. It was all about the music and the execution of it. Much of it was preconceived, at least in his own head, but then a fair amount was also improvised, and this was down to the extreme abilities of the players to take the material to a new level and to different places."

HOWARD: "Back in the early days the musicians hardly ever came into the control room, not even to hear a playback. There would be playback speakers in the studio, and they were happy to listen there. It's not that they weren't allowed into the control room, but most of them wouldn't even think of touching a console. In fact, the first artist who I can remember putting his hands on the console was Stephen Stills . . ."

154

RON: ". . . and his feet."

HOWARD: "Stephen wouldn't be afraid to grab a fader and change a level or something, but most of the others, while they might suggest this or that, would never actually physically touch the console. There wasn't a law against it, but it's just like you wouldn't walk out into the studio, pick up Eric Clapton's guitar, and start playing 'Louie Louie.' There's been a demise in the industry since the musicians have started touching the console. Now they're doing everything at home!"

RON: "Howard and I would engineer all of these sessions together, sitting side by side at the console, and we were among the first to develop the multimiking techniques that are in use today. That's how we got clients to come to us. We were creating drum and guitar sounds that no one else could create, and, because of Howard's ability to play keyboards, we also had a [Hammond organ] B3 sound that no one could create. We were always experimenting with the equipment, and over time we taught ourselves how to mike, how to EQ, and how to limit. We were putting sounds on tape and then onto disc that had never been heard before."

HOWARD: "That's right, although you also have to remember that back in the late sixties and early seventies most of the artists who we worked with already had their own sounds before they came into the studio. So, our job was really to capture those sounds rather than start coming up with all of these effects. We were just trying to make everything happen as smoothly as possible, and to capture the magic."

RON: "You see, whoever we worked with, from the Allmans to Little Richard, had their musical foundations set firmly in live performance. They made records because it was a business and they could make some money, but touring and doing shows was their initial source of income."

HOWARD: "We basically wouldn't change their music that much. We learned from Tom Dowd and Arif Mardin and Jerry Wexler that the real key to being a good producer was to make the group think it was their idea if you were going to change something, but otherwise just get things recorded. In fact, we learned that even more so from Crosby, Stills and Nash, for whom we recorded their debut album [*Crosby, Stills & Nash*], as well as the *Four Way Street* double live set and the *So Far* compilation."

RON: "With them we tried to be as transparent as possible. Especially with their vocals. Just get them down on tape. We've had the pleasure of working with such great singers and also with such great guitarists, and although the magic inevitably comes, you can never tell when that will be. A great guitar player can produce ten hours of the worst crap you've ever heard—I mean, a player in a bar band might play better Eric Clapton solos than Eric himself, except for those magical ten minutes when he's on. The same goes for vocal performance, and so you have to be ready to capture the magic.

"Our philosophy has always been that tape is cheap. We record everything, no matter how horrendous it is, because two seconds after the crap it may be magical. If you don't record it, that moment will pass and be forever gone, and artists like Stephen Stills and John 'Cougar' Mellencamp are perfect examples in that respect. As producers we wear two hats. First we have to get the artists to the point where they produce the magic, and then, once we've got that down on tape, they can go away and we can spend days, weeks, months getting that magic to sound like it happened in five minutes."

HOWARD: "At other times it can actually happen in five minutes. For example, there was Joe Walsh's lead guitar solo on 'Rocky Mountain Way.' We were getting ready to do that solo and he was warming up, and what ended up on the record was the first take warm-up. He didn't even know that we were recording him. He went to do a second one and we said, 'Wait a minute, Joe, you'd better listen to the first thing you did.' He said, 'What do you mean? What first thing?'"

RON: "What we'd often do was turn the tape machines around so that the artists couldn't see the red Record lights. Either that or, before they came in, we'd unscrew the bulbs so that they couldn't tell when we were recording. That way the pressure wasn't on. We'd never use terms such as, 'Take one. Okay, let's record.' In fact, we would sometimes calmly leave the control room with the tape machine in Record and rolling, and walk into the studio and just hang out with the guys. We'd halfway kid around, make some suggestions, do some arranging, and that would lead into fifteen minutes of trying stuff out. They wouldn't even know that we were already recording. Eventually, they'd clue in to this way of working, but it was so informal that it still took the pressure off."

HOWARD: "We worked on five albums with Stephen Stills [*Stephen Stills, Manassas, Manassas II, Right by You,* and *Stills Alone*], and, being that we were never quite sure as to how his former engineer had created his 3-D acoustic guitar sound that sort of jumps out of the tape, we set about innovating our own. We did that with these old equalizers. We'd boost the bass, cut the bass, boost the treble, and cut the treble at the same frequencies, and it seemed to work. In fact, even today, whenever we cut an acoustic guitar we still use that technique."

RON: "A lot of people have tried to emulate that sound and they've been unsuccessful, so we've had some of the fame and glory. However, it's also down to Stephen. He doesn't play with picks, he plays with his fingers, so acoustically he's always had a uniqueness. Additionally, he's playing these beautiful vintage Martins, and if somebody is trying to play the same stuff on a Guild or a Gibson it doesn't have the same effect. The kind of strings have a lot to do with it. So, there were various bits of trickery along with Stephen's own technique, but that acoustic guitar sound was monumental in terms of our success and people wanting to work with us.

"In the early days another of the acts that greatly influenced us was the Allman Brothers Band. We recorded their albums *Idlewild South* and *Eat a Peach*—which was interrupted by Duane's death—and as the Allman Band's reputation grew, so did ours. As a result of our relationship with them a lot of other acts became aware of us. I mean, they literally lived in a camper parked on the studio property! They would get up in the morning, come inside, and have breakfast. . . ."

HOWARD: "They were great to work with, really easy. In fact, it was through them that we ended up working with Eric Clapton.

He was recording in one room and we were doing some Allman Brothers stuff in another, and we just sort of put them together and that turned into 'Layla.'

"You see, Eric Clapton had already heard about this Southern guitar player named Duane Allman who had been doing sessions with people like Aretha Franklin and Wilson Pickett, and who sounded as though he was equally comfortable with rock 'n' roll as he was with the blues, and so he wanted to check him out. Well, Tom Dowd, who had produced Cream, was now working on *Eat a Peach,* and so he was the link between Duane and Eric."

RON: "We all went to see a live show by the Allman Brothers Band in Miami, and when we came back the additional baggage included Eric Clapton. Accounts vary depending on which person you speak to, but I don't remember anything being specifically preconceived. In fact, that song ['Layla'] was never actually played as one piece. Instead, the first half and the piano section were recorded separately and then they were assembled, with the half-time ending overdubbed on top of the existing piano track."

HOWARD: "The drummer, Jimmy Gordon, played the piano part on the second half of that song. We stuck some microphones in the soundboard, closed the lid, and covered it up with a bunch of blankets. The guitars on that whole 'Layla' session were recorded right next to the piano—on top of the piano, to be exact—with little Fender Champ amplifiers. There were no big amps."

RON: "We needed those little amps for the sound that we wanted to get, but the band was so loud that Duane and Eric couldn't hear them. We therefore stuck them on top of the piano [the amps, not Duane and Eric], so that, when they sat down, it was like having stage monitors at ear level. Obviously, there was a certain amount of bleed between the piano and the guitars, but that's called rock 'n' roll!"

HOWARD: "Eric was great to work with. We never had a problem getting him into the studio—we had a couple of problems getting him out of the studio—and that couldn't exactly be said when we were on the sessions for the Rolling Stones' *Goats Head Soup* album. . . ."

RON: "They were a little late arriving. One day I think we waited about twenty hours for them to show up."

HOWARD: "Yeah, that was the time when Mick Jagger hopped out of the limousine like a bunny. He hopped into the studio and kept hopping and hopping throughout the whole session. We never could figure out why."

RON: "Near the end of our tenure at 'Bacteria' [Criteria Studios in Miami] we had built the facility up to include four studios. The Bee Gees would be recording in one room, Stephen Stills would be in another, and the Eagles in another. Now, it wouldn't be unusual for Stephen to walk from one studio to the other, and for us, within the space of an evening, to have made a Stephen Stills record and also have him guest-appear on the Bee Gees' and Eagles' recordings. Stephen's a very likable guy, and the studio is his domain. He loves being in the studio and he loves making music, so if a few buddies of his were recording in the next room it would be real tough to keep him out of there."

HOWARD: "In fact, they didn't even have to be buddies. He'd just have to hear something that he liked and he'd be in there, putting his two cents worth in. There were no locked doors, no secrets. We were all interested in a common cause, to have a great time and make hit records."

RON: "Many, many times, because of scheduling conflicts or perhaps somebody getting an idea in the middle of the night, Howard and I would be recording in separate rooms simultaneously. He, for instance, could be doing a vocal overdub in one room and I could be doing a guitar overdub in another—same artist, different song."

HOWARD: "The two of us started producing in the mid-seventies, and there was a good reason for us wanting to do that. I mean, with the Allman Brothers, Tom Dowd would leave the studio at about ten o'clock at night and we'd stay there and record until three or four in the morning. The next morning he'd come in and say, 'Let me hear what you did last night. . . . Okay, that's great! Yeah, let's go on to the next thing.' Then he'd stay another few hours and leave, and we'd carry on. So, a lot of the things that we cut or overdubbed were done when the producer wasn't even there. We did years of that, until we said, 'Hey, you know, we're making these records and we're not getting the credit for them!' That's when we decided to be producers ourselves."

RON: "Well, at least Tom Dowd came to the studio to check things out. Jimmy Miller, however, wasn't in the studio or even in the same state when we cut 'Heartbreaker' [during the Stones' *Goats Head Soup* sessions], and Bill Szymcyzk wasn't in the studio or in the same state when we made "Rocky Mountain Way"! Prior to Walsh coming to Miami, Bill had recorded two or three things in Colorado that ended up on the record, and he mixed the record in its entirety in L.A. He therefore got the tapes back after the fact, as he'd never been around for the recording and producing of the vocals, guitars, or anything like that. Yet, there he was, credited as the producer. Bill's a great guy and we like him very much, but he just had a better manager than we did at that time! You live and you learn. . . ."

tom**dowd**

■

Starting as a freelance engineer in 1947, Tom combined his love of music with an expertise in physics and electronics that had been put to good use during four and a half years on the Manhattan Project, and the result would be an all-encompassing career. After making his first stereo recordings as early as 1952, he joined the staff of Atlantic in 1954 and helped turn it into one of the nation's major facilities, courtesy of not only the pioneering eight-track work that he did during the second half of the decade, but also the incredible array of pop, R&B, soul, and jazz artists that he recorded and, later on, produced. The major names are too numerous to list here, but this 1998 interview refers to quite a few of them.

"You can't hold artists to the responsibility of being easy to work with. You have to assume—and I am serious when I say this—that all artists have to be unbalanced. You see, at the time of their most creative period their equilibrium is not the same as another human being's. It can't be, otherwise they wouldn't be creative people, and whatever their motivation is, whether it's duress or stress or what have you, when they are doing what they do they are not like your average person walking down the street.

"For me, working on the staff at Atlantic was like culture shock, but I say that with tongue in cheek; I'm not complaining. There could be a day where I would be doing the Coasters at two o'clock in the afternoon and Charlie Mingus at midnight! It was like 'Hello?' You had to keep your head on straight and remember what you were doing. However, with time always as the main consideration and money as the prime factor, I must say that everyone back then was going by the existing union rules. This amounted to three hours for whatever the union scale was, and four songs or fifteen minutes of music, whichever came first. So, if the first composition you did was fifteen minutes long and you did it in the first hour, the session was technically over and you had to pay again to do another song. I mean, those were the rules, but the endeavor was to get three if not four songs in three hours, and that didn't vary whether we were doing a thirty-or-forty-piece orchestra or a jazz quartet. That was the way it went.

"The first session I did with Aretha Franklin down at Muscle Shoals in 1967, after completing 'I Never Loved a Man (The Way I Love You),' she walked out and went back to New York, and all we had were one and a half sides; we never finished the second side ['Do Right Woman—Do Right Man']. Aretha was a sweetheart. I never had an ounce of protest or any problems out of her. She was a buttercup. The walkout had to do with the climate in Muscle Shoals and the fact that in the Deep South *integration* wasn't the favorite word. We had all kinds of complications [between the white and black musicians], there were one or two drinks, and all of a sudden the fur hit the fan, nobody was talking to one another, and it was better to get out than to stay around.

"When I got back to New York, Wex [Jerry Wexler] said, 'We don't have anything to put out,' and I said, 'Wait a minute. Just give me a little time,' and I went to the studio that night and managed to hack together a concept on the second song to make it complete. We did the overdubs and stuck that track on the back side of the record, and all of a sudden we had a hit with Aretha Franklin. The problem was we only had a hit single, we didn't have anything else to put out, and, when the single hit, everybody was clamoring for more Aretha. Columbia had made some exquisite records with her, but they just weren't in the right market. The company couldn't get arrested, but suddenly everything that Columbia had in the can was selling like crazy and we pulled them out of the red in about thirty days! In the meantime, Jerry was saying, 'Man, we've got to get those musicians up here! We've got to make an album!' So, we flew the musicians in from Muscle Shoals and Memphis and crammed together a recording session, and we made the album [*I Never Loved a Man (The Way I Love You)*] with 'Respect' and 'Dr. Feelgood' and all of those things on it.

"Whenever I recorded Aretha I always tried to get her to sit at the piano and play, because for my money her input was vital. I soon discovered that when she stood up to sing she was a different artist to when she was sitting playing piano and singing. By this I mean dynamically different, and so I was always anxious to make sure that she sat down and did what she was going to do while leaving the dirty work up to me. You know, 'Don't worry about it. Just don't wander too far off the mike.' My pleasure with Aretha was to capture her. It was a challenge to capture her every time, because she never sang poorly in her life. Every time she opened her mouth to sing it was beautiful.

"Aretha would do her homework. She'd record and then we would go our own separate ways for a week, a few days, whatever, and then one day she might call up and say, 'Hey, I want to punch in a line here. I want to change that one line.' Well, there have been three artists throughout my life who I've had the pleasure of working with, to who, if they said that they wanted to change a line, I couldn't say no; Ray Charles, Aretha Franklin, Eric Clapton. If they said they wanted to change something it would be a case of 'Whatever you say!' I'm not going to argue with them, because they're artists. So, if Aretha called and said, 'Hey, I want to change . . .' I'd say, 'Fine.'

"There we would be, with this exquisite take, and I'd be listening to what she wanted to do, and I'd say, 'Okay, I can cover that. Don't worry about it, I'll punch it in,' but when I punched in and played it back the timing would be wrong. I'd be thinking, 'What the hell is wrong? How can this happen?' and then it would dawn on me that the phrasing was different when she was standing up and singing to when she was sitting down and playing and singing at the same time. All of a sudden I wouldn't have the easy job of punching in and out; I'd have to anticipate whether she was going to change the phrasing and whether she'd be moving this way or that way, because the line that she was changing wouldn't fit the line that she originally sang.

"We went through that a couple of times, but Aretha is something special as an artist. I never, never had a problem with that woman. The same thing with Ray. I mean, Ray and I joke about it and we talk about it every now and then—once he found out that I had an eight-track machine [in the late fifties] and he knew what the hell I was doing, he'd call up and say, 'Hey man! I've got a great idea! I wanna do this, I wanna do that! You got the tracks?' I'd say, 'Yeah,' he'd show up, and within half an hour he'd do three parts. Then he'd say, 'All right, partner, thank you,' and be gone! If you got three other people to do it you'd spend two days trying to get it.

"John Coltrane, on the other hand, was his own worst critic. He was a tough taskmaster on himself, but by the same token it was a case of the artist not being able to see the forest for the trees because he didn't realize that what he'd played was magical. He'd still be hearing the other concept that he had or the other permutation, but he was a master. I recorded *Favorite Things* and *Giant Steps* with John, and he was something else. John was another world, another kind of artist.

"In those days he never said too much, he was very serious about his music, and when we were doing a session he would show up an hour or an hour and a half early, and like a classical musician he would go over and stand in the corner and play so that he could hear what he was doing. He'd change reeds and he'd do this and he'd do that, and then he'd find a figure that he wanted to play and he'd find different ways of doing it, and this was all while he was standing in the corner, with not a word out of him. The musicians would be walking in and all of a sudden they'd hear what he was doing and where he was coming from, and so when it was time to start the session their minds were already set. He didn't have to play the song for them four or five times. If they got there on time and they heard him running through the song there were no questions as to how to do it.

"John Coltrane, John Lewis, Eric Clapton; if you watch them play you never see any finger pressure at all. If you observe their technique when they are playing they never press down. John Lewis would never press on a piano key, he'd touch it like a feather, and Coltrane was the same way. When he played there was never any violence or any firm, authoritative squeeze or push. He didn't even blow hard. He was the master of his instrument, and he was going to make that instrument talk his way.

"I first met Eric Clapton when I did *Disraeli Gears* with Cream in 1967, and in that setup I was the neutral ground. In fact, I never knew about the personality conflicts that existed at the time when I met them! The first meeting was bizarre. Ahmet Ertegun called me up one day and said, 'There's this group that I've signed to Atlantic and they're on tour, but they have to be out of the country by Sunday because their visas expire, and I promised that I'd record them. See what you can get out of them.' I didn't know what he was talking about! I went into my studio one morning and there was the road crew setting up double stacks of Marshall amps and two bass drums, and I'm thinking, 'I've got two drummers? What the hell am I looking at?' Then, when the band arrived and started playing, I was flying around the room trying to set everything up and I was thinking, 'Help!'

"We did *Disraeli Gears* in three days. We started on a Thursday, and Sunday at five o'clock a chauffeur came into the studio and said, 'I'm looking for a group that I've got to take to the airport,' and so I looked at the guys and said, 'See you later!' The trade rules and the exchange between America and Great Britain in terms of touring musicians was not the way it is now, so they had to leave, and, when they left, *Disraeli Gears* was in my lap and I mixed it.

"During the late sixties and early seventies I did not want to use the overdubbing features of multitrack recording. If I had a five-piece group I wanted five guys to play simultaneously, and if I had a ten-piece group I wanted ten to play simultaneously. Well, in the case of the Allman Brothers I would go up to Macon and rehearse them for a couple of days, they'd play on the road for a week, two weeks, or a month, and then Duane would call up and say, 'Okay, we've got it, we're ready to record.' When they came in they couldn't take more than a day or two off the road because that's how they made their livelihood, and they would come into the studio and it would be a matter of getting two or three songs done in a couple of days. Everything was done live on the fly, and the only things we would repair would be vocals or solos. I therefore would never take phone calls during sessions unless it was Ahmet or one of the principals at Atlantic.

"One day I was in a session for *Idlewild South* and they were doing a take, and the secretary came in and said, 'There's a Robert Stigwood on the phone for you.' I thought, 'What's he want?' I mean, I couldn't deny Robert, so in the middle of the take I picked up the phone, and when the band finished and came into the control room I was still speaking to him. When I put the phone down I apologized and said, 'Look, that was Robert Stigwood. He's Eric Clapton's manager, and I haven't spoken to Eric for some time but he wants to record here,' and Duane said, 'Do you mean the guy . . .' and he started playing these Cream licks. I said, 'Yeah.' He said, 'Oh man! Is he going to record here?' and I said, 'Well, that's what we were talking about.' Duane said, 'Man, I'm going to call you when we get back here, because when he's here do you think I could come by and watch him?' and I said, 'Well, the two of you are so congenial that I'm sure it'll work out, not a problem,' and I just let it go at that.

"A couple of weeks later Eric, Bobby Whitlock, and the guys all showed up. They started running songs by me because they hadn't formulated the final concept on them, and so I was recording everything they were doing, and saying, 'This should be the intro,' 'This doesn't belong in this song,' and we were just rapping. In the middle of doing this the phone rang and it was Duane saying, 'Hey, we're going to be in town the day after tomorrow. We're doing a concert. Are they there?' Then he heard [Derek and the Dominoes] in the background and he said, 'They're there! Can I come by?' Eric was in the control room, and I said, 'Eric, I have Duane Allman on the phone and he asked if he could come by and watch you record. . . .' Eric looked at me and said, 'You mean the chap who played . . .' and he played me the back end of 'Hey Jude' from the Wilson Pickett record. I said, 'Him.' He said, 'They're going to play a show here?' and I said, 'Yeah.' He said, 'Then we're going to see them play!'

"That's how that all materialized. That night I took Derek and the Dominoes down to the Miami Beach Convention Center, where the Allman Brothers Band were playing outdoors, and when the concert was over everybody came back to the studio. They started jamming and trading licks, and Duane was holding Eric's guitar, Eric was showing Duane how he did this part, Duane was showing Eric the bottleneck [slide technique], and it was like they had known each other all their life. Duane had to leave that night because the ABB had gigs, but two or three days later he came back when he was free of whatever obligations they had and the rest is history. We did that album [*Layla and Other Assorted Love Songs*] in ten days.

"Of course, another of Robert Stigwood's clients were the Bee Gees, and that's quite a story. Frank Fenter worked for Polygram Records and was in charge of Atlantic product coming out in the UK. When I went to Europe with the Stax tour in '67 he said,

'I've got to play you this group. They're the hottest thing around here and two or three people want them, but I've been holding them just so that you can hear them because I know you guys could make them big.' Now, I wasn't authorized to make any contractual commitments for any signing, but I listened to this recording and I said, 'Frank, we'll take it! Believe me, if I have to beat them on the head we're gonna take that band!' I didn't know who the artists were, but he just played me a couple of songs and I went, 'Incredible!'

"I tried to reach our guys in New York but I couldn't raise anybody there. I was told, 'Jerry will be back in a day or two,' and I said, 'Hey, they're pressuring me, because so-and-so wants this band.' I asked Frank to give me another day and he agreed, and finally Jerry Wexler arrived in London the day before the first concert at [the Finsbury Park Astoria], and I called him up and said, 'Hey, Jerry, you've got to hear this band. . . .' He said, 'Nah, you know I've been flying! I'm tired. I'll see ya tonight!' and he hung up on me. I was thinking, 'Oh, boy, what do I do now?' so I went looking for Ahmet, but he was on the Continent and I couldn't find him anywhere. I was beside myself and I was looking like a bum to Frank Fenter. Anyway, that night at the concert I saw Wexie and I said, 'Hey, Wexie, you've got to hear this group playing. . . .' He said, 'Group shmoop! I've just heard the greatest group around! I'm signing them.' I didn't know what the hell he was talking about. I said, 'You've got to hear what Frank has—' and he said, 'Man, forget what Fenter has! I heard this group, they're incredible, and I'm signing them!'

"The next day we were flying to Paris and I ran into Ahmet at the airport—he was there to intercept Otis [Redding] and take him to the hotel in a limo. I grabbed Ahmet and I said, 'Ahmet, Frank Fenter has a group . . .' He said, 'I just made the greatest deal in Atlantic history! Don't bother me!' He left me standing there while he took Otis away, and I was thinking, 'Now what do I do? I'm really up a tree! I mean, Wexler won't listen to me, Ahmet won't listen to me. . . .' Finally we got to the hotel and somehow or other we were all talking, and Ahmet said, 'Man, you wouldn't believe this group I've signed,' and so forth and so on, and I said, 'I keep trying to tell you guys that Frank Fenter has this outfit—' to which they responded, 'Who's Frank Fenter? Who cares what he has to say?'

"Well, we were all talking about the same goddamn group! Ahmet had signed the Bee Gees and made Stigwood their manager, I didn't know the name of the group that I'd heard, and it turned out that Ahmet, Jerry, and I were all talking about the same four guys! It was insane! Initially I didn't work with the Bee Gees. Arif Mardin was taking care of them while I was taking care of Clapton, and we would aid and assist each other so that we would make better products. We were always in each other's face because we loved the artists, we loved the work they were doing, and we loved working with them.

"The same could be said for my work with Rod Stewart. He and I got on famously. I'd be over at his house at ten in the morning having tea and Rod would be showing me these records that he had heard the night before or while listening to the car radio. 'Who played on this?' 'Where does this come from?' He was a student, and a diligent student, and he knew what he wanted.

"When I made Rod's first two albums, *A Night on the Town* and *Atlantic Crossing,* he didn't have a band. He had quit the Faces, and I was casting the musicians depending on what songs he was doing. I used studio musicians or we would go to Muscle Shoals, and I was literally acting as a casting director. You know, 'If we're going to do ballads I want this drummer with this bass player and this keyboard man, and if we're going to do hard-drive I need to use . . .' I continued in this vein after 'Tonight's the Night' became a hit and Rod got ready to go off on tour while we were remixing in England. He was auditioning musicians and asking for my advice as to who would play together best, and although he didn't necessarily agree with me he would listen and ingest what I was saying.

"Well, all of a sudden it was time to make another album. We were talking about the songs and so on, and Rod said, 'We're going to use my band.' It was like putting handcuffs on me. This is not a criticism, but I had to compromise a lot of the things that I had in mind when I had been casting the musicians myself. Now I couldn't do that anymore. I had to use the guys who he had sworn allegiance to, and this meant that some of the songs couldn't come off as well as similar songs on previous recordings. That's not a criticism, but they couldn't bend enough and there was a limit as to what some of them could do because you can't get hard-drive guys to play soft ballads and you can't get ballad guys to play hard-drive!

"For me, Rod and Ronnie Van Zant were the perfect illustration of people prepared to sing. Rod would say, 'Let's try recording tomorrow,' and he wouldn't want anyone in the studio but him and me. Not even the engineer. He'd say, 'Play me the song,' he'd listen to it once or twice, and then he'd say, 'Okay, let's try it.' He'd sing just a little bit and he'd say, 'Let me hear that,' and then he might say, 'Change the mike,' so I'd change the mike and he'd record another few bars, he'd come in and listen to the playback, and then sometimes he would say, 'I'm not ready today,' and he'd just walk out. He knew when he was in charge of his instrument, and he wasn't going to sing for five hours, sing himself hoarse, and not come up with the perfect take. Well, now I have to respect that. If he doesn't feel like singing I'm not going to argue. I'd rather have the effort even when the voice isn't at its best than the bel canto with the unhappy attitude.

"Rod was in charge of Rod, and he knew Rod better than anybody else, and Ronnie Van Zant was much the same. Ronnie would be sitting there for days on end watching us make tracks, we'd have two or three songs done, and he'd say, 'What else do you have to do?' I'd say, 'Well, we're going to change the guitar solo here and we're going to do this and that,' and he'd just look at me—and sometimes he'd be carrying around a fifth of Jack Daniels—and he'd say, 'How long's it gonna take?' I'd say, 'I don't know. It depends on what the guys are up to,' and he'd just put the cap on the fifth of Jack Daniels and he'd say, 'All right, tomorrow at two o'clock I'm gonna sing,' and he'd walk out the door, leaving the bottle on the end of the console to indicate to me that he wouldn't be having another drink the rest of tonight or tomorrow morning.

"The next day he would come in and, like Rod, he too wouldn't want anyone else around. Okay, fine. I'd say, 'I want to try this song,' and I'd put the song up, and he'd say, 'Take this.' He would be sitting on a little stool that he enjoyed sitting on when he was singing, he'd sing the song, and I would say, 'Okay, we can punch in that part. . . . ' He'd say, 'No, no, no, no, no, no! Let me hear it, let me hear it,' and he was just like Rod. He'd sit there and he would listen for two minutes, and he'd say, 'I ain't singin' worth a shit!' and walk out the door. Or he would say, 'One more take,' and he would go in and he would absolutely nail it! Then it was straight on to the next song. He knew when he was capable or not of producing the performance that he wanted.

"Ronnie and Rod were not the kind of vocalists to keep you in the studio for three days and still never give you the good performance. With these guys, when they were singing and they were on, they didn't work more than an hour and a half to two hours and the damned two or three songs were done as well as we'd ever get them done. Then they'd be ready to go home. Still, Rod was a crazy man! He was impetuous. He had the patience and the discipline to sit and watch a thing develop, but then all of a sudden he would run out of patience and say, 'Let me know when it's ready,' and he would just disappear. Then, when he came back, he'd say, 'That's not what I wanted,' and I'd think, 'Hey, butthead, if you'd been here and told me I wouldn't have done it!' He didn't do that too often, but when he did I'd think, 'Help!' "

eddy**offord**

■

As a producer and engineer, Eddy is an accomplished referee.
He's had to be. After all, working with bands such as Yes and
Emerson, Lake and Palmer during those hedonistic, overly self-
indulgent days of the 1970s often amounted to striking a compromise between a bunch of leaderless, virtuoso musicians who
were alternately in musical harmony and ideological conflict
with one another. It was the era of progressive techno-rock, and
the aforementioned artists took it upon themselves to produce
expansive opuses that pushed budgets and everyone's patience
to the limit, while also helping to redefine the previously established boundaries of Western popular music. Eddy, then on staff
at London's Advision Studios, found himself in the eye of a
cultural and technological hurricane, but he hung in there, and,
from the vantage point of a quarter of a century later and life
as an independent producer on America's West Coast, he is able
to look back without anger.

"Yes came into Advision and I engineered their first two albums,
Yes and *Time and a Word,* and those did absolutely zilch. Then they
said to me, 'Look, we really like working with you. We don't feel
we need a producer, per se, so we can just do it all together.
Would you like to coproduce with us?' Of course, I said I'd love
to. You see, at that time not a lot of engineers did produce, so we
did *The Yes Album,* and that was an immediate hit for them.

"The biggest part of my gig really was to try and keep all of
the different, opposing factions in check. There was a tendency for
ideas to conflict, for people to get upset—you know, 'I want to
do it this way,' 'No, I want to do it that way,'—and it was my
job to say, 'Well, look, I know you may be right, but we're going
to try it his way and then, if you still don't like it, we'll try it your
way.' I was kind of a referee almost! Then there'd be the mix and
obviously everyone wanted to hear their own instrument louder,
except for Jon Anderson, who wanted to bury his vocals. So, after

a while they pretty much said, 'We'll leave it to Eddy.' I mean, if they all started pushing everything up it got crazy!

"Yes used to come in with the skeleton of an idea for a song, but it wasn't properly mapped out; they'd rehearsed parts but there was no demo. At that time most bands would come in, play the song, and leave, but Yes were extremely experimental. All of the material was developed right there in the studio, and I guess they were one of the first bands to do that along with Floyd and all of the other progressive acts. They'd say, 'Okay, let's do the intro,' and so we'd spend maybe half a day on what would be like a thirty-second section, and then, once that was really perfect, they'd look around and say, 'Well, that's the intro. Now what do we do?' That's how it went, section by section, so the twenty-four-track was just a series of splices every twenty or thirty seconds. Then, once they had finished the recording and wanted to go out and play it live, they would have to go back and learn it from the studio tape.

"They never gave too much consideration to how easy that would be. I mean, as more and more overdubs went down, the keyboard setup would become huge, with strings and flutes, and at that time the whole thing was quite advanced. Well, after the *Fragile* album they asked me if I would consider going out on the road with them and help them re-create live what was on the record. That led me into a situation where I had two Revox machines with which I would cue in parts that they just couldn't quite play. So there'd be, like, a church organ section that I'd cue in or a vocal section—a little bit Milli Vanilli, but not really. They did 90 percent of the playing, and I'd just cue in the rest from the console.

"They were excellent musicians but I was always looking for new sounds, and in those days there just weren't the effects processors that everyone now takes for granted. For the guitar solo on a song called 'Siberian Katrou,' for instance, I had two mikes, one just a regular close-up and the other on a twenty-foot cord which I had the assistant swing in a circle around the studio. It was going close to Steve's amp on every cycle, and that gave it a real kind of Doppler effect [increase in the sound frequency] as it went by. That's how we would try to do something a little different.

"There again, I always loved the way that the band sounded live, and so on another occasion, after we'd just returned from a tour to do the next album, I built individual stages in the studio in order to get that wooden, acoustic kind of sound. Then there was the time when Jon said, 'Oh, it just sounds so great when I sing in my bathtub at home. What can I do?' So we built him a tiled room to do his vocals in, and that made him happy because he felt like he was back in his bathroom. I mean, the sky was the limit. If you thought of something and could figure out a way of how to do it, then you were on your way. I can recall, on a song called 'America,' Bill [Bruford] saying, 'I want to put congas through a wah-wah.' I said, 'Fine,' and we did it. After all, why not?

"The only danger at that time was the tendency to overproduce. Jon would say, 'I hear bombs for this part,' or 'I hear this,' or 'I hear that,' and then he'd do it and everybody would sort of groan. So then he'd say, 'Oh, it will be fine. We'll just put it in the background with some echo.' This would go on and on: 'Oh, we'll just put it in the background with some echo and it'll be fine,' and then one day Bill stood up in the control room and shouted, 'Why don't you put the whole fucking record in the background with some echo and be done with it?'

"My philosophy was 'Never kill an idea before you've tried it.' Even if you hate the thought of it, it might actually turn out to be something good. But then, out of that period [working with Yes] my philosophy evolved into 'Unless you're specifically going for a background effect it has to work up front, and if in doubt leave it out.' Experiment by all means, but at the end of the day be prepared to say, 'Well, it didn't really add that much.' There's nothing wrong with perfection, but there can be this tendency to lose the soul. Doing too many overdubs, drowning out the essence of the song . . . been there, done that!

"We recorded the double album, *Tales from Topographic Oceans*, at Morgan Recording Studios, and *Relayer* was done at Chris' house with a setup that I put together. Then, when we recorded the *Drama* album, there would occasionally be two sessions taking place at the same time in different studios, but mostly each of the band members would come in and do their own thing while no one else was around, except maybe for Jon. The other guys in the band would only get bored listening to Chris [Squire] do a bass part hour after hour, so there was no point in them being there.

But then at other times towards the end I think it got very destructive because there wasn't that link between them. When it worked it was good, but when it didn't it could get really weird.

"You know, there were times when Jon would be sitting in his vocal booth, surrounded by rocks, painting. He was always a space cadet, no doubt about it, and he was the only guy in the band who really wasn't a musician. His guitar playing was terrible. The rest of the guys in the band used to tease him a lot about it, and he had kind of a hard time getting any respect, but it may have worked to his advantage because he broke all of the rules when he was writing songs. At the same time, one of the hardest parts of a production is dealing with the vocals, and in Jon's case the band would lay out this kind of symphony of music and it would grow and grow and grow, and so when he had to do his vocals he'd be shaking in his boots!

"Working with Emerson, Lake and Palmer wasn't nearly as bad in terms of trying to referee. I did their first album, *Emerson, Lake and Palmer,* and then I did *Tarkus, Pictures at an Exhibition* and *Trilogy,* and I was able to concentrate more on engineering than when I was with Yes. I had a fair amount of say with some of the material, but they came into the studio far more rehearsed.

"Keith Emerson's keyboard setup consisted mostly of Hammond B3 and Moog synthesizer. The synthesizer had only recently been invented, and I was actually the one who programmed all of the sounds for him. Still, being that there were no polyphonic keyboards at that time, we had to do a lot of overdubs, and so it would take maybe ten or twelve tracks for Emerson to do a string section.

"His technical ability was just phenomenal. He could hold a conversation, drink a beer, and use his left hand to play the most amazingly weird time signature, and he often did. He was just unbelievable. He initially performed a song called 'Who Shot the Sheriff' on a grand piano, but we then decided that we wanted more of a honky-tonk, saloon-type feel and chose to varispeed the tape in order to get slightly detuned pianos on top of each other. Well, Keith did four takes of piano one after the other and achieved complete perfection in terms of double-tracking. Unbelievable. It almost sounded like one piano.

"Carl Palmer, on the other hand, also had an incredible technique—he could play the greatest kind of complex rhythms—but unfortunately, his timing from one bar to the next wasn't the best in the world. I think that came out more when you heard him play with Asia, and even on 'Lucky Man' he was a little bit up and down. He just can't play two bars in the same tempo . . . but then he comes up with the most amazing rhythms.

"Greg is also a really good guy, a great player. When I went on the road with them for the live album [*Pictures at an Exhibition*], I even got to see him sitting onstage on this £500,000 Persian rug! So, I had a lot of fun with those bands and it was really interesting. However, it turned out that there was a lot of jealousy between Yes and ELP, and at one point I was forced to choose between one or the other and I decided to go with Yes.

"Things were pretty hectic back then. I was very well known as an engineer, and someone recommended me to John Lennon. He had this studio at his home in Tittenhurst Park [Ascot], and I went there to record some of the songs on his *Imagine* album: the title track; 'Jealous Guy'; 'I Don't Want to Be a Soldier'; and 'How Do You Sleep?' It was a lot of fun, but again I had commitments with Yes and ELP, and while it was enjoyable it wasn't as challenging as the other stuff that I was doing, and so I didn't stay for the whole album even though John and Yoko wanted me to.

"The interesting thing is that I became very friendly with Alan White, who was the drummer on a lot of those Plastic Ono Band sessions, and after that we became flatmates in London. Then, when Bill Bruford left Yes, I pushed Alan in his place. Strange how those things come about. . . ."

elliotscheiner

■

Starting out in the sixties as an assistant to producer Phil Ramone at his studio, A&R Recording, in New York City, Elliot learned how to cut discs and work with film en route to becoming a fully fledged engineer. His credits in this field have included projects with Van Morrison, Steely Dan, Aerosmith, Bonnie Raitt, Barbra Streisand, Billy Joel, George Benson, Natalie Cole, David Sanborn, Luciano Pavarotti, Ricky Lee Jones, Smokey Robinson, and Fleetwood Mac, while his productions have taken in Mac, the Eagles, John Fogerty, Donald Fagen, Glen Frey, Bruce Hornsby, Jimmy Buffett, and Toto. Independent since 1973, Elliot still lives on the East Coast even though he often finds himself working out west.

"I don't listen to my old records anymore. I can't go back that far. It depresses me. It's just too long ago. I mean, it doesn't feel that long ago, but I know it was, and so I try not to think about it. I have to say, however, that I had a great time making records back then. It was so much fun. Generally, it was more fun than now, because everybody was live. There were so few overdubs. We made records very quickly. The primary thing was the music and not the sound of it. We went for as good a sound as we could get, but nobody worried about that. Everybody was just concerned with the music: 'Did we get the take? Did we get the performance?' and that was an approach that I could really relate to.

"Still, I'd often find myself asking, 'What does a producer do?' When I did the *Moondance* album with Van Morrison he was technically the producer, but when it was time to do the mix he wanted to be home for Christmas and so he asked me and the drummer, Gary Malabar, to take care of it and send copies of our work to his place in Woodstock, New York. On the next album, *Van Morrison, His Band and Street Choir,* I was supposed to be coproducing with him, but we had a falling out, and so Van and his new drummer, Daud Shaw, produced the record and I somehow ended up being credited as the 'Production Coordinator'!

"Back then we didn't know enough and we weren't discerning enough. You know, we were making rock 'n' roll records, and obviously we'd listen to the sound of them, but there really wasn't much thought put into it because we were limited as to what was available in the studio. You just went in and did it. There was no such thing as renting mikes from rental companies. That wasn't done. You worked with what you had, and if that was what the studio owned, then that was what you used. You put anything else out of your mind.

"Mixing amounted to balancing, EQ, reverb, and echoes. Everything was always cut dry. We didn't necessarily cut it flat—we'd use compression and EQ while we were cutting—but we never used reverb when we were cutting. When you hear one of those recordings now you go, 'Wow, man, there's nothing on this record!' but, you know, you forget that we really didn't put much on it. We were so unaccustomed to echo and reverb that when you put some on it sounded alien, because that's just not the way instruments sounded. You didn't hear that stuff live, there was nothing sophisticated with regard to effects, and in general people just wanted their instruments to sound on record the way that they sounded in a room, and so that's what you went for.

"I was into flanging stuff [producing a phasing-type effect by varying the tape speed], but apart from that if we wanted an effect going for live stuff we'd sometimes employ a room mike sparingly, or I'd face a guitar amp into a piano and then pick up the harmonics off of the strings. Doing stuff like that we thought was very arty . . . it turned out to be a crock of shit. People couldn't hear it anyway! You'd say, 'Oh, you know what I did here?' and they'd go, 'What? Oh, really?' Nobody cared, but it was just a case of who could be cooler than the next guy, and in that respect I think that the English were definitely more adventurous than the Americans. I remember the first time I heard Elton John's records over here, I thought, 'Geez! How did they record those strings and those drums?'

"You have to remember that in those days even the cuts didn't make the sound great. You know, we went for a vibe and we cut only when something was really bad. So, if we liked the body of a take and there was one section which we weren't at all happy with, we'd try to cut it in. We'd look for a take that had the right part and just try to edit it. You definitely could punch in back then—you couldn't punch in in the middle of a piano part, but we were pretty good at vocals. We wouldn't even attempt punching in single syllables, but we'd punch in a word or two . . . and pray.

"As part of the staff at A&R Recording, I had been bringing in more than a million dollars a year in business for them. That was a phenomenal amount of money. Meanwhile, they were paying me $40,000, and I thought, 'Gee, this isn't right!' So, I said, 'Look, I don't want to do this anymore. I want a commission for all of my clients,' and they said, 'Sorry, but no.' I then called all of my clients and told them I wasn't working at A&R anymore, and everybody canceled their sessions, so the studio called me back and said, 'Okay, what do you want?' I said, 'I want 20 percent of everything,' and they said, 'Okay,' but when my check for the first week was like $5,000 or $6,000 they called me back and said, 'This is not working!' So we ended up with a deal comprising 20 percent on time and 15 percent on tape, and that worked out pretty well. However, when other guys saw what I was making they all decided to do the same, and that was the beginning of the demise of the staff engineer."

gus**dudgeon**

■

As an engineer at London's Decca Studios during the mid-sixties, Gus worked on hit records by artists ranging from the Rolling Stones, the Zombies, John Mayall, and the Small Faces to Tom Jones and Marianne Faithful. Then he launched his own production company and enjoyed instant chart success with David Bowie and the Bonzo Dog Doo-Dah Band, before embarking on a seven-year, ten-album collaboration with Elton John that resonates to this day. While the pair joined forces again for a couple of albums during the mid-eighties, Gus also lent his ears to projects with acts such as Black Sabbath, Joan Armatrading, Ten Years After, Chris Rea, and the Boomtown Rats, and he was still as active as ever when we spoke in 1998.

"As a producer I have always wanted a high-quality sound. Previously, when I was an engineer—and not a particularly good one—I wanted to get good sounds on tape but I was never interested in how the gear worked. I went exclusively by my ears, which meant that more often than not I made bad decisions, yet I learned something out of it all by occasionally making good ones, and when I got a quality sound I knew it and I liked it.

"Working with Elton I felt that his music required that quality of sound, and I also thought that his records should particularly reflect the decision to use large orchestrations. After all, there's no point in using a large orchestration if it sounds like shit. At the time I thought that I was doing something really good, and I felt it was high quality, but now, of course, it doesn't sound particularly special and you can only judge it properly by listening to whatever else was around back then. That's not something I spend time doing.

"The thing that made me go into production was both Denny Cordell and Andrew Loog Oldham, within the space of a month, telling me that this was the area I ought to get into, not least because I had probably been interfering too much with my own opinions of their sessions. In fact, having gone out of the studio,

Andrew came back, stuck his head around the door, and said, 'Oh, and by the way, don't forget to ask for a royalty,' and left! I thought, 'Well, that sounds like a good idea,' and consequently I was on royalties before George Martin, which is pretty damned ludicrous.

"I began producing in early 1968, and the following year I got to produce David Bowie's 'Space Oddity' after Tony Visconti had told him that he didn't like the song and said that he thought it was 'second-rate Simon and Garfunkel.' I then met Elton in late '69. Steve Brown, who had produced *Empty Sky* about two and a half years earlier, didn't feel that he was up for the job of doing the following album, and that was something of a brave decision, really. We had started doing production at around the same time, and so I was no more of a producer than he was, but I had been professionally producing records for a couple of years and one of them was 'Space Oddity.' Elton and his people loved the arrangement of that song, and Paul Buckmaster, who had been commissioned to do some arrangements for the [*Elton John*] album, said, 'Well, if you like "Space Oddity" so much, why don't you talk to Gus?' So, that's what happened.

"I think Elton has improved enormously as a musician over the years. I mean, if you listen closely to 'Your Song' you'll notice that the piano isn't actually as loud as you might think it is; that's just an illusion. It's loud when it needs to be but at other times it really isn't, because his playing was a little bit messy, so it's not taken down far enough to disappear but it's taken down far enough so that you basically don't notice the fluffs. In those days he was good at vamping and he was a good player, but I wouldn't say that he was anything extraordinary. He was, however, leaning towards a great feel, a feel that I happened to like a lot, which was that whole American choppy Leon Russell sound. Anyway, the supposition was that Elton would get better as he went along, and of course he did.

"If somebody hires me I guess there's something about what I do which they like, and obviously they don't have a clue as to how it's been arrived at most of the time and neither do I, because it's all hit and miss anyway. I mean, half of the time you're flying by the seat of your pants in virtually any situation. Happy accidents happen all of the time! You just think, 'Oh, wow! Where did that come from?'

"A classic example was 'Bennie and the Jets.' That was never intended to be live, and it was never discussed at any point during the recording. First of all, when I saw the lyrics I thought it was going to be an out-and-out rock 'n' roll thing, so when it turned out to have this quirky sort of jump feel I thought, 'How bizarre.' That kind of threw me a bit, and then I was doing the mix and it just so happened that [on the tape] Elton struck a chord an exact four beats before the downbeat of the actual song, which was not something that he had ever done before, and I initially hadn't even noticed it. I suppose it was in place of a count-in, and while I was doing the mix I was just about to mute that piano part off the front when it suddenly occurred to me that every time I played the tape it made me think of something; it made me think of somebody on a stage trying to cue a band as they're about to start playing a song. This just flashed into my mind, and I thought, 'Hey, wait a minute, let's try something.' We basically threw delay on everything so that it sounded more like it was in a concert hall, and then I said, 'Oh, let's get some applause in,' and so we dragged in some applause, and then I got some people to do some whistling on it and stuff like that, and slowly converted it into a 'live' song. I didn't even say to Elton, 'What do you think?' I just got on with it, and so the first time he heard it like that he went, 'Bloody hell, how did you do *that*?' It's not that clever, actually, it's dead basic, but it sort of paid off somehow. Those things happen all the time.

"When I was an engineer at Decca in the sixties there really wasn't a lot of innovation. The sessions were very strictly timed and tea breaks were adhered to, and so it was only in the seventies that you started to have a bit of room in the studio and a decent budget so that you could mess about a bit and try a few things. I therefore doubt that I was trying to do anything that was remotely innovative in the seventies, and I guess that to some degree what I was doing with Elton was putting a theory into practice. Having done it with 'Space Oddity,' which was planned to the very last detail, I thought, 'Well, I'll have to do the same with Elton.' Then I realized that, having done it once, I only needed to do it once. I mean, having done something in minute detail, where I almost overthought it and overtheorized it, when I went to do *Tumbleweed Connection* I just threw the rules out of the window completely and carried on like that. It really was very much a case of seat-of-your-pants, and I think that produces good results. It gives things a freshness and an energy.

"I'm not a Phil Spector kind of guy; I don't create a sound that is me. What I'm trying to bring to a session is openness on the basis of 'Look, what I love about what you're doing is this, what I don't like is that.' I'll tell them very early in the process what I do and don't like, and I try to make them see that I like what I like so much that I want to improve what I don't like. However, I don't say, 'This is set in stone; this has to change or I'm out of here,' and I'm also not looking to create a compromise, because compromises are a wet wank. A compromise is solidly set in neither one thing or the other. So, if it's a compromise it's got to be because the other side is saying 'I honestly don't know; why don't you go with your instincts?' and I'll say, 'Fine.'

"Having been hired by the A&R guy, you have to make sure that you're well informed as to what's required, but of course things then get a bit wobbly when the artist quietly says to you that he totally disagrees with what the A&R man said anyway. That can happen, and it's very awkward, because you're then trying to find some common ground where it all works. In that sort of situation what you try to do—assuming that you're working in the same country as where the record company is based—is make sure that the record company gets to hear something every now and again. However, what you never do—ever—is let them have a tape at any stage, because if they do they get hooked on that particular mix. There will be something about it that they love that's completely wrong, and they'll want you to keep doing it wrong from then on.

"Obviously, at the end of the day I'm more inclined to side with the artist, because the artist's opinion in a split vote has to be the more important one when it comes to an artistic decision, and when it comes to a marketing decision which affects an artistic decision then I have to say no to what the A&R guy is saying. There are occasions when the A&R guy makes a very valid point about, say, a lyric, and he'll say, 'We can't use that. You'll either have to bleep it out or get rid of it.' Or there will be a situation where the artist wants to do a song at a slower tempo and the A&R guy says, 'Well, actually it's a dance song.' What these people are doing is they're taking in a whole load of fresh information, even if it's slightly out of whack in the balance department, and hopefully they go away loving it. All they remember is what they heard, and so when they then hear the final mix six weeks later they go, 'Yeah, but you know that was so great when the snare was hardly audible,' and you're thinking, 'But I was always intending the snare to be the biggest snare in the world!' So was the artist, and that's why it's like that now! It's difficult, because they weren't there when the decision-making process was going on and therefore their concept wasn't tried, but presumably the producer has reflected what the artist wanted. So, you have to play a certain amount of mind games every now and again, and you occasionally just have to have an orgasm without any physical stimulation!

"I'm also not a musician, never was, never wanted to be. . . . Well, actually that's not true; I would have liked to be able to play the piano, but I can't. However, even with musicians, when I'm talking to them I've always got an idea in my mind. I've never said, 'I've got no idea what to do with this. Just copy the demo.' I've always got specific things in mind, and people usually choose to work with me just because they really love some record that I've made, even though what they don't know sometimes is that a particular record that they are going nuts over is one that I've always been pissed off with because I ruined the mix! Or it was always too slow, or I wish I'd done it the way it wound up being done live, or all of the other ramifications that go with hindsight.

"I'm so grateful for the experience that I got at Decca, working with such an incredible variety of artists. Literally everything from Marianne Faithful, Los Bravos, Billy Fury, and Tom Jones to John Mayall and Mantovani. You could work with a maximum of three different acts within the same day, because there would be three sessions—ten till one; two till five; seven till ten—and every studio pretty much ran to that same schedule so that a musician could finish a session and get to the next one.

"I'd be doing [traditional Scottish singer] Kenneth McKellar followed by the Zombies, and I myself would also be swapping studios within the Decca facility. I'd do a session in the morning in Studio 1 and then move into a completely different room in the afternoon before going somewhere else in the evening! It was pretty scary, but I have to say that what you don't get as much of nowadays is the personality thing. There's a lot of artifice and consequently there's a lot of artificial personality going on, because when you sample things you know that the personality is born of a machine.

"With John Mayall I did the famous *Bluesbreaker with Eric Clapton* album, and the amount of people who talk to me about that bloody album is ridiculous. It's as if I was Eric. They all go, 'Christ, that album changed my life!' I mean, I love the fact that that album's become so important to people, I think that's wonderful, but what a fluke! My whole career has been a fluke from day one. It still is. . . . It always will be! There's no plan to it."

tony visconti

■

During the seventies and eighties, Tony produced and engineered for such eclectic rock icons as T. Rex, David Bowie, Thin Lizzy, Iggy Pop, Joe Cocker, Paul McCartney, U2, the Stranglers, and the Moody Blues, and to each project he brought his technical expertise and sharp ears for arranging. A native of New York, he spent twenty-three years in London and owned a commercial studio there before moving back to his home city, where he continues to produce and is a qualified teacher of the Alexander Technique, a mind-and-body coordination of head, neck, and spine that helps maximize economy of movement, physical comfort, and artistic performance.

"I was always able to translate artists' ideas to tape very, very easily and add something that they would appreciate, and I am getting better at that. People say that working with me is effortless, and I think that's an important factor in record production. I'm always trying to work on it. I am transparent in the studio, and everything about the artist is fully realized on tape. There's nothing standard about my approach. Every time I arrange for an artist it's a unique situation.

"In the beginning, like a lot of other producers I tried to emulate George Martin as much as possible. He was the first producer to really get involved and become a member of the group, and I think that style of production changed everything. I also found Phil Spector an inspiration, not so much as a producer but as an arranger, because even though he didn't actually sit down and write the notes on paper he was a master orchestrator.

"Every producer will say that his or her first hit record was a turning point. It certainly validates the time that you spent trying to get a hit, and of course we have to get hits in this business or else we'll be out of it. Well, my first hit was 'Ride a White Swan' with T. Rex, and in that case we did everything the same way except that we added a little string section and perhaps the song was a bit simpler and easier to understand. Whatever it was, that single went up to number two in the charts, and suddenly that encouraged a shift of consciousness for me and Marc Bolan. Everything that we did after that seemed to work—you know, instant hit records—and although I don't know if consciously I was aware of what I was doing, on a subconscious level I suddenly had the knack for making these hits.

"The T. Rex recordings brought together a lot of elements. Denny Cordell taught me how to get that bass and drum sound. He really drilled me. He was my mentor. It was a case of tuning the drums, positioning the mikes, using the room, dampening the snare in a certain way—the very live snare drum sound that people are getting these days is not the same as that thud of the sixties and seventies.

"Marc's songwriting was a bit retro, but the sound pretty much defined the early seventies. Before that the guitars always sounded clean. Now they were distorted. Then there was the use of a string section, which was an old concept, except that in our case we used larger sections and the way that I wrote for them took things a stage further. One of our big inspirations was the string part on 'Will You Still Love Me Tomorrow' by the Shirelles. I think that's the coolest writing. If you listen closely it sounds like three violins and one cello. We liked that, and so initially the strings of T. Rex were based on it. Then the string writing got absolutely insane on the later albums. Like that track 'Whatever Happened to the Teenage Dream' on the *Zinc Alloy* album; that was the most bizarre string part that I had ever written. So we kept breaking ground on a lot of levels.

"I'm not a pianist, I'm a guitarist, so I would usually sit down with my classical guitar in my lap and score paper in front of me. I was formally trained in orchestration and arranging, and by the time that I got around to T. Rex I was quite adept at strange voicings and especially the string orchestra. I know that well because I'm also a double bass player, and so I'd sit down with the T. Rex track cued up on a Revox machine in front of me and a remote control next to my right hand, and then I'd play the intro, stop the machine, scribble out a few lines, check on my guitar—or on paper—that the voicings were good, and so on. A couple of hours later I would have the whole string arrangement written, and then

I'd send the score to a copyist and a week or two later we would be in front of a string section that was playing the part.

"There was only one string chart that I actually improvised in the studio, and that was for 'Get It On' [U.S. title: 'Bang a Gong']. We didn't plan strings for that track, but I said to Marc, ' "Ride a White Swan" and "Hot Love" both had strings. This new single doesn't. Don't you think we should have strings?' He suddenly got very superstitious! I already was a little superstitious, and so I was just transferring my fear onto him. He said, 'Yeah, can you write something right now?' We were in the studio and the string players were sitting down—they had already played on one or two other songs—and so I said, 'Well, the quickest thing I can do is come up with a string line over the chorus.' The chords were G, A, E, and that's what I had everyone play, and it worked beautifully! It was just so cool. It was the missing element and I'm so happy we did that. That was the only time that I actually arranged on the spot, apart from correcting bad notes on the spot, which is something that you always have to do when you use a copyist! You know, I might scribble an A and the copyist might see it as a B.

"Marc was so often out of tune, but that was something which I couldn't even address on the first three albums. Eventually, as he began to trust me, I would adjust the tuning more and more, but I still had to do it in private. I couldn't tell him his guitar was out of tune on the talkback. He would get very obstreperous. So, I'd just take a little break, walk downstairs—say this was at Trident [Studios]—and tell him politely in his ear that his guitar needed tuning. However, once or twice when I did say it in front of other people he would tell me I was mad or tell me to 'f off.' He was a hard guy to produce on that level, but once I knew the secret I could get him to do anything.

"By the time of the *Zinc Alloy* album the last couple of singles were attracting criticism that there was nothing different and that he was copying himself. So I confronted him and said, 'What are we going to do about this?' I said, 'Why don't you take a year off and write something like *Tommy* or like *Sgt. Pepper* and learn a few new music styles?' and he agreed with me, but he said, 'I think we still need to do one more pop album for the fans.' The fans, the fans, the fans. Unfortunately, he was using copious amounts of cocaine and cognac during that period, his wife had left him, and he had a new girlfriend in the form of Gloria Jones. You'd look at it all and say, 'What's wrong with this picture?' Gloria came in at such a tail end of the T. Rex phenomenon, and Marc was trying to make her fit. Also, there was great acrimony between him and the members of the band who, after all those years of success, were still on a basic wage of between £75 and £100 a week. Here he was, giving Gloria a big break and making her a member of T. Rex, yet he wasn't really acknowledging the guys who had stood by him for many, many years.

"So, the whole thing was off-kilter. The songs were not very good, his attitude towards making records was old-fashioned, he still thought he was current when everyone was telling him he wasn't, and that was really all down to the drug abuse. I couldn't get him out of that mind-set, but he did actually agree with me that we would take a break after this next album and do something better and different. I also had a demo of this little rock opera that he had written, called *The Children of Rarn*—it was about the kind of land that Tolkien may have written about—but he said that we couldn't do that until far off in the future. We would have to make one more record for the kids, yet at the same time, during the making of *T. Rex,* the way that he treated me and the way that he treated others got to such a point that I thought the situation was irretrievable. We couldn't find that original spark or friendship ever again. I felt very put out, and I called it a day. I quit in the end, and the rest of the guys followed.

"It was a very, very sad way to end things. A few years later I met him and we had a big hug. Bowie brought him to see [Visconti's own] Good Earth Studios, and he said that he would love to make a record there, but then he died a few days later. So, there could have been a Visconti/T. Rex reunion, and it would have been the right time, too. He had already picked himself up, he was no longer using drugs, and he looked like he was in fine shape, but unfortunately he had the car accident.

"When I first met Bowie he was this long-haired guy from South London with an acoustic guitar, and I didn't realize that this was just one of his many incarnations. On *Space Oddity* I tried to take him in a particular direction and keep him on line, because we were in danger of having another silly album like his first one, which had tracks like 'The Laughing Gnome.' You know, on one track he might sound like Anthony Newley and on 'The Laughing Gnome' he might just sound absolutely ridiculous. The fact that he wasn't consistent had helped that album to be a big bomb, so consistency is what I was aiming for.

"Still, I could only work with what I had, which was a series of acoustically written numbers, and that's why I refused to do the title track. We had a whole album routined and carefully rehearsed for the acoustic tracks, and then at the eleventh hour he brought in 'Space Oddity,' which clearly had to be produced in an entirely different way. It was nothing like the other songs that he had written for that album, and I said, 'I don't think this belongs on the album, David,' and he said, 'Well, apparently if we don't record this one I don't get a deal.' I tried to talk his manager out of it, but they went ahead and recorded the song with Gus Dudgeon. In fact, they said, 'Well, if you don't do it, who do you recommend?' so I recommended Gus, who I had previously worked for as an arranger. I knew he liked David very much, and then when I heard the results my jaw dropped. I said, 'God, this is pretty terrific!'

"I wish I hadn't been such a peacenik hippie, but I had my scruples and I stuck with them, which isn't a bad thing. I was, however, surprised that David then came back and decided to do the rest of the album with me. Thankfully, it got favorable reviews, and he suddenly became much more valid as an artist than he had been previously. At the same time it was only my second album, and I wasn't very good. Sonically, I'm really disappointed with the album when I listen to it. In fact, I can't listen to it. I didn't know how to enforce what I wanted, and so I kind of bottled out and let the engineer just do it his way. Nevertheless, as a musician and as an arranger, there are moments on that album which I am very proud of; I played bass and recorders and things like that, and I also got to do my biggest orchestration to date, and so there are a few decent landmarks on that album which validate it in my opinion.

"For the next album, *The Man Who Sold the World*, we formed a group with myself on bass, Mick Ronson on guitar, and Woody Woodmansey on drums, and that was really my favorite album; that along with *Young Americans* and the seminal *Scary Monsters*, which all subsequent albums are compared to. I love *Scary Monsters*.

We had always wanted to make something on the level of *Sgt. Pepper,* and with that record I think David and I got pretty close to it.

"Again, I think I helped David by focusing him, and certainly with *The Man Who Sold the World* we paved the way for the *Ziggy Stardust* sound. That identical sound was used afterwards without me, and I helped to forge that. Also, when it came to his own writing, I would definitely help him to organize his thoughts, because a lot of the songs were simply backing tracks. For long periods of time we would just be working on backing tracks with a melody that he'd sing 'la-la' to. Then in the end that original melody would not even be used. After weeks of overdubs a track would suddenly develop a personality, and then he would write lyrics and a different melody, and I would help him with that. It was very much a cooperative thing, and he was a joy to work with.

"When David had a drug problem it screwed up his health but not his creativity. Cocaine was present on *Young Americans*—if it was around on *Diamond Dogs* I didn't notice it—but unlike Marc Bolan he was never deluded when he was on drugs. *Young Americans* had a profuse amount of drugs during the project, but it came off well, so it was no big problem. Sometimes it hurt me to see David so skinny and not eating, but through *Low, Heroes,* and *Scary Monsters* the only drug in evidence was alcohol, and that wasn't consumed when we worked. He was always intelligent and always monitoring his drug abuse, and especially in the studio he was really quite disciplined.

"We were always looking to do something different. I remember when he made that vampire film *The Hunger,* and he didn't want to go back into the studio and dub on his voice. He wanted his voice transformed into an old man's voice live on the set, so I strapped a contact mike to his neck and he wore a scarf over it. I then put it through a harmonizer and made his voice go up in pitch as he spoke live, and it worked really well, although I had to filter out the heartbeat that was coming through the arteries in his neck. You could actually hear this thumping coming through the speakers, which was his pulse, but once we filtered out the low end we got a very convincing old-man sound. Then there were the hairs on his neck rubbing against the mike—he had to shave to prevent the sound of his bristles scratching.

"Basically, he's a phenomenal singer. I've never worked with anyone better. He is the best. His mind is mercurial, he's creative, and he's very quick to see unique angles, yet one of his marked talents is to hire a studio full of talented people and to let them do their thing. He'd sit back for hours while I was working with, say, Carlos Alomar or Robert Fripp or Brian Eno, and David would just observe and maybe make a suggestion now and then. His openness is the best thing about him, and he's willing to try anything . . . as long as it's quick! We'd rarely ever spend more than eight hours at a time in the studio, but those eight hours would be concentrated on work, with no meal breaks. He would like to get in at eleven or midday and work until about seven or eight in the evening and that would be it. We'd go out for dinner, see a play, go to a film, go to a club, and then come back the next day and work another solid eight hours.

"That's how I like to work. I don't believe in wasting studio time or spending way longer on something than is absolutely necessary. There again, sometimes a project doesn't evolve in the way that you originally intended or expected it to. For instance, Thin Lizzy's *Live and Dangerous* album was recorded live, but in the end we kept very, very little of the concert performance, except for the drums. You see, being that Phil Lynott sang and played bass at the same time, he made a lot of bass mistakes. So he wanted to fix them in the studio, but then, when we tried to do that, it was very, very difficult to match the live sound. I told him it would be easier for him to play the whole bass part again rather than fixing just a few notes, and he said, 'Fine!' He didn't mind doing that. Then he said that he had to replace the vocals—'I was off-mike,' 'I was out of breath'—so we replaced the vocals.

"Everyone was doing that back then, but we did it blatantly! These things were well recorded. We were able to do a new vocal and you couldn't hear the old vocal on the audience mikes. Besides, he was so close to the old vocal anyway. That was as far as we were going to go, but then the guitarists heard that and noticed that we were able to do it without any leakage problems. So, we started doing the guitars, and it worked! It kept sounding better and better, the audience reaction was always in the background, and so we ended up with what I call a 'live-plus' album. It just kind of got out of hand. In fact, we'd given ourselves three weeks to finish it and ended up spending two months on it. We had wanted to do a quickie so that we could have product out, but it turned out to be a very well crafted studio album."

alan**parsons**

■

A producer and engineer who is also responsible for his own commercial releases, Alan started out as an assistant on many of the Beatles' later sessions, and within a few years he was at the controls for one of the landmark albums of the 1970s, Pink Floyd's *Dark Side of the Moon*. Having also engineered records by The Hollies, Olivia Newton John, and Roy Wood, he then enjoyed success as a producer during the mid-seventies with Pilot, John Miles, Cockney Rebel, and Al Stewart, before indulging his songwriting abilities through the Alan Parsons Project. Subsequently releasing albums simply under his own name, Alan has also lent his talents to film sound tracks and a stage musical.

"I think one of the reasons why current chart music is so sterile is that it's totally based on machines, and the live musician just doesn't get a look-in. It's okay to use machinery as an improvement medium rather than as a performance medium, and another good thing about machines is that they are compositional aids. Because machines are unpredictable in the same way that humans are unpredictable they can actually give you ideas.

"Everybody works better in collaboration with someone else—I'm almost incapable of working on my own—and in a way sticking one man with a machine is like having a sort of dumb collaborator. You know, if a man is not available why not take a machine? That's what I think is happening with a lot of writers at the moment; they are collaborating with their machinery and coming up with goods that they might not have come up with had the machines not been available. Nevertheless, the most important point in my view is that machines should not dominate the final performance.

"I think modern keyboards are great. The sounds that these machines are now making would have taken weeks to produce a few years back, although in a way that is also a little frustrating for the engineer in me, because it used to be part of the job, fighting to get all these great sounds. It inspired you. Now you can get them at the push of a button, and while that's benefited the overall sound quality of the music I don't think it's benefited the music itself. The focal point of any record is the quality of the songwriting.

"If you look at the Beatles, half of the strength in their music was the experimentation, and had they not spent days and nights literally just getting a vocal sound then maybe it would have turned out completely different. There again, the first two albums were recorded in a day and a week, respectively, so how can you knock that kind of output even without the technology?

"These days when you hear even the great sixties records on CD, my god, there are a few fluffs and bungles in there. I mean, the so-called Phil Spector 'Wall of Sound' may have sounded good on the radio, but if you hear it on CD it's got a few deficiencies. Most of those old records frankly sound duff, yet at the time everyone was saying, 'Oh, we've got to get the Tamla Motown sound!' 'We've got to get this sound, we've got to get that sound. . . . ' Well, they had the excitement, but technically the sound has come such a long way in the last few years that there's just no comparison. Of course, everyone acknowledges the fact there are great old recordings, but those were generally down to recording technique and the people who were on them.

"Having said that, there were great orchestral recordings in the fifties and sixties, and I think that people have now forgotten what orchestras sound like. Through the pressure of record companies it's now got to the point of not using real strings and real players because of the expense, whereas they'll pay people when their performances are encompassed in a music video. However, we mustn't lose sight of orchestral sounds in conjunction with rock music, because, if we're not careful, people will learn to like the synthesized string sounds more than the real thing. I mean, sampler technology is getting better every day, but you always know when it's real.

"Back in the late sixties you never got through three hours without some piece of equipment packing up. You know, power packs went down, mike amps in the desk used to spring out so we'd push them back in or kick them, and the early condenser mikes were always packing up. That's why, when they were putting together their own studio, the Beatles thought they would overcome all of these problems. However, [their "technological expert"]

Magic Alex's mixing console lasted approximately half an afternoon. All I can remember about it were all of these pretty colors, and from a distance you thought, 'Oh, that looks good!' But then you went up close and got a look at the workmanship, and you saw that nothing was quite straight and all of the holes had been cut wrong. It had clearly been carved by hand, and you could almost see the bits of metal hanging off. It was quite funny, and within a few minutes it was very clear that no music was going to be forthcoming from this machine.

"Still, to be involved in the creative aspects of making a Beatles record far outweighed any of the drawbacks, and it was very exciting for me. It's hard to be associated with the greatest rock 'n' roll band of all time without there being some kind of influence, but essentially I've felt influenced by everybody whom I've worked with. I consider that to be a healthy part of my upbringing in music.

"I like to think that I was one of the first engineers who had musical input. When I first got into the game engineers weren't expected to be musicians; it was a technical job. A few years before I came into it they were still wearing white coats, and I suppose I was one of the first to not be afraid of opening my big mouth and making musical suggestions. For whatever reason, that didn't seem to do me any harm—I was still getting booked as an engineer, although I can't say people were ringing me up to specifically ask for my musical ideas. Being a staff engineer at EMI, it was just down to who was available for what jobs, but I didn't ever feel that it was necessary to hold back on what I thought, and obviously that's the reason why people used to ask me. It was very much a safe job with occasional overtime.

"One of my first engineering assignments was a Hollies single called 'Gasoline Alley Bread,' which was a small hit and one of my worst efforts in the studio! Nothing beats experience, but I cringe every time I hear that record. On the other hand, my first big break was Pink Floyd's *Dark Side of the Moon*. Thankfully, I had sort of established a relationship with the band on the album *Atom Heart Mother,* which I mixed, and it was nice to get the offer. I broke my back to make sure that I managed to do every session, because again, being a staff engineer, I could also get assigned to another session, and so I'd often be working until four or five in the morning and then be in again at ten to do something else. It was hard work, but in the end I managed to do the whole lot, and it was the first time that I actually got my name as the only engineer on an album. It was a good way to start! After that the phone started to ring, not only for engineering jobs but production jobs as well.

"To be blunt, the Alan Parsons Project was probably the result of frustration at seeing how many copies *Dark Side of the Moon* shifted and seeing what I got paid for it. That was actually Eric Wilson's view on it; you know, 'You're capable of doing your own *Dark Side of the Moon*. Would you like to do it with me?' and I said, 'Yeah, why not?' So that's what our first effort, *Tales of Mystery*, was. It was a completely crazy idea, a ridiculous concept, for a producer to be making a record under his own name. It had never been known before. It was amazingly forward-thinking for the time—on Eric's part, not mine, as I would never have done it without him. I'd still be making tape copies at Abbey Road if that hadn't happened!

"The roles of the studio engineer and the performing musician are becoming really quite similar to each other now. They are both expected to have the skills of one another, and there are not many musicians around who don't know every last detail about recording techniques. That never used to be the case at all. Today everybody knows what controls there are in a desk and what digital processors do, because they've probably got the same gear in their bedroom at home anyway. So, it's hard to surprise people these days, and because everybody has access to the technology it's hard to surprise the listener as well. In that respect the job has got more difficult. It's hard to be original, but hopefully you make up for the deficiencies in sound originality with musical originality."

bill price

■

Spanning rock to pop and pap to punk, Bill's technical wiz-
ardry has lent itself to assignments with an incredible array
of musical talent. When I interviewed him in 1987, the
London-based engineer-producer was coproducing the Jesus
and Mary Chain, having already spent the best part of a quarter of a century working with anyone from Tom Jones, the
Moody Blues, Paul McCartney, Elton John, Blondie, Rod
Stewart, Stevie Wonder, Chet Atkins, Stan Getz, and ELO to
the Clash, the Pretenders, T. Rex, Roxy Music, Alice Cooper,
Pink Floyd, and the Sex Pistols.

"I would say that the majority of producers I've worked with have
been useless, and there are two main ways in which a producer
can be useless. The most offensive is for him to always insist on
doing things his way, even when he's patently wrong, doing things
that just don't work with the artist; the least offensive way is for
him to simply not do anything, saying 'Yes, that's fine,' whilst the
artist does all the work with the engineer. Years ago we had a
standing joke at Decca Studios. We were going to build an automated producer, consisting of a little box with two switches on it.
According to which switch was pressed, the box would light up
with either one of two messages; 'Come and have a listen,' or 'No,
do it again!'

"Sometimes it's difficult to know who should be credited
with what. If you look at the Sex Pistols' *Never Mind the
Bollocks* . . . album it says 'Produced by Chris Thomas *or* Bill
Price'! Basically what happened is that Chris Thomas was producing the Pistols' singles, and when he wasn't available to work
on their album I was hired to produce those tracks for the band.
The situation became very blurred, however, in terms of what
were potential singles and what were album tracks, produced
either by Chris or myself, and because this started to get to
the stage where it looked like the band's management might
try to sidestep the production agreements they'd reached with

197

both of us, we decided to pool our claims. There were songs of which we had both produced different versions, and these were getting interchanged on the paperwork and on the tape with the help of [band manager] Malcolm McLaren, who was seemingly attempting to minimalize our input and hence reduce his royalty payments! 'Chris Thomas *and* Bill Price' would have given the wrong impression that we had in some way co-produced the record, and so 'Chris Thomas *or* Bill Price' circumvented the normal procedure of having a little asterisk against some tracks and a little dagger against others. The royalties would be payable to both of us, and we could then share these out amicably!

"A lot of people said that the Pistols had no real musical talent, but that's ridiculous. You only have to listen to Steve Jones' guitar work. His sound was extremely distinctive, and he had a marvelously simple way of getting this out of his amplifier: he turned all of the knobs on to '10'—if not '11'—and off he went! He played that powerful punk style in a way that nobody else could, and he could make a simple one-, two-, or three-chord song sound really quite exciting. Steve would also often play the throbbing eight-in-a-bar bass, which generally tended to follow the guitar line. He'd put down a guitar or two first, and as he was very good at double-tracking a guitar and getting it very tight, it made a lot of sense for him to throb away on the bass.

"I like the material that I'm working on to have guts, so that even a slow ballad will sound like a rock 'n' roll ballad. Things can be light within a song, but it always needs something gutsy to mark the top and bottom of the music. I tend to produce with people where I can work together with an artist or band and work in the way that they want to, but at the same time I attempt to get the sound that I've got in my mind.

"An incredible artist is Stevie Wonder. When I was working at AIR Studios [London] in 1972 we rehearsed and recorded demos for the *Talking Book* album. It was a nonstop four-day session, and from the moment Stevie walked into the control room and asked to be shown around we were all in awe of him. He memorized every item within the various rooms, he operated the console monitor panel, and he was able to adjust and tune the drum kit himself.

He then asked me to show him where the mikes were, so I had to take his hands and touch all of the different drum mikes in order for him to avoid hitting them.

"Stevie tended to compose and record as he went along, and he would usually start off with a guide piano or a guide electric keyboard instrument. One song permanently astounded me, when he performed a guide track on clavinet. He wanted two outputs on this, one direct into the console and one through a wah-wah pedal, and he sang and played the song while whacking the pedal with his right foot. What came out was like two people playing against each other, because he was playing a fairly straight keyboard part with his hands and playing something against it with the wah-wah. It came out like a different instrument, which was absolutely amazing.

"The old Neve console at AIR had discreet transistorized electronics, and you could actually overload that desk to good advantage, whereas the better and more modern a transistorized or semiconductor desk is, the less pleasant it sounds when it's overloaded. When recording Marc Bolan, for instance, I would deliberately mismatch his guitar into the desk, and that produced a horrendous effect on his guitar pickups but also quite a cutting sound, as opposed to the kind of boomy sound you'd get if you correctly matched it. I overloaded the console like hell, getting him to play the same thing about six times, and we mixed that down to one track. Bolan's guitar style was very rhythmic and very original to himself, a very attacking, chordal style which played the song's rhythm but would sound more like a drone if plugged into an amp. So I contributed to his snappy guitar sound by tracking it over and over and over again.

"These days I personally miss the vibe of a lot of people playing at once. There is something which is technically non-reproduceable by any other means that you get when four or five guys actually play in time together. You get a power that is more than the sum total of the parts. The music actually takes on a punch of its own accord, which has nothing to do with the recording technique at all. When you overdub and try to fabricate it, it comes more under your control, and although you may get it as good or even better, you never really experience that moment of excitement when the whole band is out there and they all get it together. There's just something magical about sitting in the control room when that happens, and I miss that."

giorgio**moroder**

■

The name alone is synonymous with sensual mid-seventies disco music and late-seventies/early-eighties techno-pop. During a career that has spanned nearly three decades, Giorgio has worked with an enormous roster of artists and amassed a tidy cache of two hundred gold and platinum discs, as well as three Oscars and three Golden Globe Awards, yet today he rarely listens to his old records while dividing his time between his native northern Italy and America's West Coast.

"In the late sixties I played guitar and then the bass in a covers band, and we toured nightclubs around Europe. I also began composing, and I had a little success, and in the early seventies I was doing a lot of work in Germany when I met Donna Summer. At that time I was producing in Munich with my assistant, Pete Bellotte, and basically Donna was one of the girls in a backing band that we had used on a record. She had moved to Munich to be in a local stage production of *Hair,* and we liked her voice and the way she looked, so we recorded two singles with her: 'The Hostage' and 'Ladies of the Night.'

"At one point I then suggested doing a sexy song, almost like the Serge Gainsbourg hit 'Je T'aime . . .' and one afternoon Donna came to the office and said she'd come up with the title 'Love to Love You, Baby.' That sounded good to me. Back then I had a studio in the basement of my Munich apartment building called Music Land—which later became famous when acts such as the Rolling Stones, Led Zeppelin, and Elton John used it—and it just so happened to be empty that afternoon, so I went straight down there and composed the song. Then, a day or two later, Donna came in and we did a very rough demo.

"The way that I wrote back then wasn't much different to how I work now. In 1974 the first cheap little drum machines came out, so I would use one of those, and I also had a real-drum loop with several different tempos. I would put up a tape from a twenty-four-track, and I would have a mike for the vocal as well

201

as some sort of keyboard, a Fender Rhodes or some other synthesizer. Having established the tempo of the song that was required, I would just record the rhythm along with a guide vocal, and then go from there.

"We really just thought of 'Love to Love You, Baby' as a bit of fun. A few days after we had recorded the demo I took it with me to MIDEM [the International Record and Music Publishing Market] in the south of France, and when I played it to people the reaction was absolutely incredible. So we went back to Germany, rerecorded the song, and presented it to Neil Bogart of Casablanca Records. He took it, and then a few weeks later he phoned me at three o'clock in the morning with the idea of extending the number to cover the whole side of an album! So that's what we did, over the course of about two weeks.

"Of course, that record caused plenty of controversy, but that was never our intention. I wasn't really in touch with what was going on in England and America. I got some feedback about how the record was selling through the music papers, but I was never one for going to the discotheques. I maybe visited Studio 54 [in New York] once or twice, but I didn't follow the scene and the trends too much. At the same time, Donna originally didn't want to do dance music at all. I mean, I knew her as a great singer with an incredible voice, and so when we did the demo for 'Love to Love You, Baby' it was very different for her to be singing in that soft, breathy way. She hadn't sung that way for me before, and she wasn't too interested in disco. Ballads and musical numbers were more her style, but then that record took off and we had a bit of a problem.

"For the second album—which was moderately successful—we wanted to record disco tunes and we wanted to use her proper voice, but we also didn't want to change the formula too much. Donna therefore stayed sexy but a little less so, while using a little more voice, and then for the third album she really sang like we knew she could. After 'Love to Love You, Baby' became a big hit she moved back to America, and I followed her there. Then 'I Feel Love' attracted the attention of [film director] Alan Parker, and that led to me composing and producing the score for *Midnight Express*.

"In 1986 I worked with Roger Daltrey on the title song of

the movie *Quicksilver*. I really love Roger's singing, he's a great guy and a great artist, but in that case I made a little mistake. Unfortunately, the key that I chose for the song was too high, and in the end he sounded a little strained. I can't remember if he told me which key he wanted to sing in or if I just picked it from listening to his songs, but, by the time that he came to sing, the tracks had all been recorded. They were about half a step too high, and we couldn't really slow the twenty-four-track tape down because the voice would change. So, that was how it had to stay.

"These things happen. I produced half of Janet Jackson's debut album, and obviously at that time she wasn't a good singer like she is now. She was about sixteen, and my big mistake was that I was so busy working on movies and so on that I didn't really give all of my attention to the project, and it didn't turn out that great. I regretted that later. I mean, there was some pressure from A&M to record everything fast, but we could also possibly have chosen some better songs and been more careful with regard to how we recorded the voice. After that album she took vocal lessons and she was singing every day, but, in hindsight, when I worked with her she probably wasn't ready. In fact, I have to say that the second album wasn't much better than the first, so maybe that vindicates me a little bit! Overall, however, the whole production wasn't that great, and so basically it was my fault. I didn't do a good job.

"A lot of people know me for my synth-based sound, but although I began using the synthesizer at the start of the seventies there was not very much interest in that type of music for quite a few years. In 1970 an engineer named Robbie introduced me to a classical composer in Munich who had this incredible new instrument. It was a humongous machine with cords everywhere, and he played me this composition which just consisted of a bass tone that kept changing every half minute. That was his composition! He was using this huge machine to create what was known as 'concrete music.' There were no rhythms, no effects, and it wasn't too interesting, but then, when he wasn't around, Robbie took me aside and said, 'Look, with this synthesizer you can create more than just a low note.' He showed me a few things, and I thought, 'Wow, this is great!'

"It was the second Moog ever produced—I don't know who

bought the first one—and I was immediately fascinated by the possibilities and the different kinds of sounds that it could produce. It was two or three weeks later that 'Son of My Father' became the first of my records to feature a synthesizer, but, although I had several small hits in Europe with other records that used it, I eventually began to lose interest. You see, first of all it was quite a pain in the butt to use, because there was only one synthesizer around and the classical composer who owned it wasn't too happy about people using it as a popular instrument. He guarded it jealously, so we kind of had to sneak in when he was away. Robbie would say, 'Yeah, maybe I can do a few hours on Thursday,' and that was always a little bit of a problem.

"That's how it was for a couple of years, before several other synthesizers became available. Still, I myself noticed that people didn't want to hear it too much, so I gave up on it for a time. Then, in 1977, Donna and I did an album with some old fifties and sixties songs, and there was also a kind of futuristic song which I thought would be ideal for the synthesizer. Donna sang in a high voice, and a lot of groups seemed to pick up on that. In fact, quite a few artists—like the guy from Bronski Beat—told me that they became a singer because of Donna and that sound.

"During the late seventies and early eighties I always worked with great musicians, and I was also assisted by engineers, although I knew how to operate the Harrison desk that I had. Then, until the late eighties, I also had my own big studio in the San Fernando Valley. It was called Oasis, and that's where I recorded the sound track for *Top Gun* and so on. I therefore know my way around a console, and although I'm not a great engineer I still do all of the mixes by myself. The engineers get me the great sounds with the delays and all of that stuff, but then the final mix is definitely down to me.

"These days I don't listen much to my old records. I don't really have time for them. It's not that I don't like them, but if I listen for too long I become nervous. The major hits I don't worry about. With other songs, however, it's a different story. Oh, some of them are terrible! Absolute throwaways! I prefer to think about 'Flashdance' or 'Take My Breath Away' . . ."

langerandwinstanley

■

With Clive Langer arranging the songs and Alan Winstanley han-
dling the technology, the production-engineering team of Langer
and Winstanley was enjoying huge success when I interviewed
the pair in 1987. The two first met when Clive was recording
with his band at a small basement studio where Alan was working. Himself a former session guitarist who had engineered all
of the Stranglers' early recordings, Alan agreed to coproduce
Clive's solo album, but before they could embark on that project
they found themselves producing *One Step Beyond,* the first of
a string of hit albums that they would work on with Madness.
Thereafter they cemented their partnership by way of projects
with Dexy's Midnight Runners, Elvis Costello, David Bowie,
China Crisis, and the Neville Brothers, and opened their own
commercial facility, West Side Studios, in London.

AW: " 'Our House' was recorded in 1982, and by that time
making records with Madness was quite a long process. Their first
album was actually recorded and mixed in three weeks, and the
record was out two weeks later. That's the same with a lot of
bands' first albums, when they've been together for a couple of
years. They've been playing the songs on the road and know them
really well. Then, when success strikes and they're out on the road
all the time, they haven't time to write much new material and
you get the second–album syndrome. With Madness we were lucky.
This didn't happen until the third album!"

CL: " 'Our House' was a lot of work. We had to mess about
with it quite a lot, and it was a matter of pushing the band into
changing it and working on the rhythm. It started off as just a few
chords going 'round and 'round, so we had to expand on that. A
lot of people pick up on those key changes at the end; once you've
got three key changes, it sounds as if you're changing key again
when you come back to the first.

"Madness's songs are very visual, so they're great for production. You can let it rip. Bands like Dexy's Midnight Runners, on the other hand, are very close-knit and everything is very clearly defined as to how it should sound. It was much more satisfying for me when 'Our House' was number seven in America than when 'Come On Eileen' was laid on a plate and went to number one.

"We did a lot to shape the band's overall sound, tidying up the rhythm section and accentuating their beat. Until then, brass had been reserved for one song, strings for another, but we decided to merge the two into one sound for the group and 'Eileen' was the result."

AW: "At first I was unsure of the song's potential as a single. It sounded more like a nursery rhyme to me, but Clive was optimistic, even when it originally went under the title of 'James, Van and Me,' which was [lead singer and composer] Kevin Rowland's tribute to James Brown, Van Morrison, and himself! In fact, after he'd rewritten the lyrics as 'Come On Eileen' and recorded the vocal, Clive and I weren't too sure and thought that maybe he should go back to singing 'James, Van, and Me.' He didn't, but what we did was to change the rhythm a little bit. I heard the old record 'Concrete and Clay' by Unit Four Plus Two on the radio the day that we were going to record and I really liked its rhythm, so we made 'Eileen' lean that way."

CL: "The first session that we did at West Side Studios was for the *Absolute Beginners* sound track. That was with Ray Davies in May of 1984, and the album ended up taking a grand total of twenty months to complete, thanks mainly to all of the film and record company politics involving the finances. Anyway, one night, while we were recording the title track with David Bowie, we had to stop the session at about six o'clock in order to record a song that would tie in with a video for the Live Aid concert. The idea had originally been for Bowie to sing 'Dancing in the Street' live on stage in London while Mick Jagger did the same in Philadelphia, but that wasn't possible because of the time delay caused by the satellite."

AW: "The track was recorded and rough-mixed in three hours, just in time to start shooting the video at ten o'clock that night in the Docklands [London]. We were recording everything mainly live, and when they were running through the song it sounded like a cabaret thing until Jagger turned up, and then they all went into fifth gear."

CL: "He walked in and started jumping around like he was onstage. He did two vocals, and we used almost all of one of them, which was really good. Luckily, there was no messing about. They didn't have time."

AW: "Bowie's got a great mike technique, and he's got a great ear for the music. A lot of singers don't know when they're singing out of tune, and when you tell them you have to go back and drop in some parts they want to know why. But Bowie always knew exactly where he'd have to redo something, even before we'd have the chance to tell him. Some vocals and guitars were rerecorded on the two nights following the shoot, and the mix was then completed for the video. Bob Clearmountain later mixed for the single in New York."

CL: "In terms of chart material, I don't really understand what Americans like. It's a different sort of culture. Obviously it does cross over, and when you have a great record it's a great record whatever. When we did the song 'Absolute Beginners' both Bowie and myself thought it was an American hit, yet it was successful everywhere but the States."

terry**britten**and
john**hudson**

■

Tina Turner's astounding comeback during the mid-eighties had as much to do with the material and the innovative sound of her records as it had to do with her raucous voice and dynamic stage presence, and while numerous producers, songwriters and musicians contributed to albums such as *Private Dancer* and *Break Every Rule,* two men in particular were responsible for shaping what the *New York Times* described as "new blue-eyed soul from England": producer-composer-musician Terry Britten and engineer–studio owner John Hudson. A session guitarist during a ten-year stint in Australia as well as in his native Britain, Terry struck gold when he wrote Cliff Richard's hit single 'Devil Woman,' and this subsequently helped launch his production career. John, who had first met Terry when engineering a session that he was playing on during the early seventies, co-owned Mayfair Studios in northwest London with his wife, Kate, and it was there that I interviewed the two men at the end of 1986.

JH: "I don't arrange things or write parts, but if Terry records a part he'll say, 'Do you think that's working?' and I might say, 'Well, I think it's a bit too busy' or 'It needs to be an octave higher.' He will then try what I suggest. I might not do that all the time, but I don't just twiddle the knobs.

"When Terry was laying the track for 'What's Love Got to Do with It?' he said, 'Right, I'll do a guide bass part.' He picked up the bass guitar, didn't even bother to tune it, and I ran the tape and he just played along. That's how we record everything. At the end I said, 'That was really good,' and he said, 'Oh, well, that will do for now,' and we ended up never rerecording the bass. A couple of times we were going to redo it and he'd say, 'I'm going to do the bass properly now,' and then he'd change the strings, tune the bass and everything else, and sit there for four or five hours playing away. Obviously, I'd kept the original track, as we were working on ninety-six tracks and could afford to keep everything, and when I was setting up the mix I said, 'You know, the guide bass is the one!' Terry listened to it and agreed with me."

TB: "I only got into production because I didn't like the masters I was hearing of my own compositions, but even then I still feel a bit insecure about what I myself am doing in that respect. I remember when I did 'What's Love . . .' I listened to it and thought, 'It sounds a bit empty, a bit too sparse.' Then, when I was in America, people like Quincy Jones were saying the production was wonderful! I was thinking, 'What's going on here?' and they'd be saying, 'I just love the space, being able to hear every instrument with the voice.'

"The secret is, if you've got a voice like Tina Turner's you can have it way up and it's wonderful, whereas if you've got some Mickey Mouse band you've got to rely on a huge drum sound. I go for what's right for the song, really. The beauty for me of 'What's Love . . . ' was the size of that voice in this very tight, low-key track with a nice groove to it. Understated. I've always liked that, but then again, there's always the temptation to fill everything. If there's a hole, fill it. I used to be terribly guilty of putting everything into a track, overproducing—which most people go through—so now I've gone the other way, trying to simplify everything and just have the stronger elements come out."

JH: "Terry had strong personal feelings as to how 'What's Love . . .' should be delivered, and the fact that, against her own better judgment, Tina restrained herself on the vocal before letting it rip at the end, was a key factor in the song's success. That's one of the main things where I think Terry's an absolute genius and scored one hundred points. She kept saying, 'I've got to sing it loud!' and he kept saying, 'No, softer, softer!' She couldn't believe it. Then, when she got it right, it was fantastic, and she was absolutely staggered! She'd never sung in that way before.

"One of the problems of recording any vocals is sibilance. Now, you can sort that out fairly well if your singer is singing pretty much the same all of the time without too much change in level, but with Tina it's like one minute a whisper and the next minute 120 decibels! You therefore need to have quite a dynamic

sibilance control, and that's why I first started using two microphones to record her. That way I could split them up and compress
part of them and not the other part, and the result is that I get
sibilance control both when she sings quietly and when she sings
loudly, without compressing the shit out of the vocal. In fact, with
some other artists I also place a dummy mike in front of them so
that they don't get too close to the ones that I'm actually recording
them with. . . ."

daveedmunds

■

In 1988 I caught up with Dave, who, from his days with Love Sculpture through to his association with Nick Lowe and Rockpile, had carved out a respectable niche for himself as the roots-rock king of Britain. At the same time he had also spent much of the eighties logging production credits with acts such as the Stray Cats, the Fabulous Thunderbirds, the Everly Brothers, and k. d. lang, in addition to serving as a musical arranger for Chuck Berry, Carl Perkins, and a slew of other rock and rockabilly icons. His 1970 hit version of Smiley Lewis's 'I Hear You Knocking' revealed his penchant for the 'Sun Studios sound' of the 1950s, and the basic approach to recording was one that he still favored.

"I started producing myself when I first began recording, so I never really thought about it as taking a particular step. I just wanted to make the record, and I didn't want to go in with someone else producing and me just singing and playing. On 'I Hear You Knocking' I used different effects for each verse and chorus. It started with a telephone voice—done with crude EQ, by cranking up lots of middle and top—and then we put some rock 'n' roll delay on it, which people weren't using then. It would be dry for the next verse, then change again for the next chorus, and so on.

"I'm not very technical. When I first started recording I used to do it all myself: play all the instruments and engineer. I even used to have a mike in front of the desk in the control room, so I'd be singing away and operating everything myself! I wanted to cover all aspects of making records, but now I have no interest in that. I don't like engineering myself, and I do not think you can engineer and produce at the same time. Production is creating musical and technical ideas, combined to make people want to buy a record, and you can't do that if you're busy plugging in jacks and setting up microphones, or routing to this or that channel.

"Just turn the knob until it sounds right, that's my philosophy. I don't like sophisticated EQ–ing, and I think there's something wrong at source if you need it. I've worked with engineers whose idea of EQ-ing is to separate instruments, so that if they've added 2.5 to something then they won't add to something else because they don't want to use it twice. That's ridiculous!

"I hate spending months and months on a project. It took me about ten to eleven days working with the Stray Cats on their first album, and the Fabulous Thunderbirds' *Tuff Enuff* took about thirteen days. There's no reason for things to take a long time. I recorded the Thunderbirds live in the studio and it was great. You have to move the mikes around if something's too loud while they're all playing—you can't just sort it out later, because separation can kill records, especially rock 'n' roll records. It just takes everything away. The leakage from instrument to instrument is what creates that special sound, like the old Beatles records where you can hear the drums being picked up on a guitar mike and things like that.

"I remember when the Stray Cats recorded a song called 'How Long Do You Want to Live Anyway?' we put it straight onto two-track and didn't even use the twenty-four-track as a safety net in case it would need remixing. It took about four or five hours to set up, and then it was like, 'All hands on deck, let's go for it!' It was really exciting, just magic. Vocals and everything just go straight onto two-track, and then you can't do anything to it—it's all over. People have forgotten how to record that way.

"If you've got good songs, then the easier it is to record and to produce. It's all very well worrying about bass drum sounds, but I don't care—just mike the kit. It doesn't really matter to the success of a record. No one ever bought a record because of a great drum sound! Still, there's a fine line. When I was with Rockpile we got into some disgustingly lazy habits in the studio and we just weren't really bothering. The philosophy was 'A few rattles on the snare—it doesn't matter! That's how it should be!' and that was wrong. The records sounded like shit. They sounded underproduced and like demos. If you want a record to sound underproduced then it has to be produced that way, getting the right performance and the right take and going on a gut feeling.

"Working with people like Chuck Berry at an all-star gig in New York, and Carl Perkins when I was the musical arranger and bandleader on that TV special [*Carl Perkins and Friends: A Rockabilly*

Session], I've been able to fulfill many of my childhood ambitions. In fact, the biggest was being asked by Don and Phil Everly to produce their reunion album, *EB84*. They're the elite. Ask any musicians who have been in the business for fifteen or twenty years and they'll tell you that the Everly Brothers were the elite in pop music in their time. When they got back together for their reunion gig at the Royal Albert Hall in London I met Don, and a week later the telephone rang and he was on it, saying, 'Well, Phil and I are going to get a record deal. We want to make a record. Will you produce us?' I couldn't believe it! Y'know, why me?

"I had just spent about five or six days recording and being filmed in Paul McCartney's movie *Give My Regards to Broad Street,* and he'd given me his home number. So, when I was producing the Everlys, I was looking for songs for them and thought I'd ask Paul. It's a pretty terrifying experience to pick up the phone, dial Paul McCartney's number, and ask him for a song! It's a pretty weird experience, but he was okay and said, 'Yeah, just give me a few weeks.' And sure enough, in a few weeks he came up with 'On the Wings of a Nightingale,' which was released as a single.

"Things can still intimidate me. I went to see k. d. lang playing with her band in Vancouver, and they really knew what they were doing. A very tidy outfit, good musicians, well rehearsed, and doing something different from anyone else. Well, they asked me to produce their first album and I agreed, and then when they came over to England I was so nervous because I didn't know what I was going to do. You see, I don't know what I have to offer until I get in the studio and we start off, and then I think, 'Oh, I know, why don't we try this? What if we do this? How about doing that?' It just starts happening, and that's how it went with k. d. lang; one idea led to another and it turned out really well.

"You just wait for a bit of magic to happen in the studio, and it happens when you're working with good people. For me, the whole buzz of being in this business is working with good musicians, good singers, good songwriters—the best. You can get them if you've got a bit of a reputation and had some success chart-wise. It does help. It's like a real foot in the door."

alex sadkin
■

Alex was on top of the world when I interviewed him just before Christmas of 1986. Bob Marley, Duran Duran, Grace Jones, Robert Palmer, Talking Heads, Joe Cocker, James Brown, the Thompson Twins, Foreigner, and Simply Red were among his formidable list of production and enginering credits, all of which wasn't bad for someone with a degree in geological oceanography who had once researched the hormone growth of giant sea turtles on Grand Cayman Island, near Jamaica. There he had played bass for a local reggae band, and when the music bug had bitten harder than the sea turtles he'd returned to his native Florida and taken a course in studio engineering. A protégé of Island Records founder Chris Blackwell, Alex was dividing his time between the U.K. and the U.S. when we met at Mickie Most's RAK Studios in London. He told me that he intended to base himself in England, but just eight months later he died in a Miami hospital from injuries sustained in a car crash. He was thirty-five.

"Even though he's dead, Bob Marley is still probably my only musical idol. The things he gave me, the inspiration, are still there. I've never met a musician that powerful, who had that much control and really got what he wanted. He taught me a lot about how to build tracks and make a rhythm work, and just how musicians can come together and put together a unique hit record. He really helped to get me started.

"That guy just had so much talent. Imagine working in Jamaica and getting to organize a hit record on the worldwide scale that he did. Every record, no problem. He just had it, and he did it in lots of funky little studios. Bob moved to Miami, so I used to go over to his house, and he would play the acoustic guitar and sing stuff to me, and he knew that I was really dedicated to reggae.

"When I started at Island Records I had a lot of help from Chris Blackwell. You know, ideas on sound. The first thing that I noticed about working with him was that they always had the hi-hat really bright and loud on British records, whereas it wasn't like that on American recordings; the hi-hats would just be sort of in there, quite subdued. So I started hearing a whole different kind of sound picture. I'd heard a lot of Island records, but it wasn't until I was in the studio hearing the tapes and doing the mixes and editing that I realized I was listening to a very different sound from what I was used to.

"I coproduced quite a lot of records with Chris, and in a very low-key way he came out with incredible ideas. He's not a pushy man, he's a real tasteful, thoughtful person, and just by being next to him, hearing him yea or nay something or make some little comments, I was taking in valuable information.

"Working with Island and Chris and Bob, I did reggae and then I worked with Robert Palmer, which in turn led to Talking Heads, who were working at the same studio in the Bahamas [Compass Point]. I did the Jags, I did rock things, I did Japanese things, French punk music, all sorts of things—very international—and it just completely opened me up. So when I went to the States I had a totally different view of things. I worked with Foreigner and my ideas were completely un-American, and when I came up with them they were thought of as quite bizarre by some of the established groups I ended up working with. They wanted me because I'd come up with fresh sounds, but when we'd get in the studio and I'd suggest something they'd say, 'What?' I had just learned a different way of doing things.

"I find that for the most part American recording techniques are very samey, very traditional, whereas over here in Britain there are these great sound people who do something very individualistic, very unique. There's a handful of engineers in London who are real artists, doing sounds that have never been heard before. I don't find so much of that going on in the States. There are, of course, many specifically American ways of working that are ingrained in me, but the English groups are more open to trying things anyway, whereas in the States you'll often get actual rebellion against an idea! I've worked with American engineers and wanted to try a certain sound, plugging up certain gear that I like, and then half an hour later I've realized that they've taken that piece of gear off the sound, because they don't know how to work it and don't like the sound that it makes. They'll slowly remove those effects and replace them with the sound that they like, whereas if an English engineer can't hear the benefits straightaway he'll usually keep working on it until it makes a good sound.

"With the Thompson Twins and Duran Duran you can suggest pulling the ceiling down and recording it and they'll go for it! Especially Duran—Nick Rhodes loves to destroy a room for the sake of sound! We've hit every conceivable thing and sampled it to try to make a new sound. We've taken a classical harp player, had him play a sort of angelic sound, and then treated this so that it sounded really hard and metallic, like nothing you've ever heard before. It had been played with the technique of a harp player, and it ended up sounding like a piece of steel being struck across some heavy cables, but in tune. All done with a lot of compression, a lot of EQ, and a lot of flanging. That was done for one of the tracks on the *Arcadia* album. We've also melted plastic bags, which make a really strange sound, and recorded that. There's a percussionist named David Van Tieghern who I've worked with on several things, and he takes his instruments and puts them in water and hits them, so they'll make strange sounds and vibrate like a gong and sound like a wolfman or something!

"There again, with the Thompson Twins you can sample anything that sounds like it would add to the mood of the song. The album *Into the Gap* had a tune called 'You Take Me Up,' and *Quick Step and Side Kick* had a tune called 'I Dream in Red,' both of which had great sound effects. We had a tape with a lawn mower motor sound. We sampled a fire extinguisher sound, an anvil sound, and the sound of a lot of cattle. Some of these came off sound effects, some such as the fire extinguishers we did ourselves. That's one of my favorite sounds, giving a unique type of effect. I just get the mike at a safe distance of about five or six feet, aim it towards the funnel, give it a shot, and sample that into the AMS. It just seemed to work. A lot of the time those things become hits just because they sound different. So, if you just realize what you enjoy and start trying it, a lot of times it works. If you hate it, then probably everyone else will hate it, too!

"With the Thompson Twins we triggered that on certain beats with the snare drum. On certain hits of the rhythm you not only got the snare hit but you also got this abrupt extinguisher blast. On certain hits of the bass drum you also got lawn mower sounding like a strange sort of motor roll. Then we had certain beats triggering an anvil sample. Both 'I Dream in Red' and 'You Take Me Up' had a similar sort of approach, although 'I Dream In Red' was really more aggressive-sounding. The anvil was intense. 'You Take Me Up' was a warmer sort of song, so it had these funny sounds mixed down a little lower, just giving a vibe in there. . . . The contrast between the Thompson Twins' recordings and those of Simply Red is quite remarkable, as with the Thompson Twins not only were machines being triggered but machines were triggering machines!

"One problem that I have is that if something sounds similar to something that I have already done then I tend to shy away from it, even if it's something that I really love. Like the fire extinguishers; a lot of times I know they will be right for the mood, but I don't want to do them again. They are on an album that was done three years ago, and I don't want to be closeted with that. Neither do I want to spend longer than is necessary in the studio. I went through a period of doing some really long records; Duran Duran were great fun to work with—Nick thinks a lot like me, being very open-minded and conjuring up the same images in his head as I do from certain sounds—but everything was always drawn out. There are always lots of people around in their sessions with loads of different ideas, and they're all really intense. Another thing is that they have these incredible schedules for promotion, videos, and whatever, right from the start of a project, and so you can never predict what will happen from day to day. I'll be waiting around for five hours for them to turn up. Then, when they do come in straight from doing something else, their thoughts may be too distracted to really get down to the music. It's not really their fault; the next day their heads will be clear and they'll turn out the music.

"The Foreigner project a couple of years back, on the other hand, just seemed to go on and on. Everyone, including the band, got really pissed off with it. They're used to it, though, and I wasn't, so it just threw me. I couldn't believe what was going on! There was a problem with people not coming in; Mick, who is the leader, wouldn't show up for hours and hours, and so that obviously would really slow it down. Then the songs wouldn't be really ready—while the album was being mixed the lyrics were still being written! Things were being changed right up to the last minute, and that's what took a long time. That is why I don't want to go into the studio when somebody wants to write the stuff there. It just takes too long, and it isn't worth it; it doesn't come out right. You can't write properly in the studio because you're under pressure. How can you really be creative when you're watching the clock going 'round, burning up the money?

"Working with Robert Palmer on his album *Looking for Clues* was really great. It was done in just a few weeks, really spontaneous. Robert had everything prepared. He makes his demos at home, where he has lots of equipment, and so we just went in and did it. Talking Heads I also enjoyed. We did some of their *Speaking in Tongues* album at Compass Point Studios in Nassau in the Bahamas and some at Sigma Sound in New York, and we'd go in at seven in the evening and be out by around midnight or one in the morning. It was just quick and spontaneous, and David Byrne would just go in there and sing everything straight off. That was great!

"With some musicians the live vibe is really important. When I worked with Grace Jones on *Warm Leatherette, Night Clubbing,* and *Living My Life* at Compass Point, I made sure that those Jamaican guys, Sly and Robbie, were allowed to see each other and sit next to each other, which is how they are used to working. Most of Grace's material was done live with Sly and Robbie sitting right out in the room, while we also built a little booth for Sticky, the percussionist, who had all of his stuff hanging everywhere. He was really casual about recording—sometimes we'd start a take and he wouldn't even be there! He'd be outside having a smoke or drink or something, suddenly realize we were doing a take, come in, pick up a tambourine or shaker or piece of steel, and halfway through the tune the percussion would start! Some of the finished tunes are like that, and it always sounded right, like it was meant to start there.

"He was also the type of guy who would be playing one thing, and right in the middle of a verse he'd put that instrument down, pick up something else, and a whole new percussion instrument would come in. He would hear Grace sing a certain lyric that would remind him of a sound. There again, he might put an instrument down and not play anything for a while, and then towards the end of the tune he could think of something to do, pick something else up and start playing it and get real busy. Everyone else would get busy, and so the whole thing would speed up at the end. Now, that's what I mean by live!"

alanshacklock

WITH ROGER DALTREY

■

After Alan had produced Roger's 1985 solo album, *Under a Raging Moon,* the two men joined forces again the next year for the follow-up, *Can't Wait to See the Movie.* Released in 1987, this evidently suffered from the same lack of record company support that Roger complained about just beforehand during our interview. Meanwhile Alan, a musician and a major fan of both Roger and the Who, filled me in on the experience of working with one of rock's legendary voices.

RD: "One of the things that I always used to feel about the Who material was that it was totally undanceable for some reason. You could only ever sit and listen to a Who record. You couldn't Hoover to it or do the cleaning to it. It would grab you by the earholes and say, 'Look, fucking sit there and listen to this, c—t!' d'you know what I mean? So, with this album [*Can't Wait to See the Movie*] there's been a very conscious attempt on my part to be a bit more commercial while not compromising the musical integrity.

"In terms of the lyrics, I was looking for a bit more than just 'Ooh, I love you, baby.' As you get older the job of getting good lyrics becomes more and more difficult. I mean, when you're a teenager you'll sing about a problem and the answers to that problem are black or white, whereas when you hit forty there's this incredible big gray area that appears, and suddenly there's so much more. So, I wanted to put together an album that you could do the Hoovering to while still retaining that edge. I mean, in the end it comes down to economics, and I'm afraid it's a fact that unless you sell so many albums you do not make records. It's as simple as that, and I want to go on making records. It therefore is not a matter of compromising but of finding a niche for yourself in that market.

"What I find so strange now is that the Who had a set audience, and I'm a bit lost as to where my audience is at the moment. The market is so processed that it is very difficult to get help anywhere within the system. You're out there literally walking a tightrope and you're totally alone, and I've found that very frightening. Until the album was actually finished there was no help from the industry, and I found that very difficult. I felt that *Under a Raging Moon* was a good album for me, and it was successful, and I thought that would have given the record company the encouragement to come in with some positive energy, but there was nothing, absolutely nothing! 'Well, go and make another album.' 'All right,' and then absolutely nothing!"

AS: "What they said to me was, 'You've got to get into the Top 40 now with a hit song,' and so I then told Roger that we would have to find numbers that don't compromise him but are in that area. We subsequently went through the best part of six hundred songs, and it's very difficult to find ones for him, because he sang the best rock lyrics in the world and so, as he said, it's not going to be easy to persuade him to sing 'Ooh, I love you, baby.' We therefore have to find something that he feels he can get a hold on lyrically in terms of what he feels at this stage, and also something that crosses over, and that is not an easy task."

RD: "What I most dislike about a lot of the modern music is its lack of energy and its lack of any real passion. There's something about when you hit a note and you're feeling it, everyone knows it, and I just feel that's greatly lacking in a lot of the stuff that's on the charts at the moment. This new album, on the other hand, has got an incredible amount of energy coming out of it. It's a great record to drive to—the only thing is you'll get nicked for speeding!

"I always like drummers to be dangerous. I mean, obviously, after having worked for fifteen years with Keith Moon a drummer can never be too dangerous for me. I always say to them, 'Just go mad. I don't want to hear any pit-pat stuff. If you ever play that you're sacked!' Not really, but do you know what I mean? It actually gives them a gee up, because they feel that they can be as free as they like."

AS: "As a vocalist Roger has got to be in a room where he feels space. . . ."

RD: "If I get in a room that's too small the mikes just blow up."

AS: "We had to use a special preamp every time when he was recording, because the one on the console was distorting. I told the engineer, and he said, 'It can't be distorting! It can't be distorting!' I said, 'It is. You go and have a listen,' so he opened the control room door, Roger let out a note, and it literally blew him backwards! He said, 'Oh, yeah, it is loud, isn't it?' Roger's got a very powerful voice, and as he's said to me, singing with John Entwistle on bass for over twenty years has certainly helped develop it. That was the only way for him to get heard. However, on this album I also pushed him to sing in some pretty high keys—"

RD: "He does like to get me up there!"

AS: "He can sing high keys in full voice—"

RD: "Yeah, never mind that my throat and my stomach ache!"

AS: "All that it takes is a good bottle of painkillers!"

RD: "Actually, there weren't too many strains on this album. I like to do two hours onstage when I'm performing a live set, and these songs shouldn't be that hard for me to sing. On some of them we'll probably have to reinsert a few bars so that I can take a breath—they were edited down on the record in order to sound tighter—but the main problem for me was that, once we'd done all of the guide tracks in the way that I'm used to, Alan then went into the routine of how most people record these days, which I found to be an absolute nightmare. Jesus, it was like working at Ford's! I mean, that destroyed me."

AS: "Yeah, that's not the way he likes to work. He likes to be in and out quickly—he'll come in and go, 'Good, here we are, here's the vocal,' and then either say 'I'm feeling great today' or 'I'm not.' "

RD: "If I'm not I'll go away and think about it, and then come back and polish it up, but stripping things down and working with computers nearly gave me a nervous breakdown. I couldn't stand it. I've got no interest in that way of working."

AS: "He's never satisfied, though."

RD: "When I'm recording a vocal I don't know what I'm aiming for until I've done it. It's like planning something with lots of sketches. I do lots of sketches on tape and we'll eventually get what we call a 'finished vocal.' Then, after I've lived with it for three days and all of the little nuances have entered my subconscious, I'll go back and do a real vocal. It's a really weird process. We'll work for, like, a whole day on one song and think we've got a finished vocal, and then maybe the next day I'll go in and, just like that, be able to do one that's better. I've got a picture then of exactly what I'm aiming for. I've always worked that way."

AS: "With a singer like Roger there are several different ways you can go. I mean, he can actually take a song a whole different way from one day to the next. He's got a very versatile voice, and at times it has been difficult for me to know whether there are going to be three or four ways in which he is going to sing something. He reminds me of a guitarist during a solo; he's never satisfied with what he's done. I mean, he'll get a performance that's satisfactory and often more than that, and I'll think it's great, but he'll say, 'Oh, I can get it better than that!' I'll say, 'Well, you can get it *different* to that, but you won't get it better.' It's like a guitarist who will forever be doing that one solo again and again and again, and someone's got to go, 'Stop! You've done it,' because he can keep turning the song into something else. Well, if you listen to the composers' demos of some of the songs that we've done they're nothing like Roger's performances."

RD: "It's about finding a character. Rock 'n' roll, for me, is difficult, it's not easy. I mean, I've watched rock 'n' roll singers seemingly make no effort in coming up with the right sound, but that for Roger Daltrey is impossible. I have got a great opera voice. [He briefly demonstrates it.] It's inside me, not just in my throat, and so to get up there and sing with this sort of hoarse sound kills me. I have to be like an actor, and so that's why I have to do the vocal sketches and find my character."

AS: "He's never satisfied with his performance, and he always wants to do one more take. He'd be doing vocals in the cutting room if they had a mike in there! You know, 'Where do I plug in?' We got close to doing that!"

RD: "To me, my voice is awful. I hate it! The tracks sound wonderful until I sing on them . . . and probably a lot of people will agree with this now that I've said it! There's just something about it, and it never sounds the same to you as it does to other people. Like Alan said, you keep trying to do it better and better and better, and that's why you do it; you're really aiming for the impossible. I suppose you're really aiming to sound like someone else—'Please don't let it sound like me, 'cause I don't like that!' "

AS: "We do pick up the fifties and sixties performance element. That has got to be a part of him, because he's a performer, and that's why he hates the studio; he wants to get out there and sing live. The hardest thing is to shut him within four walls with a microphone in front of him. He does come up with the goods because he's able to do it technically, but his thing is to actually be there in front of an audience. In fact, some of the vocals that we recorded at his shows in the States, I wish we had for the record. It's not that what he did for the record wasn't good, but some of those live vocals had a magic to them and they were wonderful. I'd say, 'Why didn't you do that on the record?' and he'd say, 'Well, I did, but it was just in a different way.' "

RD: "I love performing live, and I especially love performing Who numbers. Because, you know, nobody ever covered Who songs, and I'm proud to do them, I'm proud of our career, and I'm proud to have been the singer of probably some of the best rock 'n' roll songs ever written. Music should live. It's not for hiding away on shelves, dusting off, and saying it's precious. If it's not played live it's as dead as a dodo, as far as I'm concerned, so I am proud to get out there and do it."

swainandjolley

■

During the first half of the eighties the team of Tony Swain and Steve Jolley enjoyed considerable success. A self-contained unit, these two Londoners not only produced and engineered a succession of hit singles and best-selling albums, but they also wrote the material. Soul band Imagination and powerful female singer Alison Moyet were among the beneficiaries in this regard, as was the girl trio Bananarama, which had a long line of chart smashes up to and including the *Pure Confessions* album that went gold in America. However, when I spoke with Tony and Steve at the end of 1987 they didn't feel that they were quite getting the credit that they deserved.

TS: *"Pure Confessions* was a very, very difficult album to make. Working with Bananarama isn't easy. You make a track and then they'll start saying, 'We don't like it,' and you're thinking, 'Oh, Jesus!' Like when we did 'Robert De Niro's Waiting,' they were convinced the bass track was wrong. I told them it wasn't, but I had to do six other basses to prove I was right. After a while this sort of thing just drains you! You see, they're not even united as a threesome, so you've got that problem as well.

"Selling singles is fine, but the key to the business is selling albums. The only way to do that was to make a serious effort on the songs and the production, which isn't easy when you're talking about three girls singing together. So we did this, and then to cap it all they came back to us and said they wanted to do 'Venus' and that the record company wanted them to do a cover. We got out of the situation. We were exhausted and fed up. We'd had four years of it, and enough was enough, so we just called it a day.

"They've now switched over to Stock, Aitken, and Waterman, and had a string of hits, but these guys have had the same problem that we had. Typically, the girls have said to them, 'We want to be like the Bangles.' So, they go away and write for three weeks, say 'Here are your Bangles songs, girls,' and they then turn around and say, 'We've changed our minds. We don't want to be like the Bangles!' This is what we went through for years: They wanted to be the Mamas and the Papas, they didn't want to be the Mamas and the Papas; they wanted to be sequenced, they didn't want to be sequenced. You're talking about a lot of time, money, and effort spent making tracks, and you have to make a full backing track over the course of two or three days for them to reject it! I've got eight backing tracks at home that were recorded and rejected for the last album!"

SJ: "Alison Moyet was another one who got a false sense of herself. At first she was really shy and nervous—she'd just branched out on her own after quitting as the singer in Yazoo—and when we started working together she was going on about how grateful she was for all the work that we were doing, how she was sorry that only her name would be appearing on the cover of her album, and so on. Well, that attitude soon changed after the first hit. As soon as she realized she could become successful as a solo artist, that was it. She had all the money and the power, and she became a bit manipulative. She was twenty years old and CBS gave her £2 million or something, so she employed who she wanted and suddenly she was making her own album! All of the expenses were up to her, and it was a real heavy responsibility for her on her first solo project. But, there again, that's the music business! The album [*Alf*] eventually went quadruple platinum, and all of the songs had been written in three weeks before we'd recorded the backing tracks. Still, I have to say that when we put her voice on top it belonged to the best vocalist we've ever worked with. There's a tone in her voice; it fills up so much of the track that you don't have to work so hard."

TS: "A new composition comes from one of three situations: either Steve sings it into his Walkman, says 'What do you think of it?' and 'Where can we go from here?' and we then work on it; he comes to my house—we both have home studios—and we blast something out; or I go to Steve's house and we do something there. A big problem that we previously had when we were making albums is that a lot of our equipment has been sitting in a commercial studio. Therefore, of course, any time we've had off—any weekends—we couldn't write songs. It's only since early this year that we've started to get our home studio situation together and really begun to properly write songs again. We weren't paying enough attention to our songwriting, and so it was like coming out of a room with no windows into the big wide world!"

stock,aitken,andwaterman

■

For a time in the 1980s Mike Stock, Matt Aitken, and Pete Waterman ran riot in the worldwide singles charts with their carefully crafted, highly processed, and overtly commercial dance music creations. Nearly everything that they touched turned to gold—and then platinum—as Pete kept abreast of the trends, signed artists to his PWL label, and acted as a sounding board to his two colleagues at the PWL Studios in South London: Mike, the keyboard player, chief musical arranger, and most talented composer of the three; and Matt, who composed, played keyboards and guitar, and helped out on the technical side. Bananarama, Dead or Alive, Samantha Fox, Divine, Rick Astley, Princess, Mel and Kim, Sonia, and Hazel Dean were among the stable of artists, and a team of strictly trained engineers completed the in-house picture. Nevertheless, Stock, Aitken, and Waterman's success was coupled with a fair amount of criticism from the music press, due to the clinical sound of their product and a formulaic, high-tech approach that was likened to an assembly line. When I spoke with them in 1987 they decided to hit back at their detractors while taking a few potshots of their own.

PW: "Most rock 'n' roll bands are not dance bands anymore. They are made for TV and nothing else. They are purely entertainment on a visual level, and they just happen to make records and record companies just happen to spend millions on them. We make records to entertain people for between three to seven minutes, and if they don't like them they don't buy them. If they do buy them they are doing so not because of art but because they like the records."

MS: "Every song that we produce is almost like a birth. There's a pain and a joy in doing it. I mean, everything that we release we're proud of, and it wouldn't leave the building unless we were.

Every record we do is different, and there's no formula, I promise you."

MA: "There's a difference between productivity and exploitation. Some people may want to perceive us in a certain way, but our only philosophy is to have a good song and a good beat, and everything else—apart from the artist's voice—is peripheral, really. We like listening to our own music. It's nice sometimes, having forgotten about an album track, to hear it on the radio in the car, think, 'Oh, this sounds good,' and turn up the volume only to realize it's one of your own records."

PW: "The thing is that for every track of ours you hear there are five you never hear. For instance, on the Bananarama album there are nine brand-new songs, and we wrote eighteen songs to get those. One ended up as a Sinitta single, one ended up as a Sam Fox single; Rick Astley's track came out of there. Everybody who has been successful as a composer or record producer has been prolific; that's the way it has to be. The public is insatiable. You can't make one record and say, 'That's it, I'm going to make another record in six months,' because six months later they might decide they don't want it.

"The way that we work is to constantly jot down interesting-sounding song titles on a notepad whenever one or more of us thinks of them, and to then choose from these when we write songs. Next, a guide drum pattern is laid down with a Linn 9000 [drum machine] and a guide keyboard part is recorded to set the harmonic structure. Lyrics are built around the song title as the song progresses; bass, percussion, and rhythm tracks are recorded, and then we bring in the vocalist. At least five minutes of material is recorded for a three-minute single, and so this leaves the engineer with extra music to play around with for the twelve-inch mix."

MS: "We don't know how a song is going to turn out when we start writing. The only theory we have is that if we keep on working very hard, writing and making records conscientiously five days a week, fifty weeks a year, we are going to have an output that people are going to look at as if it were on an assembly line. I'm never totally happy with anything we've done, thinking we could improve it. I also think that we're getting better, and I always have this aim in my mind that the record we're making is better in some area than the one we were working on before."

PW: "That's very true for me, too. It's like, how long is a piece of string—you know that if money was no object and time was no object you could always improve in some area. However, you can never perfect something, and so you have to let go at some point. I mean, Matt and Mike would sit for hours to perfect a little thing—you know, Mike is never happy with the vocals, Matt is never happy with his guitar solo. . . . In fact, Matt's the bloody worst! I have to tell him, 'It sounds bloody brilliant to me,' and come in and beat him up and take the guitar off him! He'd spend three days doing a guitar solo if no one stopped him, and we have constant battles about that.

"We record quickly, spending days on singles and a few weeks on albums. After all, when the pressure's on that's when you do your best work, and there's no better inspiration than somebody paying you to write a hit song."

MA: "There's nothing worse than spending eighteen months on an album with a band and rerecording every track three times. You lose all of your objectivity, and at the end of the day you might have ten tracks and just one single that you think is all right. That's okay for the band—they only come into the studio once a year; 'Let's go on holiday, let's go to the studio and have some fun'—but for us it would be deadly."

PW: "I never sit still, because I get so bored it's unbelievable. For instance, with Bananarama's 'Love in the First Degree,' Mike and Matt had written the song and I saw it in the morning as a pile of lyrics with a rhythm track that I really loved. I said, 'This is the one for me! Perfect!' The girls said, 'No, no, we don't want this!' but I said, 'Bollocks! That's the one. Come on, boys.' When I came back in the evening and heard the recording I got goose bumps. I said, 'Oh, that's brilliant! That's good enough for me!' It must have been good enough for the kids as well, because it sold really well. Still, Bananarama's the strongest band we work with. They know what they want—"

MA: "They know what they *don't* want."

MS: "They are tough women, in a sense, because they are three girls from more or less an ordinary background. That's the flag they run up the pole—'We're not going to be pushed around by the men. We're going to be tough women and businesswomen as well'—and I think they occasionally go a bit too far in that respect. I mean, they are harder on people who they're associated with than we would ever be—"

PW: "Absolutely."

MA: "They won't be bullied. You can't bully Bananarama."

PW: "We're paid by the artists to tell them what to do, but we listen to Bananarama, and it's taken a couple of years working with them to get to the point where they totally trust us now. To tell you the truth, if we say, 'We're going to do this,' they will never say anything until we've finished, and then they'll say, 'We don't like this and this.'"

MS: "There was a time when they argued before we put anything on tape."

PW: "They'd say, 'You've plugged the wrong color lead into your guitar!' "

MA: "When we did the first record with them, which was 'Venus,' they already knew the song, and it was actually recorded in about a day and a half. They wanted to do that number because they already had a history of recording cover songs."

PW: "I've always been a big Bananarama fan ever since my days as a disc jockey, because they're a great pop band, but, to be honest, we didn't want to do 'Venus.' We tried to talk them out of it, saying, 'Well, you can't beat the original,' and we came up with every excuse in the book. We attempted about five different versions of the song, slowing it down, speeding it up, using different rhythm tracks, and it just didn't work, but they were absolutely dogmatic. 'This is what we're going to do.' "

MS: "We knew we had to keep the bass line. The original was actually played by an organ and a guitar, and to us that was integral, but we couldn't see a way of turning it into the kind of high-energy dance record that they were after. In the end we managed to do so and the record was successful, but while we were still doing the mix Bananarama came in to hear it, and they said, 'It doesn't sound like Dead or Alive! It's not as exciting,' and we said, 'But you didn't ask us to make you sound like Dead or Alive!'"

MA: "So we sent them down the pub for half an hour—"

PW: "It's true. I went down the pub with them to keep them happy while Matt and Mike changed the track to how they wanted it!"

MS: "You see, they'd obviously approached us because they'd heard [Dead or Alive's hit single] 'You Spin Me Around'—"

MA: "But they never made that clear to us in the first place. . . ."

PW: "Whereas [Dead or Alive's lead singer] Pete Burns had actually said, 'Make me sound like Divine!' "

MS: "When someone says that, and you did the version they're talking about, then it's easy."

PW: "When Bananarama came and asked us to do an album with them I said, 'If we're going to do this album then there's one thing that I am going to stipulate right now; I actually control the album. I package for everybody the way that the album's going, because I believe that I, more than anybody—including the record company—love Bananarama. This is how I perceive you, these are your strengths, and I won't allow anybody to knock you because of who you are. So, if you will allow me to sit with the boys and tell them what you are, and if we all work together, then we'll have the best album that you've ever done and we'll have smash after smash after smash. On the other hand, if you're going to tell me, "We want to do this" and "We want to do that," we're not interested. It's hard enough with us three, so if we stick in three more opinions we're wasting our time. We all have to go for the same goal.' After a while that speech sunk in.

"The album took twenty-one days to make, and the record company had money left over from the budget. I said, 'Right, this is the way we're doing it: the boys are going to go away and they're going to record fifteen tracks. You're going to come in, and I want you to bring in as many sheets of lyrics as you can. You've got a task, and your task is very simple: every day you've got to write a song and record it. That's it. There's no pressure, that's the bottom line. We'll record up to fifteen songs, and anything that doesn't work we'll ditch. So, we're not going to sit around for three days on each song. You're coming in, you're going to write a song in the morning, record it in the afternoon, and if it doesn't work you'll dump it that evening. Then you'll start the next day on another track.' That's the way we did it in twenty-one days. There were only ten rhythm tracks that they really liked, so we went from top to bottom and every day there was a song written."

MA: "Pete had noticed that there had been a change in the type of beats that were coming out of Europe. The styles of rhythm tracks had changed quite a lot. He'd been doing a lot of traveling abroad, and he brought some records back for us to have a listen, and we noticed a slowing down of tempo and a difference in the implication on the bass."

MS: "It was still four-on-the-floor as far as the bass drum was concerned, but what used to be known as 'Euro-Beat' or 'high-energy'—which had an octave bass going 'boom-pah, boom-pah, boom-pah'—was now a rock bass doing eighths, like Status Quo. That really changed the whole implication, and on top of that there was also a swing element, and so when you program some of the instruments you put a little shuffle into it. There was quite a cool little rhythm going on there, and we took to it instantly. We got the direction we had been looking for, and the results were records like 'I Heard a Rumor' . . . it's not luck. We're looking out all the time for these sorts of things."

PW: "You see, it's great, because I have the roving brief in this team. My job is purely to keep us so far ahead of everybody else that they can't catch us. Now, to do that I have to do certain things; I have to be able to go to France, to Italy, to Germany, and so on, lock myself in a hotel room—"

MS: "And have a good time while we stay here and do all of the work—"

PW: "That's right! No, in all seriousness, I went to Paris, stayed in a hotel over a weekend, turned on the radio, and just listened to the top three stations for twenty-four hours each, because France was the last market that we had never sold records in. Then I came home with four records that were all Italian—they weren't French—and I said to the guys, 'Here is what it is: Italian melodies with the Euro beat and Motown lyrics.' You see, the foreign lyrics don't translate well into English. So, these were the elements for Bananarama, and it was up to the boys to make them work."

MS: "In a way this kind of hybrid approach has worked for us now on four or five occasions—it was also a hybrid with Mel and Kim, with Dead or Alive, and with Princess. I mean, we knew where we got all of our influences from, but whether the recipe would work and make a nice cake was another thing. Sometimes we put a series of different things together and it turns out disastrously!"

PW: "You see, the boys don't know. They sit and fart around for a few hours, and they fight with each other like crazy because they're trying to make a recipe without knowing precisely what ingredients to use. Then I'll walk in, and they might sing me a melody over what they've done, and I'll say, 'To me that sounds exactly like what I've been listening to on French radio!' Technically I won't know what these two guys have done or the agony that they've had to go through, because I'm like a kid; I'm not really interested. I'm only interested in whether or not the record is exciting to me.

"Nobody actually starts a trend. It's impossible. You follow one trend and that becomes a new trend, so you started it, but you can't actually say, 'I am going to start a trend.' That is presumptuous, and it wouldn't work. It's an evolution. I mean, if I was presumptuous enough to come in to the boys and say, 'I've got a great idea: we're now going to record everything at 235 bpm with Zulu drums, and that's where it's going to go from here,' it would be ridiculous of me, because people would hear it and think, 'What the bleedin' hell is he doing?' "

MS: "Things happen at street level, almost spontaneously. These 'new trends' that people always refer to have been hanging around in one way or another for years, and all of a sudden they rise to the surface. You can't control public taste."

PW: "In America they're not really concerned with making good records. They don't think of it that way at all. You know, a record is either going to be a hit or it isn't because they have decided to make it that way."

MA: "If you sell something hard enough, eventually it will get kudos in the charts and there will be a knock-on effect, with people buying the album."

PW: "American record companies treat the record industry a bit like a supermarket. They put a single in as a tester, promoting it like they do soap powder or Kellogg's Corn Flakes. You'll see it on your television every twenty minutes, and they hope that if they throw enough shit at the wall enough is going to stick. Then, if it does stick, they'll put out an album of it, so you're hooked, whereas here in Europe we don't work like that. People want exciting pop records, and they will only buy them if they like them. You cannot hear the same record on British radio every five minutes; you cannot hear the same record on British radio every hour. The most you're going to hear it in a day is perhaps five times. On American radio, however, you can hear a record twice an hour thanks to power rotation, or you can see it every half an hour on MTV."

MS: "How many independents get to number one in America? None."

MA: "American record companies are not interested in a single unless there's the album that they can capitalize on, because they don't actually make money from the single. I mean, we've seen the royalties from stuff that we've done which has been successful over there and it's pitiful."

MS: "You sell more records in the U.K.—"

PW: "You sell more records in Holland than you sell in America now!"

MS: "To get a number one in the States now is not really worth it, in terms of what you've got to spend to achieve it."

PW: "The Americans are full of their own self-importance, and they're twenty years behind the date! They're obviously not looking at their royalty statements, because we make more money in Holland than we do in America. Our worst-selling record last year was a number one American record, and that was 'Venus.' All of the British acts are now starting to say, 'What's so big about America?' You're selling 200,000 to get to number one!"

MS: "The potential there is obviously massive, but when record companies use so much power to control the market and force people to buy things that they don't really want, then the people who go out and buy it are only those who have been sold on it. In order to get a groundswell and get the kids to rush out in millions to buy something, you've got to give them something that they actually want. You can only force a few people to buy records."

PW: "The Americans are going through this whole thing about Hispanics now. They've pushed the marketplace for white teenagers down so far that they're now looking to the Hispanic population, and there are a lot of Hispanic kids, so the great white hope in America is that the Hispanic kids are going to start buying records, because the white kids have stopped. I mean, what they've done is they've forced women out of the marketplace. You know, America's a nation of wonderful clichés. They say they're a feminist nation, and they talk about fair play for all, but sorry, that is not true. They may have women A&R people, but women A&R people are not making records for women. They've forgotten that women buy records in America—they forgot about ten years ago—because the people running the record companies are students, ex-university graduates or lawyers or accountants. They ain't people who grew up buying pop records by the Beatles or Phil Spector! They're not even interested! I would say that 90 percent of American record executives don't even know what's on their own charts!

"We are realists. We come to work every day. We have a lovely job; it's called making music. It's a privilege and an honor to be able to come to work every morning and do something that we love. I worked in a factory for fifteen years, Mike struggled for fifteen years in a factory while playing with different bands, Matt's been around the world on tour ships and sat behind an office desk, so we've all actually done a nine-to-five job for a long, long time—and we know that this beats working for the electric company any day of the week!

"We don't have time to sit back. We've got to pay the rent, we've got to pay the staff, we've got to pay the overheads—we've got to pay everything back each week, and we therefore know that we've got to be here every day. We're not here for five minutes. We're not pop stars. You must remember one thing: we're on the bottom rung of the royalty scale. We're at the very bottom. We do not have the luxury that the artists have, and that's the biggest share of the royalties. What's more, if they're smart they could keep things that way, but the problem is they don't want to come to work every day at ten o'clock in the morning. They want to take their advances, buy their villas in Spain, and do an album once a year. We, on the other hand, don't take advances off of record companies. We work every time for our royalties and a small fee, and American record companies still find our deal to be weird. They're not used to that.

"We don't have the luxury of one hit bringing us in £100,000. We're at the bottom end of the scale, and we have to split our royalties three ways, so for us to earn a fabulous amount of money per year we've probably got to produce five times as many hits as any other record producer or band. We can't kid ourselves; none of us are millionaires, and that is why we have to keep doing what we're doing."

vangelis

■

Vangelis is not a man given to making light and generalized statements about the state of his art. Music has been his life and he a part of that music ever since he began composing at the age of four, and from the very start he strayed from the conventional and strived for the unimaginable. Through a list of numerous solo albums stretching back to 1972, as well as collaborations with Jon Anderson, ballets, television themes, and film sound tracks that include the Oscar-winning *Chariots of Fire*, Vangelis has continually explored the creation of musical forms, and in 1990 he took time out to talk about not only his own recording and production methods but, more specifically, his views on the technological scene.

"I am an instrument which I try to perfect more and more every day in order to interfere less and less with the flow of the moment. You see, I started at the age of four, and I don't remember ever being without music. My first memories are tied to playing the piano and any other object at home that could produce a sound. So, my contact with the outside world was always through sound, and I never felt that music was a job or had anything to do with being famous.

"When I started with music it was a kind of language, a necessity, a way to perceive and understand things, and today I have exactly the same approach. The only difference now is that because music somehow became a professional part of my life and I am involved with this 'music business,' it's a constant fight between my initial approach to music and something that is unfortunately much more calculated, with all of the wrong values. I don't want to go into details about the music business today, but most of the time it is a matter of survival. When you start out with music just being a part of you it's very difficult to find yourself in the middle of a very precisely calculated business.

"The only way in which I function is that I don't think. During the past thirty years the idea of an 'album' became something very specific; the album became a product. An album contains about forty-five to fifty minutes of music, and within this time you have to produce your new product. It's easier to sell that way; you know what you have to do and people know what they are going to buy. In other words, what I am trying to say is that music now has less and less to do with a spontaneous idea and much more to do with working within guidelines. So, I don't really have new projects. I work every day without saying 'This is going to be my new album.' Of course, every now and then I release a new album—and now, with the compact disc, you have the choice of releasing more than forty-five minutes—but I don't work with the idea of a project in mind. A very limited amount of my work is released, whereas the amount that is produced is enormous. The reason I am composing and producing music is not because of my contract with a record company but simply because this is what I do every day, and I will never stop doing this.

"A film score is different. That is something which is a collective work with a specific theme. But talking purely about music, my creating is totally free. I can never interfere, and I don't want to interfere. If you think, you interfere. The more you think, the more you are in the past. You are analyzing the fact before the fact happens. Do it first and then analyze it later. This is the way in which I function.

"There's not one instrument out today that really allows you to do anything fast enough. We are getting more and more away from nature. In the last few years sampling has become very fashionable, and it was a very nice opening for the world of keyboards and electronic music, but unfortunately the process of sampling has become very stiff. It has given us the opportunity to have 'real sounds,' but it is of no use to have the sound of a flute or a violin, or a guitar or a harp, when you can't play it properly. What makes a violin sound attractive is the player, not the violin itself, but with these new instruments the player is becoming less and less important. The sound is already there, with its own vibrato and its own expression, so when you want to play something you can't really do much. It just sounds wrong, because it's always the same. What makes my voice different is not what I am saying but *how* I am saying it.

"Let's say you play ten notes on the violin; on those ten notes you can apply ten different vibratos, instantly. Let's say you do that with a sophisticated keyboard; you can play maybe ten notes with ten different vibratos, but you have to program it, and that's ridiculous! You are interfering with the most sacred thing, the immediacy, as well as the expression. It took billions of years for the human computer to do that, and I find it so silly that we are impressed with a second-rate computer.

"Today music is more composing than creating. You see, the market is not really for music, it's for people who can't make music. There's nothing wrong with that, because everyone should be able to make music, but at the same time what I am criticizing is not what has happened with the technology but the fact that nothing has happened along with it. It's nice to give the opportunity to people to make music, but there's not a company out there that produces one instrument for pure music played by musicians. It's like they have designed a plane, but instead of using a test pilot as their adviser they have used an accountant.

"If you look at all of the instruments of the past, they have been around for centuries. Each of them—the piano, the violin, the flute, the French horn, and even the percussion instruments— has been developed very carefully over a period and perfected. Through the generations this has allowed people to become better and better at playing them, to express music better, and to develop better results. Now, opposite to this, there isn't one synthesizer that has been created and developed through the years in a better and better way. The only thing that has been created and developed is the computer, but I am talking about instruments.

"To me all of these new machines are not really instruments but just part of a library of sounds, so when I want a particular sound from the library I select the appropriate machine. We underestimate ourselves, and technology—which is a divine thing—we use the wrong way. I'm all for technology, I've never been against it, but I'm against the way it is being used. Mozart would have written a symphony in the time that it takes someone to program several racks of equipment!

"I have a complete result in one take. If you listen to my albums you'll hear that I hardly do any overdubs. Even at the start, without a MIDI system, I did very few. Sometimes, if there happens to be a mistake, I might do an edit, but [the recording of] *Symphony*

No. 3, for example, lasted about forty-five minutes and there was not necessarily the need for that. For me, that's nothing exceptional. Sometimes I may play for twenty minutes and make ten mistakes, but if the take is good why spoil it? If there is a bad note I can always cut it out, but I discover this once I've finished recording the piece, because whilst I'm playing I don't think about it.

"The piano part on *Chariots of Fire* was played straight through. For me, that is the only way. You see, I am better than a computer. I am not trying to sell myself through this interview, but a human being is able to do things that a bloody computer can't do. Anyone who says that a computer can do better than us is wrong. The only thing that can play constantly is the drum machine.

"I start playing with no specific preplanned ideas, and I do all of the parts together in one take. That way I end up with a piece of *music*. God knows what piece of music. . . . Some of my pieces have been released and people are familiar with them, and other pieces have never been released and never will be. When I'm finished playing a piece I sometimes listen to it back immediately, sometimes a month later. I don't have a specific pattern. Sometimes, with certain projects such as the Jon and Vangelis record, I will say, 'Okay, I'll put a little bit here and there,' but with all of the pure symphonic work that I've done I have never added anything. I'm not saying I shouldn't do it, but until now I have never wanted to. The musical moment, whether it was good or bad, was complete."

hugh**padgham**

■

Throughout his two decades in the business Hugh has consistently been at the cutting edge of the music scene, thanks to not only good ears, astuteness, and application to his work, but also his well-proven ability to match the sound to the talent and the direction to the material. When the talent and material belong to acts such as Sting, Phil Collins, Paul McCartney, Genesis, the Police, Melissa Etheridge, and David Bowie, that's no mean feat. The artists and the awards continue to line up for this Grammy-winning British producer-engineer, and courtesy of several interviews I have discovered why.

"Although I did learn to play musical instruments as a kid and can read scores I'm not really a trained musician. Therefore, my input with regard to making records is basically coming from the punter's point of view. Artists like McCartney and Sting don't necessarily need somebody who's a fully trained musician to come in and try to change their songs. I mean, one reason why I think Sting and I get on so well is that he presents the music and I then translate it into the sonic medium. That's where my main production values come from, being able to comprehend what the artists want to do with their songs.

"In Sting's case, the music that he writes is always quite different from one album to the next, and the minute I hear one of his songs I can 'see' the sound in my head. I can see what he's getting at, and that therefore becomes a new challenge in itself. With Phil Collins, on the other hand, while his albums don't progress musically in the same way that Sting's do, he writes these really good songs that only have about three chords in them. If you asked Sting to write a song with three chords I don't know if he'd be able to do it! So, that's where I think Phil's strength lies; a lot of it has to do with the simplicity of his approach, and that comes from many different facets, including the fact that he's self-taught.

"Whereas Phil always comes into the studio on the first day with a pile of demos, with Genesis albums we would start on day one with not one note of music! About two weeks would be spent jamming on drum machines, Phil singing 'la-dee-da-dee-da' as a vocal, and the others just messing around, sometimes without even bothering to find out what key they were in. Ideas were put onto cassettes and things then formulated from there. They had their own studio, so they weren't wasting money, and nearly everything was overdubbed, although we'd always retain some parts from a backing track that had been laid down. Say if Mike [Rutherford] played a guitar part he might keep some of it, because sometimes when you're playing without caring that's when the best stuff comes out!

"In a way I suppose I have more musical input on Phil's records, because when it comes to guitars and basses Phil hands the onus over to me. He admits he isn't expert in guitar parts and that sort of thing, and so we get good musicians in and I help direct them. For instance, Phil hasn't necessarily written a bass line to the tune, and so the bass player will come in and start playing along, and I'll tape him the parts I like and so on. Recording like that is great fun. Still, if I had to do a Sting record all the time or if I had to do a Phil Collins record all the time or if I had to do whoever's record all the time, that would be boring. It's because everybody's different in so many ways that my interest remains as high as it is really.

"The one basic thing that I still adhere to is simplicity, and that applies to my production values as well as my engineering. Using the simplest and cleanest signal path to tape is very important to me, while I also think that empty-sounding records are much harder to make than ones that include everything apart from the kitchen sink. I sometimes play a game with myself to see how little equipment I can use on a mix in order to achieve the sound that the artist and I want, and that's quite a lot of fun. I love it when a song has that minimal aspect to it, although that's not always possible.

"As songs and records go, I don't feel that they sound any better than they did in, say, the sixties. Technically maybe, nowadays, because all they had then was an echo plate, an echo chamber, and a tape machine for a repeat. That's all they had, and yet you tell me if they don't still sound good. Stick on an old Yardbirds hit or whatever and it still sounds great! I think that the producer is always at the mercy of the artist's songs. I haven't written the songs. All I'm doing is trying to present the songs that the artist has written in the way that both he and I hopefully think is the best way to do so.

"With Melissa Etheridge, I've done her albums on analog. We've gone into rehearsal and totally worked out the album before going into the studio, so then there's no screwing around in that respect. We can record it onto analog and virtually never have to edit anything, whereas with Sting that's not the way it works. With him things change during the course of recording the album. Melissa's setup is much more of a rock band kind of thing, so we work it all out, we go in the studio, everybody plays live and we record it. Obviously, it's easy to do that on digital as well, but it's very easy to do it on analog, and I think most rock 'n' roll music sounds better and warmer and thicker and gutsier that way, at least to my ears.

"I'm really not interested in working with somebody who can't sing or play. This may sound very elitist for me to say, but luckily I have always been able to choose what I've wanted to do, and so I've never got myself into a situation where I've had to do a total repair job. Now, some producers and engineers would absolutely love the idea of being able to sit in front of their Macintosh and go crazy and change it all. For them that sort of electronic manipulation would be very satisfying to do. It's like when you first get onto the Internet after weeks of messing around with applications on your [Apple] Mac—'Yes! I've done it!' I, however, can't tolerate that kind of thing. I'm not interested, and I haven't got the time for it. Occasionally, if an artist has an aberration, then okay, we can stick it through the computer and mend it, but I would never work with an artist who I initially considered to be incapable even on a good day.

"It's fantastic when you're sitting there in the producer's chair, watching and hearing someone perform and they're really into it, and you go, 'My god, that's fantastic!' It's like when Melissa Etheridge sings; there'll be 99.9 percent of it there in one take, and that's because we've got her at the right time, the sound is right, and it's a brilliant feeling. That's not to say that other people don't also have a brilliant feeling after they've spent two days or ten days using a Mac to manipulate the voice of somebody who can't sing. It's just that personally I prefer to do it in three or four minutes.

"I'm not a man who particularly likes working on vocals, because you can get bogged down in which take is the right one and whether or not it is good enough. It's magic, therefore, working with people such as Melissa, Paul McCartney, Sting, and Phil Collins, because they are so professional. Bowie is another one—he'll sing through a song once in order to remind himself of the lyrics and give a chance to get the sound, and then I swear to God you'll have your vocal take on the tape in two passes. He'll do it just like that!

"I can remember making a cardboard cutout of a guitar at the age of seven or eight, and standing in front of the mirror pretending to be Paul McCartney. So, to end up twenty years later in a studio with this guy, telling him what to do, was quite weird. Obviously, he'd need direction sometimes, like everybody does, and I've worked with enough people not to let someone's fame and reputation worry me. On the other hand, there would also be times when Paul would say something and I'd be thinking the opposite, and then I'd think, 'Hang on, this guy's got a lot more experience than I have,' but I'd just have to have a lot of confidence in myself. I'm not the sort of person who ends up having standing rows with anybody, but if there's a difference of opinion I'll sit down and talk about it.

"For [McCartney's album] *Press to Play* I was aiming for a slightly harder sound. I'd listened to some of his records and thought, 'That's a little bit wimpish. I wish he could be a bit harder and rougher in a way.' So if, for instance, someone said, 'Oh, Paul uses that mike for his vocals,' my first reaction would be, 'Okay, well, let's try another one!' Not because I didn't like his previous records, but simply because one wants to try something different. There again, when, at the start of the project, he asked me, 'Who should we get to play bass on the album?' I said, 'You've got to be joking! You're the best bloody bass player there's ever been!' He genuinely thought that there might be someone better than him, so in that case I had to provide confidence, for want of a better word.

"I don't think music breathes in the way that it used to. It was fun when it sped up a bit in the chorus or at the end, and, although

I know you can program that into drum machines now, how do you know when and where to do so? You're thinking about it, as opposed to recording five musicians who sound great just sitting on the floor in the studio and bashing away. I'd rather have a bad-sounding record that's got a good vibe and is a good song than a bad song that sounds fantastic.

"Sometimes you get demos that sound fantastic, and when you go into the studio and try to re-create them everything's clean and nice, and it doesn't sound as good. There are times when dodgy equipment can be nice, and I use quite a lot of cheap equipment—even some semipro stuff—and people come in and say, 'Wow, do you use *that*? I've got one of those in my home studio!' "

naradamichaelwalden

Since 1986 Narada's skills as a composer and producer have been responsible for a long line of number one singles, Top 10 hits, and best-selling albums, and the stars who have benefited include Whitney Houston, Aretha Franklin, Mariah Carey, Steve Winwood, the Pointer Sisters, Lionel Ritchie, George Benson, Kenny G, Natalie Cole, Gladys Knight, Barbra Streisand, Diana Ross, Elton John, Sister Sledge, Mica Paris, and Al Jarreau. Yet it was alongside guitar aces Jeff Beck and John McLaughlin that he originally established his credentials as a drummer, and it is as a solo artist that he still has a major ambition to fulfill. I spoke with Narada in 1997 at his Tarpan Studios facility, located in San Rafael, California.

"I think it's very natural for a drummer to become a producer because he's the heartbeat of the music. The rhythm comes through in the records, and if they're ballads—no matter what tempo—they're definitely spirit–oriented, which is in the beat and in the performances. I come from a background of playing with the Mahavishnu Orchestra, where all of the songs were dedicated to playing to the high spirit of life, and so if it's a pop song or whatever I still want to capture that spirit.

"When the artists are vulnerable enough to let down their defenses and let what is beyond them come out, that's when you capture magic on tape. It's a case of making the artists feel comfortable, relaxed, and trusting, just like lying on the couch in a psychiatrist's office, so that their most intimate feelings come out. I mean, if you spend a little time with a person before you start recording, you may light candles, burn incense, give them a stuffed teddy bear, massage their neck, or crack jokes. Obviously, each person is different, but what it comes down to is intimacy. Then, once the person starts singing, the endorphins start kicking in, the spirit gets really, really warm, and it wants to come right out. At that point you have to get as many takes as fast as you can, because you can't maintain it that long. You know, the voice tires, the spirit tires, so when you get that thing going you really have to capitalize on it. Even if a person sounds a little hoarse, he or she can sing through the hoarseness.

"I'm always amazed. If I push hard the first day and try to get everything, more often than not 90 percent of it is there. If you put things off until the second day, by then the artist's tired emotionally. However, if I can get 90 percent of it sounding good, then the next day the artist comes in and hears it and goes, 'Damn! That sounds great!' Now the person's encouraged and uplifted and doesn't mind punching in a few lines here and there. So, that's the trick; I try to get as much as I can on the first day, I have the artist go home, and then we compile every bit of what he or she sang. It may take me four or five or six hours to go over every bit of what they sang. Then I leave and my engineer, David Frasier, will stay even later and put it all together, so that when the artists come in the next day they're hearing a fresh-sounding recording even though they thought they were tired. That's uplifting to carry on.

"Like with Aretha, she's rehearsed the song and knows it so well that, many times, when she's ready to sing the song I'll start working with her on the vamp first, because her spirit's so strong. Then we can go back and get particular verses, bridges, first chorus, second chorus, but you'll never get anything like that if you don't get in right away when she's hot and the spirit's strong, and I find that works with quite a few singers.

"Whitney Houston is a fantastic, natural artist. To me she's still one of the greatest singers, but like all singers she needs to be pushed. That's what happens when we get together—she will let me push her. Other artists are different. Aretha, for example, is the Queen of Soul. She's taught everyone, and she'll let me get away with things a little bit, but then if I get too carried away she'll also stop me. She'll just say, 'Do you know what beautiful is? What I just sang, now that was beautiful!' And I'll say, 'Yes, yes it was.' That's when I know not to say anything more.

"The thing I've noticed about the great singers is that they love their voice. They even love the mistakes! Aretha will come back in the booth and smoke a cigarette and listen to the playback, and even if I say it's a little flat—which nobody but she and I can notice because it's so minuscule—she'll say, 'Narada, that's just the way I felt that.'

"I've worked with singers who don't like the sound of their own voice, and no matter how much perfection you go for and how much attention you give to intonation, they're still not satisfied. Well, I relish the singers who like their own voice because that makes things so much easier for me. When I come across singers who don't like their own voice, I sit them down immediately and I say, 'Listen. We're here to make some great recordings together and I believe we can do that, but you're going to hurt the process if you hate everything that you sing before I even get the chance to evaluate it. I can't work that way. So, even if you hate it, let's make a pact that, for now, you're going to try not to hate it, and, if you do, then you won't tell me. Because I may love it and be able to convince you that it is good.'

"In the first two or three hours I want to hear their interpretations and what they're going for, and then take it from there. I don't want to interfere unless they need help. I mean, even with the great ad-libbing singers like Whitney—these songs are put together like puzzles, so there are times when even I have to give them an idea as to how to make the puzzle work in terms of their phrasing and so on. Otherwise, I'm only looking to capture them, make sure it's in tune and felt deeply.

"When I compose I sit at my Roland D50 keyboard in the studio, my Korg M1 at home, or at either one of my two acoustic pianos, and, with no particular tune in my head, I touch the keys and allow the chords to inspire me. I'm very blessed that way. If I touch any kind of keyboard something will come to me. It may not be that great, but something will come, and usually, once the spirit gets warm after playing for about half an hour, I'll try to formulate that first idea and then move onto another. I'll formulate several ideas and force myself to sing a chorus. If I can sing a chorus then I can sketch or hum a verse and bridge, which lyricists can later put some words to. But if I can get a hook then at least I've got a direction. All I care about in the writing is whether the hook is strong or not. I can always change a verse, but if the hook isn't good it's like a joke with a poor punch line.

"When it comes to having my fingers on the faders and punching in individual syllables I have the fastest hands in the West. What really sells a record is the perfection with the spirit. That means the song's in tune, that it's not being rushed, that it's not being dragged, and as a result you can hear it over and over and over again and not get tired of it. If there's too much hollering and screaming going on it gets boring after a while. There needs to be a delicate balance between an energy that people really believe in and a perfection that, when a song's soft and intimate, is convincing as well.

"I don't really know what audio perfection is. I'm just concerned that a recording has enough bottom to make my heart pump, and enough top so that I can hear the crystal clarity of what's being said. You know, the hi-hats, the natural cymbals, the natural tambourines—I kind of like bright records. Plus, I've got into this whole thing of wanting to compete with what's on the radio, and that when my records come on they have a zing, a splash, an extra sizzle because that top end is cooking. On radio they compress things anyway, so by putting extra top on, say, Whitney's vocal, it'll jump that much harder and just catch your ear. Now, there are a lot of records that are dull and sound fine that way, but that's never been my thing. I've always wanted to have the cutting edge.

"In terms of the beat, I tend to mix drum machines with my own live percussion or I might drum along to the percussion track. Every song is different. It has always been the case that I listen to something and think, 'How am I going to cut this?' I almost feel like I'm cutting every song as if I've never cut a song before. At the same time I'm very inspired by the radio and I try to figure out what's hot. I mean, I may hear a good song, but then I know that the success of the song is based upon the arrangement and how it fits in with the times, because it's down to the producer—not the artist—to decide on how to best arrange the song. I mean, a number of artists can do the same song, but, based upon the arrangement, it can sound almost completely different. So, that's why I spend some time trying to think about how we can best realize what we're working on with regard to what the people are listening to.

"I have a deep desire for the recordings that I work on to enjoy longevity, to be appreciated far into the future for their inherent quality, and the only way you achieve that is by trying many different avenues and by really harnessing the singer. Like when you ride a horse, there are times when you've got to be strict and strong. They think, 'Oh, I can't go that high,' and I'll be there going, 'Yes, you can go that high! Do it again!' That's why Elton John calls me 'Sergeant Walden', Steve Winwood calls me 'Coach' and the boys in the studio call me 'Chief'!

"There is no such thing as perfection. You just do the best that you can do at the time, and that's why I do so many takes when we're recording, and that's why I go through the pain of making things more in tune with the pitching, and that's why I listen to something over and over and over again to get it as good as possible. Once it's done, it's done, and from that point on, if I hear it on the radio, all I try to do is enjoy it.

"I'm pretty tough with vocalists and with musicians. They need a certain kind of mentality to deal with me. . . . It's probably down to how I was raised. My family was real strict. I was raised a Catholic, I went to a Catholic school, and everything was discipline-oriented. Then there's also the fear of failure. Like Mike Tyson, when he walks into the ring he doesn't want to get knocked out, so because he fears getting knocked out he knocks out the opponent first. That's a big thing for me, and I therefore go into the studio feeling charged, determined to make a smash record so that I'm not defeated. Chart success is important to me because I want to keep my house. It's also down to passion, but, if I said that's all it is, I'd be lying through my teeth. I have to get myself inspired, and in that respect I find singles work the most satisfying because I want to be on the *Billboard* chart, I want to have the hits. I love that, and I also like the kind of songs that can carry an album. In fact, I'm not going to be happy until I get my own hit as a solo artist. You see, when it comes to compromising my art in the pursuit of success I will tell you what Quincy Jones told me: 'I can be bought!' "

russtitelman

■

Question Russ about his musical tastes and one quickly finds that these range from Presley to Puccini, Ry Cooder to Ravi Shankar. Dig into his past and it becomes evident that he learned a thing or two via his introduction to the music industry, working in his native New York with a certain Phil Spector. That was during the very early sixties, and since then Russ has established himself as a producer of modern music who is instilled with aesthetic values. Not averse to involving himself in the technical side of his craft, he nevertheless always gives precedence to material over machinery, as attested to by his collaborations with Little Feat, Steve Winwood, Paul Simon, George Harrison, Brian Wilson, Randy Newman, James Taylor, George Benson, Miriam Makeba, Chaka Khan, and Christine McVie. In 1991 I spoke with Russ about his concert and studio projects with Eric Clapton, as well as his earliest musical experiences.

"Eric Clapton is getting better all the time, and he's also a highly underrated singer in my opinion. When I first got involved with him I went to see him perform at the Ritz in New York with just a four-piece band, and I thought, 'What's this?' He was singing so beautifully, and he was playing at the top of his form. When we did the *Journeyman* album, however, he was uncomfortable with his singing. He doesn't consider himself a great vocalist, and I think he is a great vocalist and a lot of people do, but I remember when we got down to the mix of a track called 'Hard Times' and he heard his vocals, he said, 'I'm not used to hearing myself stick out that far.' On the other hand, when it comes to his guitar playing he doesn't comment about it, he just does it.

"I wanted to get as much of his personality on that record as possible. For instance, on a couple of cuts I'd suggest that maybe there should be more of a guitar arrangement for him rather than going for a second guitarist, and he'd then come in with all of these ideas for different parts. So, you'd get his musical brain producing, arranging, directing. It was really thrilling, and he was very definite about a lot of things. On a couple of the numbers he composed the solos—'Anything for Your Love' was a written solo—and on certain solos he'd want to have a specific kind of sound. For 'Hard Times' we were in this large room in the Power Station [New York], and we wanted to get a big room sound on the solo, so we close-miked the guitar amp and then stuck a far mike at the other end of the room, and we ended up with something that reminded me of the sort of old Bobby 'Blue' Bland sound. It was raw, but elegant at the same time.

"I think there's something that happens when you're in New York. There's an energy that happens. You have to go from your apartment or hotel or wherever you are, and you have to get to the studio, and in order to do that you go through all of this stuff, y'know? It's life in front of you all the time, and I think it affects things. There's also a certain vibe that New York musicians have and a different approach to things, and I think that's reflected in the music . . . and I like it! Collaborating with a new bunch of musicians there really worked on the *Journeyman* record, and it also worked with Steve Winwood on *Back in the High Life*.

"Eric likes live recording, so even when we'd use machines we'd have to run the machine and have the band play along to it. He doesn't like overdubbing—it just isn't natural to him—and that was the story when we did the two-CD live album, which drew on parts of his record-breaking twenty-four nights at the Royal Albert Hall [in London] in March of this year [1991]. On different evenings he played with different setups—a four-piece band, initially with Phil Collins on drums; a nine-piece; a nine-piece with orchestra; and a lineup for the special 'Blues Nights' that included Robert Cray, Albert Collins, Jimmy Vaughan, and Buddy Guy—and there wasn't any overdubbing on the record. No fixes, apart from a bit of tampering with the audience.

"I mean, on some nights they were great and on others they were like furniture; you know, 'Where did they get them?' Then again, there were three really amazing nights featuring the nine-piece band, and those audiences were all very enthusiastic. So, there was a fair mixture, and for the sake of consistency we had to do some adding in on parts where the performance was great but the audience response was not. That was the only trickery we employed, but no overdubs. I was there [at the Albert Hall] every night, grading the performances, discarding ones where there was a major mistake and noting those that really went well, Afterwards I'd sit down with Eric and go over it, discussing all of the strong and weak points, and so he was kept fully in the picture.

"Eric's performances vary a lot. It's interesting to hear. He won't stick to one way of singing things, and the guitar solos are always completely different. You never know what's going to happen. That can make things a little difficult when it comes to compiling a live album, and so at that point it means you have to go for the whole performance rather than edit different ones together. I'm always looking for the best solo, so if the rest of the performance around it is good enough I'd prefer to have that. Now, there were three nights when he was really on fire, so all that meant was that we had to choose one of three great ones—we heard all of them and everyone else heard that one great one.

"Eric knew when it was a good night, but I don't think the fact that he knew it was going down on tape affected his performance in any way, and we, for our part, tried to remain completely invisible. He and the band were there to entertain the people who had come to see them, and we didn't want anything to get in the way of the performance. We did everything we could to not interfere in any way, and so if we had little sound problems we'd correct them in the daytime. In the beginning there was some synthesizer stuff that we had to amend; some stuff was a little too brittle and so on, so we just worked on it for a couple of days and got it right. Then there was a night—the one when the BBC was filming for worldwide broadcast—where there were some tuning problems, but these things happen, y'know, and they straightened out as the night went along. That's what live performance is all about!

"A large part of the way something sounds is in the arrangement, and it doesn't really matter much if it's recorded on an analog machine or on a digital machine or whatever. Listen to some of those old records, like the original 'Hound Dog' by Willie Mae Thornton, or the early Presley records, and the sound is so amazing. They have a tremendous quality of sound. I really think that most of it depends on what the music is.

"I learned a lot from Phil Spector. I was around him in the very early days when he was doing the Paris Sisters—I played guitar and sang on their records—and before that his group the Teddy Bears used to rehearse in my living room. I was then actually in another group that he put together, called the Spector's Three, and we made a couple of records, so I got to see firsthand how Phil did it on a small scale before the big stuff happened. When the big time came around I went to some of those sessions and I played guitar on the Righteous Brothers' 'Hung on You.' I was also there when he was putting the choir on 'Just Once in My Life,' and he said, 'Go out and conduct the choir,' so I did—I didn't really know what I was doing but I waved my arms around!

"Phil is utterly peculiar—he always was—but as a producer he was inspired. In the room at Gold Star Studios he'd have, like, four rhythm guitars, two basses, a drummer, two percussionists, a horn section, and two pianos, so the place was full of musicians just slamming away, and that sound of his was there in the room. It was incredible. And then he'd lay the strings on, the voices and all that stuff, but the basic thing was all of these guys in a room that wasn't so big, together with his use of echo. Being there I got to see his style and how he related to musicians. I'd see him work parts out, and so I became very aware of how each musician, each component, fits together. At the time I was just a teenager, but I was a witness to how some great records were made. . . . It certainly was an interesting way to start a career, hanging around with a guy like that!"

keith carroll

■

The life of a concert engineer is never easy. Tetchy artists, temperamental equipment, and rowdy audiences can all combine
to make things more than a little tricky, but during three decades behind the mixing console Keith has invariably managed
to keep his cool. As a monitor engineer he has taken care of the
onstage sound for artists such as Elton John, Bruce Springsteen,
Madonna, U2, Kenny Rogers, and Julio Iglesias, as well as at
all-star charity gigs such as Live Aid in 1985 and the Freddie
Mercury Concert for AIDS Awareness in 1992. I interviewed
Keith while he was on the staff of major American pro audio
company Clair Brothers, since when he has branched out on his
own and been inundated with TV work as well as numerous
live projects.

"I'm a monitor engineer and I have a target on my forehead. In
fact, the monitor area in general is a big fluorescent target for any
artists who aren't pleased with the sound! Still, while the sound
levels for electronic keyboards mostly remain constant throughout
a tour, the vocal levels can really vary, and that's often down to
the state of health of the artist concerned on any given day. You
know, sometimes the effect that a major drinking session and an
hour of sleep have on the vocal chords is pretty obvious.

"Since Elton has stopped drinking it has made an incredible
difference to his ears. He has always had good ears for sound, and
I've never been able to fool him. He knows what he wants to hear
and he knows in what context he wants to hear it—in other words,
he knows how he wants his mix layered. Now, however, while
the monitor situation is still very loud, Elton's patience in terms of
trying new things has really got much better. In the past he was
not always that keen about rehearsals—he would basically let the
band members rehearse on their own for two to three weeks, and
then come in and run through the set in a day or two. After all,
he obviously knows the songs, he's been playing them forever. But
on the '92-'93 tour he was really concerned about wanting to

sound good, wanting to take the time to try different things—different effects, different reverb sounds, different harmonizer sounds—and so it was actually a lot easier for me to then go out on the road. We worked a lot closer together than we had in the past, and so the responsibility wasn't all on me.

"At the same time, Elton's patience has also increased in a number of other respects, including equipment failure. During his performance of the Queen song, 'The Show Must Go On,' he'd come down off his riser and move around the stage, and so for this he was using a wireless mike. Early on in the tour I had some trouble with this, because we were using a VHF radio system and between Europe and America the frequencies are not the same. Some of the frequencies in the United States translate to cellular telephone frequencies in Europe, so every now and again during a show I'd pick up a cellular phone conversation; a taxicab, or, on occasion, an oil company dispatcher! We ended up buying a UHF system in Holland and that really worked well everywhere for me, yet some things could still get to Elton. When he got fed up with the sound of an Electrovoice 757 microphone which he'd been using for about three months he took it with him after a show and threw it out of the car window as it was going along. That mike cost about $1,000, but he felt much better afterwards.

"Elton is the most important person onstage, and I really can't take my attention away from him. If he wants changes I get a very quick cue from him, and so I have to be able to interpret this immediately. We don't have any hand signals, but he'll just turn around and mouth 'More voice!' 'Less voice!' 'More drums!' 'Can't hear myself!' or whatever. The fact that we've worked together for several years now means that, as long as he does not mouth something too fast during a given song, I can understand him, and, if I don't, that's where his keyboard tech really comes in handy, because he is my extra set of eyes. In fact, we kind of rely on each other to translate things that one of us didn't pick up, and I sometimes therefore have to ask Elton to enunciate things a little slower.

"The communication between the two of us works fine, but sometimes there can be a breakdown. He is not really always able to tell me exactly what he wants to hear in terms of sounds, and it's therefore kind of up to me to try things out for him. I will take the time to work on my own with a microphone and run through different effects, and experiment with different settings, different length reverbs, different room sounds, and different EQs in the individual units themselves. You see, he is the kind of person who hears what he likes and sticks with it, and if I have three or four different things to offer he's not confused by that. He can hear the differences and he is able to pick out what he wants.

"He's basically got a big set of headphones out there, and I'm pushing between 118 and 125 dB where he's sitting at his mike position. After an hour of the show his ears have deteriorated, so he turns 'round and asks for more highs, more top, more treble—more of the problem ranges in monitoring. He's looking for S sounds and T's. I can get it very loud, but the louder you get it the more EQ you have to pull out of it, and the sound deteriorates. So, I ride the edge with him. Sometimes, with the response of the microphone we're using, if he turns his face in front of it the mike acts like a reflector and feeds back.

"On the *Reg Strikes Back* tour in '88 and '89, Elton wore hats, sometimes with a brim and sometimes brimless, and he wore glasses, so when I EQ-d I had a plastic top hat of his that just fitted me, and I used its brim as a gauge. At one stage he started wearing the top hat at the end of the show, which had a bigger brim than the hat which he wore the rest of the time, so, depending again upon where he chose to talk into the mike or how close he decided to get next to it, the pattern of feedback would change. It was like trying to defy the laws of physics.

"A standard joke in the industry is the artist saying, 'This sounds like shit!' and the engineer replying, 'I don't have a shit knob.' I was working with Bruce Springsteen, and he had three big monitors hung underneath the stage. Well, two speakers had gone out of one monitor, and you just can't foresee equipment failures like that. Sometimes things happen due to fatigue, at other times because of a mistake that either he or I have made. A loud blast or a wrong voltage and the speakers will go. Things are going to happen. Bruce kept looking at me but he couldn't stop in the middle of a performance, and so he finally came over between songs and said, 'Something's really wrong up here and I don't know what it is!' So I had to leave the console and go look. We were close to the end of the show and there was nothing I could do. I didn't have another monitor, and all of the crew members were involved in doing their own jobs at that point, so it was pretty much a 'live with it' situation. After the show was over I spoke to Bruce in the dressing room and I apologized for what had happened, but I also told him there was nothing I could do. He said, 'Oh, okay. Did I blow it up or did you blow it up?' I said, 'You did,' and he went, 'Oh, good! I like to blow things up!' And that was it, he was fine! Some people take enjoyment out of it.

"When I was doing a concert in Rome with Elton someone in the audience threw a full cup of orange drink into the air and it landed on the corner of the front-of-house console. The entire board as well as the effects and graphics rack were totally drenched, but I didn't know anything about it. We were four songs from the end, before he does encores, and there was a heavy oscillation out of the PA. Elton turned to me and mouthed, 'Something's feeding back,' but I didn't know where it was coming from, so my first reaction was to solo up all my mixes. I did this, one at a time, trying to find something that might have been hot or something that might have been out of place, and I couldn't find anything. I still didn't know about the drink, and meanwhile the house engineer was frantically trying to mop up the whole mess with towels; he'd even ripped his T-shirt off in order to soak dry the console.

"Three minutes later there was total oscillation, and so not knowing where or what it was I decided to shut down the monitors. Only then did I realize it was the PA. Elton just stopped playing in the middle of a song, and I got a call on the intercom from my house engineer saying, 'I've been hit by a drink and the console's going down!' We don't use all thirty-two channels on the second console; I think we probably only use about nine. It's basically there for the opening act, and so we shut the system down, swapped over, and the engineer had to redo his entire mix because the console wasn't labeled for the channels that he was putting on. So it took us a couple of minutes to get it together, and when Elton came off the stage somebody told him what had happened with the drink. His reaction was, 'Some stupid bastard, right? Well, can we go on?' and when we told him we could he said, 'Okay, fine.'

"Overall I have to say that right from the start, when I did a one-off benefit show for him in San Francisco in 1989, Elton and I have got on really well. Our working relationship has been pretty straightforward and very honest. He's easy to approach and easy to talk to, and he prefers that rather than having someone who he doesn't discuss anything with at all. That's my approach with anybody I work with—if there are certain acoustics, delay times, or equipment problems which need to be discussed, then I prefer to go in and tell them that right up front. It prevents a lot of finger-pointing if an artist is unhappy with what's going on but at least understands about it. Of course, that can bring about a catch-22 situation, because sometimes no news is good news, but I personally prefer to let the artists know what is happening, because they are the ones who are out onstage dealing with the public."

chris**kimsey**

■

More than thirty years in the business and still in great demand as a producer and engineer, Chris has seen things change quite a bit from the days when the producer simply arranged and the engineer took care of all aspects pertaining to the sound. Having started out at the age of sixteen, he was on hand to assist producer Glyn Johns on projects with Led Zeppelin, Delaney and Bonnie, the Eagles, and Leon Russell, before taking over behind the console for assignments with Ten Years After, Bad Company, and Peter Frampton. However, it was through his work with the Rolling Stones that Chris really made a name for himself, and in recent years he has managed to remain contemporary by working with new record company signings in addition to well-established acts.

"I engineered the Stones' *Some Girls* and *Emotional Rescue* albums and then coproduced *Tattoo You* and *Undercover* with them, and I have to say that they really did take a long time to make a record back then. Those four albums each took a year or longer to do, so all in all I was working with them for about five years. You see, they didn't get together like a normal group, writing and rehearsing all the time. They actually got together in the studio when they were paying for studio time, and that's a very costly way to do things.

"Working in Paris was a little bit of a problem because of the social scene there. None of the guys would turn up until they'd had a really good dinner, and so that meant we often didn't get started until around one or two o'clock in the morning. In the beginning I used to turn up all eager at about nine in the evening, and then I'd be sitting and waiting for four or five hours. Eventually, however, I learned my lesson; I'd wait until someone phoned me and said, 'One of them's here,' before I'd go down to the studio.

"At the end of *Undercover* I said that I would never work with the band again. There were a lot of things going on, Mick and

Keith both wanted to do their own albums, and I was very much the middle man when trying to work with the Stones. I was being pulled into this corner and that corner a little bit too much, and at that stage I said, 'That's it, I can't go on.' Also, I didn't want to spend a year making a record. It's just far too long, but then just before Christmas of 1988, while I was working in Australia and Mick was doing a solo tour there, his manager, Tony King, asked me if I would be interested in doing the next Stones album. I thought about it and concluded that I would if we could do an album in three months instead of a year, and if Mick and Keith would write together before we went into the studio, so that we'd have a really good idea as to what was going to happen and basically do a bit of preproduction, which had never happened with them for a long time. As things turned out, with a tour lined up following the release of the album, the album had to be completed in three months.

"I was working in Montserrat with Anderson, Bruford, Wakeman, and Howe while Keith and Mick went to Barbados to do the writing. I then went to Barbados after three weeks and they already had about twenty-five songs. After a total of six or seven weeks they had close to fifty ideas—not all complete songs—and I went through those, picked out the ones that I thought were the strongest, we all agreed on the selection, and eventually everybody got together and started routining the material. After having been apart for so long I was really glad to be working with the band again. We had all gone through a lot of changes, and it was great to see Mick and Keith actually go into a room and write together. I'd never seen them do that before, and it was also nice that when we got to the recording there wasn't as much jamming taking place. On previous albums they'd do a take of a track, jam for half an hour, and then do another take, but on *Steel Wheels* there was none of that. They'd do one take after the other, and then towards the end of the project one of the most exciting things was having four days to do five mixes, whereas on the other records a mix could take all week . . . and then it would be remixed.

"There are definite benefits to growing up and knowing each other so well. For my part, by the time of *Steel Wheels* I'd come into my own a bit more and I'd gotten over the whole thing of working with Mick Jagger and Keith Richards and the Rolling

Stones. Now they were just guys who had to get a job done and get it done quick, and so instead of thinking, 'Oh, I can't say that to Keith, I can't say that to Mick,' I'd just do it; I'd say, 'That's a piece of shit,' or whatever was on my mind.

"It doesn't matter how the Stones approach things, when the recording sessions actually get under way it's tremendous fun. Mick, Keith, and the rest of the guys always give 100 percent, and they basically have a good time. I've learned a great deal working with them; about feel for the music, about knowing when and when not to play, and about performing. When Mick does a vocal he gives everything. Even when he's in the studio he's dancing all over the place, just like when he's onstage. It's an amazing experience.

"Meanwhile, given Charlie's interest in jazz, his style of drumming is quite different to that of other drummers I've worked with. He hits the drums relatively lightly and prefers to play the bass drum with the front skin on because of its touch. As a result it isn't always easy to obtain a big sound from his kit in the studio, and so what I learned to do was put the bass and snare drums through a PA and pick that sound up in the room. That way the other guys, who often don't like wearing headphones, could still hear Charlie over the guitars.

"When the band was rehearsing in Barbados I called up to see how things were going, and Charlie said, 'Oh, you've been working with Bill Bruford. What's he like? What's he got?' I said, 'He's got this Simmons drum kit, a programmed computer and everything,' and Charlie said, 'Well, I've also bought some new equipment.' I said, 'Oh, really? What have you bought?' and he said, 'I've bought a new pair of sticks and a new snare head.' That was his new equipment! He was dead serious and it was wonderful, because I couldn't remember the last time he had changed his snare head, and he never changes his skins. I remember when we were working on *Emotional Rescue* in 1980, I sat down at his drum kit and I was looking at the skin, and there was all of this confetti that had trapped itself in the rim. I said, 'What's all this confetti, Charlie?' and he replied, 'Oh, yeah, that's from the Hyde Park gig.' That was the concert that the band had performed just after Brian Jones died, meaning that the drum had never been cleaned since 1969!

"When we did the *Some Girls* album I was really upset when Rolling Stones Records asked Bob Clearmountain to remix 'Miss You' for its release as a single. Back then that wasn't the norm, but as as it happens it was possibly the best thing that could have happened to me. A few months after the song had been released I was working in L.A. I was driving down the Pacific Coast Highway in a hire car which had a great stereo system and 'Miss You' came on the radio. Well, the difference between my mix and Bob's mix was that he had edited out the saxophone solo, making the track considerably shorter. So, I'm going down PCH, the song's pumping away, and I'm thinking, 'My god, this sounds amazing! This is so good. Bob really is a genius!' And then all of a sudden the saxophone solo came on—I nearly spun off the road! I thought, 'Oh, my god, I can't even recognize my own mix!' That taught me two things: One is to not get so precious about it all, and the second one is that if it's on the tape and it's in the groove then it will always be there.

"Nevertheless, the industry's becoming very rude and very short-lived in terms of its approach now. It's almost like *Vogue* fashion. The record companies aren't thinking about music, they're thinking about look, next year's sales, and how much they can pour in the pot. On the one hand they want to do an album for nothing—their dream is to pick up a production, press it up, release it, and it sells a million copies—and on the other they go nuts and lose the plot completely, inviting some top producer to work on an album when really the band should still be with the people who helped them make the first album. That's the secret of the whole thing. They hire the best accountants and the best lawyers to do the deals, and they hire the quick-and-easy, cheapest A&R scouts to find the bands. There aren't many people left who can understand and nurture raw talent anymore. Bands are signed to a label, given one shot, and if they don't have a hit they're dropped.

"I recently worked with the Gypsy Kings, who are quite unique and reminded me a bit of the Stones. It was all about performance. Seven or eight of them would sit down and perform a song, and in my best pidgin French I would say, 'That's really good, that's really fantastic. Let's take a break and we'll do it one

more time.' And when we did it one more time it was a completely
different song with completely different players! They'd all swap
around. All of the other brothers would arrive and they'd have
some other song on the boil. So, it was like a Boy Scout thing—
you'd grab whatever you could—and the result was a very ethnic,
earthy album. It was being released on Nonsuch Records in
America and Sony in the U.K. and Europe, but beforehand I heard
a test CD that had been pressed at quadruple speed and it sounded
awful. I said, 'You can't release that! The pressings have to be made
at normal speed.' Well, the same marketing team was being used
for Oasis, and basically the whole thing got stiffed. This was because
(a) I'd insisted that it be pressed technically correct, and (b) they
plugged all of their time and money into Oasis. So it just got
screwed, and it was like five months of my life—a wonderful
time—thrown out of the window.

"I can't afford to keep making albums which are dropped, left
unreleased, or not even sold properly. All of this really, really annoys
me—you know, you go into a project wholeheartedly, and first of
all they knock you down budget-wise; they want you to use the
cheapest studio, the cheapest format, whatever. Well, on some
grounds you agree to that and you sort of cheap out in some places,
but then, when it's all done, they start to come out with lines like,
'Oh, we'll have Bob Clearmountain mix it.' Wait a minute, that's
going to cost you another $50,000, and all of a sudden you're
asking, 'Why didn't you take the time and thought before you
started the project?' That's becoming more and more prevalent with
everything that I do.

"Still, so far I've basically taken an attitude of telling the
record companies, 'Okay, well, if you think that's the right thing
then you go for it.' Of course, that's not helping me, because
in terms of money I don't get paid until the record's recouped
my cost of production. However, I'm not thinking of that. I just
want to make the best record and hope that it sells, but then the
record company people make such terrible errors of judgment.
The reasons for that are either political—who they're friendly
with at the moment in terms of producers, engineers, and managers—or due to the fact that they've got absolutely no real thought
or consideration at all for the music or the artist. Well, I've now
got to the point where I just can't stand it anymore, because

deep down I know that I could run away and mix an album or do anything with an album, and if I came back and called myself Bob Clearmountain or whoever they wouldn't know the difference. It's so frustrating."

quincy**jones**

■

Artist, composer, arranger, conductor, record producer, film producer, TV producer, music publisher, magazine publisher, record company executive, and multimedia entrepreneur—in an era when many of his contemporaries are inaccurately described as such, Quincy is the real thing, a living legend. In 1998 he looked back on a career that had already spanned more than fifty years and earned him twenty-six Grammy Awards, the Grammy Living Legend Award, the Academy of Motion Picture Arts and Sciences' Jean Hersholt Humanitarian Award, an Emmy, and France's Legion d'Honneur, not to mention honorary doctorates from no less than nine universities and colleges across America.

"As a kid I used to hang around the theater a lot, and when I was about fourteen years old I gave Lionel Hampton an arrangement that I'd written for 'The Four Winds.' There was a girl singer in his band named Janet Thurlow and she kept reminding Hamp about me, and so when I was fifteen he wanted me to join the band. I went to get on the bus because I didn't want to take any chances that he'd change his mind, but his wife came along and said, 'Get that child off this bus! Send him back to school!' I was really bummed, you know. Then, two years later, while I was at school in Boston on a scholarship, they called me from New York, and I joined the band and stayed with them for three years.

"I've been arranging all my life. In the beginning I used to do all of the bebop arrangements, and we didn't have any reference. There was only one radio show out of San Francisco and *Downbeat* magazine, and the rest we had to get through word of mouth in New York, through traveling musicians. Blues bands from California would come up and Dizzy Gillespie, Clark Terry, Count Basie, and those guys would pass through, and we would be right on their butt, listening to everything that came out of there. There was no other way to communicate; there was no television.

"Eventually, I was arranging and recording artists such as Sarah

Vaughan, Ray Charles, Count Basie, Duke Ellington, Big Maybelle, Dinah Washington, Cannonball Adderly, and LaVern Baker. I used to teach Ray Charles the arrangements in Braille. These days there aren't many arrangers left in the business, but it was as an arranger that I got into producing records. You know, back in the early fifties I would tell someone like Bobby Shad that I'd just met the best alto player I'd ever heard, and say, 'You've got to sign him. He sounds like Charlie Parker. You should hear him.' And he'd say, 'No, I don't want to hear him. You write six or eight tunes for him, call up some horns, get a studio, get an engineer, and I'll see you Tuesday!' That's how I started: writing the stuff, conducting it, getting the band going, and hooking it up with the soloist.

"At that time the A&R man would come in and say, 'Take one,' and after a while you'd realize that you were doing everything that a producer does. I didn't know what that word was when I started—to me he was the A&R man, and we worked for A&R men all the time. So eventually, after conducting for all of these singers across the country and recording them in the studio, I was prepared to become a producer.

"When I collaborated with someone like Count Basie I was dealing with a legendary style, in terms of Freddie Green playing 4/4 on acoustic guitar and just what Count Basie's rhythm sound was about. He was the King of Swing, you know, no matter what they say! These people have their own style and everybody knows what the ground rules are, but the arranger has to interpret that, be it Thad Jones or Ernie Wilkins or Johnny Mandel or Neil Hefti. You have to interpret what Basie's sound is and distill it through your own personality. That's what the collaboration is about: understanding what Basie is traditionally, all the way back to Lester Young and Walter Page.

"In my case I just concentrated on the kind of music I liked to hear Basie play. I base everything on that; what will turn me on. I know it will turn Basie on. Part of a producer and arranger's role is to love the essence of a human being, which is what their music is about. The same goes for Sinatra. I knew every note he could make and could hit, and every now and then I would try to push him past what I knew his limit to be. At first he'd feel like he was jumping without a net, but the love between us was so strong that there would be this total trust in each other. He'd know that I'd never embarrass him, and that if it worked it would only be better.

"The same thing happened with Michael [Jackson]. We added a lot of things to Michael, including an extra fourth on each end of his range, because when he was with the Jackson Five he was singing high bubblegum stuff all of the time, and so I had to bring him down. For instance, when we first did 'Don't Stop Until You Get Enough' I said, 'Now, Michael, I would like to do the melody down in this register,' and he didn't understand this until he actually heard it. Everything was in octaves, and I needed him to do solo ad-libs down there to show the difference in the range. So, at first there was a little resistance, because he was nineteen, he'd been recording since he was eight years old, and he'd got into certain habits. Everyone does, especially if they're successful, not thinking that there's even more room to grow. Eventually, they get it.

"I met Michael when he was twelve, Little Stevie Wonder when he was twelve, Tevin Campbell when he was twelve, Dinah Washington told me about Aretha when she was twelve, they told me about Whitney when she was sixteen, and I first saw Patti Austin when she was four years old! She was awesome, and she still is. When they've got it that early, boy, you know that they're not playing around! There again, some still have it real late in the day.

"During the sixties I spent three years conducting and arranging for Frank Sinatra, and he was the man back then. One night when we were on the plane on our way to Vegas, he decided to put 'The Shadow of Your Smile' in his show. There and then I said I would write the arrangement, and I asked, 'Do we have the lyrics?' He said, 'By the time you have the music I'll have the lyrics,' and he took out a legal pad and wrote the lyrics down eighteen times to plant them in his subconscious. I'd never seen anybody do that before. Frank was something else.

"Then, in 1984, I produced and conducted the album *L.A. Is My Lady,* and you know, even though his voice was no longer in quite the same shape, his instincts as an artist were as sharp as ever. He'd know when something was right. Inside he'd know. He'd look at me and say, 'I guess you want to do another take,' and I'd say, 'No, not necessarily, but I think *you* do.' You see, a guy like Sinatra you can't coach like an ordinary person, because he's such a legendary stylist. Your suggestions are minimal in that respect, just peripheral to the area in which he is working, and so at each stage you feel him out. You feel out what he's open to hearing feedback on—you have to be sensitive to that, and if he's not open to feedback then don't volunteer it.

"After all, when there was something that he was off on he was still hardly off, and he didn't go off too often. His instincts were awesome. He overdubbed bits of *L.A. Is My Lady* and he didn't like to do that, so he came back to L.A. and he wanted to take another shot at it, otherwise he wouldn't be happy. I'll never forget, as he finished the last take he knew he had it nailed, and he winked at me and he just said, 'Well, I guess I'll unpack my bags and stick around here a little while longer!' It was so cute. That just fell out of his mouth.

"As a producer I like to leave in rough edges and search for the truth all of the time. I remember I had the song 'She's Out of My Life' for about three or four years after it had been written. A lot of people thought it was for Sinatra, but I held on to it and then when Michael [Jackson] came along I thought it would be perfect for him, because he'd never sung that kind of mature song before. Well, we recorded about ten or eleven takes and he'd cry every time we'd end it, so I thought, 'The hell with it! Leave it in, let him cry.' That's what he felt, you know, and I couldn't even appreciate how he was identifying with a mature relationship like that, because he was nineteen or twenty years old. So I just left the tears and everything in there. I mean, if it's the truth, man, the truth is gospel and you let the truth come on out.

"In the studio the trick is to know when a session is working and when it's not working. If it's not working then why isn't it working? I mean, if I don't know what's wrong but I just don't like it I can't tell the musicians that. A major thing that is necessary for a good session is chemistry. People who enjoy working with each other have a sense of the sum being bigger than the parts, so it's a case of knowing how to play that kind of team game. Then there's the right material; it all starts with the right material. It's all about the song. You know, without a song there's nothing to talk about, and I think that half of a producer's job is to find the right songs from the beginning.

"At the same time, when it comes to film scores every film

tells each different personality exactly what it wants to be. Thirty different composers will score it thirty different ways. Of course, you look at it and you deal with the technical restraints in terms of synchronization, click tracks, and so forth, and then, once you decide on what the technical peripheral boundaries are, you go on to the emotional side and go with the images, and every time it's different. Musically it puts you in a zone that you'd never go to with records. If you heard the score to *In Cold Blood* [1967] on a record you'd probably run out of the room! I had a housekeeper quit me when I was writing that. She said, 'No more!' She was fed up with murder.

"I've seen everything that's been going on in the last fifty years, you know, and we started with 78s. I used the very first synthesizer on the *Ironside* theme and the very first Fender bass with [William 'Monk'] Montgomery in Lionel Hampton's band, and without the Fender bass there would be no rock 'n' roll. The electric guitar and bass are what made rock 'n' roll. Experimentation is so important to me, not just with instruments and recording equipment, but also with combining different musical styles.

"Man, you know, it's just like eating a meal. I like to mix up apple sauce with sliced bananas and peanuts and cookies and sliced peaches and roasted pecans to see how many tastes can be different yet compatible in one batch. I love that; the compatible richness. What I enjoy most is changing and doing different things, because a change is like a rest to me. I always try to transcend past standards and that's the hard part; I did this before, so how can I do it different and better? That quest is really what it's all about, as well as breaking down musical categories. I don't like categories at all.

"Every day I learn something new, and the older you get the more you realize you don't know. If you put a lot of energy into the beginning of your life and career, really grabbing onto the one thing that you love, then that's everything. I did that since I was twelve. You know, I love writing music, orchestrating, and arranging, and I've put a long time and all my energy into trying to be the best at that. I've worked with almost every pop singer and instrumentalist in American music, and what I've learned has provided me with the basis and discipline to approach anything else, be it film, television, magazines, whatever. After all, the principle's the same: trying to find excellence and having a real careful eye for detail. . . . There may just be 12 notes, but a lot of great people have done a lot of great things with those same twelve notes!

"It's wonderful and it's been an amazing life. I mean, you only live one time. You have 29,000 days if you live to eighty, and you've got to do it now, man! You can't say, 'I think I'll wait till later and come back.' I don't know what I'd do just lying around fishing for eight months a year. That's too simple for me. I had two brain operations, I almost died twice, so I don't look at life like that. I want to know I came through here and really be sure!"

bruceswedien

■

Not quite as easy to pigeonhole as many of his music industry peers, Bruce has made his name as an engineer while also producing, arranging, and composing for artists as diverse as Muddy Waters and Michael Jackson. Fast approaching his sixth decade in the business, and with the credits still rolling in, he spoke to me about a body of work comprising pop, classical, jazz, blues, movie scores and almost everything else in between.

"There's a tendency in music to think that we're educating people or coming up with a cure for cancer, but we're not. The only thing you can do to music is listen to it, and I have always felt that the real value of what I do as an engineer or as a producer lies not in the technical or acoustic sense but in what the music signifies to the people who listen.

"As a kid in Minneapolis I would sneak into a black church with a friend just to listen to the singing, and when I was ten my father gave me a disc-recording machine and ten minutes later I decided on music recording as a career. I worked evenings, weekends and holidays in a small basement studio when I was fourteen, and later on, after graduating from high school, I bought a Magnacord PT-6 pro tape recorder and recorded local jazz groups, choirs, polka bands, and radio commercials. I also studied electrical engineering with a minor in music at the University of Minnesota. So, I knew all along what I wanted to do and I pursued that goal.

"In 1957 I moved to Chicago and worked at RCA Victor for just under a year. While I was there I recorded the Chicago Symphony and then I got a job at Bill Putnam's new Universal facility. It was there that I got to work with a lot of my jazz idols, people like Lionel Hampton, Count Basie, Stan Kenton, Duke Ellington, Woody Herman, Oscar Peterson, and Sarah Vaughan. Bill could be called the 'Father of Recording.' Many of the techniques that we use today originated in his mind. He believed in me as a kid, and for the first few weeks at Universal I would follow him around, bring him his coffee, set up mikes, and generally try to learn how things were done. I would sit down and get the song started and Bill would finish things up. We were doing a Stan Kenton session for Capitol, and he must have arranged something with Kenton, because at one point Bill said, 'Bruce, come on, you sit down and do this song. I've gotta go take a leak.' I didn't see him again for five years! So that was my baptism of fire. Evidently, he thought I was ready, and so did Stan, because I did the rest of the record.

"The first time I really got excited about pop music was when I discovered that it was possible to use my imagination. That had come with a record which I myself didn't work on; Les Paul and Mary Ford's 'How High the Moon' in 1951. Up to that point the goal of music recording had been to capture an unaltered acoustic event, reproducing the music of big bands as if you were in the best seat in the house. It left no room for imagination, but when I heard 'How High the Moon,' which did not have one natural sound in it, I thought, 'Damn, there's hope!' You see, being a Scandinavian from Minnesota, it was okay to like your life's work but not to get too excited about it. Well, I was absolutely in love with music and with what I was doing, and when I got to Universal in Chicago and did the first couple of albums with Duke, and I had the chance to talk to him and to spend a little time with him, all of a sudden he made me realize that it's perfectly all right to love what you do.

"So, things evolved from there and I did some experimenting with Basie's band, Ellington, Woody Herman, and Quincy Jones, and they were all very supportive of what I was trying to do, which was to include a bit of myself in the recordings. That evolution took a long time, and, as a matter of fact, it was when I started working with Quincy again in the late seventies that I began to realize reality was not an important part of music recording and probably wasn't even desirable. I kind of see my mixes as sonic sculptures—I would like them to be in this world, but not of this world, and in that sense I think Quincy's *Back on the Block* album was my most satisfying project, especially the title track. To me, music mixing is an extension of arranging, and I actually once got an arranging credit on a Sergio Mendez album.

"The late fifties and early sixties were a great time to be working. We were learning so rapidly and things were moving so quickly. I remember the moguls of the big record companies saying that there was no future in stereo, and they took it to the point where they'd refuse to pay for the tape to record some of these incredible bands in stereo. So, a bunch of us guys—myself, Phil Ramone, Al Schmitt, and so on—paid for the tape ourselves. In fact, I have a lot of stereo recordings of Oscar Peterson, Duke Ellington, and all of those major artists that I worked with in Chicago, and now the record companies come to me, of course, to see if I have a certain recording, and I'm always happy to sell it to them!

"I basically see my role in the studio as that of the fortunate student. Quincy told me early on when we began working together that every element about the music and the sound is important. Every little detail. Anything you can do to enhance the image is important, and I admired that approach so much early on that it's kind of become a part of my everyday life, and it drives people crazy! Something else that Quincy brought home to me is to learn to listen to my instincts and believe in them, while from Duke Ellington I learned a lot about listening for the primitive elements in music and being sure that none of them are overlooked. Primitive is important, and I would hate to be the first person in the world to make a perfect record. I don't think that would be very interesting.

"It's all about feeling responsibility to the music that we're working on, because anything that we do in a studio is, for all practical puposes, carved in stone. I mean, it will be there forever if it's important enough for people to examine, and like a good photographer I always like people to look at my best pictures. Music has only two categories: good and bad. Working with a great artist and great material brings more responsibility to a project, and I think the single most important thing that I've learned from Quincy is to never take that lightly. We've worked together for over forty years, and I promise you there is no one like Quincy in terms of the quality and the musicality and the good taste that he brings to every project. In the beginning I was twenty-one and he was twenty-three, and one of the first recordings that we did was Dinah Washington's 'What a Difference a Day Makes,' which was not a bad start.

"Both Quincy and I bring all of our experience to every session, and so another thing I've picked up from him is that the kaleidoscopic approach is really where it's at. When you play one of my mixes, for instance, you can hear it in a certain way, but then you can play it again and listen for something else. I mean, they're still trying to figure out some of the techniques that I used on *Thriller,* and I've got stuff buried in there that people will be studying for years!

"There again, I don't believe in secrets, so when I give lectures I talk about the techniques that I use and I'm criticized by both Quincy and Michael [Jackson] for that. Michael especially. He'll say, 'Bruce, you can't go telling people all this stuff!' But I don't believe in that, the reason being that I have yet to find anybody who really understands what I'm talking about! As a result, I am more concerned about finding people who will understand my approach to what I do than I am about anyone stealing ideas. That's never been an issue. So, microphone technique, multitrack recording technique, I go through all of them.

"There's the song 'Thriller' itself, for instance. On the intro there's a little rhythm track that commences the music, and I purposely limited the bandwidth on it so that as you listen to it your ear adjusts to that spectral response. Then, all of a sudden, the real bass and kick drum come in and the effect is really startling. So far I've told people about this but nobody has verbalized to me how it actually happens. Still, I do love to hear the imitations! Then there's 'Billy Jean.' Before we rolled tape Quincy told me, 'Okay, this piece of music has to have the most unique sonic personality of anything that we have ever recorded.' Now, that's a hell of a way to go into a recording! So I thought and thought and thought about it, and when it came time to do the rhythm track—consisting of drums, bass, and so on—I did everything I could imagine to really make it sound unique.

"This included borrowing a superhigh-quality recording console, using a specially built drum platform, and having a special bass drum cover made. I took the front head off the drum kit, put cinder blocks in there to hold it still, put the cover on, and slipped the microphone through. Then I made a special little isolation flap that went between the snare mike and the hi-hat mike in order to give much better imaging. Consequently, I think that track really is unique, because see if you can think of any other piece of music where you can hear the first three drumbeats and know what the song is. That's what I call sonic personality.

"Michael is a doll in the studio. You could not possibly ask for anyone better to work with. At the same time, I'm an only child, and I would love to have Quincy for a brother. The same goes for Burt Bacharach. Oh, man, the list just goes on and on. . . . Sometimes I kind of think that I would have loved to work with Sinatra, but Quincy worked with him and so did my pal Phil Ramone, and as a result I think that it's better if I just remember his music! I recall a time when Quincy and Phil were working with him while I was in L.A. producing a band named Missing Persons, and they called me and said, 'Bruce, just be glad you're not here!'

"I can't be in the control room when Michael listens to a mix. He plays it so loud. We'll be in the middle of one of our huge mixes and he'll turn to me and say, 'Bruce, hurt me!' So I'll turn up the speakers and leave the room. He'll then leave me a little laundry list, signed 'Love, Michael' at the bottom. . . . You see, I have been very, very careful to preserve my hearing, and I have very critical monitoring parameters that are set up in the studio before I start. There are certain volume levels that I won't go beyond, and I've worked that way for twenty-five years. Of course, when we're doing an R&B track or a big kick-ass thing I like to play it loud once in a while, but if that's the case then I'm very careful not to listen to it for more than five minutes out of the hour. . . . It's like an old joke that I share with Phil Ramone: every Christmas we used to call each other and say, 'Up is louder!' and hang up.

"As the saying goes, 'The first million hours in the studio are the hardest, and after that it gets easier.' I love this business just as much today as I did the first day I walked into Studio A at Universal when I was twenty years old, so what else would I do? I guess I could drive a tugboat, but I'm such a junkie."

trevor**horn**

■

Things sounded different before Trevor began producing. A multi-award-winning innovator, his eclectic catalog of high-tech work has taken in projects by Seal, Simple Minds, Frankie Goes to Hollywood, the Art of Noise, the Pet Shop Boys, Malcom McLaren, the Buggles, Band Aid, Barry Manilow, ABC, Yes, Grace Jones, Godley and Creme, Paul McCartney, Rod Stewart, Marc Almond, and Mike Oldfield. Managed by his wife, Jill Sinclair, Trevor spoke to me at one of their London studios when their ZTT Records label was celebrating its tenth anniversary in 1994.

"In this business it's very difficult to disentangle the technology from the music, whether you like it or not. You know, Elvis wouldn't have sounded like Elvis without the tape slap, and religious music only used to sound the way it did because a choir of eunuchs was singing in a huge church where there was this fantastic reverb. That's using technology in music, and so have I, although I think I'm a bit less interested in it now than I was back in, say, '78 or '79. Then I was obsessed by it and I had all kinds of visions about it and I was even writing songs about it! There were much fewer ways to make records, whereas now there are so many. If you listen to some of the records that I was making with the Buggles or with Dollar, I was trying to make records sound like records sound now, before all of the technology existed. I'd be editing multitracks to wipe reverbs in a way that made everything cut off dead and doing all sorts of strange things, whereas nowadays I'm more interested in working with better musicians for a start.

"As I get older I don't want to spend days on end waiting for somebody who can't play very well trying to get it right. I haven't got the patience anymore, and when you've worked with people like Wendy and Lisa—who are just such natural musicians—it's difficult to revert to the other way. Also, when you're working with people who are limited as players, that can make you do quite a lot of gimmicky things to get around the problems. So, I don't have the same angle on the technology as I used to.

"You have to realize that this whole business has moved so quickly. I can remember [engineer] Steve Lipson and I doing a track with Propaganda called 'Dr. Mabuse,' for which I had this idea that we wouldn't use any tape. Back in 1983 this was a pretty radical idea. We got a Linn 2 drum machine and various different samplers, hooked them all together, and programmed the song into each of them. At that time there was a very specific device called a conductor, which enabled you to synchronize a Linn drum machine with a Fairlight sampler, and to us it was the most incredible thing ever. So we programmed this song into all of the machines with the idea of the girls singing live, us pressing the button, and the whole thing being performed without going onto tape. Of course, it was a complete catastrophe, because it kept breaking down and losing sync with itself. In the end, we had to put it all on tape.

"Steve was a great guy to work with, because he'd be constantly coming up with ideas. He turned me on to digital, and I'll never forget the day when I came into the studio and he said, 'Watch this. I want to show you something.' He'd copied a multitrack and offset it eight bars, and it was like 'Wow! Let's use this on "Welcome to the Pleasure Dome!" So he and I were basically upstairs for three months doing that track, which had started out as three minutes long, and we just kept overlapping it on itself and lengthening it and doing all sorts of stuff. We had a lot of fun together and our partnership lasted five years, which is a long time.

"I've been doing this for nearly twenty years now, and in that time I've had some pretty hot tracks up and going, and I knew they were kinda hot. It's therefore difficult to kid yourself when the track isn't hot. So, if the song isn't working, and if the recording isn't working, sometimes it's best to just dump it, wipe the multitrack, and start again. Occasionally this may happen three or four times before you find just the right way to cut a song.

"With the Frankies we cut 'Relax' four times. Back then that seemed extraordinary, and I think everyone was completely worn out with it, but now it's a lot more common and a lot easier to do. Seal, for instance, has got a great voice, and, if you get the right bunch of people behind him, on a good day he'll get the vocal in the first couple of takes. It will be your master vocal, you won't have to sweat over it, but at other times it can be difficult. From the current album [*Seal*] sessions I've got alternative versions of some of the songs that are really cool, but they didn't quite make it and so we dumped them and started again. I do therefore have a tendency to do that sometimes if I think a better version's possible. In the end, however, you can be as clever as you like, but the thing that determines a record's success is how much people like it.

"The only reason [Frankie Goes to Hollywood] didn't play on 'Relax' was because the guys weren't there. They'd gone back to Liverpool. If you want to hear what the Frankies actually sounded like, two tracks to listen to are 'Born to Run' and 'Krisco Kisses.' That's absolutely them, playing live in the studio, and they were good! You know, 'Born to Run' is not bad if you listen to it. They worked it all out, and it's got some great bass playing. On something like 'Two Tribes' that was Mark's bass part, but we put it through a sequencer, and it was the same on 'Welcome to the Pleasure Dome.' They were better than people gave them credit for being.

"With 'Relax' we did a complete swerve. It was around lunchtime on a Wednesday, and we had worked for two weeks on a version on which the band had played, but it wasn't really happening for me. It was neither the band playing live nor a good sequenced version. It was somewhere in between, and because we'd messed with the way the band played it, it wasn't comfortable. One lunchtime I suddenly threw a bit of a wobbler and said, 'This isn't working. We've got to start again.'

"It was just one of those things; the guys weren't there. Then by the end of that Wednesday we had completely rerecorded the track. It all happened in the space of fourteen hours. We scrapped this version that we'd worked on for two weeks and the main record of 'Relax' was done incredibly quickly. It was played live onto the tape along with the lyric, and although we did about three takes the first take was the one that we used. Don't forget, you couldn't lock things up afterwards with the same kind of ease that you can now, and so I was manually changing the drum patterns as we played the song.

"When we did 'Two Tribes' everyone more or less agreed that we would record the band playing it and then we would see what we could do with it. On 'The Power of Love,' however, that is the band playing. So, I always think it's one of those media clichés to say the band didn't play on the record. People get obsessed about it over here [in the U.K.]. That's one of the faults we have. The Americans pull just as many stunts, if not more. People don't just go into a studio and play and it comes out sounding like Nirvana! The most incredible amount of work and production goes into making it sound like that, but people over here don't seem to understand.

"With *Liverpool,* it was the second album, the songs weren't as good, the band and the singer had fallen out, and really the only thing wrong with the record was that Frankie didn't keep going. The album made it to number one in Germany, they made a load of money on the tour, and we did about a million units worldwide, which wasn't bad. It did nothing in America—the Americans didn't like it, but then the band hadn't exactly behaved themselves there and so there was a bit of a backlash against them—but if they had made a third album then *Liverpool* would have been a normal second album. If you listen back to it some of it's not bad at all—there are about four or five really good songs on it—but you could never keep that kind of intensity going that was so vital.

"One of the reasons we did all the remixes of 'Relax' was that the initial twelve-inch version of that track had something called 'The Sex Mix,' which was sixteen minutes long and didn't even contain a song. It was really Holly just jamming, as well as a bunch of samples of the group jumping in the swimming pool and me sort of making disgusting noises dropping stuff into buckets of water and so on. We got so many complaints about it—particularly from gay clubs, who found it offensive—that we cut it in half and reduced it down to eight minutes by taking some of the slightly more offensive parts out. Then we got a load of complaints because the single wasn't on the twelve-inch. I didn't see the point in this, but I was eventually put straight about it.

"When I was out in New York doing Foreigner I went to Paradise Garage. The Art of Noise was happening, and I'd just done 'Owner of a Lonely Heart,' which was huge in America. There was a great remix of it which made number two in the dance chart there, and yet it was only when I went to this club and heard the sort of things they were playing that I really understood about twelve-inches. Although I myself had already had a couple of big twelve-inch hits, I'd never heard them on a big system. So I then went back and mixed 'Relax' again, and that was the version which sold a couple of million over here.

"So, the point is that I wasn't being clever. It wasn't some great scheme that I dreamed up to make three different twelve-inch remixes, but I was just desperately trying to get the record right. At the same time, I had a kind of ethic with twelve-inches. I never wanted them to be boring, even though they were going to be nine minutes long. I didn't see that as an excuse for them to be self-indulgent or boring, and so we would work quite hard on them in order for them to make sense as pieces of music. I don't hear much of that nowadays.

"At the time of 'Relax' or 'Two Tribes' there was no 'techno,' there was no 'house music.' These were all terms that people came up with. When we did 'Relax' I hadn't been to a club in years, but I'd had a certain amount of exposure to black music in New York working with [Malcolm] McLaren. When we did 'Buffalo Girls' the only scratching record before that, I think, was 'Wheels of Steel' by Grand Master Flash, and I was no great guru of grooves. I just said to them, 'What's your favorite groove? Sing it to me,' and that took about eight hours, because I kept misunderstanding what they said!

"So, I had a bit of a grasp of what people were dancing to, but 'Relax,' for instance, was a drum pattern that I had in my Linn 2. It was like my pet drum pattern which I fiddled about with, and I thought it was more like an English square dance than anything else, but when I saw the effect it had on the guys in the band I realized that it was probably going to be a very good dance record.

"Actually, when I was in New York I did this one track with Malcolm [McLaren] called 'She's a Hobo Scratch,' which was a nine-minute scratching track over a beat and probably one of the most hard-core things I ever did. My wife didn't like it at all, but I said, 'Look, I know it's a little bit repetitive and boring, but certain people will like this in New York.' Then, one day, I was walking in Greenwich Village and there was this little black break-dance group on the sidewalk dancing to 'She's a Hobo Scratch.'

I'd just been to a meeting and so I was standing there and watching them, wearing a shirt and tie, and I remember thinking, 'If I go up and tell them I did that record they'll never believe me!'

"My wife's got great ears. When we were mixing 'Crazy' on the first Seal album she came in and made me mix him really loud. We had him quite loud, but then she came and said, 'I don't know why you're even bothering to listen to the backing track. I'm only interested in *him*!' She was the person who actually signed Seal to ZTT in the first place, and she was really enthusiastic about him. If you ever listen to 'Crazy,' Seal is absolutely bone dry. There isn't an effect on him. He's also flat, there's no EQ on him, and he's incredibly loud, while the whole track is compressed around him. That's a technique we use a lot. We very rarely put on any EQ, and we try to keep the whole thing digital from the minute he sings until it ends up on the CD, without his voice going through any analog process.

"Being a producer is a huge job, you know. I don't want to sound arrogant about it, but it's like you just see the tip of the iceberg, whereas with some people it's only the tip of the iceberg that exists. I've got a good instinct for arranging things. I've got a very low boredom threshhold, so I'm probably not too good at doing indie bands. I like the kind of records that you can listen to loads of times, because they take you off on some kind of a journey, and so that's what I always try to make. At the same time, I also like clarity.

"Things either work out pretty quick or they take a long time. If it comes quickly then I'm not going to mess around with it, but it isn't always like that. I have been known to spend quite a long time on things. Working in this business, you get to hear loads of songs, and I don't necessarily always like those that are written by professional songwriters. You really can be quite bored by a 'well-written' song even before you've started working on it, because you know that it's not real, it's not true. The person wrote it for the money or to get a cover, but it's far more of a challenge to take something that somebody's written out of an actual feeling inside and try to turn it into something commercial. It's genuine, it's the real thing. I draw a very big distinction between what I consider to be a composition that's real and something that's bogus.

"The original version of 'Relax' that I heard on television was absolutely from the heart. Without a doubt! All of Holly's stuff was. I mean, whatever differences I might have with him, all of his stuff was very much written from the heart and that's what I liked about it. In fact, 'Relax' was a very interesting song, because it was a kind of nonsong. I'm sure I'm not denigrating it in any way by saying that it was an advertising jingle, and a brilliant one. I mean, how can you resist a line like 'Sock it to me biscuit'? That's a brilliant line! You don't get that doing—God bless him— Michael Bolton, even though Michael Bolton has a terrific voice. You would never get that kind of originality in that area. But, of course, with it also comes the baggage that it isn't necessarily going to be tailored for the mass market, and so it's a lot more of a challenge to turn that into something that will compete with people like Michael Bolton. That is what it was like with Frankie, but that stuff was the genuine article.

"I worked with Rod Stewart in Ireland on 'Tom Traubert's Blues.' I set up a studio in a house over there, but the main reason for that was because I'd had to spend a lot of time out of England working with Mike Oldfield in Los Angeles. So I thought I might as well make it into a tax year, and that's why I did Rod's record in Ireland. We also recorded Simple Minds [in a home setup] years ago and it's quite a nice way to work, but only to a degree, because the problem is that you don't know what you're hearing half the time. I still like big control rooms in recording studios.

"In terms of the artists who I prefer to work with I tend to like singers. I think Sting is brilliant; without a doubt one of the best singers we've got about at the moment. If someone's a really good singer then every time they sing something it's different. With Seal's singing, for instance, I always approach it like recording a jazz saxophone player. Every time he sings it, it's going to be slightly different. If you actually listen to his phrasing it is quite brilliant, and you can't teach someone that.

"In fact, on the new album the first verse and chorus vocal of the opening track ['Bring It On'] were recorded in Wendy and Lisa' s bathroom, and if you solo up the track you can hear the cat scratching and the toilet running a little bit. Seal was sitting in the bathroom and he completely overloaded their board, because he's got a pretty strong voice. So, there's all this distortion, but it's such a great piece of singing that I had to keep it.

"It was just a guide vocal for the demo. I hang on to everything, you know. I can remember which vocal he did such-and-such on, kind of like an archivist. That's the part I like, because it's real, and I guess that since I've got older I've become more interested in that than the kind of whizz-bang stuff. At the beginning of the eighties I was into whizz-bangs and lots of mad productions as I didn't know if people would pay any attention if I didn't do that.

"The Seal record is a kind of hybrid of loops and people playing all sorts of things. That's what we tend to do nowadays and that's what can be so confusing. Take any one record and there are so many different ways to do it. I think that at the moment we're kind of in an era where you can do anything. You can play live if you want to, you can use computers, and people will accept it. You can do what you want. There's no specific way to do anything.

"During the past twenty years certain great songs wouldn't have been so great without then-novel sounds which gave them their feel. I mean, the Frankies won an Ivor Novello Award [for most performed work] for 'Two Tribes,' but before we made the record everyone was saying, 'What are we going to do for a second single? There isn't another song there.' It was only when you put it in the right context, gave it the right arrangement, and organized it properly that people saw what a good song it actually was. So, I wouldn't necessarily say a good song's a good song; I would say a good idea is a good idea."

don**was**

■

Born and raised in Detroit, Don is one of the world's most pro-
lific and respected producers, working with Bob Dylan, Bonnie
Raitt, the Rolling Stones, Elton John, Carly Simon, Michael
McDonald, Iggy Pop, Paula Abdul, Willie Nelson, David Crosby,
Lyle Lovett, Jackson Browne, Neil Diamond, Brian Wilson, the
B-52s, Bob Seger, Michelle Shocked, k.d. lang, and Roy Orbi-
son. As an artist Don experienced success in his own right with
Was (Not Was), the band that he formed with childhood friend
David Weiss before turning to production as the primary focus
of his career, and his reputation is now such that, to quote the
New York Times, he "bridges a gap. He takes people that were
good all along and distills them into the best versions of themselves." It was shortly after he had finished distilling the Stones
for their *Voodoo Lounge* album that I spoke with Don in 1994.

"The preproduction sessions for *Voodoo Lounge* took place at Blue
Wave Studios in Barbados. [Engineer] Don Smith put together a
small setup which Mick and Keith could use for their songwriting,
and within six months they came up with fragments of seventy-
five songs which were in various states of completion. As a matter
of reference, people should know that having seventy-five fragments
written within a six-month period is sensational. It's amazing for
any band at any stage in its career to have that kind of raw material
exploding out, and I think it bodes really well for the creative ways
in which Mick and Keith are writing.

"Out of all the song fragments, thirty-two complete numbers
were recorded at Windmill Lane [Studios in Dublin]. Now, out of
those, fifteen eventually ended up on the finished album, but I
have to say that there really wasn't a pronounced difference in
either quality or feel between those that did find their way onto
the record and those that didn't. There were some incredible things
that didn't get used, although if the album had a few less tracks it
would have been stronger to me. Still, having read some reviews,
I can't find any consensus of opinion. A lot of people like the songs

that I probably would have eliminated, and so it's all subjective. It was because there wasn't any consensus within the band that we just figured, 'Well, we don't hate any of these, so let's put the lot out.'

"In terms of coproducing with Mick and Keith, out of the three of us I was the one who didn't have to walk the plank! I think it's important to have someone holding the kite string with both feet on the ground. That goes not just for the Rolling Stones but for any artist, because if [as an artist] you're doing the job right you're floating around on a creative asteroid, and someone's got to keep track of where you are.

"In this case, I never felt that my job was to impose creative concepts on them, but just to help distill the wealth of ideas that they had. I mean, I would point out if I didn't think something was going to work, but I didn't think it was my position to say, 'Here, Keith, give me your guitar for a minute. I'll show you what to play.' Man, that's one thing you really don't want to do! Not because he's going to bite your head off, but just why on Earth? You know, it's like grabbing the sax from Charlie Parker! Keith's got so many ideas and they're all so original that I couldn't come up with them in a hundred years. That's the amazing thing—the simplicity of what he does is so deceptive. With Keith, there's so much happening within a few notes. People think they can just take the sixth string off the guitar and tune it a certain way, and yes, you can play the chords to 'Brown Sugar' pretty easily, but can you come up with new parts and interact with musicians in the way he does? The answer is no.

"When Mick and Keith write and routine their material they are like guys who keep working with the clay, over and over. Especially Keith. He may play a riff for an hour, just trying to get inside of the thing. Listening back to all of the tapes, it's amazing to hear the very roughest demos and then trace the evolution of each song. The songs certainly did flower in the studio, but we were pretty rough on them; they weren't ready until they were ready. Personally, I don't believe anyone ever fools anybody with production techniques. You know, you really can't hide a shitty song, but you can try, and that's what some people do.

"A lot of the songs definitely have that classic Stones feel, but it really wasn't a case of 'Let's sound how we used to sound.' With any artist's work there is usually a thread of consciousness which is easily identifiable, so maybe 'Out of Tears' is reminiscent of 'Angie,' but there again, it's been written by the same guy, so why shouldn't it be? Let's not fight that, let's not try to disguise it. 'New Faces' was written by Mick on a harpsichord, and the encouragement I provided was to say, 'Don't fight it. If you wrote it on a harpsichord, who cares? So what if you used one twenty-five years ago?' The fact that there's a thread of consistency through the years is a plus. It just means you have a consistent vision.

"Don Smith and I worked together on Keith Richards' solo albums, and for this new record, after we'd spent a long time talking about how it should sound, I pretty much left him to his own devices and he did an incredible job. The record sounds very natural and intimate. Sometimes, just given the nature of the technology, you almost have to create an illusion of smallness. Maybe a room is larger than you want it to be and the sound is too big, so to get it tighter requires some maneuvering, and this is not as simple as it appears to be.

"For most of the basic tracks the whole band played together in the studio, positioned close together in a semicircle with Charlie sitting in the middle. That was when he was playing what we referred to as the 'upstairs drum kit,' because for some of the songs Charlie played a different kit which was positioned at the bottom of a three-flight square stairwell. The stairwell was concrete and it had tremendous echo. We put his kit in there for 'Thru and Thru' and 'You Got Me Rocking,' and it produced a really huge, natural sound.

"I think the Stones' basic intention was to capture the fact that it's a band and capture the intuitive playing that takes place within a band. The sound of *Steel Wheels* was a bit monolithic in terms of how everything was big, as well as dense with echo and texture, and that tended to obscure the subtleties of an ensemble playing. That said, *Steel Wheels* was made in a period when that kind of record was fashionable—that whole Bon Jovi/Bruce Fairbairn/Aerosmith sound was a huge, produced sound. So, I respect guys who try to change things, and in this case it was, 'Okay, we did that. Now let's go back to the essence of good band playing, utilizing a raw, Chess Records kind of recording technique.'

"Also, there was a period of time, around *Beggars Banquet* and

Let It Bleed, when they were adventurous texturally, and so in this case, once the band sound had been captured, they did want to extend the textures and try different things. They didn't just want to have a five-piece band playing and then the next thing it's mixed. So on every song we tried to apply some extra texture. Like on the intro to 'You Got Me Rocking,' Keith is playing something called a 'mystery guitar,' which is actually just a wild sound that he got from playing an old fiberglass dobro with a stick that he found in the yard at Ronnie's house. It makes this kind of clanging effect in the background, and it just gives the song some dimension and a unique texture.

"Perhaps the best example, however, is 'Moon Is Up,' which has everything from Charlie banging on a garbage can with brushes to Ronnie playing his pedal steel through a Mutron, Keith playing his acoustic guitar through the Hammond organ's Leslie cabinet, and Mick singing through his harmonica mike which had phasing on it. Every sound on there was dramatically altered.

"The difference between the Stones and session guys is that you drive session musicians like mules. You know, you crack the whip and get them to keep playing over and over and over until they get it right. But with the Stones there's this kind of mystical feel—everyone's got to feel like doing it—so after a take they may go shoot pool or watch a football match and then come back and do it one more time. It was rare for us to get good results by performing a song back-to-back, twice in a row.

"As for Mick's vocals, it would take him a minute to warm up but you always knew when he had it, because he would cut to the essence of the thing. Sometimes you really have to strain to tell if someone's deep inside a song, but with him it's really remarkable: his voice leaps off of the tape and out of the speakers like no one I've ever heard. It was a phenomenal experience. He projects this huge character. I mean, if you close your eyes and listen you can actually visualize the sort of caricature that may appear in *Rolling Stone,* where someone has drawn the huge lips and so on. He becomes that person, and he cuts right to the heart of the song, like an actor giving a great performance. He'd give it the full stage bit, and in fact it was so awesome I had to keep looking down at the console, because I didn't want to be wowed too much! I mean, I used to wait in line overnight to get tickets to see these guys, just for some shitty seats, and now I had them about five feet in front of me, on the other side of the glass, and I didn't want to be biased in my assessment of his vocal. So, I had to look down and just listen to make sure it was working, because otherwise I could have lost my objectivity.

"For me the track that best embodies the spirit of the entire project is 'Sweethearts Together.' Mick and Keith both played their acoustic guitars in an isolation booth, and then they sang a duet standing eyeball-to-eyeball, about eighteen inches apart. They did this incredible Everly Brothers–type [harmony] all the way through the song, and I thought it was very cool, but the people in the control room who had worked with them for ten or fifteen years were like, 'I can't believe this is happening!' That moment epitomized the collaboration which characterizes the album, and I think that's why it's a better record than others that they've done in recent years."

phil ramone

■

During a production and engineering career stretching back four decades Phil has worked on international hits ranging from Stan Getz and Astrid Gilberto's "The Girl from Ipanema" and Billy Joel's "Uptown Girl" to Harry Nilsson's "Everybody's Talkin' " and Paul Simon's "50 Ways to Leave Your Lover." Then there have been the recordings with anyone from Dusty Springfield and Dionne Warwick to Paul McCartney and Barbra Streisand. Not for nothing is he known as "The Pope of Pop." In 1993 Phil resumed his working relationship with Frank Sinatra when he produced *Duets,* which was notable not only for being the best-selling album of Ol' Blue Eyes' career, but also because the then-seventy-seven-year-old singer never actually crooned together with any of his duetting partners.

"Liza was recorded in Brazil, Bono in Dublin, Aznavour in London, Gloria Estefan in Miami, Tony Bennett in New York, and Aretha and Anita Baker were in Detroit. So it was fantastic being able to make use of the new EDNet [Entertainment Digital Network] system. By way of the fiber-optic lines running into all of these cities, it enabled us to work direct with the artists in different studios. The nice thing about it is that you can't tell the difference between those who used it and those who actually came in to the studio. Without this technology we wouldn't have been able to make any kind of deadline. We'd still be recording!

"Frank recorded all of his parts first, and going back to the Capitol Records Tower in Hollywood after so many years was like a walk down memory lane for him. The studio has been totally refurbished but left acoustically pretty much the way it was. They've joined Studio A and Studio B, which were never that way before, and made a larger control room. They've got this dividing wall which you can open up and obtain a uniquely big sound.

"On the day of a session we had a rehearsal with the orchestra before Frank got there and then he'd just walk in and sing. He's very demanding about how he records. He does one or two takes,

291

and then says, 'Let me hear that.' If he likes it he just goes, 'Next!' It's not a wiseguy thing, the way he speaks, but he just won't labor over it. He doesn't overdub, refuses to overdub. When he says, 'Wheel it back,' that comes from the old school of telling the orchestra to go back four bars, continuing, and then making the edit. Editing between two takes is fine with him, but he's just not comfortable overdubbing. To him it's hokey.

"So, there are no punch-ins for Frank. You go back or you recut or you do another take. When I'd go out of the control room to talk to him those steel-blue eyes would look right at me, and I'd know that the only way to deal with him—and the only way I ever work with artists—is to be direct and honest. He'd listen to a playback and say, 'No, let's do it again.' I've been brought up around that live performing thing, so it doesn't frighten me. It's actually the best pressure that you could ever have to make a record.

"We sometimes tend to get a little lethargic making a record nowadays, and so at first we generously thought, 'Well, we'll do two songs a night. Don't push the old man.' But it was baloney, because once he got rolling and started to perform in that room, he managed to do nine songs in one night. Three of those, which ended up on the album, were done in one take. That was on the third night. He first came in on a Monday night and agreed to record in a booth, but after working out on a couple of songs he was back out of there, telling me that he was going to work in the way that he was accustomed to, in the main room with the band. I really wasn't keen to do that because of the leakage, so the next night I had Frank wearing headphones and overdubbing his vocals onto prerecorded instrumental tracks, but again he wasn't happy, and the Capitol executives were now starting to get nervous. He didn't come in on the next night but he came back on the Thursday, and at that point we placed him in the kind of setup with which he feels most comfortable, sitting on a low stage with the same hand-held, wireless Vega microphone which he uses in concert.

"Because he would choose either to sit or to stand within the band, it would be almost impossible to have recorded him with a hanging mike, whereas, because he's been performing for eight or nine years in this setup, the comfort factor came into play, enabling him to feel a lyric, to move, to kid around with his piano player of forty-two years [Bill Miller], who was seated right in front of him at a Steinway grand. So, while I'm sure the audiophiles will be on my case for working this way, it's what works best with Frank. The mike he uses is a hand-held transmitter and it performs the job required of it. I mean, any technician would go crazy when I tell them about it, but the rejection of the outside material around the mike is quite heavy. And it gives him freedom, because when he starts to move to a tune he's really into it. When he's doing a ballad, he will sometimes wave his hand in the most beautiful conducting manner, because he feels where the phrase is going, and the conductor will actually follow every movement of his hand. So he doesn't want to be bothered with some stupid microphone standing there. This isn't the 1960s. He can do what the hell he wants.

"A couple of years ago [A&R man] Don Rubin and I spoke with Frank's manager, Eliot Weisman, about him recording a new album. He was interested, so we then flew to Palm Springs and presented Frank with two ideas, *Duets* and *Live at the Rainbow Room*. Well, he loved the idea of *Duets,* and so we started coming up with some names and it was then that he said he had met Bono in Ireland and perhaps he might be interested.

"That line on 'I've Got You Under My Skin' where Bono sings, 'Don't you know, y'ol' fool, you never can win . . .'—we had a substitute line prepared for our own protection. We were worried, because Bono said, 'I don't want to offend him.' You know, to him Frank is the ultimate rock 'n' roller, and therefore that line is very much what a young punk would say to an older guy. It's not about disrespect, but they're singing about a woman getting under their skin and it's father to son, brother to brother, very conversational. Frank's reaction when he heard it was immediately positive, so there must be something about being a bit of a rebel with a cause. There again, after Barbra Streisand sang, 'You make me blush, Francis,' near the end of 'I've Got a Crush On You,' we went to his dressing room just before a concert near Chicago and had him sing 'Barbara' into a DAT machine. We then used that to replace the word *baby* on his vocal so that it would sound like he was responding to her in the song.

"During that first meeting with him in Palm Springs, Frank had said, 'You know, the gals don't have the same range as the boys, so we may have some problems, but if I have to adjust, I'll adjust.' So, in a few cases, we did end up modulating down and making very subtle changes. Then there were also a lot of times when we wondered who should sing where—him or his partner— but it was safer for us to let him perform most of the song. And as it turned out, he sang almost every song all the way through. After all, he's a fine actor, so he knows that if he reads a line in a certain way then someone else may respond accordingly. He's very generous in that way.

"After he'd finished cutting the tracks I then prepared the other artists by sending them a tape of their alloted song. In several cases, this also featured a stand-in doing the appropriate vocal harmony part, and so by the time each of them arrived in the studio they had a fairly clear picture of what was required. They all realized the value of what they were doing, and so every single one of them just left their egos at the door and got on with whatever it would take to make it work.

"For his part, Frank is amazing. He's not going to sing out of tune, and if he has trouble singing to that high note it's not about having the chops which he had when he was thirty or forty or fifty. After all, at his age most singers that we've ever heard of have faded away, and as he doesn't sing with less enthusiasm or less musicality than before it's not a problem if he does struggle for a note. That's where the voice is at today, and I promise you that if we thought—and he thought—it was a drawback, he would drop it right now.

"Anytime I've recorded Frank with a pair of microphones, one overhead, one underneath, he's always asked me, 'Why two?' and my response to this has been, 'Well, I need one spare track of vocal, because I know you ain't coming back, and besides, my bootlegger likes the other track!' "

hanszimmer

Hans is not a man to mince his words or compromise his music. An Oscar and Grammy-winning composer-producer, he has helped pioneer the successful integration of digital synths, electronic keyboards, and advanced computer technology with the traditional orchestra when creating music for television and films such as *Thelma & Louise*, *Rain Man*, *Driving Miss Daisy*, *Black Rain*, *Green Card*, *Backdraft*, *A League of Their Own*, *Crimson Tide*, *Broken Arrow*, *Muppet Treasure Island*, *The Preacher's Wife*, and *The Lion King*. In 1997 I visited this multi-talented German at the multifaceted entertainment facility which he co-owns in Santa Monica, and talked to him about his innovative techniques and trend-setting film scores.

"When I moved to London in the seventies my first professional work was producing radio jingles, and then I teamed up with Trevor Horn and Geoff Downes to form the Buggles. Spending two to three years making records with Trevor Horn convinced me that I just cannot last eighteen months working on a single project. I'm not built that way. There again, the stuff that I wanted to write couldn't be done in rock 'n' roll. You know, the problem when you're in a band is that first of all you don't get a deal, and then, if you do get a deal and actually have a hit record, you inevitably have to stay within the parameters of that style.

"It was when I worked in London with the film composer Stanley Myers that I became convinced about the importance of incorporating electronic music with classical. The two of us set up Lillie Yard Studios together and worked on films such as *Insignificance*, *Castaway*, and *My Beautiful Laundrette*, and then I branched out on my own. In 1986 I worked with Ryuichi Sakamoto and David Byrne on the sound track of *The Last Emperor*, and after I composed the music for a small-budget film called *A World Apart* I was then asked to write the score for *Rain Man*. I arrived in Los Angeles in 1988 completely broke.

"The great thing about films is that nobody will tell you not to do something, so you can use your imagination. Still, with film music there are certain rules for how you are supposed to work. You know, don't make a big noise because it will block the dialogue. Well, the dialogue is my enemy. I don't give a shit about the dialogue! I'll make a big noise and it can then be turned down in the dub if necessary. I'm just trying to write a tune that fits in with the film.

"I do everything wrong. Every time I work with a blues band I want to introduce an orchestra, and every time I'm writing orchestral stuff I want to get all of these synths going. I get restless, and so I sometimes pick projects largely because they allow me to do things that I have no idea about. I will spend several days talking with a director about a new film in order to find out exactly what his views are, but then I will go away and attempt to write precisely what I think is required. My job is to knock his socks off and write something that he can't even imagine, otherwise he'd be doing it himself. I mean, you can either become a musical secretary or you can do your own thing.

"You will have arguments and fights about things, but nobody sets out to make a bad movie. There has to be an element of trust to start with, and the knowledge on the director's part that I'm not just trying to write a symphony because I feel like it but because I'm actually trying to serve the film just as he does. . . . You know, it's a funny thing, but once you start working on a film it dictates the direction and you find yourself just hanging on for dear life!

"A perfect example was *Driving Miss Daisy*, where the director [Bruce Beresford] is a big opera buff and he wanted more of an orchestral score for a period picture. I, on the other hand, could hear this synthetic sound coming out of a sequencer because it felt right to me, in line with the main character. It had nothing to do with the period in which the film was set. So, that was a bit of a struggle.

"You have to remember that it's scary for a director. I mean, he's used to seeing his picture, he's probably heard the temp track or some stuff in his head, and now suddenly you are completely turning his film on its head. He thought that car chase was going to be all fast and frantic, and here I am writing this slow tension piece. Directors have a terrible time when it comes to the music. After all, they've been in control all along—you know, they can write a bit, they can act a bit for the cast, but then what are they going to say to me? 'A nice C major chord in here would be just the thing'?

"Anyway, having watched the rough cut of the film and talked with the director, I will then go away and write, say, a ten-minute section that creates the kind of atmosphere that I'm after, regardless of how well it fits a scene right down to the last frame—at this stage there is still a lot of editing to do. The danger here is writing to spec, because I really try to avoid using the same formula that worked well with another movie not too long ago.

"I was working on a film being produced by Steven Spielberg. Well, Steven loves *Crimson Tide*. In fact, I think *love* is too weak a word; he'd love to marry *Crimson Tide*! After the first time he saw that film he said, 'Don't change a note! Well, okay, change the notes, but you know what I mean!' At the same time, I couldn't write *Crimson Tide* again because I was bored with it, so then I was trying to find out what it was about *Crimson Tide* that made it work and how that could apply to this new film. It's like a sample, you know. A sample is a boring thing, because it was done at a different time for a different purpose, and *Crimson Tide* didn't really fit onto this film. So, I really struggle with that, and sometimes I succeed and sometimes I don't.

"Take action movies. Part of the way they now sound is due to what I did on *Black Rain* back in 1988, and so I have been battling to reinvent myself for an awfully long time now with varying degrees of success. All of the drums and the percussion stuff—it would be great to figure out a way of saying that without using that. It's about inspiration, and there are bad days and there are good days . . . although there are a lot more bad days.

"A lot of the time I write in my bathtub. Lying there for an hour in the morning I have tunes going through my head, but I won't write them down or sing them into a recorder. I firmly believe that if I can't remember a tune by the time that I arrive at the studio then it can't have been that good. At the same time, when I have a tune in my head or I'm working on something, I need people to be quiet. The other night I was in here, struggling with four bars, and a friend of mine who was sitting a few feet away very carefully picked up a box of matches to light a cigarette. Well, I heard the matches rattling in the box and I whipped around and fixed him with one of these evil looks, because you start taking on the character. In fact, when I was working on *The Fan* I had to move out of the house, because I *was* the psycho killer!

"So, my team here knows when it's safe to come into the room and when it's not, and the reason why I work here—and why we built this place—is that it gets awfully lonely. You just want to walk down the corridor and see some other composer having a really tough time, because then you know you're not the only idiot! I mean, just for ten minutes I would like to be that person who everybody thinks I am; you know, that incredibly talented guy who is just knocking out these pieces of music. Because if I was that guy for ten minutes I would have the whole thing written as opposed to still sitting here until eight in the morning, working on the same three bars. At some point, of course, I do get over the hump, but it's so scary because, while other people sit in front of a sheet of paper, I sit in front of a blank computer screen.

"When you're writing you want to be distracted by the technology as little as possible. I mean, the real problem that we all have when we're writing with computers is the mouse, because while you're still in a certain state of mind you have to pick up the mouse and search for the cursor, and so your brain is switching between emotional and analytical all of the time. It's a real bummer. The reason why my suite at the studio is so excessive in terms of keyboards and samplers is because I don't want to think about loading in a sound. I just want it to be there, and so my fake orchestra does take up rather a lot of room. I sit here all day, so why shouldn't I have something that sounds good and inspires me? I mean, this is how I'm spending my life.

"I write an orchestral score with certain tried and trusted musicians in mind, and so after I've completed it I fly to London to record them at a facility such as AIR Lyndhurst. I used to be on their sessions in London and now I'm on the other side of the glass. Once you've played with those people it does something. AIR Lyndhurst is like a home from home, and I also get to see all of my friends! I have to say that the musicians in London have been incredibly helpful, letting me sample them, and I have an agreement with them that I will never use the samples without using real musicians. You see, film is the only place left where we have the budgets to use big orchestras, and I don't want that to stop. Sometimes it's a bit of a fight, because yeah, I can make things sound really good, but with real musicians there's that thing that happens, that unquantifiable magic.

"Like when I was working on this animated film with Elton [John] named *El Dorado*. I'd done all of the demos using samplers, and while all of the lines were there and all of the percussion was there it didn't move me. Then I brought in these two guitarists— they were playing the same patterns, the same lines, but suddenly there was a passion about it.

"When all I had was a Prophet V [synthesizer] and everybody seemed to think that you could achieve any sound in the world with a synth, I would be asked to get a string sound and have to think about what it really sounded like. That's how I learned about orchestration and what the individual instruments do. After I'd done my bit I would hang around at the sessions and watch and listen to what the other guys—the real players—were doing. I wasn't a player, I was a programmer, but when I was asked to get the 'Tower of Power' brass sound I'd say, 'Well, guys, they don't actually live in this box. They live in America.' Still, I'd get close to what they wanted.

"My orchestrator now is Bruce Fowler, who was formerly the trombonist in Frank Zappa's band. He can play anything. Of course, when I ask Bruce if the musicians can play a part that I've written he will say, 'Yes,' because he himself can! We always rehearse the band when we arrive at a session, and part of Bruce's job is to somehow make the piece playable for them. Occasionally he will phone me up and say, 'On this part here maybe we should just use the samples,' because in a way the samples are a safety net for the guys. When I go to the orchestral session all of the stuff that I've done is on tape, and I play it to the orchestra and say, 'Just follow your parts.' They can actually hear the whole piece and know where they are within it, and if the dynamics make sense then the notes suddenly make sense.

"At first it was a bit of a struggle playing session guys things on samples. On *Crimson Tide* the brass parts were really pretty outrageous, and so they were saying, 'Hang on, why don't you just use the machines?' I'd say, 'No, guys, I know you can do this,' like it was a challenge. In fact, sometimes I'll purposely write things which are a challenge. You know, there'll be a scene where there's a struggle going on, and I'll therefore write something that's a bit of a struggle for the musicians as well. That way you can actually smell the fear in the room and it heightens the whole atmosphere.

"Take the choir parts on *Crimson Tide*, which were incredibly difficult to sing. I was working against type all of the time, and so whenever it got really tense I would just make it very, very quiet and have it go down to the chorus. They are human beings, and it's so obvious that it's a voice, but you can hear the struggle that is going on and it just gives you that extra bit of tension. There's a scene at the end where Gene Hackman and Denzel Washington are just sitting there, and he has two minutes to prove his point, and the note just lasts forever. You see, the most difficult thing for most players is not to play fast, it is to play slow, and to play long notes.

"I don't believe any musician should be at the mercy of the studio gear or have a problem trying to explain how he or she wants a particular part to sound, so I know how to engineer. I mix my own music, working mainly with Alan Meyerson, and I move away from the console whenever the need arises. Usually, by the time we've done the orchestral sessions there's some piece that I've forgotten to write, so I'm in my suite writing while Alan mixes all of the cues next door, storing everything in the computer. He gets everything to sound really good and then I go in there and start pushing the faders around. At that point he actually leaves, and it's great to not have him in the room. When he returns he does so with a fresh perspective, and he'll say, 'You know that bass drum there? I think people will throw up in the cinema!' He therefore becomes the conscience. The whole movie process is always down to teamwork, and so Alan is not just the engineer. He will say, 'That tune sucks,' and that is great. 'Okay, I will try to write another one.'

"There was a film called *I'll Do Anything* for which I wrote two scores. It was originally conceived as a musical with songs, but then that didn't work and so the songs were cut out and I wrote another score which made no reference to them. We were so behind schedule on that project, but then on the day I finished the score I dreamed the whole opening sequence as a completely different tune with a completely different feel. I woke up and phoned the director, Jim Brooks, who was happy that things were over, and I said, 'I want to withdraw the score.' He couldn't believe it, but I went ahead and the thing that I ended up with was completely mad.

"I mean, there were things in there that you would never do if you were just sitting writing music, but in a dream you don't care about major and minor! It had the oddest lineup—there were, like, eight violins, a baritone saxophone playing much too high, an 808 drum machine, a gospel choir—and chords that I was totally unfamiliar with. Just weird, but it worked. Of course, I hadn't dreamed the piece to the right length, but I went and did it and when we put it up against the picture we suddenly had a movie, or at least more of a movie than we'd ever had before.

"As I said, it's all about inspiration. Sometimes this inspiration chooses to come at an inconvenient time, but when it does come you have to grab onto it and follow your instincts. You see, those are the moments that can make all the difference."

bob rock

■

Bob first made a name for himself in his native Vancouver, Canada, during the early eighties, when he recorded various provincial new wave acts. This work soon brought him to the attention of top local producer Bruce Fairbairn, and thereafter the two men collaborated on projects by acts such as Bon Jovi, Aerosmith, and Loverboy, before Bob quit engineering in the middle of the decade in order to begin producing on his own. The Cult, Mötley Crüe, Cher, Bon Jovi, David Lee Roth, and Metallica have all subsequently benefited from his endeavors in this field, and in 1996 I spoke with Bob about his work with Metallica on the *Load* album, which had recently been recorded at a facility in Sausalito, California, close to where the band members were living.

"Since the Mötley Crüe project I've been using the same engineer, Randy Staub. You know, to be a producer and to also engineer is a little much—you end up doing so much technical stuff that you don't really concentrate on what the band needs. So, the collaboration with Randy has turned into a great relationship; he's grown into knowing what I want and how I do things, but even though he pretty well engineers everything I still get my hands in there and I kind of oversee the engineering.

"Lars [Ulrich] was so happy with the drum sound on the *Black Album* that he just wanted to stay with that. James [Hetfield], Kirk [Hammett], and Jason [Newsted], on the other hand, have all changed their setup. There was one track, 'Mama,' which was a recut, and what happened there was that after we had cut everything we started editing the drums and recompiling them. The song, however, was just so one-dimensional in terms of Lars' drum sound. It seemed very bombastic, very big, and it didn't have a lot of soul to it. There were not enough dynamics and the drum kit had to be played really hard just to sound good, and so I told Lars that maybe he should have another go at it using the 'hot sticks,' those sticks that are made up of strands and look almost like brushes.

I bought him a pair of those and said, 'Why don't you try doing the same song using these?' He agreed, and so we all set up really quickly one night towards the end of the sessions, and we ran through it, and the band loved it. It's turned out really, really, really cool. So, that was the last track, but it also really opened up some doors for Metallica.

"While this album contains fourteen songs we actually ended up cutting twenty-nine, and oddly enough we were going to finish all twenty-nine. Now, we cut all of these in three main sessions; the first one consisted of about eight songs, and so we'd get that edited, getting drums, bass, rhythm guitar, and vocals, and the funny thing is that the songs that are not on the album were the first ones that we cut. So, we did a whole pile of work before getting to the songs that are being used.

"We'd get the drums and the bass—Metallica's always done the guitars before the bass, but in this instance I suggested fixing up the bass first by using whatever we could from the basic track and then fixing up anything else that we wanted to add. There was quite a different approach on the bass from Metallica, a lot more of a bass line vibe rather than just doubling what the guitars do, as had been the case for quite a while previously. So the bottom end, especially with Jason, ended up being quite different, and they're all happy with it. Then we'd do the rhythm guitars, a rough vocal, and move on.

"In the years since the *Black Album* the band members had compiled riff tapes and songwriting tapes. Then, about six to eight months before we went into the studio, James and Lars—who are the main organizers of song material—gathered all of the riff tapes from everybody and went through them. There were in the neighborhood of between 300 to 350 song ideas, and they just went through them and indexed them and put them together in sequences. Basically, what James and Lars do is put things into a song form between themselves in Lars' basement, then from there James works on the lyrics and it was in this way we ended up with twenty-nine songs.

"We therefore worked *through* the songs in the studio. We rehearsed eight songs at a time, came into the studio, and ran them down. So, if there were any arrangement changes—perhaps due to my perspective or because of lyric ideas that James had come up with—we'd end up maybe honing a little more on the bottom end before then building through the choruses and instrumental sections. The guys really wanted to have a lot more of a free-form feel, not as rigid. They wanted to round out those straight edges that they've had in order for it to be a lot looser, and so we ended up having quite a lot more playing going on.

"The vocal approach was just about the only thing that was different from the *Black Album*, where we got out of this very studious kind of approach of James doing a line and then doubling it. I ended up getting multiple takes and having him compile them, and I freed him up from headphones, because he seemed to like using a pair of out-of-phase speakers, and he got used to that. This time we ended up bringing him into the control room and he actually just used a hand-held mike. Obviously, this is not the best thing to do in terms of leakage and the general sound, but what it did do was capture the performance, and it was great being able to communicate that well. He was right beside me, and so the communication factor and the whole vibe was the reason why we did it this way. I had tried it with Jon Bon Jovi on *Keep the Faith* and I had really liked it, and I told James about it and asked if he wanted to try it. Afterwards, when we weighed up what we lost in terms of the fidelity against what we gained in terms of the performance and the vibe, there was just no comparison.

"I mean, as a producer, if I was just looking at it from a technical standpoint and Bob Rock wanted to win a Grammy, then I'd probably not go with this method! Actually, the 'Mama' vocal ended up being recorded out in the studio because in that case it just wasn't working, but with most of the other stuff the vibe and the performance were the thing. As a matter of fact, when [James] was out in the live area doing 'Mama' he was complaining the whole time that he had all of these things in front of his face! He hated it. He actually got mad and threw a mike stand right across the room!

"The whole band would play together on a cut like that, doing several takes, and from those we would then compile the different instrumental parts [using a computer workstation] and cut in the best performances from Lars. That way you can get some really good character and some really good performances, rather than doing maybe five or six takes and compiling the drums. You seem to get a better vibe, rather than laboriously doing all of these takes to try to get the timing right and thinking about fills. Lars can just sit there for the eight takes and play kind of free-form, and then [with the workstation] we can put those takes together and get, like, one really good take. It just becomes like taking the whole thought process out of playing, and I use that with regard to vocals and with drums just because it sets musicians so much at ease. You know, they don't have to think about, 'I've got to get this in one take! It has to be the magical one!' They can just relax, play what they want, and not feel the pressure.

"On the live takes, the fact that James is sitting there and singing live whilst generally playing his guitar is really there to help Jason and Lars with feel. However, we did actually end up getting one track that we kept from the studio floor, which is a song called 'Believe.' Otherwise, with regard to guitars, until now Kirk generally hasn't played a lot of rhythm on Metallica albums. On this album there are actually only two rhythm guitars; James plays one on one side and Kirk plays on the other side, and that is very much a stretch for these guys, but that's what they wanted and so I was game for it. They just wanted to have two guitar parts and that was it, and James, being the competent kind of guitar player that he is, needed just one take to run all the way through the song.

"So, rhythm-wise the guitars were really easy, whereas on the *Black Album* everything was doubled and tripled and we had to get every nuance right. This time around we'd do maybe three takes until there was one that was cool, and then maybe there would be one bum note, and so we would just punch that in. However, as I said, James is such an incredible player rhythm-wise that his parts were pretty much all complete takes.

"The thing with Metallica this time is that the whole band wanted to simplify. I mean, I can't imagine a band that has done more busy or complicated stuff ever, but now they are changing. They've got different tastes and they want to do different things. We wanted to move on and make a different album. And it's definitely a lot different; it's a lot more open and just not as studious . . . or anal! It's a lot freer-sounding, and I really like that.

"Generally there are a lot more rough edges, even in the approach to the mixing. It's not all about 'me' in the sound of the kick drum and the snare anymore, but it's more about how the song sounds and how it works as a whole. That's tough for the guys to swallow, but this is what they wanted to do, and we've tried to achieve that for them. Having been recording for ten months and not mixing every day, Randy and I have to first find our footing, and the initial mix is the one on which the band and ourselves find the approach and the overall feel that we're going to go for. So, the first mix is usually the longest.

"These days I don't employ a lot of effects in the mix. You know, having gone through the eighties and used more than my fair share of effects and reverbs and everything, my approach now is to collect vintage instruments, amplifiers, drums, whatever, and to present them to Metallica and most of the bands that I work with. It's a performance-orientated kind of record, and we try to pretty much capture that character on tape."

brucefairbairn

■

Bruce is a producer who derives much of his in-studio enjoyment from the process of capturing not only the sound but also the natural energy of a live band performance on tape, and his work with Bon Jovi, Aerosmith, AC/DC, Poison, the Scorpions, Blue Oyster Cult, Van Halen, Chicago, and INXS is a testament to that. A man of many musical talents, Bruce is undeniably one of the hottest producers of the nineties. I spoke to him at the start of 1997, just after he had completed production on INXS's *Elegantly Wasted* album.

"A band defines its own sound in the studio. What comes off the musicians' instruments is what we basically record, and so unless there is a major problem in that something is either unrecordable or it sounds terrible when it goes onto tape, I think it's my job to try and capture the sound of what is being played.

"Being a musician myself, I have a good ear for songs, for arrangements, and for music, so I try to bring all of that to a project, providing songwriters and musicians with a sounding board on which to base their material and their performances. I think that reflects my experience over the years, being part of a band. That's how I learned to play, and so that's why I'm really not that interested in working with bands that don't—or can't—perform live. For me that's all part and parcel of giving the consumer a product that is true. I really have a problem with records where the end result doesn't represent either the human performance of the artist or any ability on the part of the artist to actually perform that song. I think that's musical fraud, so I stay well away from that.

"Before I got together with INXS they'd rented a tiny little studio in Dublin for a week or so and done some writing there. Then they'd done some other writing in London, and they had nine or ten songs that were reasonably well along. Actually, they sent a few of the demos to me before I flew over to London, and they sounded pretty good. I was quite impressed with the feel and the different sounds that they had been using. They hadn't labored over them, but they'd stumbled on some really good things, and so I actually ended up suggesting that we might want to save some of that stuff because the chances are that when we were back in the studio we wouldn't be able to re-create that vibe.

"Andrew Ferris is very meticulous in his musical work, and my thinking was that, given the time to reassess some of the parts that he'd already played, he would probably change them and they may well suffer as a result. That was especially so with some of the vocals, where Michael Hutchence, after a few glasses of wine, wanted to sing, and I really captured some good energy there. I'm always a believer in hanging on to those small gifts. I didn't really coproduce with the band, but the record was produced with Andrew. He was certainly a player at the demo stage, and as we ended up keeping some of the stuff on the demos I felt that it was fair to recognize his contribution in some way.

"They had just come off a record, *Welcome to Wherever You Are*, which had been very well received critically—by the press and by their closest fans—but which really hadn't been able to achieve much success commercially. So, what they wanted to do was make a good band record that was also more commercially accessible, while as high in quality as the previous album. That was the dilemma, trying to get the best of both worlds. When I suggested that we use the demos as the basis for what we were going to be doing over the next few months the guys were quite pleased with that.

"Then it became a question of getting the band involved and getting band performances down. We also cut several songs from scratch, so there was a nice balance there. Overall, however, with a vengeance and a passion they wanted to get the band back in the public eye, and to do that we were really going to look hard for good songs, especially some singles that would fly at radio, and also make a record that would have some depth of character and integrity from a song point of view.

"One of the things that I was most excited about was when John Ferris came to play drums on top of some of the existing tracks. He's an uncanny drummer in that he's able to lock in with an existing track, and he's deadly. It was almost unnatural the way that he was able to play on these tracks and make them feel good. When most drummers play to a click or to an existing instrumental track they will rush or slow down, but John has this amazing ability to be in there and on the mark consistently, as well as to add a really good feel. So, I was just so happy when he came in and laid his parts down on some of these songs.

"Another thing that I really enjoyed about the sessions was that Andrew doesn't tend to choose what I would call mainstream sounds to work with. He's always exploring and trying different things, and he's a fountain of ideas. You know, I would go in there and say, 'Gee, the second verse could really use something to give it a bit of a lift,' and within the space of about five minutes Andrew would have three or four different possibilities on the go. He'd say, 'Well, listen to this. What do you think?' and he'd have this great countermelody, and then he'd go, 'Well, what about this?' and there'd be something else, and so it was really an inspiration to work with that kind of input as a producer. I didn't have to sit around humming and ha'ing for a couple of hours, waiting for him to find a part. If anything, there were too many on the table, and I think that by and large one of our biggest challenges was to take these songs and make them work with just the essential ingredients. Of course, when you have forty-eight tracks available there can be a tendency to fill them up just in case, but I'm very against carrying the excess baggage along and so housecleaning was always a big thing for us.

"Still, Andrew was really excellent at coming up with good ideas, and of course as a singer Michael shot straight from the hip. His vocals were just full of weird things that he could do. For example, we were in Spain, where we did a lot of the vocals, and the vocal booth window of this studio looks right out over this big cliff towards North Africa, and on one day it was really strong and it started whistling through the window. Michael was singing and he paused, and all of a sudden this wind made a really loud whistling noise and Michael just jumped right on it and sang along with it, using this wind almost as a instrument as it came through the glass! At the end we all looked around and said, 'What was that?' Then we said, 'Okay, let's hold it. Let's wait a minute. This wind is going to come again and we'll record it again, so we've got another one.' Of course, it never came again, but Michael, God bless him, was there!

"I'd come down into the studio at three in the morning and

there would be Michael in his pajamas kind of jamming on a vocal. He was always down there stirring the pot and working on new ideas for himself. I think he was very happy with this record, because for once it wasn't a situation where the last thing to be done was the singer writing the lyrics. You know, the singer's in there grasping at straws, trying to get anything that makes sense so that the record can be completed. Basically, Michael had 90 percent of his lyrics completed before I got involved, and for him it was really a good experience because all he was dealing with now was performing and revising lyrics. He didn't have to try to generate completely new ideas. He'd already gotten that down, and I think it gave him the luxury of really concentrating on his performances without being pressured to go down to the wire.

"They weren't out to make a real audiophile kind of record, spending a year to break new ground in the recording business. Instead, they wanted to go with energy and performance over nit-picky advancements in sound quality; what was going to make the songs work, concentrating on the material and the performances, without spending two weeks getting a drum sound together or three days choosing the right mike for Michael to sing into. That took three minutes. With such a great voice he could make a little clip-on mike on your jacket sound like a million bucks.

"I think every record I make is a different animal, in that each band has a distinct thing that it is trying to create with its music. So, I like to gain the first impression of a band or a song and then say, 'Okay, let me throw a few things into the pot and see if I can contribute something worthwhile that will cause the band or the writer to try something a little different.' For instance, with Van Halen's ballad 'Not Enough,' I wasn't responsible for changing it around completely, but I was responsible for putting enough ideas out there after I'd heard Ed [Van Halen] sit down and play it on the piano to get them thinking seriously about actually recording a ballad. I then worked on the lyrics with Sammy [Hagar] as well as on the overall arrangement, and this definitely affected how it came out.

"That song has a really bizarre introduction to it, featuring Ed inside a grand piano and dragging all kinds of stuff across the strings, plucking and banging them. He was hitting that instrument with spoons, dumping marbles in there, and scraping it with knives, and it was Marvin Hamlisch's piano! Ed had been staying at Hamlisch's house as a guest for the weekend while Hamlisch was away and he had asked if he could play the piano. Hamlisch had said, 'Okay,' and Ed went nuts on it, and then after all was said and done Hamlisch went, 'Yeah, great, I can see you had a good weekend! It's gonna cost you $20,000 to restring and repair my piano.'

"So that was that, but what Ed had got out of it was, like, hours of this totally bizarre piano wierdness which I thought would be great at the front of this ballad. So we edited it down to around a minute of great stuff, and maybe that's something which those guys would never have thought about using. It really transformed the song's intro. We also tried some string parts, which were something quite different for them, as was the way in which we tackled the overall arrangement, and the end result was really a team effort, but I'm also happy to say that as a part of that team I brought in some interesting ideas.

"I think it pays to keep your ears open when you're working with really talented people. I learned something from everybody I work with, and so in certain situations I may find myself thinking, 'Okay, what would Steven Tyler do here?' or 'What would Joe Perry do in this case?' or as a songwriter, 'What kind of a bridge would Jim Vallance put in this song?' I don't like to take anything specifically from one project and apply it to another, but I am undoubtedly influenced by the extremely talented people I'm working with, and so I'd be a fool not to learn as I go.

"Of course, there will be times when we disagree over how something should take shape, but I think it's that kind of friction which makes for some good creative sparks, and I'll certainly encourage that kind of friction up to the point where I think it's going forward. As soon as it starts to take a left turn and looks like it's not being creative anymore, then it's time to sit down and make a decision.

"I'm more of a compromise kind of guy. I like to find the road that everybody's happy with. Occasionally I'll be real up-front and say, 'Listen, this is how I hear it,' but that's not to say that I won't record it if it doesn't go down that way. I'll just be real clear as to my preference for something, and sometimes the band will say, 'Hey, that's not what we thought,' and so I'll say, 'Well, you know, take a look at it and maybe it'll surprise you.' There again, more often than not what they come up with surprises me, and I'll think, 'Gee, I had no idea this is what they were hearing! It's really great!' So, there's a lot of give and take, I think, in being a good producer."

will mowat

∎

A keyboard player, composer, programmer, and producer, Will did session work with Living in a Box, D-Mob, and Dusty Springfield during the late eighties and early nineties. This preceded a five-year stint with Soul II Soul, for which all of his musical talents were called upon in collaboration with Jazzie B. Since then he has branched out on his own again, and in 1994 I spoke with Will at the Soul II Soul studio and learned about his work within that state-of-the-art setup, as well as with luminaries such as James Brown and U2.

"In the autumn of 1984, just when MIDI was coming in, I was coerced into flying to Dublin to program an Oberheim for U2, and I was shitting hot bricks because I really knew bugger all about MIDI. So, I read the manuals on the plane over to Dublin, and then when I arrived at U2's place it was a case of—without having previously heard the music—transferring the same sounds which Brian Eno had produced on the Fairlight over onto the Oberheims for Edge to trigger. After that they did their first warm-up concert at the Academy in Brixton [South London], and I went there to fine-tune a few things, and off they went.

"The band's tour manager, Dennis Sheehan, was actually quite miffed when I said I couldn't carry on, because at the time I was managing [London recording studio] Aosis. I had this terrible thing called a sense of responsibility, and so I couldn't give up the studio just like that, although with hindsight maybe I should have done. So, anyway, that was my first true programming session, and it made me realize just how much power you can wield as a technology guru. Of course, if artists genned up just a bit more about their gear then they could do everything themselves, and that's largely what's happened now.

"In terms of the creative process, what comes first is the idea. That spark which sets the whole thing on its way. Technology—hardware and software—is just one piece of the puzzle. Now, for some people it's a fairly large piece of the puzzle and for others it's a tiny, tiny piece. Let's say, for instance, that you just write chords, melody, and lyrics at the piano, then technology doesn't come into it. It's only a certain section of the public which likes to major on technology and make this the most important factor, whereas the healthy way, the right way, is to have the idea first and then set about discovering what you need to bring this idea to fruition.

"I suppose if you look at what I have done you could say that technology has played a fairly major role, but that's only because you can't see what's going on inside my head and my heart, which is what really counts. You know, the equipment that I have here in the studio and at home doesn't count if I don't have the ideas to drive it, both as a writer and as a producer. Okay, as a musician you get your head down and play with your technology, but in absolute terms the technology is simply there to help you achieve what you've got inside your head.

"The whole entertainment business is sourced on ideas, nothing else. Tape recorders, consoles, agents, managers; they're all there to help you get that idea across to the public. Now, if as a by-product the technology allows you to experiment with the idea and do different things with it, that's another ball game. So, for me, the creative process is down to chemical reaction between people, as well as that sort of instant reaction when my hands are on a keyboard, I hear a chord and that sets me off. I'm not a purist. I do take my technology and make it happen for me, but then that's it. I don't submit myself to the studio and then allow the studio to dictate how the material should develop.

"I think melody is still around but it's on a back burner at the moment, because the commercial market doesn't really want melody, it wants rhythm. At the same time there is this thing about perfection, and technology has pushed us into making perfection a sort of religious cult. I'm most probably as guilty of this as other people, and it's got to a point now where you deliberately try to put the rough edges in and keep them in. . . . Not that they are necessarily there to start with! There again, I suppose there are some people who don't mind if things aren't perfect, but I just like things to sound the way that I want them to, and it's only when you're a producer that you can definitely achieve this. When you're a musician, a session player on an album, you're just one of the stages in the overall process. You can try to sneak in something which you like and hope it won't get noticed, or in my case with Soul II Soul you try to tie up as many loose ends as possible before the producer walks in!

"I'm in the fortunate position where I don't always have to rely on technology. You don't need to use technology if you don't want to, provided that you've got the budget. That's the crunch; having the budget to do what you want. I've always wanted to use a real drummer, a real bass player, real strings, and so on, but they're horrendously expensive to hire in and so you have to wait until the budget is there. Then, if you are in that situation, you *can* treat technology with a certain amount of disdain because you don't have to use it. You can wake up in the morning and say, 'Well, I don't think I'm going to use my computer today,' whereas, if you've got a home studio, you're the only musician and you want to make some nice music, you have to use technology, and you have to buy very, very wisely. So, the less money you have to spend, the more important the technology is to you, and I think that is definitely the equation.

"Working on James Brown's *Universal James* album was really like a dream. He's always been a hero for Jazzie, and when Mr. Brown—because that's what we called him; even all of his entourage call him Mr. Brown—read some complimentary things which Jazzie had said about him in a book, he contacted Jazzie and said that he would like to work with him. Due to other commitments we had to pass on that, but when the next album came around Mr. Brown contacted Jazzie again and asked if we would like to write and produce a couple of tracks for it. 'Yes,' went back the answer, and so then Jazzie and I looked through our collection of ideas to see if anything would be suitable, and, sure enough, there were two.

"You see, back in February of '91, soon after I had begun working with Soul II Soul, I spent a month at Jazzie's house knocking out loads and loads of thirty-second ideas with him. Basically, Jazzie would play me something, I would sample up a bar or two, and this would provide us with some basic ideas as to a bass line and chords which I would then lay down. Jazzie would express his thoughts on this and I would flesh these thoughts out. So that's how we first collaborated on the writing, and we ended up with literally hundreds of ideas, and amazingly we still refer to them now.

"Anyway, what we initially did was to consciously go back to the early seventies, listening to some of the tracks with the idea of doing modern versions of them. So Jazzie just gave me a load of records and I listened to maybe two songs, but already I knew that here was a chance for me to not so much re-create what James Brown had been doing but rather to come up with something that I myself wanted. It could always be toned down if it wasn't accepted, but I really wanted to do something of my own.

"So, as I mentioned, we then went back to a couple of our ideas from '91, which were really nothing more than just a groove, and began to build on them. Haitch [of Soul II Soul] wrote the lyrics, and we got in Bazil Meade from the London Community Gospel Choir to voice those lyrics in a James Brown voice, which he did amazingly well. We then sent what we had done over to James Brown, and they were accepted, and his people asked for one more. Then they came back and asked for another one and then they came back and asked for another two, and so in the end Jazzie, Haitch, and myself cowrote six songs for the James Brown album. And it really was like a dream, because after the first two songs it was a case of, 'Oh, look, he's asked for another song,' 'Okay,' and a couple of hours later there it was.

"We already had an idea of how his voice sounded, we knew what Soul II Soul were about, and we felt that we wanted this one to be a bit more up-tempo than the last ones. The way I often tend to work is to start with a drum sample, and then chords and then bass, so I did this and that then triggered something off in Jazzie's mind to go and look for some totally left-field ideas on the records which we could incorporate, and this in turn triggered Haitch to come up with a theme. The first brass lines that came into my head were all accepted, and it turned out in the end that I had to score them for a brass section. So, from the germ of an idea, layers and layers of other things were added on until it became almost larger than life, and the song was able to walk out of the door on its own.

"Everything was done here [at Soul II Soul] but the vocals were recorded at Bobby Brown's studio in Atlanta and at A&M in L.A. Jazzie, [engineer] Eugene Ellis, and I flew to Atlanta and recorded Mr. Brown, and then flew back to London and mixed the first three tracks here. For the next batch of three songs we then flew off to L.A. to record him. He walked into the room with his lyrics—having practiced to the demos we'd sent him—went behind the microphone, gave us about five versions of each song, and left. And that was it. He was incredibly nice, and because we were going to him with humility, as fans and as genuine disciples, he could really appreciate that, and so he was able to give us a few pearls of wisdom from his experience.

"He didn't touch the music and hardly touched the lyrics. He just put in a few different words that he thought suited him better, and then he added all of the ad-libs that make him great. However, I really got the impression that, because he had complimented us by asking to do our songs, we were his guests in a way and so he was being very, very nice to us, whereas I imagine that if we had been doing his songs it would have been a different ball game. The man's tough, he's a bed of nails, you can see that.

"Very soon after the recording sessions we were asked to support him on the German leg of his tour, which we did in December of '92, and that was great. He's an amazing guy, he looks great for his age, and every night he performed for two hours onstage. I remember in Frankfurt he walked off stage, saw me, called me over, we walked arm in arm to his dressing room followed by the crowd of people in his retinue, the stage personnel and the German press, and he immediately started talking about the mix that we'd just done for the first single. He said that he wasn't going to go with the version that we'd done featuring real brass, but he was going to go with my original synthesizer brass, because he felt that it somehow suited the song better. He said that that was what I had originally intended and the real brass dragged it down a bit. This was after two hours onstage and we hadn't discussed it for six months, and there he was talking to the right man—me—about the right thing. Astonishing guy, but then, I suppose you don't expect anything else.

"I don't think you can successfully pass off synthesized piano, brass, or strings as the real thing, although it depends on how much they are being used. I mean, you can do brass stabs which sound just like the real thing, but you see, going back to what we were saying before, if I wanted real strings I would bloody use real strings.

We've had a session of ten string players in this room, and what a beautiful, beautiful session that was. We'd written something out on the synthesizer using the sampler, we had our arranger in, and then the musicians came in and played and it was *fantastic*. You just can't get away from that real sound. So, provided that you are able to choose between the real thing and the technology thing, it doesn't matter that technology hasn't got it right, because you can ring your fixer and get brass and string players in. Therefore, from the purist's point of view, it doesn't matter, and it's very useful that you've got different sounds. If, on the other hand, one accepts that technology is trying to get it right, then we're on the way but we're not there yet.

So, if an artist uses a synthesizer trying to make it sound like real strings and people can hear that it's not real strings, then he's a fool. You should only use the technology if you're ready to accept that it's another sound in its own right. That's the only way to treat synthesizers, although I don't think everyone does. Take your typical MOR-type artist—easy-listening stuff—who has record company money behind him and who can therefore use the London Symphony Orchestra if necessary, yet on his latest record you can hear that they've just gone out and got a synthesizer and sampler. That really jars. You know, you've got this so-called beautiful melody and well-modulated tones of the singer, and then you've got this nasty synthesized background which really is so crass.

"It's not so bad in the U.K. because, like it or not, we do come up with fairly good quality productions here. But you listen to some of the European productions and it's an embarrassment! The buying public there don't know jack shit about production and music. They are far less critical about music than the British. The British actually have a very critical ear, and if you talk to any performing artist, classical or pop, they'll always prefer working in Britain—or the States—to anywhere else in the world.

"Now, when I did the brass parts for the James Brown record, okay, I layered two brass sounds which I thought would sound as realistic as possible, but I never intended to pull the wool over anybody's ears. Actually, they weren't even intended to be heard by anyone, because they were intended as the guide for the real brass, and for some of the songs we did do that. But for a couple of the songs we left the original brass parts as they were, simply because the feel was right and they sounded great for that particular production. They sounded like fucking shit compared with the real stuff, but the sound was absolutely right for that production. Now, when you're talking about commercial music you can do that sort of thing, but there's certain other music where that really, really jars and you do need to have the real stuff.

"Certain things can never be synthesized, can never be sampled properly; sax is incredibly difficult to do, guitars, solo violins. I'm certainly as guilty as anyone else of replacing people's jobs—we can do sessions now without seeing another musician—but that's because we're working in a certain field where you can get away with Moog synth sounds and you can get away with pad sounds on the sampler and so on. Yet, there are always certain instances where you need the real players, not just because they've got the real sound but also, of course, for their input, for their soul, for their beauty.

"In everything I do as a musician I always try to put myself in that position where I will get a lump in my throat. I can't deny it. I can be as cynical as I like, but there are things in almost every song which I want to be there, and that's even more so when you're a producer. I have a physical thing too: when I play a certain combination, when something is so right, I get a cracking sound in my right ear. Now, this may well be down to me tensing myself, but this only happens when I have a certain feeling, and so if I hear that cracking sound I know that I've hit it.

"An example of that is the James Brown track 'Moments,' which is an incredibly long song with lyrics by Haitch. It's basically a sermon, and in the background there's just some percussion, a pad, and then there's a brass line that comes in which we had doubled in L.A. with some real players. Now, it doesn't come in as often as I originally wrote it, but it's the chemical reaction between this very intense talking and this driving pad—because I really love pads—and then the brass comes in towards the end, and it's really almost everything that I've ever wanted to do in a few notes.

"There again, on the Soul II Soul *Just Right* album, right at the end of 'Intelligence,' over the fade, a pad comes in, and once again it gets me every time. Inside of me I don't know any more than you do as to why a certain song has come out this way, but it has and I'm just glad that it's me doing it and not some other guy!"

obieo'brien

■

As the all-round audio man to Jon Bon Jovi, Obie produces, engineers, and even masters for him, in addition to simply being on the spot as a consultant to other producers and engineers whenever necessary. A drummer before becoming an assistant engineer during the late seventies, Obie worked on a lot of blue-grass, country, and gospel records in the southern United States. Co-owning a studio during the next decade, he then came into contact with acts such as Nils Lofgren, Ozzy Os-bourne, Skid Row, Cinderella, Lita Ford, and Bon Jovi, and it was when the facility closed down in 1988 that Jon came to the rescue.

"Any time Bon Jovi have done a live TV show or radio broadcast I've flown to wherever they are and done the job. I mean, I've been around the world a few times with them. There again, aside from working with them, Jon is one of the closest friends I've ever had. Primarily I'm his friend, and then after that I'm the guy who works with him—if I had to choose between the friendship or the work I would take the friendship, because very few people are lucky enough to have a friend like him.

"This is a working relationship that I will never have with anyone else and I know it. First of all, I'm never going to work with anybody who's as talented and smart as Jon, and while that's a funny thing to say, it's not intended to put down anyone else who I've ever worked with. It's just that this guy knows all of the nuances of the business of making music, and he's always four steps ahead of everyone else. That, in turn, makes me better.

"On his solo record, *Destination Anywhere,* I engineered about half of the tracks and I then mixed the entire album, in addition to producing, scoring, and mixing the accompanying forty-five-minute TV movie. We demo'd about twenty songs at Sanctuary Studios, which is in the basement of Jon's home in New Jersey. For the most part, he locks himself away when he's writing a song, and he'll then emerge to tape the number with just voice and guitar. He writes out his chord charts and lyrics for himself, keeping one big book with all of his ideas in there, and while he's writing he'll envisage the other parts and make notes of them. Then, when it's time to do demos, he'll bring in a couple of guitar players, bass, drums, and keys, and we'll cut live, which I really love.

"As a matter of fact, on *Destination Anywhere* a lot of the bonus tracks and B sides are recordings from the demo sessions that didn't make the album and which I just pulled out of the vault. To me those tracks always end up having so much character, because there are no overdubs on them, and the vocals haven't been done three times in order to get the perfect take. They can also be really sparse—one guitar, one cheap keyboard pad—because at that stage we're not concerned with getting all of these great sounds. At the same time, I also leave in all of the stuff where he's saying things like, 'Go to the "B" section now,' and I think the fans really like that, because it shows you the process. You know, here's what it started out as, and here's what his vision ended up being.

"With Jon's compositions the actual structure of the song doesn't change that much. He gets in these producers who have a great overview of the songs, and then he has these terrific players who come up with all of these different parts and ideas. That makes sense to me, because I've never understood why you would hire a great guy and then tell him exactly what to do. You should use his brain, and then if it comes out great take all of the credit for it, and if it comes out rotten blame it on everyone else!

"Jon's written so many hit songs. He writes a song and he knows how it should be put together. He knows the basic mood of it. He knows how to move the parts around. He's just got that instinctive talent, and that's the pleasure of working with an artist who's been around. It isn't like pulling teeth when you get to the production stage. Instead, it's a case of having a very good foundation and then putting all of the little bits together.

"We recorded at a few different studios. Dave Stewart produced the tracks that I engineered, and Stephen Lironi produced the others with Niven Garland engineering. Still, the album was so eclectic that I didn't need to go for sonic parity. I mean, it wasn't like a Bon Jovi band album, where all of the songs sort of have to fit together and I have to concern myself with the guitars sounding the same, as well as the overall sound. Every song was so different, and you therefore really hear that difference.

"Much more time and effort was spent on microphone placement than cranking the knobs to try and get the sound that we'd want. That would be down to trying a different guitar, trying a different amp, trying different microphones and microphone positions, and that's another reason why I think the record sounds cool. It wasn't just a case of 'Oh, shit, I don't like this. Turn the knob, turn the knob, turn the knob. . . . Give me the pliers so I can turn it a little bit more!' We would always try different things, and that was a great thing about both producers and Jon. They'd let you take the time to dick around. A lot of guys aren't like that. You say, 'I don't like the sound,' and they go, 'Well, come on . . .' Jon, however, is the ultimate pro.

"Aside from when he sang live along with the band, he would usually attempt two or three complete vocal passes for each song. I would then use as much of a complete pass as I possibly could and punch in the odd line. It would take maybe half an hour to get what we wanted, and a large part of that was because Jon knows how to work a microphone. It may sound funny to say that, because you normally think of it more in a live context, but in the studio Jon knows which line he's going to convey a certain feeling with, and he knows how to get intimate with the mike at that point. He also knows when to turn his head and do the throwaway line. It's really easy doing vocals with the guy. He knows the routine, he knows his job, and it's easy to get spoiled working with him.

"When we mixed we made a conscious decision to let the songs themselves set the mood. The music called the shots, and it was kinda weird. You'd just start putting the faders up and the thing would take on a life of its own. The style, the song, and the players pretty much dictated the way that the final mix would sound. It was very easy to mix this record. It was *really* easy! After all, just having good players makes it easy for a start. People call me up and say, 'I love the drum sound,' and I tell them, 'I didn't do anything! Kenny Aranoff did it!' His playing, his technique, his fills, and his creativity make the drums sound great.

"I like to enjoy myself when I'm mixing. There will be a big-screen TV linked to a VCR that is playing my favorite movies, and this will be hooked up to the automatic talkback system of the console so that, whenever I rewind or stop the multitrack tape, the audio for the movie will come over the speakers. That keeps me in a really great mood, because you're like a rat most of the time, in a room without any natural sunlight, and that wears on you.

"When Stephen Lironi and I were mixing here in New York I had the studio guys put up black lights and Jimi Hendrix posters, and I got one of those psychedelic oil projectors. Then, for a couple of the songs—like the track 'Naked'—I hired two go-go dancers to do the Frug and the Hully-Gully. For four hours, every time I started the tape these girls would be doing the Frug! My wife is a wigmaker, and so I had her make up some sixties pageboy-style wigs for Stephen Lironi and me to wear in the control room along with blue sunglasses, while the oil lamp was projecting all of these shapes and the two girls were doing the Frug! We had a great time! It's got to be fun.

"Like when we were recording the album, we'd be in there fifteen hours a day, and Jon, who was writing, recording, and doing everything, would be exasperated. Well, I'd wait until he was ready to blow his top, and then I'd ask, 'Can I have a pony?' That became sort of a running joke, and every time he'd tell me to go screw myself. Then, when I was at Trevor Horn's Sarm [West] studio in London to do the first mix of the Dave Stewart stuff, I sent Jon the mix of 'It's Just Me.' I didn't hear back from him, but the next day when I came into work the woman downstairs called to say 'We've got a package for you. Can you come down?' So I did, and there was a friggin' pony standing in the lobby of Sarm! Jon and his wife had rented it for me! That's how I knew he loved the mix.

"I really like doing the solo stuff, because you can branch out so much more. You can go wherever you want to go. You know, Bon Jovi have a particular sound that people expect, whereas when Jon does something solo he doesn't have to conform to that. There again, I also love the band setup. My favorite bands have always been those with the two main guys: Lennon and McCartney, Mick and Keith, Joe Perry and Steven Tyler. Well, Jon and Ritchie [Sambora] also have that magic thing happening.

"When you have a band situation it is a meeting of the minds. With any one song each individual member will have his own vision of it. I mean, Jon or Ritchie will write the song, but everybody hears it slightly differently, and then you've got the producer's view on top of that. The producer becomes more of a referee in that situation, whereas when you're only working with Jon you've just got to get his vision. You're a little bit closer to the creative process, and you don't have to take four ideas and try to figure out the best one to use.

"I went out on the last Bon Jovi tour, and I recorded and mixed the video of the band's performance at Wembley Stadium in London. Now, let me tell you; I've heard these songs a million times, but I still found myself dancing around the truck to 'Living on a Prayer'! After all, what rock 'n' roll bands are left? This whole alternative scene has come along, with the angst and everybody hating their life because they grew up in an upper-middle-class family with two cars and colored televisions everywhere. . . . I always say to Jon, 'Don't ever let this band die. There aren't many guys carrying the torch!' With Bon Jovi there's no pretentious bullshit. They're a rock 'n' roll band playing their nuts off. I love that and I don't want to see that end. I'm a fan!"

dave reitzas

■

In his thirties, Dave already has a list of engineering and mixing credits that others twice his age would easily trade their faders for: Michael Jackson, Whitney Houston, Barbra Streisand, Frank Sinatra, Rod Stewart, Linda Ronstadt, Quincy Jones, Toni Braxton, Michael Bolton, Cher, Celine Dion, Gloria Estefan, Tony Bennett, Aretha Franklin, Vanessa Williams, Natalie Cole . . . All in all, a fair haul for someone who, although a professional for little more than a decade, is reaping the rewards of tens of thousands of hours spent in the studios, not to mention several years of invaluable training alongside musician-composer-producer David Foster. Since 1995 Dave Reitzas has worked independently, and the recording of three songs for Madonna's *Something to Remember* album led to his assignment to cut and mix most of the vocals for the *Evita* record.

"A lot of people consider the manipulation of vocals to be my specialty. Nobody really needs to know what goes into the production of a vocal. We all have our techniques of punching in and compiling and so on, but in my work with David Foster we've taken these to the highest level possible while keeping in mind that the end result should have that one-take feeling. So, even though the artists are aware of it, it's kind of like our little secret.

"I get to move things by milliseconds, borrowing from other places, using a syllable here and there. Basically, I save the artists from having to fix something, because if it exists somewhere else then they don't have to redo it. For example, after singing the first and second choruses of a song, somebody may suggest that the vocalist then doubles them. Well, I'll grab the first chorus and put it up against the second chorus, and I'll usually find that about 80 percent of it is already close enough to be a double. The other lines can be fixed. So, why struggle to try and match a vocal when they've already given me enough to work with?

"Even though they sometimes like to focus on a certain section, I'll generally have artists sing a song six times from top to bottom, and while they're singing I'll be taking notes. Then, when they've finished, they'll come into the control room, and, although there may be some instances of weakness in the performance, we'll work from the notes to produce a pretty good vocal performance. You know, after a take the artist will be saying, 'Oh, I screwed up that line and I've got to do it again,' and I'll say, 'But you did a great version of that line on track two!' Singers are not necessarily as keen to remember where the good lines are, but if you know what you have on tape then you can usually make something work. . . . I usually have more to work with than most people even realize.

"I figure that if you're going to use one line from another take then you can certainly use one word, and if you're going to use one word then you can certainly use one syllable, and if you're going to use one syllable then you can certainly use an *s*, and if you can use an *s* then you can certainly use a fraction of the *t* sound. . . . So, it's like how small can you go in order to give it that extra 5 percent? It isn't cheating. These are wonderful singers who don't even need any help.

"The *Evita* project amounted to one hour and fifty minutes of music and twenty-five different vocal contributions by Madonna. Being that the movie has no spoken dialogue, that means her voice can be heard for about 75 percent of the time. It's just so unusual, working on a full-length motion picture which consists purely of singing all the way through. We recorded everything first, but then, when they shot the film, our work was constantly being updated. At times it could be manic, but it also gave rise to many memorable challenges.

"The original scores were reworked to make them more contemporary. At the point when I came onto the project back in October of '95 the scripting had all been done and so we knew which songs we had to work with. These were based upon the earlier recordings, and so it was just a matter of rearranging them. David Caddick, Nigel Wright, and David Cullen did most of that.

"The entire music sound track was recorded at three studios in London. Madonna cut most of her vocals in Studio 2 at Whitfield Street, and she loved doing them there. It just had a great vibe to it. She recorded her parts in a booth, and these went pretty much according to plan until she had to record the big deathbed scene. You see, the most difficult thing about this project was that the film was not shot until the music was completed. They were shooting to whatever had been sung, and so the vocal performances always had to take the visual aspects into account.

"Well, when Madonna attempted to sing 'The Lament,' where her character, Eva Perón, is dying, she just couldn't get into the part and her performance suffered. I soon figured that the fact that she was standing up and wearing headphones probably had something to do with it—I mean, I doubt if Eva Perón was standing and wearing headphones on her deathbed—so after everybody left I had the assistants bring in two big couches. We put them together, put blankets down, and I then had the techs bring in oscilloscopes as well as a plastic bag which was hooked up as if it was a morphine drip. Next to the 'bed' we had a Neumann U47 [microphone], and so now the atmosphere was better suited to getting the right performance. By singing lying down Madonna sounded perfect for that scene. That's what you hear on the album, whereas in the movie they used her live on-set performance. It would have been too difficult to lip-sync to an emotional scene like that.

"About a month was spent recording all of the vocals. Most of the large choir performances took place in the huge room at CTS Studios, consisting of a hundred people singing together on the first day followed by several different-sized groups. When you're dealing with a hundred session performers you've got to go by your gut instincts to judge what the room is going to be like, and then use your knowledge as to which microphones would be best for the sounds that you wish to capture. Obviously, before the session I'll test the individual mikes to make sure that they're all up to caliber, but then it's just a case of balancing as quickly as possible. When I'm working with David Foster and we're doing an artist vocal, I've got about three quarters of the first line in which to get the sound right, because you have to be prepared for that spontaneous first vocal performance. So, that's just down to experience and gut instinct.

"We did a little bit of everything at every studio. Even up to a week before the end of mixing there were still orchestral parts being overdubbed, and a lot of the work last year was being taken care of by engineers such as Robin Sellars while I was working on vocals with Madonna.

"When I worked on the album mix I started in one room at

Larabee North in Los Angeles. Then I found that I needed two to keep up with the workload, so I would start one mix, go to the other room to kick off another for a different song, and then just travel between the two. At some points I was even working on a big mix in one room and three little mixes in the other, splitting the console into thirds, and I have to say that it certainly was a lesson in focusing.

"There were moments when it was slightly overwhelming, but, due to deadlines, it had to be done. Most of the logistical problems had to do with timing everything so that, when Madonna came in to listen, I could play her four things rather than one and have her return or wait around. There again, sometimes I would also be in there and almost forget which room I was in. I would say to myself, 'I thought I had an effect on the bass,' and then I would realize that was in the other room! Fortunately, however, Larabee was the perfect place to do that because the equipment is identical in each room. I'm pretty good at visualizing what's going to be required, and so it worked out fine. The mission was accomplished!"

arthur**baker**

■

From Afrika Bambaataa and Soulsonic Force's 'Planet Rock' to
Freez's 'I.O.U.,' from mainstream remixes of Cyndi Lauper's
'Girls Just Want to Have Fun' to Bruce Springsteen's 'Born in
the U.S.A.,' and from projects with artists such as Bob Dylan
and Hall and Oates to the *Sun City* anti-apartheid album, Arthur
certainly made a name for himself on the New York music scene
of the early-to-mid-1980s. A remixer in the days when techno-
gear was still only used as a means of enhancing a song rather
than as its basic raison d'être, he now feels that modern dance
remixes often make too much use of the equipment that is so
easy to handle. When I spoke with Arthur in 1997 he had recently relaunched his Minimal Records label and was enjoying
a string of big club hits in the U.K.

"Computerized editing and sampling is pretty cool, but I'm still
more into finding a good song and a good groove. All technology
does is give you more control. At the same time it also cuts down
on innovation, because everyone has the same tools now, whereas
years ago if someone had a new piece of equipment it was novel
and people didn't necessarily know about it. Everything was more
secretive and you had to discover for yourself, but now it's just a
case of here are your sample CDs, here's everything handed on
a platter.

"I'm not saying that there aren't people who are making cool,
innovative music, but I don't know if technology really helps the
whole process. It just makes it simpler. Electronic records have
always been enriched by real instruments, because a purely electronic record is, for the most part, boring. I mean, there are definitely exceptions to that rule, but in my case I would always have
live piano, live bass, and live percussion even if we were using
drum machines. You see, synths can't really replace things such as
live brass or live strings, but real drummers are completely replace-
able. You can put feel into drum programming, and while some
drummers are great players they can be difficult people to work

330

with. I don't know what it is about drummers. I know I'm making a generalization, but especially now, being that they are so insecure with regard to what they have to offer, I'll spend more time working with them than with anyone else!

"You know, things go in cycles. Something that was totally naff five years ago may now be in, and when people get bored and look for something new the things that can seem new are sometimes old. At the moment there's the resurgence of electronic music—or 'electronica'—and I just love it. It's the genre of the day! Nothing ever went away, but it's just a name for white people making electronic dance music. Electronica—white home boys doing their thing!

"Sampling is fine as long as it isn't abused. With black music there has always been a history of cover versions and answer records. It's like when a jazz musician would take an old melody, incorporate it into a new song, and do quotes. Well, when sampling started it was more like that, but now it's pretty much a case of stealing. I mean, I've had so many people sample my stuff—anything out of Miami has usually sampled the Soulsonic Force record—and the thing that I find bad about it is that a lot of people are just sampling and not learning their craft as musicians. That's the problem with hip-hop; hip-hop's killed the black band. Before hip-hop there were hundreds of black bands, signed and having hit records, whereas now in terms of funk bands there are none. I can go to my collection and pull out a hundred records by bands that had hits and were well-known, but now that whole scene is dead really. It's been replaced by people sampling records, and that means the roots are going to be lost.

"After all, how many times can you loop 'The Message' or loop James Brown? A perfect example is that Puffy Combes record; it's just 'The Message,' and he can't even fucking rap! He's shit, y'know! He's shit, he can't rap, he's just stolen 'The Message,' there's not even any credit on it for 'The Message,' and it's absolute crap! Someone did 'The Message' last year and now they're sampling it again, so the time cycles are getting shorter and shorter. Eighth-generation samples! It's absolutely killing music. There are no black bands at all, and they're just going to run out of samples. Maybe in five years someone will say, 'Hey, let's get a really great black band together, use the hip-hop element, and we'll clean up,' but right now it's just so easy for someone to go in with a turntable, a sampler and rapper, and make a ton of money.

"The whole thing is that it's not killing white bands. It's not killing rock bands. There are more rock bands than ever. In the sixties there used to be all of these vocal groups, and then the black bands came along in the seventies and killed off those vocal groups. Now, with the rappers, we're kind of back to the vocal groups again and no bands.

"I'm not going to say that there's no talent in some of the people who use samples to create. It's obviously a different type of talent, but it's a talent for making money, that's for damned sure! It's a talent for knowing what people want. The guys who make rap records are really in touch with what's going on. They know what people are going to like, what samples they're still into, and if you really know your market then it's not brain surgery to do that. Like when I made 'Planet Rock,' I knew my market back then. I knew that people were playing [Kraftwerk's] 'Trans-Europe Express' in the park, and I knew that 'Numbers' was a big record, so we decided to combine the two of them and come up with something new. Combining different elements to come up with something new is great, but if you just do the same old shit then it's just the same old shit and you don't get any innovation. Most of the stuff now is just pretty safe and standard.

"I hate gangsta rap. I mean, what do these people gain by promoting violence? Biggie Small dies and we hear, 'Oh, he was this, he was that,' and everyone's giving him accolades, but the guy was a crack dealer and a gangster who beat up people with baseball bats. Now it's supposed to be society's fault, but the fact is that the guy made all of this money and he wasn't smart enough to just remove himself from that whole scene.

"Personally, I love the idea of doing A&R, even though when it's your own label it's also your own money that you're dealing with. The main thing that I'm looking for when I'm considering an artist is the material. You see, I've passed on working with bands because I didn't like the material—I passed on doing the first Happy Mondays record because I just thought the songs were shit. Sitting in the studio listening to something for three months and not liking the song . . . it's not worth the effort.

"For the most part I go to clubs and hear sounds and hear

grooves that I like, and if I can find out what the record is I'll go out and buy it. I also buy records to just try to stay in touch with what's going on, but nothing's really blown me away. Unfortunately, the deejays are more apt to play the dubs nowadays, and so you don't hear the songs anymore, which is totally different from when I started. When people like Larry Levine and François were deejaying, the song was of major importance and there really weren't that many dubs. People would relate to the lyrics and get off on them, whereas now you can go to a club and never hear a song. It's an endless beat and it's really boring.

"I've never done a remix where I haven't at least attempted to maintain the actual song. Back when I started remixing that's what the job was, but now record companies don't care if there's, like, one little yelp remaining, as long as it's a hit. So now, when I'm doing an album, it's a case of really trying to strike a balance between keeping the integrity and also having some mixes that the knuckleheads will play in the clubs."

trina**shoemaker**

■

Female engineers aren't too numerous in the recording industry, and neither, for that matter, are women producers, so it was a neat break with tradition when Trina Shoemaker and Sheryl Crow fulfilled these respective roles for the latter's eponymously titled album, released in 1996. Following on from her auspicious debut with *Tuesday Night Music Club*, the *Sheryl Crow* album confirmed the artist as the creator of her own success— a point that some had previously disputed—yet at one time it had looked as if the record might never see the light of day. Crow had opted to record in New Orleans as a means of avoiding the distractions of everyday life in her adopted hometown of Los Angeles, but just one day into the sessions she'd had a blowout with producer-engineer Bill Botrell, and Botrell had walked. . . .

"I'd stopped by the studio to pick up some piece of gear that I needed and there was a bit of a heavy scene. Sheryl was introduced to me and told that I was a local engineer who knows the room and could therefore help her out. I could have been anybody at that point, but Sheryl just needed someone to step in and say, 'Hey, even though no one quite knows what happened yesterday, and you've been left feeling angry and upset, you still make records. I make records. Let's try to do that together.' So that's literally what we did, initially on a one-day basis. She said, 'Will you record me? I'll fly in my guitar player tonight.'

"Of course, I agreed, and A&M Records gave Sheryl the green light to produce the record on her own. She has perfect timing, perfect pitch, she can play by ear, and is a musician of the highest order, so who could be better to produce the album? I guess A&M initially had more of a problem with my involvement, being that they'd probably never even heard of me!

"I had spent most of the eighties performing as a musician, serving in record stores, working at record companies, and generally hanging out in studios. I quit working at Capitol Records in 1989 to become a full-time assistant engineer, but, aside from a job at a small sixteen-track studio named Dominion Sound, work wasn't easy to come by in L.A. It was a case of 'Girls don't do this.' You know, 'You've got to be a dude and have a funny hairdo.' Still, I had a mind for this kind of work, and so, even though I was broke and depressed, I went to New Orleans on a romantic notion and got a job at a studio called Ultrasonic . . . as a cleaner. I was grateful just for that, but almost immediately the house engineer, David Farrell, invited me to assist him on a session with the local artist, Gatemouth Brown, and after that I started doing other sessions at a number of places in the area, including Daniel Lanois' Kingsway Studio. I eventually became the chief engineer there, and then in 1994 I went independent.

"Anyway, on that first night with Sheryl it really was a case of 'C'mon, let's just go into the studio, set up a few mikes and see what happens.' She was a little freaked out, and I was definitely freaked out. There was a heavy atmosphere and I didn't want to clean up somebody else's mess, but I sat down and did my job, which was to hit Record. Sheryl didn't know that I was recording. I went through about six reels of tape on that first night. She thought that we were just going to something like DAT, but of course a song happened—which was 'Home'—and she said, 'You know, we need to start rolling tape, because this is turning into a song.' I said, 'Sheryl, we already have that,' and I could see a click in her eye. I think she liked the idea that I was doing what I was supposed to do without bugging her and asking her questions. She suggested that I could come in the next day and do some overdubs. I said, 'Sure,' and then that stretched out into most of the record and the rest of the year—the only tracks that I didn't engineer were 'Redemption Day,' 'Hard to Make a Stand,' 'Superstar,' and 'Ordinary Morning.'

"The studio that we were in at Kingsway is open-plan, so we sometimes set up the four-piece band behind the console, in the 'wood room' next to the console, or in the area behind the control room. Some bands like REM and Pearl Jam have set up in the large room on the other side of the house in order to achieve the isolation that they're more accustomed to, and I will do the same if the artists don't want a record that's real live and captures the beauty of the leakage.

"Anyway, the drum kit for the Sheryl sessions was sometimes

even set up on a small piece of marble flooring directly next to the console, and so, as you can imagine, it was loud! In that kind of situation you wear headphones and you just guess! You see the meter, you think, 'Okay, it's at the tape machine. What does it sound like?' and then you track, you stop, you listen back, and you kind of cross your fingers!

"On Sheryl's record everything kept changing as she was writing in the studio, and I can safely say that every song involved different musicians and was a whole different cup of tea. Much of the material was loop-driven, and so, depending on how the loop was going to sound, the drums, for instance, would either be miked so that they would have a real roomy, boomy sound or we'd build this little foam hut over the whole kit so that it was as dead as we could possibly make it. Sheryl came to the studio with several loops already created, and three or four of these made it onto the record.

"Her whole notion was superlive yet superdead, superfunky yet superpop, while also loop-driven, and at first that dichotomy appeared to be impossible, yet she pulled it off. That's when I thought, 'Wow, she knows what she wants! Just follow her and go there with her.' It was by trying a million things that didn't work that we arrived at this one perfect dichotomy, like 'Maybe Angels,' which sounds completely live but is, in fact, a loop.

"In telling me that she needed a loop, Sheryl said, 'The loop cannot swing, but I want to swing over the top of it.' You try doing that! We'd work on a load of different rhythms and she'd be saying, 'No, the loop is swinging! Can't you hear that?' 'Uh, no.' 'Well, it is, because I can't swing if *it* swings!' So, finally we came up with a loop pattern that had just enough of a swing in it to create the illusion of swing, and which she could also swing the instruments over. It started with Brian MacLeod playing a drum groove and also hitting something metallic to give a ringing sound, which was then mixed into the normal, dry, organic loop which I created. The result doesn't sound as if it swings, but it actually does, and that's what makes that song so groovy.

"Sheryl brought a multitude of toys to this project, including the harmonium and the pump organ and the Mini Moog and the Wurlitzer, and that's where her organic soulfulness emerged. In her heart she's basically a soul fan, yet she also wanted things to sound cool. She did all of her vocals in the control room with me—if the singer will allow it, that's the way I really feel comfortable recording vocals, because then the communication is unbeatable—and she would also often play an instrument at the same time.

"She did that on quite a few of the songs, playing acoustic guitar or Hammond B3 organ while tracking. There again, on 'Home' she sang and played bass right next to me at the console, while Brian was in his drum hut in the performance room and Jeff Trott was literally lounging on the couch near us with his acoustic guitar and a Shure SM57 mike overhead. Sheryl made up the song as she went along, and what was kind of strange was that when we went back and listened to it only about eight of the twenty or so lyric lines contained actual words. The rest were just scat, and so later we had to drop in and try to match up the kind of murmuring that she was doing when she was still writing.

"She could sing so loud that she would immediately blow up the microphone, but she also didn't want to sound really small. So I just devastated her vocals with the 1176 [Urei compressor], and they came out sounding big. . . . There's hardly any EQ on them. They're pretty much raw. Sheryl's also a good doubler of vocals, and a lot of the nice richness of her sound is because of that.

"There were always different guitar players showing up, and so it was often a case of 'Hey, stick the amp over there, wherever it's convenient. Yeah, that's cool. Come on and sit down. Here's the song. . . .' We'd grab a mike, stick it in front of the amp, run back into the control room, and get started without messing with EQs. We'd sometimes have to be real fast because a certain musician would only have an hour. In any case, I rarely spend a lot of time getting sounds. It seems that I often work with artists who are really anxious to just get things going—'Are you rolling?' 'Yeah, I'm there!'

"Our biggest problem was finding a good bass, not a good bass player. For some reason we were plagued with bass problems. None of the instruments sounded good. It would be, like, 'Hey, we've found this $8 billion old gold-plated Fender. I'm sure it'll sound great.' But then, when we'd plug it in, it would sound like crap! It seemed like every person in the world with an expensive bass was cruising by the studio—'Hey, I heard Sheryl Crow needs a bass'—but we just seemed to end up with these dorky basses, none of which sounded good, aside from a few exceptions such as the brand-new Precision which Dan Rothchild showed up with. That sounded great and made its way onto 'If It Makes You Happy.'

"More than twenty-five songs were written and cut for the album, and while all of this was going on Sheryl was also trying to learn how to produce herself. She already knew how to produce for other people, but it's another thing doing it for yourself when the eyes of the world are looking at you. She knew that everybody was pointing at her and saying, 'We want to know what you did on that first record. We want to know if others wrote it for you or if you really were what you were hyped up to be.' She had every intention of proving herself to the world, and as a result there were a lot of roads that we went down that some people would have considered to be huge wastes of time and money. We, on the other hand, regarded it as the means of her finding out what the record should be and how she could make it great.

"For example, during the first few days of recording we worked on a song that never ended up making it onto the album. It was real interesting, it had a vibe, and it was potentially going to be pretty cool. There was this great drum part on it, some cool guitar, Sheryl played this really weird, eclectic bass line and sang some interesting lyrics, and we spent weeks on that song. I'd say, 'The bass is out of tune,' and she'd say, 'Oh, well, we want that exact bass line.' 'Okay, let's play it again.' 'No, I can't play it again. Can you pitch-shift it?' 'Well, Sheryl, it's gonna be really hard to pitch-shift a whole bass line.' 'Yeah, but if I play it again it'll lose the vibe.' 'Okay, then I'll try to pitch-shift it.' So, that took me, like, a hundred years, and then she said, 'That still sounds out of tune,' to which I replied, 'Well, it always is going to be out of tune because it's essentially . . . out of tune!' 'I hate this song!' 'Okay, me, too. Let's move on.'

"A week later that song reappeared, and so we spent a lot of time on material that we both sort of knew was not going to be on her record, but she just wanted to wrestle the mother to the ground anyway. She needed to make the point to herself, if only to find out why the song wouldn't gel in the studio. In that way she was learning, and so I would go there with her even if I perhaps should have said, 'You know what, this is a waste of time. It will not work technically. I cannot pitch-shift an entire bass line.' Basically, we would try everything, and in that way she would know that, when she'd have to say that a song was off the record because she couldn't make it work, we'd left no stone unturned.

"If a bass has intonation problems that is the producer's call. You might cut a brilliant track with it but you can't use it, and in the case of that initial song it was the basis of what everybody was inspired to play to. When we removed that bass the song fell apart, yet it was out of tune and Sheryl couldn't sing over it. So, that was the kind of production call that she learned about. All of the instruments should be checked before the session starts. Often nobody but the producer thinks of that. Everyone just says, 'Hey, let's roll! Here we go!' but next time around she'll know better."

glen**ballard**

■

Glen is nothing if not versatile. As a songwriter, producer, musician, and engineer, he has found success at the top of the pop, alternative, R&B, adult contemporary, jazz, and country charts. He has worked with artists such as Michael Jackson, Quincy Jones, Van Halen, Aretha Franklin, Aerosmith, Natalie Cole, George Strait, and Barbra Streisand, and in the process amassed 100 million record sales and several Grammy Awards. Three of these were for his work as the producer and co-composer on Alanis Morissette's multiplatinum album, *Jagged Little Pill*, which, together with the follow-up, *Supposed Former Infatuation Junkie*, Glen and I spoke about in the middle of a hectic schedule.

"There are fewer restrictions working with a new artist and it's more liberating. What I've done best, and what I continue to do best, is really to recognize talent at an early stage and give it an opportunity to blossom. I take pride in doing that and I really enjoy it, because in every case I think that I learn as much from new artists as they do from me.

"Alanis is very intelligent, very curious intellectually, and we were just compatible with each other right from the downbeat. I hadn't heard the record that she'd done in Canada when she was much younger—I didn't want to hear it, and she didn't really want me to hear it. I don't think it reflected what she wanted to be as an artist. She knew that I'd produced a lot of hit records but she wasn't there because of that. I think she was just looking for someone who she could collaborate with on a meaningful level, so we didn't really spend any time listening to each other's songs. We just had a cup of tea and went straight to work.

"I immediately had a sense from her that she was willing to go where we felt we should go and not where we thought we should go. I think I brought that out of her and she brought it out of me, too, and so we kind of dived in the deep end and started writing just for the pure joy of it. I picked up a guitar, and, when

340

the smoke had cleared, we'd written a song that I thought was very special. Just hearing her voice I thought, 'Oh, my god, she's an incredible singer!' That first song never made it onto the album, but to me it was a preview in terms of her potential and what we could accomplish together. It was incredible. We would walk into the studio with nothing planned. She had a notebook full of poetry and ideas, and I always had bits and pieces of music lying around, but it was never a case of 'Okay, here's the lyric' or 'Here's some music.' It was always created on the spot, and I'm still amazed by how quickly we did it.

"We'd write a song and record it on the same night. Her lead vocal would be done last, it would require one or two takes, and without exception those were the vocals that made it onto the album. She never touched them again, and that still blows my mind. I mean, the ink wasn't even dry on the page! She'd be singing through the melody all day long as we were writing, but the lyrics wouldn't be complete until later in the day or maybe after dinner, and then she'd go out and have total command of this material. It was quite remarkable. We never changed anything, and she wouldn't even let me change any of my parts. It was like, 'This is the moment' coming right off of my guitar, right out of her mouth. I've worked with a lot of talented people, but I've never worked that quickly before.

"In fact, on 'You Oughta Know' I didn't have the vocal level right and I sort of distorted it when I was getting it down on tape, but the performance was so good that we thought we'd just leave it that way with a couple of hot spots. I was overdriving the preamp a little bit, but, being that the take was so good, I only had one pass at it. Afterwards, people were asking me, 'How did you get that effect?' and I had to tell them that it was unintentional distortion. I couldn't do it again if I tried!

"It wasn't really until we'd been working together for about two months and produced quite a few songs that Alanis and I acknowledged we were actually making a record destined for commercial release. We had just been writing, recording, and having a good time with the music. I don't think we ever went over twenty-four-track on anything, and in some cases twelve or thirteen tracks were enough, because it was real simple. I played my guitar parts in one take, usually to a drum machine, and I'd have an idea in my head as to how the track should turn out. Then we'd layer it, one thing at a time, and within a couple of hours we would have a track that she could sing to. In large measure that is how the album was done.

"When it comes to songwriting I don't have a set template. For me it often depends on what makes my cowriter comfortable. I mean, I can write in any way that it needs to be done; starting with the lyrics, starting with the music, writing a track and having someone else write the lyrics, having someone else write the track for me to then write the lyrics—I've done it almost every way imaginable.

"Many times when I'm writing with someone we're the only two people around, so it falls to me to record a lot of what we do and then that quite often ends up being on the finished album. I certainly understand the process and I'm more or less qualified to do it, and as a result I sometimes find myself playing, programming, writing, engineering, and producing all at once. Because I understand equipment I'm able to do all that, but I have to say that I do prefer having an engineer there, and that's always the case when we're no longer involved with the writing process.

"Alanis recorded her vocal overdubs at my studio, and the most demanding song in that regard was 'All I Really Want,' which required sixteen tracks of backing vocals. She also changed a verse on 'Ironic,' and so she had to re-sing that, and she sang 'Mary Jane' a second time just because she was unhappy with her original performance. However, all told, including original performances, she never sang any song more than three times.

"That's also how it was for the second record, which we certainly made very quickly. We spent twenty-five days together writing twenty-five songs, and a lot of the recording was done during that time, too. Then we spent two weeks with her band in the studio and another two weeks finishing it. So we made it in under two months. I didn't want to get too intellectual about it, because what was special about what we had done on the first album was the fact that we were kind of channeling this wonderful energy. We weren't trying to be trendy, we weren't trying to really do anything other than what we do, and so I certainly didn't want to spend a year and a half in the studio working on the follow-up, going over ten or twelve songs, dotting every *i* and crossing every *t* . . . although I've made records that way, too. To me, the pure power of Alanis singing from her heart and from her soul has always got to be the most important element. I've got to make sure that I'm providing these complex lyrics and these complex emotions with the right support.

"This voice and these words are just stunning, so that sort of makes it easy for me to see what should be at the center of it all. I mean, when I hear her singing it sort of solves a lot of problems. On the first record I always felt that it was important to have her vocal out front and intelligible, because the lyrics were great and she articulates wonderfully. One reason why it reached a lot of people was because they could actually understand what she was saying.

"The only difference on the second album was that from a lyrical standpoint she was exploring some different issues and different structures, and this was something that she had been thinking about for the past couple of years. The music therefore conforms to a lyrical excursion that she's taken which is much less structured, with a lot of words. In a few cases she had somewhat complete lyrics, but in most cases she just had journals of ideas—poems, fragments, observations—and out of that wealth of material she sort of formed the words, so they completely shaped the music, even more than on the first record. She'd hear some music that she liked, she'd sing something that she liked, she'd have a chord that she liked, a sequence of notes, whatever, and once she found something that she felt good about she'd go into a trance and was really able to write lyrics on the spot. A lot of them were based on ideas that she'd been exploring, but at that point it was also really a kind of channeling and a case of her getting lost in the music.

"For my part, I came in cold on the project. You know, I'm always trying to grow as a musician, I'm always listening to all kinds of music from all over the world and trying to get better, and some of those influences are probably reflected in what I was able to bring to the record to whatever degree. However, it was mostly about what she wanted to do lyrically and me trying to serve that, because I think she is all about what she has to say. My first job as a writer with her is to serve that interest, and as a producer it's to make it all kind of fit together.

"Clearly, for the follow-up there is an expectation out there among millions of people who like her music, but I have to say that Alanis was true to her artistic inspiration, and she first really wanted to say something and not worry about that expectation, especially the commercial expectation. You know, could we sell 28 million records? I think we both knew the answer was no, and if that had been the goal then we would have approached this whole thing differently. However, it wasn't her goal and it really wasn't my goal. She had made a startling kind of statement on her first record that really did define her as an artist in a certain way, but it would not be appropriate for me to keep her right there and say, 'Okay, let's do something that is very similar to *Jagged Little Pill* so that we can sell 28 million records.'

"That would have been the last thing that she would have responded to. She was not interested in that. She was really interested in trying to do what she does and to speak what's on her mind, so making this record was not unlike making a record with a new artist. I mean, she didn't want to write 'Ironic' sideways. She's a very strong artist, and she's got a very clear idea of what she does and does not want to do and how she wants to represent herself, and so I really took my cue from her. It was also the case that she coproduced this record with me, and so her approach to it was different from exactly what I would have done had I been doing it on my own. There again, what I would have done without her influence is probably irrelevant. She as an artist wanted to have more of a contribution on the production side because I think she wanted to make sure that the musical expression was in sync with what she wanted to say, and I welcomed that and embraced it. To me it represented growth of an artist, and that's always good."

butch**vig**

■

A key figure on the so-called grunge scene of the nineties, Butch is a producer, engineer, remixer, writer, and musician whose innovative use of studio equipment as part of the instrumental lineup has made waves via bands such as Nirvana and Smashing Pumpkins, as well as the neo-punk techno outfit Garbage, of which he is a member. Butch and his fellow Garbage men, Duke Erikson and Steve Marker, co-own Smart Studios in their hometown of Madison, Wisconsin, and it was there that he spoke to me at the start of 1997.

"I think a large part of Nirvana's appeal was the intense passion that came out of Kurt's singing and his writing. To a certain extent, when you heard the band play live or even their stuff on record, it was almost kind of cathartic, as if there was something trying to get out. There are very few artists who have that kind of sensibility inherent in their nature, and that's part of what made Kurt so amazing and also so much of an enigma at the same time. He didn't know exactly what the hell he was trying to say, but he was definitely trying to get it out.

"He really had an amazing voice, too. He could scream and it would just have this great rasp and tone to it, and yet he could also bring it down really quiet and make it sound so world-weary and exhausted and intimate. It's one of those things that are hard to put your finger on it, but there are not many artists who have that kind of charisma and voice and persona. Kurt, you see, had this brilliant pop sensibility in terms of melodic structure and phrasing, and yet he loved the attitude of punk, and those are the two things that collided and made Nirvana so special.

"I was producing a lot of stuff for Sub Pop when Nirvana came into Smart to ostensibly record their next album for the label. At that time Dave Grohl hadn't joined the band, so they still had the original drummer, and I don't think they were necessarily very happy with the lineup, or at least Kurt wasn't. Still, we recorded six or seven songs and they were going to come back and do some more, but this was right around the time when all of the major labels took an interest in them, and they subsequently jumped from Sub Pop to Geffen. So, really, the stuff that I had recorded with them primarily became demos and they got bootlegged real fast.

"Anyway, when it came time to make the record I think that Geffen wanted a known producer—someone who had more major label credits—but the band held out for me, and so I was lucky. The only track that made it onto *Nevermind* from the original sessions at Smart was 'Polly,' which was a fairly stripped-down acoustic song. Then, after Dave Grohl joined the band, the new stuff was recorded at Sound City in Los Angeles.

"The band and I were cocredited for engineering the album, but actually they did none of it. At the time almost every project that I was involved with had me coproducing and engineering. Being that I had kind of grown up in the punk scene, when a lot of the bands wanted to have a say in everything, I didn't particularly care if I had solo credit for that kind of stuff. In fact, if you look at a lot of the records that I've done since then many of them say that they are coproductions, whatever that means. The band may have a very small amount of input, but I still like to collaborate.

"In the studio, I used a fair amount of compression on Kurt's vocals so that I could control his dynamics, and I also got him to do some double-tracking. I'm a big fan of doubling, particularly on choruses, and he did that quite a bit on the record, and that's part of what the sound is. Andy Wallace, the mix engineer, had a little bit of tight slap echo—almost a double echo—on a couple of the songs, and a little bit of reverb in the mix, but for the most part the vocals were fairly dry. That really was the approach that the band and myself wanted to take. We didn't want to have it too washed out with reverb or echo, and it was the same with the drums and the guitars; we wanted everything to be fairly dry and in your face.

"I actually started getting more and more into recording everything very dry when I worked on *Gish* with Smashing Pumpkins. Everything would be really in your face, and then if you wanted to add reverb or echo later you could. You could put it farther back in the mix, but if we wanted something to be way up front in the mix you could also do that. That's how

I've worked on pretty much all of the records since then. I don't really like to record with a lot of ambience, particularly on vocals or guitars.

"Back in the eighties, Duke, Steve, and I worked on a lot of things together after we'd started our studio, but then I began producing full-time and we were all doing our own projects. Well, eventually I got kind of burned out on doing really long records, and so in '94 Duke, Steve, and I started collaborating on remixes for House of Pain and Nine Inch Nails and U2 and Depeche Mode and bands like that. When we did a remix we would erase all of the tracks except for the vocals and record all new instrumentation, but instead of doing a club mix we would basically write a song. There would be lots of hooks; we would write new guitar hooks and new bass grooves and change the chords, and it was the first time that I was writing and playing again. It was really fun, and it really kind of inspired us, and that was the sensibility for us to start a band.

"We wanted to take that remix sensibility and somehow translate it into all of the possibilities of a band setup. We also thought it would be cool to work with a woman singer, and Steve saw Shirley [Manson] on MTV with her band, Angel Fish. I think they played her video once, and Steve happened to tape it that night and showed it to us. I just fell in love with her voice, because instead of screaming or singing really aggressively she sang the opposite way, really low and understated, and to me it was much more intense than a lot of other singers who scream all of the way through songs. So, we called her up and asked her to come and sing on a couple of songs, not really knowing what was going to happen. We thought that maybe we'd work with different singers or that this just wouldn't work out, and it was a little awkward at first, but we soon realized that there was this chemistry going on and she ended up joining Garbage.

"We made the record with the intention that we were never going to tour, because that would really free us up to record tons of stuff. We ended up having forty-eight tracks of samples and loops, and all sorts of strange processed sound effects and weird guitar overdubs, and then through the mix process we'd add and subtract until we'd get to a point where the song still comes across. However, we then also realized that if we were going to have a successful record we'd have to go out on tour and promote it, and we therefore spent pretty much all of 1996 on the road. We actually went out and did fourteen months of touring and played over two hundred shows in twenty countries, so it was a long, long haul.

"It was kind of daunting. We really had no idea how to use the technology and duplicate some of these songs live. Initially, we thought we'd get some samplers, get a deejay, get a bunch of extra musicians, and somehow keep it simple, and so we found a bass player from Los Angeles called Daniel Shulman who joined the band for touring and is also going to play on the next record. He has a hip-hop background—he's worked with Run DMC and other bands in Los Angeles—and so he helped right away because I think he really glued everything together.

"I mean, we didn't do all that much live playing on the record, and I'm not necessarily a great musician, either, so I was thinking, 'Holy shit! How am I going to go out and play some of these songs?' Anyway, what we ended up doing was getting a pretty massive sampler, and through trial and error I figured out what grooves I was going to play, and then I sampled some of the sounds from the album that I could trigger live, as well as sampled sound effects and loops that I could play along with. At first I tried to just use monitors, cranking them up, but in the end I basically had more of a studio setup, with a headphone mix enabling me to hear very distinctively what I was triggering and what I was playing along with.

"Duke and Steve took all of their guitar pedals as well as their Kurzweil samplers, and they loaded in all of these samples that they had concocted in the studio, while they were also able to trigger some new things and keyboard sounds. Like, Steve did a lot of multiple things—he played guitars as well as having a key pad underneath at the same time.

"As for Shirley, she just sang. We decided that we didn't want to sample vocals or sample stuff extensively from the record like that. We just wanted to go out and have all five of us play as a band. So with Shirley, for instance, at the end of 'Fix Me Now' there are three or four parts all overlapping, but she just decided to sing whatever she thought was the main part. In fact, at some point in the song she sang all of those different parts separately. We just decided that we wanted one mike onstage, and Shirley kind of ran the show.

"We'd started recording our debut album [*Garbage*] in the late summer, early fall of '94, and then we finished it around May of '95. Everything was written in the studio. Basically, the way that we work is that someone will bring in a loop or a sample, and then we might jam for a couple of hours, find one bar that is kind of cool, load that into our samplers, jam on top of that, Shirley will ad-lib, and then we'll take that home, come back, jam on it some more, record some more things, add and subtract. Often, by the time that a song was finished all of the original ideas were gone and the song had somehow mutated into something completely new.

"We try to take the approach of utilizing studio gear almost as instruments. I got bored spending so many years recording really fast, straightforward punk records, and so that is why we didn't want to approach the Garbage record from the angle of a band playing live. Instead it was like, 'We can record forty-seven guitars on this song, mix it down to a stereo sample, then run it backwards, record another twenty guitars, and process them so that they sound like a percussion instrument.' You see, the guitar is still pretty much the rock 'n' roll instrument that I love. Duke and Steve are primarily guitarists, and so, as much as we used samplers and keyboards, there are a lot of things on the Garbage record that originally came from a guitar.

"We just wanted to see what we could do, utilizing the studio and the gear there, to create something that sounded fresh. It's impossible, I think, to do something new in music, but the exciting thing is that you can take elements from different genres and try to combine them and process them and mutate them so that they sound new and fresh. That's kind of what we wanted to do on the Garbage record, and there definitely were some sonic arrangements that we came up with that at least were exciting for us.

"Take 'Stupid Girl,' for example. The whole song was written around that bass groove. We wanted to have a song that had a very thumpy and repetitive bass line, with the bass line acting almost like a hook. Well, we actually recorded most of that song in Steve's basement on a little eight-track A-DAT using an Akai machine, a couple of small amps, and a small drum kit. We had a bunch of stuff going on, and Steve took a loop from the Clash, the bass went down, Shirley started ad-libbing vocals and came up with a mostly finished lyric, and then we started incorporating all of these noisy little mistakes. Like at one point Steve was trying to dub something from one track to another track on the A-DAT, something happened digitally, and he got this scratchy feedback. He thought, 'Oh, this sounds cool,' so he sampled it and managed to tune it into the song, and that almost became a hook. In fact, we're as much into things that aren't necessarily musical but can still become hooks.

"The same applied to the start of 'Super Vixen,' which has all of these stutters and stops, and which was totally an accident. We were working on some guitar part at the start of the song and we put the tape machine into a loop—you know, pick up and rewind and play again—and after a while the tape was parking, and again we thought, 'That's kinda cool!' So then we decided to do that every time, but because a lot of things played through those pauses we had to do some extensive muting with the automation in the mix in order to get them supertight. So, basically it goes to dead air and in a way it's just silence, but that also becomes a hook. As it turned out a lot of people commented that they thought their CD players were broken when they first put it on, which is cool!

"The sampler is probably the thing that has changed music more than anything else during the past five years. Originally, hiphop and rap were the only forms of music to be really influenced by that technology, but now everyone's using it, and it's really cool to see these different styles of music all intertwined. That's one thing that utilizing the new technology can do for you.

"A lot of times we don't know what we're doing. It's like trial and error, and a lot of error. I mean, we never really sit down and say, 'Here's a plan, let's do this.' We really do experiment a lot and it's difficult, because we're a disfunctional democracy! All of us have opinions and everyone has an ultimate power of veto. If someone hates something then we'll discuss why. The good thing is that there's a certain sensibility that the four of us share, and so when something really connects with one person it's usually going to connect with all four of us. Not always, though! There were some great arguments in the studio, let me tell you! Still, with any band, I think that kind of creative tension is healthy. You have to be able to put it away and not take criticism personally. That can be hard to do, but it's healthy when you can deal with it."

INDEX

■